A Companion to Wolfram's 'Parzival'

Studies in German Literature, Linguistics, and Culture

Edited by James Hardin
(*South Carolina*)

A Companion to Wolfram's *Parzival*

Edited by
Will Hasty

CAMDEN HOUSE

Copyright © 1999 by the Editor and Contributors

All Rights Reserved. Except as permitted under current legislation,
no part of this work may be photocopied, stored in a retrieval system,
published, performed in public, adapted, broadcast, transmitted,
recorded, or reproduced in any form or by any means,
without the prior permission of the copyright owner.

First published 1999 by Camden House
Reprinted in paperback and transferred to digital printing 2010

Camden House is an imprint of Boydell & Brewer Inc.
668 Mt. Hope Avenue, Rochester, NY 14620, USA
www.camden-house.com
and of Boydell & Brewer Limited
PO Box 9, Woodbridge, Suffolk IP12 3DF, UK
www.boydellandbrewer.com

Paperback ISBN-13: 978-1-57113-458-5
Paperback ISBN-10: 1-57113-458-1
Hardback ISBN-13: 978-1-57113-152-2
Hardback ISBN-10: 1-57113-152-3

Library of Congress Cataloging-in-Publication Data

A companion to Wolfram's Parzival / Will Hasty [editor].
    p. cm. — (Studies in German literature, linguistics, and culture)
Includes bibliographical references and index.
ISBN 1-57113-152-3 (alk. paper)
    1. von Eschenbach, Wolfram, 12th cent. Parzival. 2. Perceval
(Legendary character)—Romances—History and criticism. 3. Arthurian
romances—History and criticism. 4. Grail—Romances—History and
criticism.   I. Hasty, Will.   II. Series: Studies in German literature,
linguistics, and culture (Unnumbered)
PT1688.C66 1998
831'.21—dc21

                                                               98–31482
                                                                   CIP

A catalogue record for this title is available from the British Library.

This publication is printed on acid-free paper.

Cover: Depiction of the battle between Parzival and his brother
Feirefiz. MS Heidelberg Universitätsbibliothek, cpg. 33g, fol. 540.
Courtesy of Universitätsbibliothek Heidelberg.

Acknowledgments

I WOULD LIKE FIRST to express my gratitude to the contributors for their knowledgable, conscientious, and cordial collaboration during the work on this volume. My thanks also go to Jim Hardin and Camden House for the opportunity to work with Wolfram's fascinating text, and to Jim Walker for his help with the preparation of the manuscript. Permission to use the reproductions of the illuminations from *Parzival* manuscripts was kindly granted by the university libraries of Heidelberg and Munich, while the town of Wolframs-Eschenbach generously provided Willy Riedel's photos of the Wolfram monument and the Wolfram Museum brochure. Finally, for their love and support, I would like to thank Bàrbara, Isabel, and Natalie.

W. H.
November 1998

Contents

Acknowledgments	v
Introduction *Will Hasty*	ix
People, Places, and Things in *Parzival*	1
Gahmuret and Herzeloyde: Gone but not Forgotten *Francis G. Gentry*	3
Ideals of Flesh and Blood: Women Characters in *Parzival* *Marion E. Gibbs*	12
The Significance of the Gawan Story in *Parzival* *Martin Jones*	37
Doing his own Thing: Wolfram's Grail *Sidney Johnson*	77
Wolfram's Art of Narration	97
Fiction, Plot and Discourse: Wolfram's *Parzival* and its Narrative Sources *Adrian Stevens*	99
Wolfram von Eschenbach: Modes of Narrative Presentation *Neil Thomas*	124
Cultural Contexts	141
Parzival and the Theology of Fallen Man *Brian Murdoch*	143
Tournaments and Battles in *Parzival* *W. H. Jackson*	159
Reading, Writing, and Learning in Wolfram von Eschenbach's *Parzival* *Albrecht Classen*	189

Otherworlds, Alchemy, Pythagoras, and Jung: Symbols of Transformation in *Parzival* *Winder McConnell*	203
At the Limits of Chivalry in Wolfram's *Parzival*: An Arthurian Perspective *Will Hasty*	223

The Modern Reception of Wolfram's *Parzival*   243

Wolfram, Wagner, and the Germans *Ulrich Müller*	245
Works Cited	259
Notes on Contributors	279
Index	281

Introduction

WOLFRAM VON ESCHENBACH'S *PARZIVAL*, composed in the first decade of the thirteenth century, was the most popular vernacular verse narrative in medieval Germany and one of the most vibrant of the High Middle Ages. *Parzival* expands and transforms the Arthurian tradition as it existed in the works of predecessors such as Chrétien de Troyes and Hartmann von Aue into a grand depiction of the medieval cosmos around the year 1200, a depiction that demonstrates detailed knowledge of astronomy, natural sciences, medicine, geography, theology, and philosophy. The brilliance, boldness, and astonishing originality of *Parzival*, along with the allure of its forceful but elusive author, contributed to the ongoing popularity of Wolfram well into the fifteenth century, when Wolfram's works were first published by Johann Mentelin in Strasbourg (1477), and to the ongoing fascination *Parzival* has continued to exert on modern readers since the rediscovery of Wolfram's works in the eighteenth century. At the close of the twentieth century, Wolfram continues to be held in the highest regard. He has been considered Germany's greatest poet (Bertau 9) and his *Parzival* is included in Harold Bloom's *Western Canon* alongside the works of Virgil and Dante (500).

Despite the regard in which Wolfram was held in the Middle Ages, there is no extra-literary reference to his life. Although this is the rule rather than the exception with the authors of epic narratives in Germany (Bumke 1991,1), it is unfortunate that Wolfram's works, which reveal so much of the medieval cosmos, yield so little clear information about the life of their author. Only the vaguest of outlines about Wolfram's life can be conjectured on the basis of these works. References to contemporary events such as the military conflict between Philip of Swabia and Landgrave Hermann of Thuringia in 1203 (*Parzival*, verses 379,18-20) and the coronation of emperor Otto IV in 1209 (mentioned in *Willehalm*, verses 393,30-394,5), along with the death of Wolfram's possible patron Landgrave Hermann of Thuringia in 1217, suggest a period of literary productivity falling in the first two decades of the thirteenth century. This was a time of social and political turmoil in the German speaking regions of the Holy Roman Empire. The first Hohenstaufen emperor Frederick I ("Barbarossa"), who had reigned from 1155 to 1190, had succeeded to some degree in asserting imperial power by working against the centrifugal aims of the powerful territorial princes in Germany. Frederick's son Heinrich VI wielded a degree of power similar to that of his father, but upon his death in 1197, the rivalries and conflicts of the German princes reemerged. Since Heinrich's designated heir Frederick was only four years old, the princes rushed in to fill the power vacuum with Philip of Swabia (Heinrich's brother) and Otto of Brunswick (the son of the powerful Welf duke Henry the Lion) each claiming the emperorship. Military conflict between these two contenders and their supporters coincided with Wolfram's composition of *Parzival* in the early years of the thirteenth century and some scholars have believed that Wolfram's depictions of military matters may have been based on his own involvement in this conflict.

Wolfram probably came from the Frankish town of Ober-Eschenbach, which renamed itself Wolframs-Eschenbach in 1917 in honor of the famous son it claims for itself. This claim is based primarily on numerous places (Abenberg, Nördlingen, the Sant near Nuremberg, to name only a few) in the vicinity of this village that are mentioned in Wolfram's works. There are also historical documents of a family named Eschenbach in this town beginning in the latter part of the thirteenth century. It was long thought that Wolfram himself had been interred in the town cathedral, the Liebfrauenmünster, and an epitaph with his name was said to be in the cathedral as late as the early seventeenth century (Bumke 1991,3). A fountain and statue of Wolfram, donated by King Maximilian II of Bavaria, were erected in 1861 across from the cathedral. The town currently has a museum dedicated to Wolfram, which imaginatively addresses the question *Kann man Literatur ausstellen?* (Can literature be exhibited?) by "staging" culturally interesting aspects of Wolfram's verse narratives and lyrics.

Despite the forceful way in which he frequently presents himself in his works, Wolfram remains in many respects an elusive author. He claims, for example, to be illiterate, and thereby suggests a polemical attitude toward the Latin clerical culture of learning. This however stands at odds with the vast amount of learning his *Parzival* seems to contain, which normally would have been obtained in a monastery or cathedral school. Wolfram proudly claims to be of chivalric heritage in the same section of his *Parzival*, the much interpreted "self-defense" at the end of Book II (114,5–116,4). In this section, Wolfram defends himself against the enmity of ladies in his audience, which was allegedly caused by an expression of anger Wolfram made toward his own lady on account of her infidelity (assuming this is an autobiographical statement rather than a literary theoretical reflection, the historical details are unknown). Consistent with this assertion of chivalric heritage is the high regard in which chivalry is held throughout *Parzival* as well as the detailed knowledge that Wolfram conveys about chivalric life and medieval warfare, but Joachim Bumke, in what can be regarded as the standard German language introduction to the medieval poet and his works, points out that it is difficult to know exactly what Wolfram's social rank and status were (*Wolfram von Eschenbach* 1991,4–7). It is possible that the activity of Wolfram was supported by patrons close to his hometown during the early work on *Parzival*, which is considered his first verse narrative, and that Wolfram later worked at the large court of the powerful Landgrave Hermann of Thuringia, a generous patron of literature who held court in the Wartburg castle near the Frankish town of Eisenach. Support for such a view is based on the mention of the count of Wertheim in Book IV of *Parzival* (184,4–6) and of Hermann in Books VI (297,16–23) and VII (379,18ff.) of *Parzival* and also in Wolfram's other, presumably later verse narratives. But lacking clear indications from Wolfram and extra-literary references to Wolfram's whereabouts, definitive statements about where Wolfram worked and who supported him remain difficult.

There is a single extant image of Wolfram from the Middle Ages, which is contained in the Manesse Codex from the early fourteenth century. In this image, Wolfram is depicted with a coat-of-arms consisting of two brown axe-like weapons. There is no other document of a such a coat-of-arms, and Bumke points out that this is likely the invention of a later age, since coats-of-arms were not yet very developed during the lifetime of Wolfram (1991,4). Thanks to the very rich transmission of *Parzival* (sixteen complete manuscripts and more than eighty fragments) — perhaps the best testimony to its popularity in the Middle Ages — the editorial work on *Parzival* has not posed the same kinds of problems as many other medieval German narratives. The first critical edition, that of Karl Lachmann (Berlin: Reimer, 1833), is still widely regarded as authoritative and it is the edition cited in this volume. It is Lachmann who divided *Parzival* into sixteen Books, based on illuminated initials in the St. Gall manuscript upon which his edition is largely based. The division of the narrative of *Parzival* into units of thirty verses probably goes back to Wolfram himself (see Bumke 1991, 148–150).

On the basis of his other verse narratives and lyrics, which show a comparable degree of originality and expressive power, Wolfram would have been a famous poet even if he had never composed *Parzival*. In his lyrics, most of which are Dawn Songs, Wolfram sings of the illicit lovers' parting with a daring, if not shocking degree of emotional and erotic force. *Willehalm* (ca.1210–1220) was Wolfram's very independent reworking of the Old French *La Bataille d'Aliscans* (*The Battle of Aliscans*), based remotely on the deeds of Count Guillaume of Toulouse, a grandson of Charles Martel, who fought against the Saracens in Southern France and Spain around 800. Perhaps the most striking feature of the unfinished *Willehalm* is its very positive portrayal of the Muslim adversaries as a courtly and chivalrous people — which stands in stark contrast to the highly pejorative portrayal of them in the chanson de gestes tradition. This "humane" portrayal of Muslims — which echoes Wolfram's very tolerant treatment of infidels such as the Baruc and Feirefiz in *Parzival* — seems extraordinary for an age that was very much shaped by the militant Christian ideology of the Crusades. The unfinished and fragmentary *Titurel*, which was probably composed around 1217 in a flexible stanzaic form apparently of Wolfram's own design, and which was also the first courtly work not to have an earlier source (see Wynn 1994,204), presents the story of the character Sigune prior to her appearance as the *klôsnærinne* (anchoress) in the presumably earlier *Parzival*. Focusing on the difficult position of children and youth between the conflicting demands of love and society, Wolfram describes in this poem the tragic outcome of the love affair between Sigune and the knight Schionatulander, who ultimately dies trying to earn the consummation of their love with chivalric deeds.

As significant as his other works may be, it is on *Parzival* that the greater part of Wolfram's fame rests. Although Wolfram states that he is following the correct version of "Kyot," and not that of Chrétien de Troyes, the current scholarly consensus is that Books III–XIII of *Parzival* were based on the corresponding sections of Chrétien's *Perceval* or *Li Contes del Graal*. Little is known about the life of Wolfram's famous French predecessor beyond his association with the courts of Champagne and Flanders. The dedication of Chrétien's *Lancelot* indicates that this poem was written for Countess Marie de Champagne, the daughter of Louis VII of France and Eleanor of Aquitaine, and *Perceval* was commissioned by Philip of Alsace, who became count of Flanders in 1190. Chrétien's works, which include a translation of Ovid, indicate that he was well educated, possibly a cleric. Although the chronology of Chrétien's works is uncertain, the unfinished *Perceval*, which is presumed to be his last one, may have been composed around 1190. For his Arthurian works Chrétien, just as Hartmann and Wolfram after him, was apparently in a position to draw on materials from a multifarious Arthurian tradition that included written texts such as the *Historia Regum Brittaniae* of Geoffrey of Monmouth and its vernacular reworkings, the so-called "Bruts" (most important among which was Wace's French verse translation, in which the Round Table appears for the first time), and orally-transmitted tales told by wandering storytellers. Characteristic of the Arthurian romances of Chrétien, and those of his German successors, is the narrative interweaving of two main perspectives. One is that of King Arthur and his court, which for the most part represents a communal principle of festive courtliness and chivalric solidarity. The other significant perspective involves a shift of the narrative focal point away from the Arthurian court: a single knight rides into unknown regions in order to undertake a series of adventures, or military encounters. Although they typically bring the hero back to the court of Arthur, these adventures — in fantastic landscapes populated by renegades, giants, dwarfs, dragons, and other adventuring knights — occupy, by virtue of the amount of attention given them, the central position in the romances. In their depiction of the Arthurian court, the romances give literary expression to the courtly and chivalric interests and values of the lay noble audiences for which they were produced, while their emphasis on the adventures of individual knights — however beholden to the Arthurian ethos they remain — suggest the increasing importance of the individual vis-à-vis communal forms of identity that is also visible in other cultural spheres in the High Middle Ages.

Initially, the Arthurian romances treated problems arising from within the courtly/chivalric world. In Hartmann von Aue's *Erec* and *Iwein*, which Wolfram knew and to which he frequently refers, the hero's adventures have been seen as achieving a balance between the conflicting demands of military activity on the one hand, and the knight's amorous obligations to his lady on the other. If the earlier Arthurian romances were about balancing *âventiure* and *minne*, the Perceval/Parzival story, by virtue of its introduction of the grail kingdom with its new religious dimension, seems to operate at another level altogether, at which the worldly demands of chivalric life have to balanced with the spiritual demands of God. In this we see signs of the Church's increasing influence on the nobility's basically military understanding of itself in the High Middle Ages. Around 1200 this self-understanding had been influenced by the ideology of the Crusades, one of the effects of which was to endow fighting with a higher spiritual purpose. Even if the Crusades are not explicitly mentioned in the

Arthurian works (the closest reference is Wolfram's use of the word *templeise*) apparently based on the Knights Templar, to designate the grail knights), the subordination of fighting to a higher spiritual purpose that was an ideal of the Crusades, if not always a reality, doubtless left a mark on the grail narratives of Chrétien and Wolfram, although it must be stressed again that neither of these literary works adopted the demonization of the Muslim adversaries that was a conspicuous aspect of Crusades literature and propaganda. The Peace of God (*pax dei*), mentioned by pope Urban II in 1095 in Clermont as he called for the first Crusade (Le Goff 1965, 54), may also have been of some importance in shaping the self-understanding of feudal magnates and their knights. The Peace of God placed certain categories of people such as monks, priests, and the poor, and certain material things (e.g., church property, peasants' means of livelihood) under protection, while the ensuing Truce of God (*treuga dei*) called for cessation of armed conflict on specified holy days. We may see a literary reflection of the Truce of God in Book IX of Wolfram's *Parzival*, when the grey knight rebukes Parzival for being armored and armed on Good Friday. By relating fighting in these different ways to higher religious purposes, the Church endeavored to control and redirect the disruptive aggression of the feudal magnates and their retinues, which found its typical form in feuding.

The aspects of *Parzival* that justify its inclusion in Harold Bloom's *Western Canon* and account for the high regard in which this work has been held since the early nineteenth century are perhaps best circumscribed by the term "originality." Despite Wolfram's indebtedness to Chrétien, and also to earlier German authors such as Heinrich von Veldeke and Hartmann von Aue, Wolfram sets himself apart from earlier courtly authors in so striking a way as to support the assertion that he has no identifiable "poetic father." If Wolfram's statement that he does not know a single letter of the alphabet can be construed as a chivalric polemic with clerical culture altogether — however learned Wolfram may have in fact been — then his position vis-à-vis earlier literature seems all the more singular. The works of predecessors such as Chrétien and Hartmann, and of contemporaries such as Gottfried von Strassburg, however innovative in their own right, qualified themselves by demonstrating their ambition to adhere to formal and stylistic standards of grammar and rhetoric as transmitted by the Latin clerical culture of learning from late antiquity through the Middle Ages. In the prologues of two of his narrative poems, *Der arme Heinrich* and *Iwein*, Hartmann von Aue, the most significant courtly author in Germany prior to Wolfram, pointedly refers to his education, as if clerical learning were a necessary prerequisite both for the composition of a narrative and, by implication, for its favorable reception by his audiences. Like other authors such as Gottfried von Strassburg, Hartmann respects the authority of tradition, thereby adhering to another clerical ideal by naming and more or less faithfully following his sources. By contrast, Wolfram pointedly asserts his independence from clerical learning, saying that his knowledge is based on experience and insight rather than on books. And where other authors loyally follow in the footsteps of hallowed predecessors, Wolfram puts forth the uniqueness of his own work and his independence from sources in a way that seems almost scandalous. Even if the Kyot who Wolfram says was his source is something more than an outright fabrication, Wolfram stresses that the adventure he relates is his own. What has come to be known as Wolfram's "dark style" — the emotionalism, impulsiveness, and obscurity with which his story often seems to be told — is also doubtless an aspect of his apparently critical attitude toward the clerical culture of books.

Hartmann's originality in his treatment of his sources has been the subject of spirited debate. Frequently with a thinly veiled nationalistic agenda, scholars in Germany and France have considered either that Hartmann's *Erec* and *Iwein* are unique renditions, despite their closeness to Chrétien de Troyes's *Erec et Enide* and *Yvain*, or that they are more or less deficient translations thereof (see Hasty 1995, 82–84). Wolfram's originality, by contrast, remains unquestioned. Even those parts of his *Parzival* that are assumed to be based on the corresponding sections of Chrétien's *Perceval* have been changed so much that it is not always easy to dismiss Wolfram's claim that he is not following Chrétien's text at all. The issue of Wolfram's originality, although articulated in numerous different ways, has remained an underlying idea in scholarly assessments of *Parzival* since the nineteenth century. Earlier critical appraisals grounded this originality somewhat unsystematically in what were considered to be the life and personal attributes of the author, whose words about himself (the *Selbstaussagen*) and his literary activity were taken at face value. Wolfram's words that he was poor and illiterate, for example, were not doubted. Goedeke assumed that, because Wolfram used French sources, he must have first had them read aloud and possibly even translated (1884, 94). For Goedeke, Wolfram's lack of learning did not prevent him from becoming "the greatest poet of the German Middle Ages, a poet full of depth and manly dignity" (94; translations of the German literary histories are those of the editor). Wolfram's staunch advocacy of chivalry in the "self defense" and elsewhere in *Parzival*, which Gervinus saw negatively as an elitist mentality (1853, 389), Leixner more favorably as the proud expression of Wolfram's "chivalric manhood" and of his fostering of "bold deeds and weapons" (1910, 51), was also taken as a statement of personal engagement rather than as a literary theoretical statement (see below). Leixner even went further, seeing in Wolfram's positive depictions of the chivalric life indications of the author's "proud nature," which would have made it difficult for him to stand in the service of magnates such as the count of Wertheim (51–52).

Since Wolfram's statements about Kyot were taken at face value as well, Wolfram's "originality" was also that of the mysterious Kyot, who, as Wolfram tells us, found the story of the grail in an Arabic manuscript in Toledo (453,11–12). Gervinus considers that the depth given to the character of Parzival, the weight placed on the "inner purification of his being," the spiritual conception of the grail question, and the "higher synthesis of the ascetic-contemplative with the active-military life" are ideas that are first achieved in the grail poems of Kyot and Wolfram (386). Like other nineteenth-century appraisals of the great medieval courtly poets, Gervinus's view is largely shaped by an ideal of folk poetry to which an epic narrative such as the *Nibelungenlied* was seen as corresponding more perfectly than the seemingly random and chaotic chivalric adventures of the Arthurian narratives. It is the more modern, novelistic aspects of Wolfram's work — the eclectic abundance of events and information conveyed frequently in great detail — that made it somewhat objectionable to Gervinus, whose ideal is the epic poem in which, as with Homer, all of the elements seem to flow from the same inexhaustible poetic source. Even in Gervinus's somewhat negative appraisal, which is exceptional in the early scholarship and reveals interesting parallels to Wagner's criticism of Wolfram (see the article of Müller in this volume), a central idea is seen to save *Parzival* from the "aimless activity, egotism, and violence" of chivalric adventures (394). In *Parzival* the seemingly chaotic and violent randomness of chivalric adventuring is ultimately overcome by a higher, spiritual instance — the grail — and to an inner spiritual yearning in the hero. Gervinus thus articulates one of the most abiding ideas of Wolfram-scholarship, which is that the chivalric adventuring of heroes in previous Arthurian narratives is seen by Wolfram as insufficient, as a mere artifice or convention, that has to be rejected in the form of a higher, deeper, truer kind of spiritual life that is represented by the grail. Similarly, Leixner, some sixty years later, writes that service for the grail rests not on external, formal ceremony, but rather on the "sanctification of life" and the "fulfillment of moral obligations" (54). Somewhat typical of other early critical assessments is Leixner's view of

Gawan as the representative of an external, ceremonial courtly knighthood, to which the more significant inner quest of Parzival stands in a relationship of opposition (53). Such a view may account for the fact that Leixner, along with many other early scholars, has relatively little to say about the Gawan Books and their significance.

The assessment of Helmut de Boor (1953), published a century after that of Gervinus, presents a view of the medieval author and his masterpiece that is in many ways exemplary for trends in *Parzival*-scholarship in the decades following World War II. Doubt had long been expressed about the seriousness of Wolfram's invocation of Kyot as his source. Anselm Salzer, for example, although he took most of Wolfram's statements at face value, had considered that Kyot may have been Wolfram's own creation, designed to make his tale believable by satisfying his audiences' demand for a source (1926,151). For Boor there is no longer any doubt. By contextualizing the references to Kyot and observing that they are made in episodes containing information that is generally "fantastic" and "scarcely believable" (93), Boor concludes that Kyot is equally fantastic, the product of Wolfram's own imagination. From this perspective it could be said not only that the "originality" of Wolfram is no longer that of another historical author named Kyot, but also that the biographical or historical value of *anything* Wolfram says about himself and his work has to be assessed with a much greater degree of care than was previously the case. The recognition that Wolfram the historical individual and Wolfram the narrator/performer are not necessarily identical has introduced an element of speculation into the understanding of Wolfram's statements: are they declarations about his personal, biographical situation, embellishments of his stories, or metaphorical declarations of positions in literary theoretical debates? Wolfram's declaration that he does not know a single letter of the alphabet is not without some biographical value for Boor, even though this scholar argues that a statement such as this cannot be taken *literally*, but rather has to be understood as a "humorous, exaggerated declaration that he lacks a regular education" (92). Wolfram's words on chivalry in the same context, which have been understood as a straightforward advocation of deeds of arms, came to be understood by some scholars as a literary theoretical statement amounting to an attack on what Wolfram presumably saw as exaggerations — particularly the prostrate attitude of the singer/knight towards his lady — in many of the love lyrics of his day. Whatever biographical/historical value Wolfram's statements about his sources and himself may *also* have, it seems fair to say that they have increasingly come to be seen primarily as an element of his narrative art.

In the appraisal of Boor, the increased skepticism with respect to the biographical value of the *Selbstaussagen* coincides with a shift of critical focus to the conceptual and aesthetic aspects of Wolfram's works themselves. Much like earlier scholars, Boor seeks and finds a unitary aesthetic conception in the idea of the religiously inspired chivalry of the grail kingdom, to which the Arthurian world leads and is ultimately subordinated. Boor concedes, in a manner that is reminiscent of some of the earliest critical appraisals (e.g., that of Gervinus), that this idea does not pervade all aspects of *Parzival*, that the youthful Wolfram sometimes seems to fall victim to the "Fülle seiner Einfälle" (= "profusion of his ideas"), although "jumps" and "contradictions" in the narrative are not seen as detracting from the overall value of the work (95). Boor's assessment of *Parzival* is also representative of numerous others in the decades following World War II by virtue of the emphasis it puts on the hero's sinful guilt, or *Schuld*, which is seen as consisting in the hero's adherence to a strictly feudal and strictly Arthurian kind of relationship to God. Achieving the grail involves for Boor and many other scholars giving up this external, purely "formal" relationship and adopting an internal, truly Christian one, which occurs during Parzival's sojourn in Book IX with his uncle, the hermit Trevrizent. According to this higher spiritual aspect in the adventures of Parzival, Boor sees the adventures of Gawan in a way that is somewhat similar to the earlier assessment of Leixner: "Gawan is a continuation of Hartmann (von Aue); Parzival is the completely new addition of Wolfram" (96).

Views similar to those of Boor continue to be typical in more recent scholarly appraisals of *Parzival*. A quarter of a century after Boor's assessment, Bernd Lutz viewed Wolfram's words on his lack of education as "derisively ironic," intended to represent the author not as "uneducated," but rather as "free of the ballast of Latin culture" (*Deutsche Literaturgeschichte* 1979, 32). Similarly, Kyot is seen by Lutz as a "fantastic stratagem, with which a mysterious secret authority is feigned," and Lutz stresses the conceptual uniqueness of Wolfram's work by viewing the religious dimension of the Parzival story, just as earlier scholars did, as a significant step beyond the more strictly worldly, Arthurian orientation of Hartmann von Aue's *Erec* and *Iwein*. Even as views such as these continue to be prevalent, recent years have seen a variety of very different approaches to Wolfram's work which in some cases question some of the most basic assumptions. A recent example is the book of Arthur Groos, which advances a Bakhtinian understanding of Wolfram's *Parzival* as an open-ended narrative, a dialogue between clerical and chivalric cultures, that is "fundamentally decentered and pluralistic" (1995, 3). The implications of such a view have yet to be considered fully, but the idea of *Parzival* as a "decentered" narrative seems inevitably to "de-center" the long-standing hierarchical understanding of the relationship between religious and chivalric values according to which many aspects of Wolfram's work have been interpreted. If the contribution of Wolfram's *Parzival* is seen not primarily in terms of a unified religious/spiritual conception that lifts Arthurian romance to a "higher" plane, but rather in terms of a vastly greater variety of cultural, generic, and linguistic elements in an open-ended dialogue, then some of the basic questions posed by Wolfram's work — the relationship between religious/clerical and chivalric values in the literary performance of Wolfram, between the grail kingdom and Arthur's court in the adventures of the hero Parzival, and between the import of the adventures of Parzival vis-à-vis those of Gawan — may require answers other than those heretofore proposed.

Given the originality of Wolfram's *Parzival* as outlined in the last few paragraphs, it is not surprising that an interest in this runs like a leitmotif through the essays in the present volume. Written by Wolfram scholars working in Europe and the United States, these essays provide a definitive treatment in English of significant aspects of *Parzival*. This volume is divided into four general sections. The first focuses on some of the significant people, places, and "things" (as which Wolfram designates his grail) in *Parzival*, the second on Wolfram's narrative art (i.e., his treatment of his sources and other aspects of his much discussed style), the third on broader cultural aspects of *Parzival*, such as its relationship to medieval theology, to the culture of books in the context of the so-called "Twelfth Century Renaissance," to otherworlds and alchemy, to the Arthurian tradition, and to the material culture of jousting and warfare, and the fourth on the modern reception of *Parzival*, which has been very much shaped by Richard Wagner's *Bühnenweihfestspiel* (Sacred Stage Festival Play) *Parsifal*. Since this volume is intended to introduce significant aspects of *Parzival* to readers who may not be familiar with it or know German, parenthetical translations of Middle High German passages from the medieval works and, occasionally, of modern critical assessments by German scholars, have been provided. With the same audience in mind, I have asked the contributors to devote their articles to a discussion of Wolfram's text itself, along with some of the most significant scholarly appraisals, and to make references to the secondary literature parenthetically. Although this format may have the effect of reducing the scope of discussions of the vast critical literature — for which I have to ask for the indulgence of Wolfram-specialists — the articles nevertheless convey an impression of the current state of scholarship and, beyond this, point in new directions for the future study of Wolfram's incomparable rendering of the quest for the grail.

The Wolfram monument in Wolframs-Eschenbach.

From the Wolfram von Eschenbach Museum in Wolframs-Eschenbach.

People, Places, and Things in *Parzival*

FRANCIS G. GENTRY

Gahmuret and Herzeloyde: Gone but not Forgotten

THERE ARE MANY TALES IN WOLFRAM'S *PARZIVAL*, the main ones, of course, being those of Parzival himself and his ultimately successful attempts to win the grail. Further, there are those of Parzival's friend Gawan and his likewise successful quest to free the four queens and four hundred maidens held in the Schastel Marveile. More smoothly than in Chrétien's *Perceval*, the two narratives and their respective heroes intersect and connect at crucial junctures in Wolfram's romance. There is, however, yet another narrative thread that is of almost equal importance, but which has not been subject to the detailed analysis lavished on the others. Here I am referring to Wolfram's major addition to the story of Parzival, the episodes dealing with Parzival's parents Gahmuret and Herzeloyde.

Scholars have long recognized that there is a connection between the Gahmuret and the Parzival narratives, beyond providing the obvious account of Parzival's biological beginnings and his antecedents who provide him with the necessary relationship to the Arthurian and the grail worlds. Much of the scholarly discussion of the Gahmuret story (Books I and II) has focussed on determining which narrative model the account appears to follow: either that represented by the *Eneas* of Heinrich von Veldeke (see D. H. Green 1970 and Tax, "Gahmuret") or that illustrated by the classical Arthurian romance — with modifications (see Stein). There have, of course, been other voices, and the main currents of research have been clearly summarized most recently by Holger Noltze (7–32). And while all are agreed that the Gahmuret story acts as a sort of prelude to that of Parzival, there is little scholarly harmony as to the precise purpose of Books I and II.

That the Gahmuret story stands in a typological relationship to the Parzival adventures is clear. For example, reminiscent of the later experience of the young Parzival who comes of age in Soltane "an küneclîcher fuore betrogn" (118,2= "deprived of [his] royal heritage") and who leaves his familiar life to become a knight, Gahmuret, too, leaves home after his father Gandin's death. As the second son, Gahmuret inherits nothing and, thus, feels compelled to strike out on his own. He was not forced by others to do so. Indeed the peers of the realm advised his brother Galoes to convince Gahmuret to remain as a beloved brother, a wish to which Galoes quickly and graciously acceded. But Gahmuret is adamant about making his own fortune. And like his son many years later, he, too, must say farewell to his mother Schoette. She, like Herzeloyde, attempts to persuade her second-born to remain:

> 'fil li roy Gandîn,
> wilt du niht langer bî mir sîn?'
> sprach daz wîplîche wîp. (10,15–17)

('Son of King Gandin, do you not wish to remain any longer with me?' asked that womanly woman. — Translations are mine.)

Seeing that he is firm in his intentions, she laments greatly, believing (correctly) that she will never see her son again. As Parzival learns from Trevrizent about the death of Herzeloyde after the young hero's departure, so also does Gahmuret hear the sad news from Kaylet about the death of Schoette. In both instances, the heroes are told that their respective mothers died from grief because their sons were no longer with them. True, Schoette passed away after her husband Gandin and elder son Galoes had also died. Nonetheless Kaylet makes clear that Gahmuret's absence was the final blow and that he is at least partly to blame for her death:

> 'dô ir erstarp Gandîn
> und Gâlôes der bruoder dîn,
> unt dô si *dîn* bî ir niht sach,
> der tôt och ir daz herze brach.' (92,27–30 — emphasis mine)

('When Gandin died and your brother Galoes [too] and when she observed that *you* were not with her [either], death also broke her heart.')

Trevrizent not only does not spare Parzival the news of Herzeloyde's death but also assigns him the direct responsibility for it. After castigating Parzival for having killed Ither who was Parzival's cousin, although the young man had been unaware of the relationship when he slew the Red Knight, Trevrizent goes on to lament:

> 'got daz erbarmen müeze
> daz de ie gefrumtest selhe nôt!
> mîn swester lac ouch *nâch dir* tôt,
> Herzeloyd dîn muoter.' (476,10–13 — emphasis mine)

('May God always be merciful [toward you in view of the fact] that you brought about such sorrow! My sister, Herzeloyde your mother, also died *because of you*.')

Interesting here are both the similarities and the dissimilarities between the two episodes. Both father and son have abandoned their mothers to seek their fortunes in the world; both mothers do not want their sons to leave; both mothers die, whether as a direct or indirect result of their sons' leaving. Dissimilar is the level of responsibility placed on Gahmuret and Parzival. Gahmuret is admonished by Hardiz to show his manliness and grieve in moderation. Following this advice, Gahmuret sheds some tears and is up the next morning ready for mental jousting with Herzeloyde. There is no indication that anyone believes that Gahmuret has done anything for which he should atone. Not so with Parzival! After he explains to Parzival the entire story of the grail and the many people involved, Trevrizent returns to the matter of Parzival's responsibility for Ither's and his mother's death:

> 'mit riwe ich dir daz künde,
> du treist zwuo grôze sünde:
> Ithêrn du hâst erslagen,
> du solt ouch dîne muoter klagen.
> ir grôziu triwe daz geriet,
> *dîn vart si vome leben schiet,*
> die du jungest von ir tæte.' (499,19–25 — emphasis mine)

('Sadly I must tell you that you bear two great sins: You slew Ither [and] you must also lament your mother. Her great love and devotion brought it about that *your journey* which you last took from her *parted her from life*.')

Of course, this is not the only similarity between Gahmuret and Parzival: both are exceptionally handsome; both represent (apparently) the epitome of chivalry; and both rescue women beleaguered in their cities (Belacane and Condwiramurs) whom they eventually marry and then desert — for different reasons, of course. Gahmuret comes upon the siege of the city of Patelamunt and is at first repelled, then intrigued, and finally erotically attracted to its dark-skinned queen, Belacane, a process which may be viewed as demonstrating a medieval cliché regarding the supposed overwhelming sexuality of black people (see Ebenbauer). Whatever the reason may be, he is sufficiently interested to fight on her behalf and then to marry her after military victory has been assured. A few months into the marriage Gahmuret is seized by a wanderlust for adventure and flees surreptitiously — and, thus, not very honorably — from his queen who is by then pregnant with Feirefiz. Inconsolable, Belacane bears the child but later dies of grief. Gahmuret also leaves his next wife, Herzeloyde, in order to seek adventure. She, too, is pregnant. She, too, is inconsolable, but bears Parzival and lives until he departs for Arthur's court.

Parzival likewise comes upon a besieged city, Pelrapeire, ruled by a queen, Condwiramurs. Parzival, too, is attracted to this lovely woman, falls in love, and succeeds in lifting the siege. They marry and, at least one year later (according to Weigand), Parzival requests leave to visit his mother and seek adventure. After he is gone, Condwiramurs bears him two children, Kardeiz and Loherangrin. Thus, like his father, Parzival has two sons. Condwiramurs and her children are later reunited with Parzival at Munsalvaesche.

Here, again, neither the similarities nor dissimilarities between the two episodes can be overlooked. And as in the first comparison mentioned above, it is the dissimilarities that are more arresting. One is the lack of overt sexual passion in the Parzival/Condwiramurs story — certainly as opposed to the Gahmuret/Belacane marriage (see below). They are both innocents, quite unlike Gahmuret, who was a man of great sexual experience, so much so that he had the queen of France at his beck and call, or so it would appear! Nonetheless, the most obvious and telling difference is that Parzival did not steal secretly from his wife, but rather requested her leave and received it.

Of course, in some ways, one would be completely justified to assert "like father, like son." To do so, however, would be merely to observe the surface similarities. The distinctions between the similar adventures of father and son are much more revealing about the purpose of the Gahmuret story within Wolfram's great work. This is a point to which we shall return in due course.

Concluding our discussion of correspondences, it should be noted that other characters, too, stand in a typological relationship, the most obvious pair being Belacane and Sigune. Both women, for example, bring about their lovers' premature deaths. Both Belacane and Sigune refused to grant their love to Isenhart and Schionatulander, respectively. Instead they persistently tested the devotion of their knights. Thus, in order to demonstrate their love, both men undertook risky and — in the final analysis — fatal chances. To prove his love for Belacane, for example, Isenhart sheds his armor and seeks out adventure completely unprotected except for shield and lance. Clearly, this was a valiant, but foolhardy gesture, and Isenhart died in a joust with one of Belacane's men. Similarly, the cause of the brave Schionatulander's death is a trivial one, although we do not learn this in *Parzival*, but rather in the second *Titurel* fragment. In this work we see Sigune sending Schionatulander on a deadly and ultimately selfish quest to retrieve a runaway dog and its leash upon which was written a tale of love. Schionatulander, who was unarmed, suggested that she should forget this "wunderleash" and allow him to read to her of love from French books. Sigune goes into what can only be described as a pout and unmistakably threatens her friend with the loss of her favor should he not undertake this task. If he does do her bidding, she adds coquettishly, she will do everything for him that a maiden can do for a dear (male) friend (Leitzmann ed., strophe 168). Schionatulander sees this as an offer that he cannot refuse and starts to chase after the leash and the dog attached to it. In *Parzival* Wolfram only describes the result of the chase: Schionatulander was killed by Orilus in a joust. Assuming Wolfram has already conceived the whole story of Sigune and Schionatulander, we are not given more information in *Parzival* about the circumstances of the latter's death, on the one hand no doubt because the picture of a flighty young woman whose impulses must be humored would detract too greatly from the tragic and, ultimately, noble figure as which Sigune is portrayed in *Parzival*, and on the other hand because they are basically not important. For the intent both of the Isenhart episode as well as the Schionatulander scene is not to describe a chivalric encounter, but rather the senseless loss of a great champion because of the whims of the woman he loved. Both incidents depict the principle of chivalric *minnedienst* run amok. But as with the Gahmuret/Parzival comparisons, here, too, it is more instructive to note the dissimilarities between Belacane and Sigune. While she is in great mourning, and doubtless sincerely so, Belacane soon falls in love again, this time with Gahmuret. Life does go on. Only with the desertion of Gahmuret does Belacane go into a deep anguish from which she does not recover. For Sigune the death of Schionatulander means nothing less than the death of love itself. For her there will be no other.

Of course, it could be argued that a more suitable pair of characters for the purpose of comparison would be Belacane and Herzeloyde in that both married Gahmuret, both bore him a son, and both were abandoned by him. And that assertion certainly has validity, viewed from the perspective of the women. There can be no denying the depth of the love they display for Gahmuret, especially when he leaves (Belacane) and when he is killed (Herzeloyde). Nonetheless, when observed from Gahmuret's position, we see that the two situations are not similar (see Wynn 1984, 321–327). He rescues Belacane and then marries her with a mixture of passion and longing, fully in keeping with his desire to perform chivalric deeds for the love of a lady. Herzeloyde, on the other hand, arranges a tourney with herself as first prize. After Gahmuret has defeated everybody before the tourney even begins, Herzeloyde declares him to be the winner and demands that he claim the prize. Gahmuret brings up every excuse that he can think of: his marriage to Belacane and his obligation of chivalric service to Ampflise, the queen of France, only to have them brushed aside by Herzeloyde. Finally, after a hastily-assembled legal procedure, Herzeloyde's own judge rules that Gahmuret must claim Herzeloyde as his prize. They marry, but without any real ardor or erotic attachment. True, their union becomes affectionate and can be characterized by fondness, but the intensity, the mutual longing that characterized the Gahmuret/Belacane marriage is simply missing. Viewed from this angle, the Gahmuret/Herzeloyde union is perhaps not so different from the Parzival/Condwiramurs match.

At this point in the tale, it is difficult to imagine that these two individuals are slated to be the parents of the future grail king. While there can be no doubt that the product of their union is exemplary in all respects, even if he is "træclîche wîs" (4,18= "slowly wise"), definite reservations arise when considering the early history of Gahmuret and Herzeloyde. Fickle, untrustworthy, willful, arrogant, and superficial are among the adjectives that could be used to describe either the one or the other. For as Joachim Bumke indicates, their behavior before Gahmuret's death does not show them off to their best advantage (1991,58). Wolfram, however, describes their personalities only positively. In his epitaph, for example, Gahmuret is described as one who gladly helped his friends, bore the burden of love, is mourned by Christians and Saracens, and as one who is an enemy of falseness (108,5–28). Many years later at Arthur's court, Cundrie praises Gahmuret in the midst of her denunciation of Parzival for his failure to ask the question at Munsalvaesche (317,22–24), and toward the end of the work when Feirefiz and Parzival are discussing their father, it is in the highest terms: "nie bezzer rîter wart" (750,29= "There was never a better knight"); "triwe ân wenken" (751,13= "loyalty without wavering"); "er kunde ouch wol verkrenken / alle valschlîche tât" (751,14–15= "he knew how to vanquish all falsity").

Herzeloyde, too, is praised by Cundrie as a model of selfless faithfulness (317,20). Further, her portrayal after Gahmuret's death is truly spectacular and, in a word, heroic. In her lament for Gahmuret, Herzeloyde does not indulge in private grief or hysteria, as Marianne Wynn cogently notes (1984,336–341). Rather she mourns publicly, together with and for her people, becoming in the process herself the glue that holds her land together. Finally, when the young Parzival rides off to seek his fortune at Arthur's court, and she drops dead from grief, Wolfram extols her with words of highest praise: She is a "root of goodness and a bough of humility" (128,27–28).

Thus it seems obvious that Wolfram wished his hero's parents to be viewed as exemplary, and with few exceptions modern scholars have hastened to follow Wolfram. For the distinguished British literary historian, Margaret Richey (1923), Gahmuret is "charming" if not always very admirable. At the other end of the spectrum of reaction is Blake Lee Spahr (1991) who considers Gahmuret to be a "bounder" and a "cad," who meets his match in wiliness in Herzeloyde. Parzival's mother, too, fares well at the hands of most critics. Typical, also of more modern scholarship, is Marion Gibbs's description of Herzeloyde as a "gentle woman" (1972,19). And, following Karl Bertau's model, Lydia Miklautsch views her both as *regina lactans* and *mater dolorosa* (58). Even Wynn appears to succumb to Herzeloyde's not so subtle charm (although she is a bit more critical vis-à-vis Gahmuret) by asserting that the motivation for her behavior in the scenes leading up to her marriage, including forcing Gahmuret to claim her as his wife, is prompted by "altruism, recognition of the demands of privilege, and disregard of self" (1984,322).

It is clear that many commentators on *Parzival* are not placing equal importance on the entire development of Herzeloyde and Gahmuret and are, instead, relying primarily on the very positive statements by other characters or by the poet himself. It is this tendency to take an overly sentimental view of the events and characters in the romance that has made it difficult to view the Gahmuret story as an integrated part of the narrative whole, even though, as mentioned above, Gahmuret appears as the topic of a discussion between Feirefiz and Parzival shortly before Cundrie informs the latter that he is to be the next lord of the grail. Indeed, in the last thirty-line unit in the work Wolfram relates that Kyot, as opposed to Chrétien de Troyes, told the tale of Parzival to the end: "wie *Herzeloyden kint* den grâl / erwarp, als im daz gordent was, / dô in verworhte Anfortas" (827,6–8 — emphasis mine= "how *Herzeloyde's child* gained the Grail, as was determined for him, after Anfortas had lost it). In this connection, it should also be pointed out that Parzival is consistently referred to as "Gahmuret's son" or "Herzeloyde's child" throughout the work. Consequently it is quite evident that Wolfram did not intend that his listeners should forget Gahmuret and Herzeloyde or the important role they played in bequeathing to their son those traits and virtues which were necessary for him to win the greatest prize, the grail.

The question then remains whether it is possible to harmonize the tale of the parents with that of Parzival while taking into consideration their seemingly incongruous conduct as well as the positive descriptions of their characters. In other words, can one take a more holistic view of the introductory Books without neglecting that which does not seem to fit in.

Possible approaches have been hinted at in several studies, but especially those of Wynn (1984) and Ina Karg. Wynn points to Wolfram's achievement of adding yet another world to those of Arthur and the grail, namely the non-Christian world of Outremer, which has the effect of emphasizing the universality of Parzival's quest and its "relevance" (341). Karg is not as sweeping in her analysis as Wynn, but rather concentrates on the differences between the chivalric ideologies of the pre-Arthurian world of Gahmuret and the Arthurian world in which Parzival finds himself (173–175). Unlike Arthurian knights, Gahmuret cannot embark upon a quest and, having completed it, return to court, for, according to Karg, there is no center about which all the quests revolve. As a result there is a continual search for adventure that can only end in death. Parzival, as an Arthurian knight, however, has a different context in which he can perform chivalric deeds like his father, but which he can also — unlike his father — utilize for reflection (175). While both interpretations have merit, Wynn's is the more convincing because she does not see the necessity of reviving the discussion of the "crisis of chivalry" that was so popular in critical discussion in the 1970s. Essentially, however, both Wynn and Karg correctly point out that Wolfram has constructed a third sphere of activity; whether it is labelled as "Outremer" or "non-Arthurian" is immaterial. Important is only to note that it is *there* and that it is *necessary*. If the grail world can be viewed as a type of sacralized Arthurian society, one in which the development of the chivalric ideal has progressed to a higher level — Munsalvaesche as a cloistered Camelot — then Gahmuret's world, of which the young "pre-Arthurian" Arthur was also part, represents a first stage of development out of which evolved the Arthurian court. One should not forget that it is also on this level that Parzival himself begins. When he rides from Soltane toward Camelot, he has only the advice of his mother as a guide. As a result, he makes terrible mistakes with Jeschute and Ither before he is taught the essence of Arthurian knighthood by Gurnemanz. And even then it takes a long time before he has truly acquired the skill of reflection — and that only with the help of Trevrizent — that will enable him to progress to the grail and become its king. As is the case with any journey, so also this one begins with a step. Parzival's progress to the grail begins with the combined heritage and wisdom of Gahmuret and Herzeloyde, just one step, but a very necessary one.

This determination leads us, then, to the concluding observation concerning the suitability of Gahmuret and Herzeloyde as the parents of the future grail king. If one observes only those actions of the two that took place before they married, it would be difficult not to arrive at the same conclusions as Spahr (see above). But Wolfram does not limit his gaze just to this period. Likewise, if one ignores the actions of Herzeloyde and, especially, Gahmuret prior to their marriage, one ends up with just as lopsided a perspective. Both aspects of their characters, the base and the noble, the vain and the meek, the courageous and the cowardly (Gahmuret's desertion of Belacane), the flighty and the steadfast are all necessary components of their personal makeup. All have been blended and passed on to their son. Without them Parzival would not have been successful in his quest.

The Gahmuret Books are not separate from the rest of the tale any more than the Gawan adventures. All are skillfully and, one could say, seamlessly interwoven into an aesthetically pleasing whole. When confronted with seeming incongruities, we would do well to remember the beginning lines of the prologue:

> Ist zwîvel herzen nâchgebûr,
> daz muoz der sêle werden sûr.
> gesmæhet unde gezieret
> ist, swâ sich parrieret
> unverzaget mannes muot,
> als agelstern varwe tuot.
> der mac dennoch wesen geil:
> wand an im sint beidiu teil,
> des himels und der helle. (1,1–9)

(If uncertainty is the heart's neighbor [sc. in one's heart], that will become bitter to the soul. The spirit of the steadfast man is scorned and praised [in like measure] wherever it is mottled like a magpie [i.e. black and white]. But he can still be joyful, for both heaven and hell have a part in him.)

Wolfram's insight and humanity as revealed here at the start of his great romance should serve all readers as a guide to an understanding of his complicated yet at the same time simple world view. For modern readers, Dylan Thomas expresses it best in his play *Under Milkwood* in the words of Reverend Jenkins's sunset prayer: "We are not wholly bad or good who live our lives under Milk Wood . . . ."

MARION E. GIBBS

Ideals of Flesh and Blood: Women Characters in *Parzival*

A SURPRISINGLY LARGE PROPORTION OF WOLFRAM'S multitude of characters are women, and indeed women perform very significant roles and exert substantial influence on the progress of the narrative. That this should be the case is not altogether surprising, given the crucial function of women in the narrative works of Wolfram's predecessor Hartmann von Aue and, inevitably, in Gottfried von Straßburg's *Tristan*. With good reason, too, the Middle Ages appears to have viewed the *Nibelungenlied* as "The Book of Kriemhild." The case with *Parzival* is different, however, for here we have a vast array of women who people the poem, as it were, in all shapes and sizes and contribute to its diversity and marked human interest.

Their significance goes further, for Wolfram has laid his cards firmly on the table when he defines the poem in terms which are superficially very simple, but in reality complex and profound. His story is to tell of the relentless courage of one man, the bold hero slow to wisdom whom he greets while assuring us that he is not yet born (4,18–26). However, this as yet unnamed man is linked in these early lines with another acknowledged theme, and another whole dimension of the poem, for he declares that the story will tell of the special nature of women, the *reht* which Wolfram identifies as true devotion, that *triuwe* which is unmistakably a keyword, arguably *the* keyword of the poem (4,9–11). The juxtaposition is important, and when Wolfram now launches into the colorful story of Gahmuret, he does so not least in order to demonstrate that Parzival emerges as the product of the fusion of two ingredients, the steel-like valor of his father and the gentler, self-sacrificing devotion of his mother. In the future grail king both strands are needed, and in Parzival they will transcend their origins in the different genders and merge to create a unique being capable of fulfilling a unique role.

Even after thirty years, during which many perspectives have changed and been modified in the light of continuing thought and some persuasive arguments, the present analysis will not seek to retract my adherence (in *Wîplîchez Wîbes Reht*,1972) to these lines as a significant statement by Wolfram himself of his own position regarding the nature of woman, a statement which is taken up again at the beginning of Book III, when he addresses womanhood itself, declaring that its true nature is *triuwe*:

> wîpheit, dîn ordenlîcher site,
> dem vert und fuor ie triwe mite. (116,13–14)

(Womanhood, your proper nature is now, and always has been, loyal devotion. — Translations are mine.)

What Siegfried Christoph dismisses as a "tag-line" and "not clearly delineated" ("Couples," 233) is an important definition of an ideal which is largely attained on various levels by the female protagonists in Wolfram's poem. Nor should the focus on the women characters be dismissed as "well-nigh unavoidable in the climate of our times" (*Choice*, June 1973, 230), when we have Wolfram's own statement of intention, his manifesto as it were, to guide us. The important position accorded to women by Wolfram is no figment of the second half of the twentieth century, but a reality which has firm support in his own utterances. Not least among his achievements is to combine his conception of an ideal with the creation of women of flesh and blood, and to show that, if along the way some of them fall short of the ideal, this does not negate the ideal but is rather a sign of the complexity of human beings of which he is so aware. (The co-existence of the individual and the idealized, very much an aspect of Wolfram's depiction of character, is clearly brought out in the large-scale study by David Blamires.)

If, on the whole, Wolfram elects to display the positive aspects of his characters, to the extent that most of them — and especially the women he depicts — achieve his ideal, this should not be taken as a sign that he does not know of the existence of the opposite kind. Women who do not deserve his praise will not receive it, no matter how beautiful they may be, as he tells us in his prologue (3,12–14). In practice, rather than assess such women negatively, according to their true nature, like paltry blue glass albeit set in gold, Wolfram appears to prefer to refrain from mentioning them. His famous "self-defense" suggests that at least on one occasion he may have let down his guard and spoken disparagingly of a lady, thus incurring the wrath of other women and living to regret it, but this is explicitly not his custom, nor something which he intends to repeat (114,8–114,25). One may speculate on the circumstances which gave rise to his criticism, but that is actually not relevant to the overall view of his women characters as conforming to an expressed ideal.

At the conclusion of Parzival's journey, Wolfram sums up what he has related: he has told how the child of Herzeloyde struggled for the grail and achieved it, as he was destined to do (827,6–7). It is through Herzeloyde that he is a member of the select family, related to Titurel on his mother's side and thus the heir to the kingship, the only male child of his generation. Important as this is, it is a technicality compared with his more abstract inheritance from Herzeloyde, that capacity for love which is manifested in him most explicitly when, departing from the group of pilgrims in Book IX, he softens a little in his attitude towards God and allows Him to guide his horse. Wolfram assures us that it is as the child of Herzeloyde that he rides away, with a myriad of emotions prompting him to think for the first time in many years of the Creator (451,3–22). The encounter with the virtuous young girls acts upon his "manlîchiu zuht" (451,4= "courage and courtesy") to evoke a similar "kiusch unt erbarmunge" (451,5= "purity and compassion") in him, but what is even more explicit is that his young mother Herzeloyde had given to him a legacy of *triuwe* (451,7). It is this which stirs deep in his heart and prompts him to regret his obdurate attitude to God, and to recall that he has been assured — by his mother (119,24) and by Sigune (442,9–10), and now, implicitly, by the Pilgrims — that God's help is at hand for those who ask for it.

Within himself, then, Parzival possesses that all-important quality of *triuwe* which Trevrizent will tell him is the very nature of God (462,19), and he has inherited it from the mother whose own *triuwe* permitted her to abandon the court and withdraw into the wasteland of Soltane in order to protect her son from the fate of his father. It seems entirely inappropriate to deny that this is what Wolfram means when he says that a woman, clearly Herzeloyde, endured poverty for the sake of love and loyalty (116,19); a fuller discussion of the negative views of Herzeloyde's behavior occurs below. This is another matter on which Wolfram is adamant, both at the beginning of Book III, when some critics would blame her for depriving her son of his knightly heritage, and at her death, which he actually characterizes with the adjective "getriulîch" (128,23= "loyal").

Parzival's *triuwe* is innate, but it needs to be encouraged, and never more so than at the beginning of Book IX when, lonely and estranged from his wife and from God, he is geographically very close to the grail, yet spiritually divorced from it. Thus Sigune, who, at their first and second meetings respectively, has praised his *triuwe* (140,1–2) and accused him of lacking it (255,14–16), is herself the very essence of *triuwe* in her love of God which has its roots in her grief and love for Schionatulander (435,13–18). The ring on her finger is a token of both forms of the same emotion and will, she firmly believes, assure her passage into the presence of God (440,13–15).

When Wolfram comments that her entire life is a prayer (435,25), he raises her, as he does Herzeloyde, to the very personification of that most prized of human attributes. Not long afterwards, when the young girls urge their father to abandon his cold teaching and offer instead hospitality and love to the lonely stranger, Wolfram does not define what it is which prompts them, yet it radiates in their beautiful red lips, and it is quite explicitly that which leads them to gaze after the young knight as he rides away from them: "ir triwe si daz lêrte" (451,26= "They were loyal-hearted people").

If a single virtue is shown to dominate Parzival's nature and his progress, it is expressed in this word *triuwe* which has so many manifestations and seems in addition to embrace the other virtues of *kiusche* (= purity) and *diemüete* (= humility) and *erbarmunge* (= compassion) which Wolfram identifies as the essence of God and of those who would serve Him. Thus the principal characters in terms of Parzival's progress towards the grail — Parzival himself, Trevrizent, Herzeloyde and Sigune, Repanse de Schoye and Condwiramurs — have these virtues explicitly associated with them. The word *kiusche*, purity on all levels, is as inextricable from Trevrizent (452,15; 452,20; 452,28) and the virgin grail bearer, Repanse de Schoye, as it is from the grail itself, of which Wolfram tells us, as early as Book V and in connection with the special function of Repanse de Schoye, that the person allowed to carry the grail must eschew all falsity (235,28–30). We have already seen that Herzeloyde and Sigune are the very personification of *triuwe*, and the same is true of Condwiramurs, whose devotion to Parzival, as indeed his to her, is expressed in the two words *triuwe* — most significantly during the episode of the blood in the snow, at the end of Book XIV when he rejects all thought of other love, and during the battle with Feirefiz — and *stæte*, the steadfast commitment which binds them mutually to one another (192,3; 202,3; 743,4).

If Wolfram bestows upon his women characters so much of the abstract virtue which is seen to be crucial to Parzival's nature and to his attainment of the grail, this does not by any means imply that they are saintly paragons. Sigune's passage to the next world, where she will be united with her earthly lover and with God, is fraught with conflict and passion. Anger and grief rack her body and destroy her beauty before she arrives at the heightened state when her whole existence is one of prayer. Before she reaches that calm which allows her, at their third meeting, to commend Parzival to God and hope against all expectation that he may yet come to the grail again, she attacks him verbally in the most forthright terms when they meet on the second occasion and is relentless in removing from him all possibility of making amends. That her extreme reaction stems from her belief in him and from her yearning for the release of her family from suffering is understandable, coupled as it is with her own bereavement, and in the fullness of time her apparent rejection of him can be seen in a positive light, a contributory factor in the suffering which is essential to his ultimate success.

Scholarship has concerned itself, perhaps too much, with the question of Sigune's guilt, based on her anguished cry when she accuses herself of foolishness in withholding her love from Schionatulander (141,20–21), yet she has apparently done no more than was expected of her within the courtly convention. Moreover, we must say "apparently," since neither *Parzival* nor *Titurel* supplies much detail about the circumstances in which Schionatulander met his death. Siegfried Christoph is doubtless right to shift the focus from Sigune's perception of her guilt for the death of Schionatulander to her grief-stricken awareness that, as a member of the grail family, she partakes of its despair ("Wolfram's Sigune"). The passage of Sigune is thus less a self-imposed penance than a gradual coming to terms with despair until Parzival at last removes this despair from her, the whole family, and, indeed, from himself. Already, of course, Sigune has come a long way in her progress through grief when she is able to direct Parzival to God at their third meeting, by which time the *triuwe* which showed itself in her anguish at their first meeting and her fury at their second is being directed towards God and the hope of the next world. What appears to be her totally destructive reaction to his revelation that he asked no question has its place in the positive progress of them both, but that this is so emerges, like so many of the major insights of the poem, only when the time is right.

More explicitly, Wolfram appears to be expressing the same idea when he warns of the approaching Cundrie that her natural courtesy is distorted by rage (312,4), assuring us of her reputation for *triuwe*, the loyalty which leads her to reproach the child of Herzeloyde and Gahmuret so bitterly for his failure to demonstrate precisely that emotion towards Anfortas. When she weeps at the conclusion of her outburst, Wolfram again emphasizes the *triuwe* which prompts her grief (318,9–10). Although the word is not applied to her again at her second visit, it is doubtless this quality which makes her the appropriate person to announce the reversal in Parzival's fortunes — when her plea for his forgiveness is again accompanied by tears, not this time of anger, but of remorse and desperation lest he refuse her: "si warp al weinde umb sînen gruoz" (779,24= "weeping copiously she begged for his greeting") — and then to escort him, with Feirefiz, to Munsalvaesche.

Even Herzeloyde, the very epitome of that humility and sacrifice which are contained within the concept of *triuwe*, does not escape negative appraisal, though this comes more from recent critics than from Wolfram himself who leaves no doubt that his own ultimate assessment of her is positive. Only the comment that Parzival is "an küneclîcher fuore betrogn" (118,2= "deceived of his kingly way of life") betrays a touch of explicit criticism, redressed by Wolfram's assurance that everything that Herzeloyde does — from her over-protection of her son in the wasteland seclusion, to her somewhat bizarre idea that if she dresses him in the clothing of a fool and gives him an inferior horse to ride he will come running back to her, fleeing from the mockery of the world outside — is motivated by love. That, anyway, would appear to be the implication of the passage which opens Book III and seems to be Wolfram's way of countering in advance any adverse view of her behavior. When he asserts that she is totally without falsity — der valsch sô gar an ir verswant, / ouge noch ôre in nie dâ vant (117,1–2= She was so completely devoid of falsity that neither eye nor ear ever discovered any in her) — one might imagine that he is defiantly making it inappropriate for observers to criticize her actions, just as his praise of her at her death would also seem to represent his final and authoritative opinion.

However, it might be held that this defiant view on the part of Wolfram has encouraged rather than allayed the negative assessments of more modern critics, who see her behavior as selfish, essentially self-centered and often as the product of a woman crazed by grief and incapable of proper judgement (see in particular, most recently, Gertrude Jaron Lewis and the studies of David Yeandle.) Some see her actions following the death of Gahmuret as all of a piece with her ruthless determination to secure him as her husband in the first place, ignoring the scruples he expresses and the claims of the other two women in his life. The very title of the article by Gertrude Jaron Lewis suggests a deliberate attempt to sweep aside the view of Herzeloyde as a saintly, long-suffering woman, but she surely goes too far in her determination to expose her. Her insistence on the deception which Herzeloyde practices, conceded just once and in passing by Wolfram when he speaks of Parzival's being *deceived* of his kingly way of life, leads to — or perhaps stems from — her interpretation of the word *flühtesal* as "deception," rather than, more gently and with greater linguistic justification (see

Yeandle 1985, 38) as "refuge" in the telling lines which explain her motive for leaving the court: "si brâhte dar durch flühtesal / des werden Gahmuretes kint" (117,14–15= "She took the child of noble Gahmuret there in search of refuge"). It is not difficult to distort the subsequent actions of Herzeloyde once one has assumed a wilful betrayal on her part of her duty as the mother of a king's son.

In comparison, the long and balanced separate study of Herzeloyde by David Yeandle (1981) examines the portrayal in detail and probes the problems which it poses with much greater restraint, although he too attributes less than worthy motives to her, arising not least, he assumes, because she has become "a confused, grief-stricken character who has all but lost her powers of reasoning" (10). Yeandle is by no means alone in seeing the widowed Herzeloyde as mentally unhinged by her loss of Gahmuret, an assumption which not only suggests a limited understanding of the complex process of bereavement but also seems to fly in the face of what Wolfram actually tells of her deliberate and reasoned decision to leave the court, which has hitherto been very important to her, and seek out a different kind of life (117,7ff.). Nor is it enough to say that she has "a dim presentiment of Gahmuret's legacy breaking out in Parzival" (14): on the contrary, she *knows* with absolute certainty that this legacy must and will break out in time, hence her desperate attempts to put off that time. Her behavior may be unwise, uncourtly, but insane it is not.

For all their well-argued attempts to set the record straight with regard to Herzeloyde, neither Lewis nor Yeandle arrives at a conclusion so far divorced from the one which Wolfram appears to wish to encourage. Thus, for example, Lewis finds that in spite of her intriguing, her desire for sympathy, her arrogance and selfishness, Herzeloyde emerges as a phenomenon rare in courtly literature: a convincing character such as would not have been possible had she been depicted exclusively as an ideal (485), and Yeandle writes: "what emerges from the narrative concerning Herzeloyde in Book III as a whole is not a blatant discrepancy between positive and negative aspects, but a subtle fusion of the two ...." (1981, 28). Eventually, then, one might compromise on the view that Wolfram was fully aware of Herzeloyde's shortcomings but sought to treat them with characteristic compassion and understanding and ultimately to redress any apparent negativity by the emphasis on the intention behind her actions. After all the dissection of the text and even the avowed process of iconoclasm undertaken by Lewis, Herzeloyde emerges as what she is: a woman with all the complexities of any human being, placed in a tragic situation and responding in the only way she knows how to circumstances as they arise. With that in mind, one can see Wolfram's portrayal of her as harmonious, showing a development rather than an abrupt and unacceptable disjunction between the worldly young woman who wins Gahmuret and the grief-stricken mother who will go to extremes to protect her child, and the exalted ideal which Wolfram would have us see.

Indeed, we are shown in Herzeloyde a woman who develops to a greater extent than any other female character in *Parzival*. Her behavior as a young widow towards her handsome visitor Gahmuret is unseemly, as Wolfram acknowledges when she ignores the claims of her other guests in her desire to greet him and pulls him unbecomingly close to her (84,3–7); her ruthless dismissal of his protests that he is already married to Belacane and that he owes his allegiance as a knight to Ampflise (94,11–20) do not endear her to the onlooker, although Wolfram remains objective in his own presentation of her behavior this time, and Gahmuret himself needs little persuasion. In fact their love is never brought into question, and this is as it should be, given that its product will be the future grail king. The spontaneous effect of seeing Herzeloyde for the first time speaks volumes for Gahmuret's response to her radiance (64,4–6), and although he may struggle for a while with thoughts of Belacane, and even of Ampflise, he cannot withstand the overwhelming passion he feels, which Wolfram finds it necessary to attribute to his "art von der feien" (96,20= "fairy nature"). No such supernatural heritage prompts Herzeloyde, yet she too appears to be guided by an ineluctable force, a ruthless determination to get what she wants, if one views it in a negative light, or perhaps, more kindly, a deep consciousness of her destiny.

However one interprets their origins, Herzeloyde is elevated by the intensity of her love and grief, and again this is appropriate in the mother of the future grail king. Scholarly attempts, particularly by Schröder (1963), to draw analogies between Herzeloyde and the Virgin Mary have been taken to extremes and often discredited (see Kratz 484–491), yet it cannot be denied that Wolfram himself introduces the comparison, or allows Herzeloyde herself to do so, when she refers to her decision to suckle her own child (113,17–26). This, combined with Wolfram's praise of her as "a root of all goodness and a veritable stem of humility" (128,27–28) justifies a passing comparison, though there is danger in adducing too many other instances, for in Herzeloyde Wolfram creates an individual who may partake of qualities expressed through Marian symbolism, but who possesses also her own claims to be seen as an ideal (see Blamires 93–96 for a well argued view of this question). We should surely not disregard the fact that both Sigune and Trevrizent speak explicitly of her reputation for *triuwe* (140,18–19;

499,23), nor dismiss it on the grounds that both have a personal reason for viewing their close relative in a positive light.

Herzeloyde is a woman who responds to her inner promptings rather than to anything more rational, and so she needs to be persuaded not to place on her own body the stained and torn garment which the page brings back to her with the news of Gahmuret's death (111,26–29), and she orders the killing of the birds which appear to have caused her child's tears, yet responds just as quickly to his pleas that they be spared. If her religious education of her son leaves much to be desired, this is less a question of deliberate neglect of duty than another instinctive reaction, this time to a question which takes her off her guard. It is not Herzeloyde's fault that time is not on her side and that her son rides away before she can fill in the details which might have made all the difference to his future behavior: details of his duty towards God, his relationship with women, and his own lineage, crucially his destiny within the dynasty of the grail. Of course, saying this assumes that, given more time, she would have wished, or even would have been able, to supply such detailed information. As it is, as Yeandle puts it, "at the eleventh hour Herzeloyde goes some way towards compensating for her having brought up Parzival in total ignorance of the outside world and the world of chivalry, by giving him elementary advice and information" (1981, 23). The *list* (= knowledge) which in the event she undertakes to teach him (127,14) is, of course, incapable of redressing the *tumpheit* (= foolishness based on lack of knowledge or experience) for which she is also, however unwillingly, responsible, and the bigger issues which might have made all the difference to his early progress are postponed to a much later date. (On the much discussed subject of Parzival's *tumpheit* and Herzeloyde's responsibility, see Alois Haas 56–71.)

If two of the principal women characters in *Parzival*, Sigune and Herzeloyde, develop as the narrative progresses, they are the exceptions, and their development cannot be separated from their function within the account of Parzival's own growth. (This is not quite the same as the contention of Blamires which sums up an essential part of his finding about the main characters: "It is thus a dependent individuality they possess which derives from their relationship to Parzival" [473].) Other women, equally powerfully characterized and hardly less significant, are more static figures, though that description should not imply anything negative.

Belacane is the central female figure in the first Book, the heathen queen who so captivates Gahmuret and who is recalled perhaps above all for the strength of her grief, first in her lengthy account to Gahmuret of the death of her beloved Isenhart (26,9–28,9) and then when she laments that Gahmuret himself has left her, apparently because of the difference in religion between them which she would gladly have redressed with baptism had she known that this was what he wanted (57,6–8). The picture of Belacane is a charming vignette, focussed on these two pictures which cannot be separated from one another. Gahmuret has looked at her, with tears pouring down her dress (28,16–17), and he has recognized the essential goodness in her which means that, for him, she is as much a Christian as any woman formally baptized. The difference in religion cannot be what takes him from her, as he at least has the grace to admit to Herzeloyde (97,3–4), and the cruel deception does little to enhance the picture of Gahmuret, ruthless in his search for knightly adventure. Posthumous reparation is sought by their son Feirefiz who tells Parzival that he has come looking for his father, and it seems to be bestowed by Wolfram in an appropriately conciliatory way, when Feirefiz seeks and receives baptism out of love for the grail bearer. Even so, Wolfram cannot really soften the anguish of the woman left at the end of Book I to cradle her black and white son. Belacane is, as far as we know, his own creation, certainly without counterpart in his source, and she both contributes to his array of virtuous women in *Parzival* and anticipates his much more extensive treatment of Gyburg, the central female figure in his *Willehalm*, the heathen woman who converts to Christianity for the love of Willehalm himself. Siegfried Christoph is probably right when he excuses the speed with which Belacane "turns her womanly charms . . . towards Gahmuret" on political grounds, since, following the death of Isenhart, she is in dire need of support ("Wolfram's Sigune," 64), but Wolfram leaves us in no doubt that her love for Gahmuret banishes her grief, sincere enough at the time, for Isenhart, rather in the way that Gahmuret himself is able to find consolation for the loss of Belacane once he has met Herzeloyde. In both cases, *the* great love has the overriding power.

The desertion by Gahmuret of Belacane and his later departure which leaves Herzeloyde a widow combine to form a memory which is, as it were, reversed when Parzival's own wife gives him unconditional leave to go in search of adventure, which is as much life's blood to him as it was to his father. It is also significant that Parzival expresses to Condwiramurs his desire to find his mother and see how she is faring (223,17–19). Although the listeners have heard of Herzeloyde's falling dead to the ground when her son left her, and although Trevrizent may designate this responsibility among Parzival's sins, Parzival is innocent of the ruthless desertion which marred his father's reputation, and Condwiramurs herself is a different kind of woman from her counterparts in the previous generation. She allows him to go even though she herself has everything that she could desire in her marriage (223,1–4). For her, love is enough; for him, as for his father, love must be joined with *âventiure* (knightly exploits), is indeed inextricable from it. For both Parzival and Condwiramurs love and chivalry will be tested in a way not experienced by their predecessors, and she is capable of fulfilling such a role in his development as was never asked of Belacane or Herzeloyde. The memory of her sustains him through all the years of suffering which lie ahead and ensures that he remain true to her; and the picture of her which ultimately endures is of the mother lying asleep in her tent with her twin sons by her side next time Parzival actually sees her (800,20–23). Not for nothing does the grail insist that its king should be married, and married explicitly to a pure woman, as Trevrizent tells Parzival (495,9–10), and it is important that the name of Condwiramurs appears side by side with his in the inscription on the stone, together with that of their son Loherangrin (781,17–19): she is not simply an accessory but a vital ingredient of his success, his indispensable consort and the custodian of the future of the grail family. As such she can be evoked on several occasions during their separation. The drops of blood in the snow which cause Parzival to fall into a trance are a reminder to him of her beauty, and they are also the inspiration to his paean of praise to God the Creator (283,2ff.). In response to Gawan's commendation of him to God, he may reject that same Creator, but in His place he puts woman, the abstract being who will guide him in the future but who is, in tangible terms, his own wife, for whose sake at crucial turning-points he will reject the blandishments of Orgeluse (619,4–5) and the temptation to find passing solace in female company (732,1–7).

If some of the central female characters can be seen first and foremost as the embodiment of qualities which are vital to Parzival's progress and eventual achievement, this should not suggest that they are not also distinctive as individuals. Herzeloyde's capacity to develop and Sigune's demonstration of her outstanding positive quality in what appears to be its negative aspect of anger, ensure that one cannot consign them to the stereotypical, and the same is true of the other women, too. However, it is in the Gawan action that Wolfram produces women characters who challenge some of the preconceptions one might adopt from other areas of the poem. Obie and Obilot, Antikonie and Orgeluse, all derive to a more obvious extent from Wolfram's source, and sometimes one senses that they may have presented problems to him, in the way they appear to oppose his conception of an ideal. A closer look shows that, with them as with Gawan himself, he is operating in a different realm in which different ideals hold. Yet just as the worlds of Parzival and Gawan overlap and touch, so do the "heroines" of the Gawan story possess qualities in common with the major women characters already discussed. If Gawan experiences *zwîvel* (= doubt, or even despair) when he is uncertain whether he should proceed to Bearosche (349,30) and is subsequently persuaded to serve Obilot by his memory of Parzival's commendation of him to the hand of woman (370,18–19), so too do the somewhat wayward women whom he encounters work their way through to a semblance of the ideal propounded by their more rarified counterparts.

One of the consequences is that Obie and Obilot, Antikonie and Orgeluse are more complicated figures, sharing with the Gawan narrative in general that greater variety — confusion, one might almost call it — which distinguishes it, and them, from the smooth passage of the much deeper story of Parzival. By "complicated" I mean here, not of course more profound, but contradictory, even discordant in some respects. Obie and Obilot are two women who, in different ways, are struggling with the courtly conventions which govern their lives and the world in which they live. When Obie demands that Meljanz serve her before she will consider offering him her love, she is doing no more than is her right, following in the footsteps of the tragic Belacane and the tragic Sigune, but Meljanz himself has transgressed the norm of courtly behavior in demanding reward without service, unlike Isenhart and Schionatulander whose deaths came, as far as we can judge, as a consequence of their adherence to the chivalric code. That all ends well for Obie and Meljanz accords with the lighter tone of the Gawan action, but it might have been quite otherwise.

Similarly, the gentle outcome to the "relationship" between Obilot and Gawan owes much to the respect of each for the conventions by which they live. Obilot may actually be more at home playing with her dolls (372,18) or at the childish game of rings (368,12), but Gawan has the tact and good sense to play the game of courtly love, hopeless though it must be in this case. When Gawan embraces her on parting "like a doll" (395,23), Wolfram returns Obilot to her proper place, as a child who has some years in which to grow up to the proper courtly lady he anticipates. Meljanz predicts, "Obilôt wirt kranz / aller wîplîchen güete" (394,12–13= "Obilot will become a garland of all womanly virtue"), but Wolfram also gives Gawan his due recognition, acknowledging his reputation as the lover *par excellence*, scrupulous in his pursuit of chivalry; the knight, indeed, who was sensitive to Parzival's plight when he stood gazing at the blood in the snow and who also had the maturity and experience to know how to alleviate it.

When, immediately afterwards, Wolfram allows this paragon of chivalry to find himself in a distinctly compromising situation, this is no doubt primarily out of loyalty to his source, which supplied the figure of Antikonie and the episode which contains her. However, there are times in the course of this adventure when one suspects that he is quite enjoying a situation which both represents a sharp contrast to the delicate play-acting of Gawan in his service of Obilot and further lightens the action before he comes to the profound events of Book IX. Even an audience tut-tutting at the forwardness of Antikonie and the opportunistic behavior of Gawan was probably also diverted by this account of erotic attraction at first sight, while the chess-set battle from the tower, this irreverent travesty of chivalry, may well have prompted some laughter, albeit somewhat uncomfortable laughter. Equally, though, one senses that Wolfram is not entirely happy, as he struggles to present a favorite hero in a positive light and must adapt an ideal of female behavior which he has established elsewhere to accommodate the decidedly unconventional Antikonie. To some extent he has already done this with Obie, a young woman who reacts spitefully and pushes events to the edge of tragedy, and who could almost be accused of abusing her power. He will also face the same problem with Orgeluse, whom he will transform from the counterpart figure in his source into a woman of special significance, not only to the career of Gawan, but, more importantly, to the whole poem.

Antikonie may thus be seen to fulfil a function which is both structural and thematic in a work which is remarkable for its subtle structure and its multiplicity of themes. However, that does not diminish her importance as an individual. On the contrary, she stands out among Wolfram's women characters, and not only for the colorful and somewhat risqué events in which she finds herself. Possibly Wolfram sensed that he needed to defend her very forcefully, and certainly he does this in a number of passages which owe nothing to his source (403,26ff; 404,24ff; 427,5ff; 431,12ff.) and which go beyond any support he gives to his other characters. It is striking, too, that he uses terms to describe her which are applied, with more obvious reason, to these others and which appear to take on a new dimension when applied to her. On the face of it, the word *kiusche* (= purity, chastity) would not seem to be the most appropriate, yet its extension here to cover the integrity of Antikonie, her total commitment to the support of Gawan and her unflinching regard for the truth, shows that Wolfram can be quite flexible in his assessment of what matters in human behavior (see 404,27; 409,14 by implication applied to Antikonie; 414,23; 427,6). Similarly, the word *triuwe* which is inseparable from his ideal and which, as we have already seen, can embrace a variety of other valued attributes, is not out of place in the description of Antikonie (406,6; 409,15). It is thus not so "incredible that anyone should want to compare the two characters Herzeloyde and Antikonie," as David Duckworth assumes people might think at the opening of his article (1987/88). On the contrary, as he goes on to make clear, the two women are closely linked by the praise which Wolfram heaps on both of them, possibly in both cases anticipating that the instinctive initial response of the audience to their behavior may be a negative one. As if to underline his purpose in both cases of redressing a possibly unfavorable reaction, Wolfram significantly uses a phrase which explicitly contradicts a negative quality to characterize the two women: thus, Herzeloyde at her death is described explicitly as "diu frouwe valsches laz" (128,20= "the lady lacking in falsity") and Antikonie is called "vor valscheit die vrîen" (427,8= "the woman devoid of falsity"). Just as Parzival himself, at the nadir of his fortunes, is described as avoiding "den rehten valsch" (319,8= "real falsity," "wrongdoing"), so too is neither Herzeloyde nor Antikonie, in their very different ways, remotely false. What protects Parzival is "scham ob allen sînen siten" (319,7= "shame in all his being"), a somewhat difficult phrase because it clearly attributes an essentially positive quality to the sense of shame, and both the women, too, are protected by *kiusche* and *triuwe* in their widest senses which appear to embrace integrity and honesty of purpose. Antikonie is no saint-like figure fit to be the mother of the grail king, but, as she stands by the side of Gawan in the tower, and, even more, when she subsequently defends him verbally, she earns for herself both the enthusiastic praise of Wolfram himself and Gawan's own assertion that she has triumphed over falsity (431,13).

With all this in mind, one has little difficulty in accepting the depiction of Orgeluse who represents, perhaps along with Sigune, the most remarkable example of Wolfram's use of his French source to recreate a female character. Although he does not attempt to soften the spiteful taunting of Chrétien's counterpart figure, he implies early on that there is an explanation for it (516,1–8) and leads his listeners to expect that all will be made clear. In the meantime, until they learn how matters stand with her heart (516,8), they should refrain from judging her actions, a caution which resembles the one he has already offered in respect of the behavior of Obie, similarly motivated by love (366,2). The explanation, when it eventually comes — or rather, in the manner of Wolfram's narrative, emerges from a series of hints and half-explanations — is a moving one, which places Orgeluse alongside the other devoted women in the poem. She differs from them in her relentless active pursuit of revenge for the death of her beloved Cidegast. Her ruthlessness in rejecting and equally in enlisting the service of other knights is yet another manifestation of *triuwe*, and it is significant that Wolfram's most explicit definition of love as true loyalty is embedded in the story of Gawan and Orgeluse: "reht minne ist wâriu triuwe" (532,10= "benign love is true fidelity"). Of course it would belong just as well, perhaps more obviously one might say, within the Parzival action, but it says something very important about his conception of Orgeluse that he places it here, in this tragic love story which has important repercussions and spills over into the main action of the poem. Leaving aside most of the much discussed and very important issue of the relationship between the Parzival action and the Gawan action (for a résumé of some of the scholarly work in this area, see Kratz 556–569, Bumke 1991, 84–118 and 189–191, and Jones in this volume), we should note here the masterly stroke of Wolfram in making Orgeluse responsible for the transgression of Anfortas and thus for the tragedy which afflicts the whole of the grail family. Although she ultimately belongs with Gawan and with the Gawan action, Orgeluse in this way nevertheless attains an extraordinary dimension and must, moreover, contribute significantly to the consideration of the relationship between the overlapping realms of the work.

The view of Orgeluse as a tremendous figure in the poem, limited only by the context from achieving overwhelming stature, is supported by one of the most moving moments in the poem, when Orgeluse tells Gawan of her encounter with the Red Knight who refused her, saying that he had a wife more beautiful and dearer to him, the queen of Pelrapeire (619,3–10). From the beginning she has been compared with Condwiramurs, the only woman more beautiful than she (508,22–23), and it is left to Gawan, who was so nearly defeated in battle by Parzival, to console her. What she has perceived as a rejection is nothing of the kind, and Gawan himself is appropriate compensation. Nevertheless we are left with the sense that the woman who was pursued by Anfortas, even if in doing so he threw the grail kingdom into turmoil, and who was spurned by Parzival, is somehow bigger than the mold to which she now returns. This is no example of an unparalleled weakness in Wolfram's characterization (as Marianne Wynn argues [1976/77, 128]), but, on the contrary, of its power. Thus, bridging as she does the two main areas of the poem, the Arthurian and the heightened realm of the grail, and given this inherent stature, Orgeluse attains a unique quality which distinguishes her from the spectrum of women formed by Herzeloyde and Sigune, Belacane and Condwiramurs, and supported by such relatively minor characters as Liaze, Jeschute and

Repanse de Schoye. For all her intrinsic similarity with them in some respects, she is unique in Wolfram's depiction of character.

At the other end of the scale from this almost larger-than-life figure with her apparently contradictory behavior and her tragic past, are some of the women who make quite fleeting appearances, or even appear in person not at all. Some of these are extraordinarily vivid. One thinks of Schoette, the widowed mother of Gahmuret who must watch her son ride away from her and of whom we later learn that she died of grief when she lost her other son (92,27–30). She foreshadows other more major characters, like Belacane, Herzeloyde and Sigune, in her loss and her inevitable acceptance of chivalry with all its pain. Secundille, beloved of Feirefiz and his inspiration in the great battle with Parzival, makes an impact on the poem without ever appearing in it. There is color and glamour in her, shadowy though she may be, and in this she matches the exotic Feirefiz until she is superseded by Repanse de Schoye and the greater power of baptism: even then, Wolfram softens her fate by allowing her to die before Feirefiz brings his bride home. Although the memory of Belacane hovers, Wolfram avoids a tragic replay of her fate; the two women appear to represent the same situation, yet the outcome is different.

Another "invisible" woman of some importance is Ampflise, the mysterious liege-lady of Gahmuret. Indeed she is so vivid a character that one perhaps feels the need to check that she never actually appears in person, but this is certainly the case. Instead Wolfram builds up a picture of a captivating woman who exerts a powerful influence on Parzival's father. The first mention of her passes almost unnoticed: she is the "friundin" (= "lady friend") of Gahmuret who has bestowed gifts of precious jewels upon him (12,11). This early reference is revived when Wolfram speaks of a woman whom he has already mentioned (76,1), but even now it is not Ampflise herself who appears, though her identity as queen of Franze and her name are now revealed to us, but her messengers with a letter, the very sight of which, with her familiar writing on it, produces a strong reaction in Gahmuret, who bows. That she and not Herzeloyde is his true inspiration in the jousting which wins him Herzeloyde is an aspect of the irony which is inseparable from her, just as Gahmuret himself asks her, via her messengers, to accept that he must adhere to the code of chivalry which she taught him, although this means that, on one level, she must lose him. This time the life of chivalry exacts its toll from a woman but in a different way. In the vast array of women in Wolfram's poem, one might suggest that Ampflise is at the opposite end from Orgeluse: two subtle depictions of powerful forces in the lives of their men, the one a shadowy, abstract force, the other a vivacious creature of flesh and blood, yet both quintessentially feminine and both bound by deep commitment.

We never learn how Ampflise responds to Gahmuret's decision, though the tears of her messengers may perhaps anticipate her anguish and one would need to look to Wolfram's *Titurel* to expand just a little on our understanding of this intriguing character (see my own article "Ampflise im *Parzival* und im *Titurel*"). A gentler fate is granted to Cunneware who for a time assumes the role of liege-lady to Parzival, receiving his defeated opponents, his messages, and his assurances of his service. Although she may be mentioned for her beauty in the same breath as Condwiramurs (187,15), and although she performs the parting service to him when she helps him mount his horse as he leaves Arthur's court (332,19–30), there is no suggestion that she rivals Parzival's wife in his affections. Indeed Wolfram seems to be removing any doubt about this when he has her marry none other than Clamide, the rejected suitor of Condwiramurs (332,25–26). This may seem like poor compensation, but actually it serves to clarify the situation: Parzival and Condwiramurs are the perfect pair and unassailable, but the woman who recognized Parzival's excellence as a knight is well matched with the man whom he defeated in his first major encounter, and it affirms Clamide's reputation when he is paired with Parzival's own liege-lady. This is a telling decision with an important message, quite unlike the somewhat unseemly haste with which couples are married off at the end of Book XIV, at the conclusion of the Gawan action.

Cunneware, of course, stems from Wolfram's source, where the unnamed maiden laughs when she returns Perceval's greeting as he rides out of Arthur's court (Hilka, ed., verses 1034ff.). Characteristically, Wolfram increases her role and endows it with a special quality, for Cunneware is condemned to a life without laughter until she sees the greatest of all knights. This phenomenon, with its touch of the magical, the fairy tale, is nevertheless firmly bound to reality, for the way has been prepared by Cunneware's own brother, none other than Orilus, who revealed it in the course of his angry onslaught on his wife Jeschute (135,14–18). Moreover, in Wolfram, the breaking of the spell which binds Cunneware has the domino effect of causing the dumb Antanor to speak and, like Cunneware herself, to be beaten as a result, a further development of Chrétien's version which has the unnamed jester cry out in pain when he is hurled into the fire by Keu for having frequently in the past declared that the girl would only laugh when she saw the greatest of knights (1053ff.).

The manner in which Wolfram uses his source, often taking up hints which Chrétien unwittingly provides, repeatedly leads to a remarkable expansion of the French poem, and Cunneware is one such example among the relatively minor female characters. Another is Jeschute herself who fulfills an important role in the overall account of Parzival's progress. The episode of the unnamed lady in the tent is already important in Chrétien's story, and the elements it contains — the clumsy embrace, the repeated kisses, the theft of the ring and the eager consumption of the food, the conventional words of farewell, the return of the woman's lover and his threat of the hardship he will impose on her in future — are all taken up in some way by Wolfram. Yet there are significant differences and additions. The ring will be restored to Jeschute when next they meet, but meanwhile the fact that it had no firm symbolic value to Parzival, largely because Herzeloyde had failed to associate a ring with a genuine relationship, is stressed by his additional theft of her brooch, the object which he will use to bribe the rogue who agrees to direct him to Arthur's court (143,1–2). As already mentioned in connection with Cunneware, Wolfram creates a family relationship between the knight (i.e., Orilus) and the maiden who laughs at Arthur's court (Cunneware), an idea doubtless prompted by the fact that, in the French version, after he has been defeated by Perceval, the knight journeys with his lady to the court and fulfills his obligation, the condition on his release, to deliver Perceval's message to the assembly and above all to assure the maiden that he remains conscious of the debt he owes her (3975ff.).

Perhaps the insistence on the family relationship does not much change the situation, though it is very much in line with Wolfram's overall pre-occupation with family ties, but of considerable significance is the setting chosen for the reconciliation of Orilus and Jeschute, explicitly in Wolfram a married couple. Parzival takes them to a holy cell which he knows to exist close by and there he takes a solemn oath declaring her innocence. Two factors are significant here: the very solemnity of the occasion which, in a sense, erases this early misdemeanor of Parzival's at a time when he is laden with new and more complex guilt, and the location, the place which time will teach us is the scene of Parzival's sojourn with Trevrizent who will give him his most important religious education and where Parzival will acknowledge his failure before the grail. Characteristically, too, Wolfram will link the two events and provide a clear indication of time when Trevrizent tells Parzival that it is four and a half years and three days since he removed Taurian's spear, a gesture which had at the time of that first visit seemed relatively meaningless but which now assumes an importance in establishing the link and the length of time. The role of Jeschute thus takes on a new dimension in the whole narrative. An early victim of his *tump-*

heit (= youthful inexperience), she also marks the beginning of his lengthy path of atonement, and though she never resurfaces physically after the end of Book V — except fleetingly at 646,19 — the memory of her echoes through this tangible reminder in Book IX.

Another woman who might be assigned to the ranks of the "minor" characters — though it has already become evident that many of Wolfram's minor characters are accorded quite substantial functions — is Liaze, apparently invented by Wolfram as his own addition to the sojourn of Perceval with the old knight who, among other things, warns him not to ask too many questions. That Gurnemanz, unlike Gornemant, has a lovely young daughter accords with the tradition of the Arthurian romance (among other examples are Koralus and Enite, and the daughter of Kalogreant's host in *Iwein*), and her presence enhances this important episode in a number of ways. The addition of Liaze contributes an important dimension, and her charming treatment of Parzival certainly represents a pleasing aspect of his early process of learning. There is considerable delicacy in Wolfram's depiction of their brief acquaintance which brings home to us both Parzival's innocence in sexual matters and his instinctive understanding of his knightly obligations. The human understanding which allows Wolfram to touch on the eager expectation of the household that Parzival will marry their young mistress (175,10ff.) and on the disappointment of the old father when he realizes that this is not to be (178,8–10) extends also to the emotional conflict in Parzival as he rides off, deeply moved by this "companionship without love" as he calls it (179,29), yet eager for the chivalrous challenges which may, but in the event do not, permit him to return to claim Liaze as his bride. Although Liaze will not appear in person again — and in this respect there is never any question of a going-back for Parzival — her impact on him pervades his next encounter, the only real love of his life. It is again typical of Wolfram that he understands how the young man's preoccupation with the woman he has just left will color his first meeting with another woman, to the extent that in his confusion he actually thinks Condwiramurs *is* Liaze (188,1ff.). Moreover, it shows Wolfram's realism that, though he dismisses the idea by declaring that Liaze is nowhere near as beautiful as Condwiramurs, he allows the possibility of a family likeness by making the two young women first cousins (189,27). Further still, when Condwiramurs comes to appeal to Parzival for help against Clamide and Kingrun and their forces, she herself has the perspicacity to mention the name of Liaze (195,6), and Parzival responds to the mention of the name by agreeing to help her. The emotion stirred in the young man by his first acquaintance with a lovely young woman will be transferred to this second woman, and the surpassing love of Parzival for his wife loses nothing in the transition, so subtle is Wolfram's depiction of Liaze and her almost indefinable influence on her father's visitor. It is important, too, that it was Liaze's father who first expounded to Parzival the nature of the relationship between man and woman (173,1–6), in the powerful lines which Parzival explicitly recalls when he is about to express this generalization in real terms through the consummation of his marriage (203,4–5).

This consideration of some aspects of Wolfram's depiction of his women characters has thus returned to Condwiramurs, arguably and perhaps inevitably the most important of them all as far as the interpretation of the work is concerned. In her Wolfram merges his two techniques, creating, as we have seen, someone who is the personification of the power of love and the power to be loved, yet who is also very much an individual. One of the aspects which is important here is that Wolfram not only develops a character from his source but actually changes it, to the extent that his Condwiramurs is a very different being from Blanschefleur, her counterpart in Chrétien, and is called upon to fulfil a very different function which her changed nature allows her to do. Bearing in mind Wolfram's interest in names — he gives names to characters unnamed in his source and to relatively minor figures who could just as well have remained anonymous — it immediately arouses interest that he takes the unusual step of changing a name completely in this one case. Two explanations have been offered: that he wanted his creation, the woman who becomes Parzival's wife, to be completely separate from Perceval's beautiful *amie* in Chrétien's romance, and that he wanted her to have no connection, even via a name, with the mother of Gottfried's Tristan, a woman associated with a very different kind of love, clandestine, outside society, and first and foremost based on physical attraction. Possibly both objections led Wolfram to change the name, and change it to one whose meaning, particularly in the form in which it occurs just once — *Condwiren âmûrs* (327,20) — expresses one of her most important functions, to lead Parzival towards love and to lead love to him. Just once is her name combined with a circumlocution which recalls her predecessor in Chrétien's version — "Condwîr âmûrs, / diu geflôrierte bêâ flûrs" (732,13–14) — but this is so late in the poem that the comparison has become irrelevant.

This is, however, a case where comparison with the source brings out very clearly the intention of Wolfram, and, given the fragmentary nature of Chrétien's work, comparison must be based largely on the meeting between the hero and the maiden in the castle under siege. The very nature of the respective episodes establishes their place in the careers of the heroes, for while Perceval rides away from this first real test of his chivalry without marrying the lady of the land, the natural consequence for Parzival of his tremendous display of knightly prowess is marriage with Condwiramurs and a settled period during which he rules over her land. For Parzival, this episode is the foundation of a stable relationship which will in its turn be the foundation for his future as grail king. Whether Perceval ever returns to Blanschefleur as he says he will remains untold, of course, but the episode, for all its length and, in some respects, its charm, does not achieve that special quality of the inevitable and the fateful which characterizes Wolfram's account. Yet many of the details are there already in the French version, but differently used by Wolfram. Above all, the nocturnal visit of Condwiramurs explicitly lacks the sexual motivation which is so much a part of the French version. Condwiramurs comes to Parzival to plead for his help in her dire need, and, though he cannot have failed to notice her beauty, it is the mention of Liaze which seems to prompt him to offer his help, in a somewhat absurd question which suggests that he has hardly taken in anything she has told him, or anything of her situation: "vrouwe, hilft iuch iemens trôst?" (195,13= "Can anyone help you, my lady?"). Indeed a kind of childlike ingenuousness characterizes the whole scene, emphasized not least in Wolfram's assertion that both of them are ignorant of sexual matters and that nothing remotely physical occurs between them: "wênc si des gedâhten," he insists (193,14= "they were not thinking of that at all"), though one cannot fail to be impressed by Adrian Stevens's analysis of the episode which demonstrates the contrast between the innocence of the two young people and Wolfram's own worldly-wise view of the potential of the situation: "But if the protagonists are naive and innocent, the same cannot be said of Wolfram the narrator or of the reactions he expects from his audience" (Stevens 1993, 253). One recalls Chrétien's lengthy account of love-making which, pleasurable though it is to both parties, lacks any depth or commitment. In contrast, the chaste night which Parzival and Condwiramurs pass together ends with his promise of help and her expression of thanks (195,27–196,4). It leads straight into the religious service and thence into Parzival's defeat of Kingrun. This, in turn, leads Condwiramurs to embrace him publicly and declare that no one else will be her husband (199,26–28). Her conviction and the immediate movement towards their married state reinforces the sense of the inevitable about this relationship which will henceforth play such an important part in Parzival's destined progress. A somewhat different view is taken by Arthur Groos, who highlights the lack of passion in the couple and sees this as an aspect of a very different kind of relationship from that which exists elsewhere in the courtly romance (1993,265–268). However, though his analysis seems more negative, he too arrives at the positive conclusion that what Wolfram has produced is a marriage which hints at "a religious and ascetic component," allied to that present in Sigune's view of her relationship with Schionatulander (267).

Although Condwiramurs appears as the instigator of events at first, her role in Parzival's future takes on a special quality which is characterized by passivity, or, more precisely, by absence. It is in separation that the strength of the love of Parzival and Condwiramurs reveals itself, and it is a love which requires no analysis and raises no questions. Unlike Herzeloyde, Condwiramurs does not develop; unlike Sigune there are no signs of transition in her character or her influence; we are not faced, as some may be in the case of Orgeluse, with any contradictions. The praise of Condwiramurs comes, moreover, not from Wolfram, as it did with those other women, but from Parzival himself. It is his awareness of her power which causes him to remain transfixed by the blood in the snow and to praise the Creator of such beauty; it is his knowledge of her steadfastness which sustains him and permits him to resist all temptation, whether it be from Orgeluse or from any other woman who might afford him companionship in his lonely state at the end of Book XIV. When Gawan urges his friend to rely on God in the struggles ahead, Parzival rejects God's support and explicitly replaces it with the support of woman, though he is at that very point aware that physical reunion with his wife is out of the question for the foreseeable future. At the crucial point in his career, when his chivalry is being tested to its uttermost in the combat with Feirefiz, even the thought of Pelrapeire is enough to inspire him, and his wife's love traverses four kingdoms on its way to him (744,4–5). Her role in this final spurt of energy which causes his sword to break on the helmet of his half-brother needs no explanation: the death of Ither can be put behind him at last, and reconciliation, with his opponent and ultimately with God, can take its place through the healing question to Anfortas. Only now does the grail recognize him as its king, but the magic inscription names Condwiramurs as well, giving tangible expression to Trevrizent's information that the grail king must have a pure queen and, more broadly, bearing out Wolfram's own thesis about the nature of the ideal woman.

Wolfram has fulfilled his early promise of telling of the nature of womanly woman (4,11), demonstrating the surpassing value of devotion in its various forms throughout the poem by making it the intrinsic virtue of the central women characters. More than that, he has shown that his hero, the veritable stem of the tale (678,30), possesses that same quality, whether by inheritance or by the influence of those he meets. The God whom he serves through the kingship of the grail is the very essence of devotion according to Trevrizent, who tells Parzival that he should practice *triuwe* without faltering, "sît got selbe ein triuwe ist" (462,19= literally "since God Himself is a devotion"). The question which he asks Anfortas is the expression of *triuwe*, or so we may justifiably conclude from the assertions by Sigune (255,15), Cundrie (316,2) and Trevrizent (488,28–30) that he was lacking this when he failed on the first occasion. The word itself eludes proper translation: love, loyalty, devotion are all ingredients of the quality in its most perfect form, but implicit also are other facets of human relationships, in which compassion, humility and service all play a part, and even that sense of duty which imbues Parzival's progress. What is not elusive is Wolfram's message. His announcement early on that he will tell a story about the special nature of both men and women, the unswerving courage of the former and the great devotion of the latter, is borne out again and again, and on different levels, and reiterated most powerfully in the juxtaposition of the names of Parzival and Condwiramurs on the grail inscription which proclaims the ideal nature of both.

*Herzeloyde with the young Parzival in the wilderness.
(Parzival manuscript n [fifteenth century] —
Heidelberg, Universitätsbibliothek, Cpg.339, fol.87ʳ)*

Parzival finds Sigune holding the body of Schionatulander in a linden tree. (Parzival manuscript n [fifteenth century] — Heidelberg, Universitätsbibliothek, Cpg.339, fol 185ᵛ.)

MARTIN JONES

The Significance of the Gawan Story in *Parzival*

IT IS A VITAL FACTOR IN THE BROAD AND INCLUSIVE picture of the human condition that Wolfram von Eschenbach projects in his grail romance that he affords space and depth to characters besides the hero Parzival. This is evident both in the way that minor figures who remain flat and functional in his source are given a name and a history which individualize them and in the distribution of the narrative as a whole among three leading figures, each of whom follows his own distinctive course of action. When Parzival is "mæreshalp noch ungeborn" (4,24= "still unborn as far as this tale is concerned"), the first two Books of the work are devoted to the life of his father Gahmuret, from the time of his leaving his home in Anjou to his death in the East. With Book III, Parzival's own story begins, extending over three blocks of narrative — Books III–VI, IX, and XIV–XVI — which trace his progress from the isolation of his forest upbringing to the grail kingship. Embedded within the story of Parzival are, finally, a series of adventures of the premier knight of the Round Table, Gawan, which occupy Books VII–VIII and X–XIV. In Book XIV Parzival appears in the forefront of the action again alongside Gawan, though the events of this Book are primarily concerned with bringing the Gawan story to a conclusion. For the purposes of the numerical data presented in the next paragraph, Book XIV is regarded as forming part of the Gawan story.

When Wolfram makes the transition from the Parzival story to that of Gawan at the start of Book VII, he marks the shift of narrative focus in a prologue which begins with some reflections in justification of this procedure:

> Der nie gewarp nâch schanden,
> ein wîl zuo sînen handen
> sol nu dise âventiure hân
> der werde erkande Gâwân.
> diu prüevet manegen âne haz

> derneben oder für in baz
> dan des mæres hêrren Parzivâl.
> swer sînen friunt alle mâl
> mit worten an daz hœhste jagt,
> der ist prîses anderhalp verzagt. (338,1–10)

(He who never acted shamefully will now have this story at his disposal for a while, the noble and famed Gawan. This story takes friendly note of many beside or beyond the lord of the tale, Parzival. Anyone who lauds his friend to the skies all the time lacks words of praise for others. — Translations are based on those of Hatto.)

Wolfram here invokes a principle of even-handedness which allows that, however dear the hero may be to the story-teller's heart, there can be others who are no less deserving of his attention. Such a one is Gawan, who is to occupy the forefront of the action from this point onwards, with the exception only of Book IX, for little short of 10,000 verses. This portion of the work devoted to Gawan represents some forty percent of its total length and is only 2,000 verses shorter than that which deals with Parzival himself directly (that is excluding the parental story in the first two Books). The proportions are such as to suggest that Gawan could be thought to rival Parzival, but Wolfram seeks to forestall that possibility by his insistence on the preeminence of Parzival, who is "the lord of the tale."

Wolfram no doubt had good cause to preface his account of the adventures of Gawan with reflections to guide his audience, for compositions which juxtapose the independent stories of two leading figures who are contemporary with one another (as opposed to stories placed in succession on the genealogical principle, as with Gahmuret and Parzival) were a rarity at the time. Indeed, the *Doppelroman*, the romance with two heroes, was a recent innovation within the context of medieval literature, having been evolved by Chrétien de Troyes in his *Perceval* (or *Li Contes del Graal*) as the last in a series of adaptations to the form of the Arthurian romance which he himself created with his *Erec et Enide* (see Schmolke-Hasselmann 9). Chrétien's grail romance, which was Wolfram's principal source for *Parzival*, combines the adventures of Perceval with those of Gauvain, introducing the latter, as in *Parzival*, part of the way through the Perceval story. The text was not finished by Chrétien, but as it survives, approximately equal numbers of verses are given to the adventures of the two heroes. It is impossible to say whether this balance would have been maintained if Chrétien had completed the work. Equally imponderable is how the two narrative strands would have been coordinated in the latter stages of the work. As they stand, the adventures of the two heroes simply alternate in the sequence Perceval — Gauvain — Perceval — Gauvain, until the text breaks off at a point corresponding roughly to the middle of Book XIII of *Parzival*. There is no attempt to harmonize their adventures chronologically, nor is there any indication that their adventures are connected, though each of them does have a mission relating to the grail.

With his *Perceval* torso Chrétien left to posterity a fascinating but difficult legacy. A number of French poets were inspired to compose continuations, the earliest of which could have been known to Wolfram, but there are signs of his diverging from Chrétien's narrative well before the extant text breaks off, and there is no reason to believe that in adapting Chrétien's work and carrying it to a conclusion Wolfram was guided by anything other than his own conception. This included the synchronization of the Parzival and Gawan actions and the tracing of Parzival's movements in the background of the Gawan narrative until, in Book XIV, the two figures are brought together in combat. It is probable that the idea of making the two narrative strands coincide in this way was inspired by the example of Hartmann von Aue's *Iwein*, where the hero returns to the Arthurian court and encounters Gawan in combat before proceeding to his ultimate goal at the court of his wife Laudine, just as Parzival finally goes on from the Arthurian court to the grail castle.

In having Parzival come into contact with the Arthurian court in Book XIV, Wolfram makes the story of his hero conform to the structural pattern typical of Chrétien's earlier Arthurian romances, *Erec et Enide* and *Yvain*, which were known to German audiences through the adaptations by Hartmann. That is to say, the story of Parzival is (in part) structured according to a bipartite scheme of action involving three major scenes at the court of King Arthur, with two cycles of adventures undertaken by the hero falling between these scenes. Up to the point in *Parzival* at which the Gawan episodes commence at the start of Book VII, the first two Arthurian scenes have been played out, in Parzival's visits to the court in Books III and VI respectively. In shaping the course of Parzival's career beyond the point at which Chrétien's narrative breaks off, Wolfram completes the Arthurian structural pattern to the extent that he brings his hero back to the court in Book XIV. However, between Book VI and his return to the court in Book XIV the adventures which claim most of our attention are devoted to Gawan and not to Parzival, who, with the exception of Book IX, leads a shadowy existence in the background of the Gawan story. Thus, in a structural sense at least, Gawan is made in *Parzival* to substitute for the hero for a time, releasing him to pursue his own distinctive course.

In this disposition of the narrative material, which locates the Gawan story within that of Parzival, we can identify two of the functions which the Gawan episodes fulfil in Wolfram's work. First, they point up the exceptional character of the path which Parzival has to follow after Book VI, a path on which progress is dependent not on such deeds of prowess in the service of society and love as are the stuff of the Arthurian hero's story but on the attainment of insight and the radical inner change which are the subject particularly of Parzival's encounter with the hermit Trevrizent in Book IX and related to his specific vocation to the grail. Secondly, by absorbing the audience's attention for the two major blocks of narrative in Books VII–VIII and X–XIV, the Gawan adventures provide an experience of the extended period during which Parzival is engaged on the quest for the grail and isolated from society; this is an important consideration, for Wolfram clearly conceived time as a factor in shaping the process of change that Parzival undergoes and took trouble to map the chronology of his career. The significance of the Gawan story is, however, much greater than that of a contrastive filler within the account of Parzival's progress. Wolfram devoted much attention to the elaboration of the Gawan episodes and to establishing links between them and the story of Parzival. To appreciate this we must examine Gawan's role in detail. At the outset it is necessary to express the indebtedness of the present examination to the work of Wolfgang Mohr (1957, 1958, and the two articles in 1965) and to the essay of Marianne Wynn (1962). General accounts of the Gawan story are also to be found in the books by Sacker, Blamires, Ruh, and Bumke (1991), and in the article by Rupp (1983), while Busby (1980) provides an overview of Gauvain in Old French literature.

Gawan first appears directly in the action in Book VI in the context of the Arthurian court, but it is typical of Wolfram's predilection for investing his work with chronological depth that he makes mention of him already in Book II, when he is present at the tournament at Kanvoleiz which leads to the marriage of Parzival's parents. Gawan is at that time a boy, not yet of an age to bear arms though already eager to do so. He is there with his father King Lot of Norway, the brother-in-law of Arthur. Arthur himself, not yet king, is absent from Kanvoleiz, engaged in the quest for his mother (65,29–66,22). This proves to be an allusion to the abduction of Arthur's mother Arnive, from which Gawan will eventually rescue her in the course of the adventures described in Books X–XIV. Of more immediate interest is that the reference to the young Gawan identifies him as the nephew of Arthur and of the same generation as Parzival though older than he.

It is the presence of Parzival outside Arthur's camp, entranced by the image of his wife which is evoked by three drops of blood on the snow, that brings Gawan into the action in Book VI. By this time he occupies the place he conventionally holds as the premier knight of the Arthurian company, as would have been familiar to Wolfram's audience from Hartmann's *Erec* and *Iwein*. He has the reputation of being the model of Arthurian chivalry, "der tavelrunder hôhster prîs" (301,7= "the glory of the Round Table"). The role which he plays here — that of befriending the hero and persuading him to join the court — is also one with which he is conventionally associated.

Gawan's approach to the allegedly threatening figure of Parzival contrasts with that of Segramors and Keie, whose challenges have ended in their ignominious defeat. Unmoved by Keie's typically rancorous suggestion that he is so subservient to women that he lacks the courage to tackle the stranger outside the camp, Gawan rides out unarmed to investigate (299,2–12). Parzival is lost in the contemplation of his wife's image and fails to respond to his greeting, but undeterred by this, Gawan draws on his own experience of the power of love, and by the simple expedient of dropping a cape over the drops of blood he breaks the spell and is able to engage Parzival in conversation.

In this first example of Gawan in action, we see two qualities which are of relevance to his later adventures, namely an aversion to unnecessary aggression and a secure sense of his own worth which enables him to maintain self-control in the face of abuse. Noteworthy is also his experience in matters of the heart, exemplified in the reference to two earlier incidents, the first of which involved him stabbing himself in the hand with a knife when he was in thrall to love, while the second saw him rescued from death in a joust by the lady who loved him (301,7–25). Neither of these incidents is preserved in any of the stories of Gawan that have come down to us, indeed it is possible that Wolfram invented them (see Draesner 258), but this does not detract from the importance of the allusion at this early stage to Gawan's susceptibility to the power of love and its capacity to place him in dangerous situations. As Keie, with his knack of wrapping truthful observations about others in exaggerated abusiveness, has hinted, Gawan has a weakness for the opposite sex, a point which would not have been lost on those familiar with the part played by Gawein in *Iwein*.

Equally indicative is Gawan's reaction to the charge of murder which is levelled at him later in Book VI. No sooner has Cundrie delivered her tirade against Parzival which provokes him to undertake the quest for the grail than Kingrimursel arrives to accuse Gawan of having killed his lord treacherously and to challenge him to a judicial combat forty days hence at the town of Schanpfanzun. Gawan makes no direct response to this, but when he refuses his brother's plea to be allowed to deputize for him in the combat, his words convey, on the one hand, certainty of the falseness of the charge made against him and reluctance to fight without good cause and, on the other, a determination to uphold his honor: "ine weiz war umbe ich strîten sol, / ouch entuot mir strîten niht sô wol: / ungerne wolt ich dir versagn, / wan daz ich müesez laster tragn." (323,27–30= "I do not know why I should fight, nor do I much care for fighting; I should be loath to deny you were it not that I should be dishonoured").

The effect of the allegation made against Gawan is to place him in a situation similar to Parzival's insofar as both have been subjected to public condemnation, and this invites comparison of them. In reality, of course, their cases are far from similar, in that, as Parzival himself is aware (330,29–30), there is some substance to Cundrie's castigation of him, however much she may have overshot the mark with her imputation of wickedness on his part (319,4–11), whereas Gawan is completely innocent of the charge of murder. And yet comparison is valid and instructive, for while Parzival is so profoundly shaken by Cundrie's accusations as to sever his contacts with society and to rebel against God, claiming that He has failed to honor his service to Him, Gawan experiences no such existential crisis, even though he is genuinely the victim of injustice. In his wish that God will favor them both (331,25–30), Gawan reveals a quiet confidence in the fundamentally benign ordering of the world, however much the vicissitudes of human affairs may make that seem improbable. It is no contradiction of this optimism that Gawan should prepare himself carefully for the task that lies ahead of him, selecting shields, horses, and lances of suitable quality (335,1–23), and (as emerges later) taking a number of squires with him: trust in God's power and goodness is no excuse for being ill-equipped to confront the challenges that life presents. By contrast, Parzival, who has renounced trust in God and relies on his own strength, rides out from the court alone with only his personal equipment.

When Gawan sets out from Arthur's court it is with the limited objective of reaching Schanpfanzun within forty days and defending his innocence in combat, after which he would presumably return to court. But things do not turn out that way: the judicial combat is never fought and he is absent from court for more than four and a half years. During that period he is above all involved in incidents centered on three separate locations — Bearosche (Book VII), Schanpfanzun (Book

VIII), and the region comprised of the duchy of Logroys, Terre Marveile, and the kingdom ruled by Gramoflanz (Books X–XIV); for a time he also undertakes the quest for the grail, placing him directly parallel to Parzival, but barely any attention is paid to this motif, which like that of the judicial combat ultimately proves to be primarily functional, providing among other things a reason for Gawan to be absent from court.

The first episode in the Gawan story begins an unspecified number of days after he has left the court, but he has ridden far enough on his way to Schanpfanzun to have entered a country in which he is unknown to the people whose affairs will briefly engage his attention. Halted in his progress by a large army marching through the countryside, Gawan learns from a squire that the motley company is making its way under the leadership of the young King Meljanz to attack the town of Bearosche, the seat of Duke Lyppaut, who is the loyal vassal of Meljanz and who had raised him in his family since he had been orphaned. The cause of the impending conflict is a lovers' quarrel. Obie, the elder of Lyppaut's two daughters, has rejected the wish of Meljanz to be granted her love in return for service, insisting that not even five years of service to her in deeds of chivalry would merit such a reward (345,27–346,14), though in reality she already loves him. No less headstrong than she, Meljanz has accused her of arrogance and jumped to the conclusion that her father was behind her rebuff. In the ranks of the army raised by Meljanz is the knight Meljacanz, a notorious abductor and violator of women (343,23–30), who also appears as such at the start of the Parzival story (125,1–16). His presence implicitly underlines the threat of violence against women to which Meljanz has resorted, having seen the path of service for the reward of love apparently blocked by Obie. For her father the situation is doubly distressing: not only has he had no hand in Obie's rejection of Meljanz, as the young man alleges, but he is also obliged to take up arms against his lord, towards whom he has acted as a father.

Having learned of this topsy-turvy situation, Gawan feels himself in a dilemma. On the one hand, it would reflect ill on his reputation if he were to be a mere spectator of the fighting that is to take place there, but on the other hand, participation in the conflict could jeopardize his ability to present himself for the judicial combat in which he is to clear his name. He resolves the uncertainty in so far as he decides to ride on towards the town, putting his trust in God to keep him safe: "er sprach 'nu müeze got bewarn / die kraft an mîner manheit.' / Gâwân gein Bêârosche reit" (350,14–16= "He said 'May God now preserve my manly vigour.' Gawan rode toward Bearosche"). He takes up a position under the walls of the town, from where he can hear the dispute which arises between Obie and her sister Obilot about him. Obie claims that he is a merchant, referring to the large number of horses and large amounts of equipment which Gawan and his company have, but her sister, young as she is, recognizes his knightly status immediately and declares her determination to prove her point by having him serve as her knight (352,19–26). Having fallen out with the man she loves, Obie is in a confused state emotionally — the narrator urges his audience not to be hard on her for this (366,1–2) — and this manifests itself in her continuing insistence that Gawan is a swindler and counterfeiter. She seeks to mobilize the burgrave and her father against Gawan, but they, like Obilot, recognize his quality and admit him to the town. In spite of Obie's false allegations, Gawan remains unruffled throughout, showing only in a brief flash of anger when she sends a squire to ask if his horses are for sale (360,10–28) that there are limits to how far he will allow himself to be misrepresented.

Gawan is approached by Lyppaut to lend him assistance. Initially he refuses, explaining that he can do nothing which might prevent him from maintaining his honor in the forthcoming duel, but on hearing Lyppaut's account of his distressing circumstances, he becomes less certain and promises to consider the matter and give him a decision before evening. This provides the opportunity for Obilot to come to her father's aid and to realize her ambition to engage Gawan as her knight. Having thanked her for the defense of his honor in the face of Obie's aspersions, Gawan listens as she, with a sophistication beyond her years, employs the rhetoric of courtly love in an attempt to win him over. She offers him love as reward for service, talks of their being one, and throws herself, a damsel in distress, on his mercy (369,1–370,7). Gawan is conscious of the claim on his compassion and honor but seeks to deflect her plea with a reference to her immaturity, which makes any thought of love's reward for service unrealistic (370,8–17). The matter is, however, settled in her favor, when, remarkably, Gawan recalls that as they parted in Book VI Parzival had urged him to be guided in battle by a woman rather than by God:

> nu dâhter des, wie Parzivâl
> wîben baz getrûwt dan gote:
> sîn bevelhen dirre magde bote
> was Gâwân in daz herze sîn (370,18–21)

(Now he remembered how Parzival trusted women more than God. His [= Parzival's] commendation was this maid's angel in speaking to Gawan's heart.)

It seems unlikely that any critical reservation about Gawan's decision to act as Obilot's knight is implied in this allusion (see Bumke 1991, 86), as there is no sense in which the service of God and the service of women are in opposition in this situation. More to the point might be the reflection that whereas, for Parzival himself, trusting in a woman meant trusting in his wife, Gawan has no such established figure in whom to trust. In the present instance the decision to serve woman leads to a peaceful outcome, one that has God's approval, but it remains to be seen whether the position is always so uncomplicated.

Released from his dilemma, Gawan throws himself wholeheartedly into the role prescribed for him in the love relationship with Obilot, which she in her precociously imaginative way has conjured into being; it is for him a fiction — for her it is altogether more serious — but it has the function of enabling him to step out of his real identity temporarily and leave thoughts of his obligation at Schanpfanzun aside. He affirms his unity with Obilot, announcing that when he rides into combat it will be she who will be fighting in his stead. For her part, she hastens to obtain a love-token which she can bestow on Gawan — a dress is made for her, one sleeve of which is not attached but is sent to him after it has touched her arm. Gawan attaches the sleeve to one of his shields (375,19–23).

Thus protected by the token of Obilot's love and fortified spiritually by attendance at Mass and physically by God's strength in the field (378,21–27; 380,11–13), Gawan excels among the supporters of Lyppaut in the fighting before Bearosche on the following day. He takes Meljanz prisoner and delivers him to Obilot, his true conqueror (394,17–20). On her young shoulders rests the burden of deciding what should be done with him, and she entirely fulfills the trust that Gawan reposes in her when she commands Meljanz and her sister to be reconciled with one another, a judgement with which they have no difficulty in complying as "frou minne" (= "Lady Love") creates affection anew in their hearts (396,21–24). Obilot's adjudication accords with Gawan's wish that the conflict should be ended by a "suone" (392,18= "reconciliation") and is described as being of God's inspiration: "got ûz ir jungen munde sprach" (396,19= "God spoke through her young mouth"). Amicable relationships between Meljanz and Lyppaut now also having been restored, the episode ends in that most potent symbol of social harmony, a marriage, as Meljanz and Obie are united. Only Obilot's distress at being abandoned by Gawan as he turns to face the reality of his impending combat and resumes his journey to Schanpfanzun qualifies the scene of joy that he leaves behind him.

In the course of the fighting before Bearosche on the second day, we learn that the knight who most distinguished himself among the attackers was "der rôte ritter" (389,4= "the Red Knight"). He had joined Meljanz's army three days previously, and he leaves the field as soon as the fighting is over, taking Gawan's horse Ingliart, which had strayed away when Gawan was fighting Meljanz, to replace his own wounded mount. It is not until the hostilities are over that Gawan hears of this knight and recognizes from the description of his armor and the fact that he requires those he defeats to seek the grail that it was Parzival. He thanks God that they had been spared confronting one another in battle (392,24–393,2). (By contrast, Parzival appears never to realize that there was a danger of his fighting with his friend and kinsman Gawan at Bearosche, i.e. that he might have found himself in a situation like that which led to his acquiring the red armor and becoming known as the Red Knight, when in killing Ither von Gaheviez he unwittingly took the life of a kinsman.) By incorporating Parzival into the Gawan action in this way, Wolfram takes the first step in synchronizing their movements since they left Arthur's court, and establishes a material link between the two via Gawan's horse. Most interesting, however, is the indication of their different orientations. Gawan has allowed himself to be drawn into the fighting with some reluctance and only after acquainting himself with the nature of the conflict sufficiently to know that he is giving support to the side which is more deserving of it, and the outcome of his involvement is the restoration of order and sanity to a situation which had got seriously out of kilter. By contrast, Parzival is eager only to fight, in the belief that this will further his quest for the grail (390,9), and is so indifferent to the ethical dimensions of the situation as to have engaged himself in the service of the aggressor. This is not the only occasion on which Parzival will show himself so preoccupied with his own particular goal as to be oblivious to the needs of others, whereas Gawan is drawn to tackle them.

The Bearosche episode is a fine example of how Gawan functions, in Wolfgang Mohr's memorable phrase, "gleichsam als Katalysator der Menschlichkeit" (1958, 14= "so to speak as a catalyst of humaneness"). The effect of his presence there is to enable the characters who have become locked into an antagonism which betrays their true feelings to regain themselves and to re-establish right relationships: the lovers love one another, vassal and lord — "father" and "son" — are joined in mutual respect and affection.

The central factor in this transformation, beyond the person of Gawan himself, is love, which manifests both aspects of its great power in this episode. On the one hand, it lies at the root of the problems experienced here, in that the social convention by which love's power should be controlled — the postponement of love's reward until proof of worthiness is given through service — has been tested to the breaking-point by the two young and inexperienced lovers, Obie and Meljanz. On the other hand, it furnishes the solution of those problems, when Obilot engages Gawan in her service in the name of love. This is a partnership of unequals: a girl, too young to give love's reward, motivated by a vision of love not colored by passion, and a man, mature and experienced in love, conscious of her immaturity, unite together in a de-eroticized love relationship which, through his victory on the field of battle and her wise adjudication, brings about reconciliation and harmony. The union of these two is a charming fiction, a romantic flight of fancy, which can claim no normative status, but it does raise the question whether love can be so salutary in its effects where the partners are equal and the power of the erotic is not suspended.

Gawan reaches Schanpfanzun, the goal of his travels since leaving Arthur's court, at the start of Book VIII, where he comes upon the young King Vergulaht, son of the man he is alleged to have murdered, hunting with falcons on the plain before the town. There are clues as to what lies ahead in the comparison between Gawan's approach to Schanpfanzun and that of Aeneas to the Carthage of Queen Dido (the story of Aeneas was known to Wolfram through the *Eneasroman* of Heinrich von Veldeke, and there are numerous references to Heinrich in the course of *Parzival*). One of a number of allusions which associate Gawan with Aeneas in the course of his story, this instance (399,11–14) points forward to Gawan's reception in the town by Vergulaht's sister, the lady Antikonie, who, like Dido with Aeneas, is willing to let him enjoy her love without any prior service (see Draesner 315). The meeting between Gawan and Antikonie is instigated by Vergulaht, who does not trouble to ascertain who Gawan is, before bidding him enter the town and seek the company of his sister, an invitation which is accompanied by more than a hint of a possible sexual adventure (402,19–30). He does this in preference to accompanying Gawan to Schanpfanzun himself, as etiquette might be thought to demand, because he does not wish to break off from his hunting. This, taken together with the impetuosity of Vergulaht, which has led to his getting a drenching in the course of rescuing his falcons, suggests that Gawan is entering a situation in which all is not in the best order (see the article of Schnell).

It is not clear what strategy, if any, we are meant to understand Gawan to be pursuing on his arrival at Schanpfanzun. He appears to be anxious to preserve his anonymity for as long as possible. Perhaps, knowing "that he is in enemy territory" (D. H. Green 1982,142), he fears that he might be assaulted, in spite of the safe conduct granted him by Kingrimursel until the time of the combat, as indeed does happen. He does not offer his name to Vergulaht, and in response to Antikonie's enquiry, he says: "ich sage iu, frouwe, daz ich pin / mîner basen bruoder suon" (406,14–15= "I tell you, my lady, that I am my father's sister's brother's son")! It is, however, possible that his evasiveness in the latter instance is prompted by the wish not to spoil his prospects with Antikonie rather than by any thought of enhancing his safety. His acceptance of Vergulaht's offer of hospitality increases — at least it *should* increase — his security, as the status of guest bestows the right to protection, and if Antikonie is to be believed (415,1–5), being in her presence should offer some kind of immunity from attack. However, if it was his purpose to gain security by these means, the strategy goes badly wrong when he allows himself to be drawn into a blatantly erotic encounter with Antikonie. He responds so eagerly to her enticing words of welcome that already the kiss of greeting that they exchange is "ungastlîch" (405,21= "not that customary between strangers") and soon afterwards he is so intimate with her as to be touching her thigh under her cloak. Caught in this compromising situation, in which she is an equally willing partner (407,9), by a knight who recognizes Gawan and raises the alarm, he quickly becomes the object of the fury of the mob, as people from the town storm the turret next to her room in which he and Antikonie take refuge.

The scene that follows is not without its comic dimensions. Gawan substitutes the bolt used to bar the door for his missing sword and a chessboard for his shield to defend himself, while Antikonie hurls large chess pieces at the attackers, earning herself comparison with the women shopkeepers of Dollnstein who fight in armor at the Shrovetide revelry (409,5–9; nothing is known of this Shrovetide in Dollnstein, a place in Franconia not far from Wolframs-Eschenbach — see Nellmann 1994,648). In a parodying variant of the motif of the knight drawing inspiration from the sight of his lady during combat, Gawan's courage is increased "swenne im diu muoze geschach" (409,23= "when he has the leisure") to admire the beauty of Antikonie, whose extremely narrow waist is emphasized by grotesque comparisons with a hare on a spit and an ant (409,23–410,6). But the humor cannot fully disguise the fact that the situation does little for Gawan's dignity as a knight, nor can it escape notice that the convention of the knight fighting in order to win the love of a lady has been so far perverted that he and his lady fight alongside one another to ward off the consequences of having given way to their desires too quickly. Wolfram does not explicitly condemn the behavior of either of them in any way, but it is clear that it is the opportunism of the sexual adventurer that has landed Gawan in this unflattering and dangerous position.

The plight of Gawan and Antikonie is worsened, when Vergulaht returns from his hunting and joins the attack on them, completely disregarding the obligation which lies upon him to safeguard the welfare of a guest in his town. The arrival of Landgrave Kingrimursel on the scene shortly afterwards adds to the sense of Vergulaht's disgraceful infringement of the norms of acceptable behavior, for he is outraged that the safe conduct which he had issued to Gawan has been violated, despite Vergulaht's agreement that it should be granted. Kingrimursel joins Gawan and Antikonie in the turret, determined in peril of his own life to ensure Gawan's safety. The sight of Kingrimursel supporting Gawan leads the townspeople to abandon their attack and to urge upon Vergulaht the impropriety of his conduct towards his guest and his sister, in response to which he declares a truce.

A series of discussions now follows concerning Vergulaht's behavior and what should be done with Gawan. Antikonie and Kingrimursel join forces in upbraiding Vergulaht for his treatment of Gawan and, by association, of them too. It is here, as also in her earlier active support for Gawan when under attack, that Antikonie justifies the narrator's persistent praise of her moral rectitude, which critics have often found hard to reconcile with the looseness of her sexual behavior. In the scale of values which Wolfram applies here such laxity seems to weigh less heavily than the unfaithfulness to obligations of which Vergulaht has been guilty. In the criticism which Kingrimursel makes of Vergulaht we see something of the political implications which the erratic and unreliable conduct of the king can have, as the landgrave complains that his trust has been betrayed and hints at reprisals on the part of the great lords of the realm if Vergulaht does not prove more trustworthy. In this tension between the older vassal Kingrimursel and his impetuous young lord we may detect an echo of the problems experienced at Bearosche between Lyppaut and Meljanz. The deliberations are joined by another of Vergulaht's leading vassals, Duke Liddamus, who represents a cynical and self-serving ethic opposed to the sturdy set of honest values embodied in Kingrimursel. When it comes to deciding what should be done with Gawan, Liddamus urges that they should take advantage of his being in their power and kill him immediately in vengeance for the death of Vergulaht's father, but Kingrimursel insists that Gawan should have the opportunity to defend his innocence and finally wins agreement to a postponement of the combat for a year, when it will take place at Barbigoel. Gawan can do nothing other than consent to this. Vergulaht then makes report of a joust which he had fought in the previous week with a knight who had defeated him and charged him to seek the grail on his behalf (424,15–425,14). Liddamus leaps on this to propose that Gawan should assume the undertaking to find the grail in Vergulaht's stead, confident that it will lead to his death, since the grail territory is so stoutly defended. Vergulaht's adversary was, of course, Parzival, whose movements are again plotted by reference to those of Gawan, while the kinship between Vergulaht and Parzival, of which the audience is aware, though neither of them realized it, keeps alive the issue of the hero's propensity to endanger the lives of kinsmen. As with the postponement of the judicial combat, Gawan has no choice but to accept the commission to seek the grail; thus, after sending his retinue back to Arthur's court, he departs from Schanpfanzun to become for a year a solitary seeker of the grail like Parzival.

Throughout the exchanges and negotiations which occupy much of the latter part of the Schanpfanzun episode Gawan plays a passive role. Insofar as Vergulaht, whose conduct comes in for particular censure, is brought to see the error of his ways and to amend them, this is the achievement of his sister and Kingrimursel, arguing as much on the grounds of their own grievances against him as on behalf of Gawan. As for Gawan himself, the decisions about his fate rest entirely with others, and it is characteristic of his good fortune that he should have such powerful advocates as Antikonie and the landgrave to ensure that he emerges from the situation unscathed. It may be said that the affection which he inspires in Antikonie and the respect which Kingrimursel has for him as a knight lend eloquence to their arguments, but at the practical level he is unable to help himself other than by remaining calm and composed in the face of his adversity. It is Liddamus who shrewdly characterizes Gawan's position, when in one of the many images from bird-hunting which occur in this Book, he says to Vergulaht "der vederslagt ûf iweren klobn" (425,21= "he is beating his wings on your fowling-stick"). The bait which has led Gawan to be caught in this trap is the beauty of Antikonie, of whom the narrator says earlier, "minne gerende gelust / kunde ir lîp vil wol gereizen" (409,30–410,1= "her body could very well arouse love's desire" — see Schnell 264–265). That she certainly does in Gawan, and tempted by the prospect of an effortless conquest, he becomes the victim of his own unregulated desire; the price is subjection to the will of others.

When the Gawan narrative resumes at the start of Book X, it is evident that the postponement of his combat with Kingrimursel was to his advantage, for in the year which precedes the encounter at Barbigoel it comes to light that, as the narrator had informed the audience already in Book VIII (413,13–20), a certain Count Ehcunaht was the slayer of Vergulaht's father, so that Kingrimursel readily forgoes the combat which Gawan had always been reluctant to undertake (503,16–20). The kinship of Gawan and Vergulaht is also cited as a reason for abandoning the combat (503,12–15), but why this was not recognized already at Schanpfanzun and deemed then to eliminate the possibility of a combat is not clear (on this "minor inconsistency," see D. H. Green 1982, 144–145). Gawan now continues the quest for the grail, for reasons which are not explained. This too is a blind motif, in that Gawan abandons the quest to become involved in other matters, but it does serve to indicate that different spheres of activity are peculiar to him and Parzival. Although we learn nothing of his grail quest, it lasts for several years, for the resumption of the detailed account of Gawan's actions again in verse 504,7 is located after Parzival's stay with Trevrizent in Book IX (as becomes retrospectively apparent from the chronological information contained in verses 559,9–10 and 646,14–18).

The action which begins to unfold when Gawan comes into close focus again in Book X runs without major interruption through to Book XIV, constituting a single large block of narrative. All the action occurs in a region dominated by three figures, each with his or her own territory: the necromancer Clinschor, who is lord of Schastel Marveile and of an area extending for eight miles around the castle, known as Terre Marveile; Orgeluse, who is the widowed Duchess of Logroys, a land which borders onto Clinschor's territory; and King Gramoflanz, the slayer of Orgeluse's husband, who rules over a land which is not named but has Rosche Sabins as its capital and is contiguous with both Terre Marveile and Logroys. While Orgeluse and Gramoflanz live in a state of constant and open hostility to one another as a result of his killing of her husband Cidegast, each maintains a truce with Clinschor, a figure who never actually appears in the action but whose brooding presence is felt in much of it. Each step that Gawan takes further into this unfamiliar region is accompanied by warnings of the dangers which it holds for him, and indeed he is confronted here with his severest tests as he becomes embroiled in the complex and dark histories of the three ruling persons and their interrelationships.

The action of Books X–XIV is highly elaborate in construction, and it is impractical to trace the events in sequence; rather it will be necessary to examine as discretely as their overlapping and interlocking nature permits the three major strands of narrative in this portion of the text. These are, in the order in which they will be treated: (1) Gawan's conquest of Schastel Marveile and his liberation of those held captive there by Clinschor; (2) Gawan's relationship with Orgeluse; (3) Gawan's surprise reunion of members of the Arthurian family on the field at Joflanze and the resolution of the problems associated with the combat arranged to take place there between himself and Gramoflanz.

The adventure of Schastel Marveile is flagged as a challenge of particular concern to Arthurian society long before it becomes the center of attention in Book XI. As has already been noted, there is an allusion to the abduction of Arthur's mother, one of the captives in the castle, as far back as Book II in the days of Gawan's childhood, when we learn that Arthur had been seeking her for three years, obviously in vain. Schastel Marveile is first named in Book VI, when Cundrie, as her parting shot at the Arthurian court, refers to the castle and to four queens and four hundred ladies held there, describing the adventure as one which surpasses all others (318,13–24). A little later in the same Book a visitor at the court, Clias the Greek, recounts his own experience of a joust before the castle when he learned the names of the four queens, these being, it later transpires, from three generations of the Arthurian family and closely related to Gawan himself: Arnive, Arthur's mother and Gawan's grandmother; Sangive, Arthur's sister and Gawan's mother; Cundrie and Itonje, daughters of Sangive and sisters to Gawan (334,11–22). The knights of Arthur's household set off to undertake the adventure, probably in two contingents, but their efforts are also fruitless (334,1–10 and 23–30). It is more than likely that Gawan was still present at court when Clias revealed the names of the queens (see D. H. Green 1982, 154). Thus, when Gawan learns from the ferryman Plippalinot, with whom he lodges, that it is Schastel Marveile that he sees before him, he is aware that he has the opportunity to tackle an adventure which has defied the efforts of the Arthurian knights for many years and which, in the event of his success, would liberate his own kinswomen (557,6–9;19–22).

The background to and nature of the situation at Schastel Marveile which now confronts Gawan are revealed only gradually after he has overcome the challenge there and become lord of the castle and Terre Marveile, displacing Clinschor. It is above all Arnive who is informed about Clinschor's history and who recounts to Gawan how he had been caught in an adulterous affair with the queen of Sicily, in punishment for which he had been castrated by her husband (656,25–657,25). Clinschor had then abandoned his Christian beliefs and gone to the East to learn the black art and become a practitioner of demonic magic (see McFarland 286). He had acquired powers with which he gave vent to his hatred of mankind, imposing his will on others in many places, including Schastel Marveile, where he imprisons both men and women but denies them any contact with one another, thus creating conditions of sterility which mirror his own lack of sexual potency. Among the many powers of this necromancer are control of all spirits between the firmament and the earth, apart from those whom God is willing to protect (658,26–30). From this account Clinschor emerges as a Lucifer-like figure and as "the principal personal embodiment of active spiritual evil in *Parzival*" (McFarland 287).

Gawan is ignorant of these deeper dimensions of the challenge that Schastel Marveile enshrines when he gazes up from his lodging with the ferryman at the castle. Indeed, were it not for his questioning of Bene, Plippalinot's daughter, whom he reduces to tears with his persistent enquiries, and of Plippalinot himself, he would not even learn the castle's name or know of the task of liberation that awaits to be performed there. Both of them are extremely reluctant to enlighten him, fearing for his life if he should attempt the adventure: "vrâgets niht durch got: / hêr, dâ ist nôt ob aller nôt" (556,15–16= "Do not ask, in God's name! My lord, there is anguish surpassing all other there") is Plippalinot's response, when Gawan turns to him for information. But Gawan is not to be deterred, however dire his host's warnings (558,1–11), and he learns from him much about what to expect in the castle and how he should conduct himself at a practical level. Thus, hoping in God's assistance (562,11–14) and armed with a stout shield borrowed from Plippalinot, Gawan makes his way as instructed to the castle, through the empty palace and into the chamber which houses the Lit Marveile, the "bed of wonders," and in which the adventure will be won or lost. Obviously charged with erotic associations, which link the trial of the bed with Clinschor's adultery and Gawan's turbulent relationship to Orgeluse, it is above all a test of courage that Gawan faces here, as the bed hurtles around the room with him lying on it, crashing into the walls, amidst the most deafening din. All that Gawan can do is to cover himself with his shield and entrust himself to God's care (567,29–568,11). When the bed finally comes to rest in the center of the room, Gawan is subjected to bombardment from above by five hundred stones, then an equal number of crossbow bolts, some of which penetrate the defense of his shield and chain mail and bruise him severely. Then a ravenous lion, as tall as a horse, enters and lunges at him with a paw, embedding it in his shield. Gawan is able to hack off the leg and amidst much blood from the wound finally to sink his sword up to the hilt in the lion's breast, bringing it down (for a consideration of the symbolism in this episode, see the article of McConnell in this volume).

The image of Gawan on the Lit Marveile covering himself with both the shield of knighthood and the shield of faith is a vigorous expression of the combination of courage founded on chivalric prowess and courage founded on trust in God's assistance which is needed to overcome the demonic power of Clinschor's magic. Gawan appears here as the champion of good in its struggle against evil, combatting the consequences of Clinschor's illicit passion and the devices of his diabolical invention. This incident represents Gawan's supreme chivalric challenge, a test of both physical and spiritual strength in which the ideal of a Christian chivalry is validated. It also exemplifies the role of the knight in relation to womankind, in that no fewer than four queens and four hundred ladies — emphasis is placed throughout on them rather than on the hundreds of men also imprisoned in the castle — are liberated from oppression. But the act of liberation has wider implications, for in denying to his prisoners all contact with the opposite sex, all affection and fruitfulness, Clinschor has imposed upon them a perversion of the natural order. This state is ended at the feast that is held at Schastel Marveile after Gawan has recovered from the wounds sustained in the challenge of the Lit Marveile and has himself won the love of Orgeluse. For the first time the ladies and knights mingle with one another, eating and talking together, and finally they join together in the movements of the dance under the eyes of their new lord, Gawan, and his lady, Orgeluse, who on that same night consummate their love for one another for the first time (636,15–644,6 — see Bumke 1994, 105–109). As in the Bearosche episode, Gawan's action brings order and humanity into a segment of society whose personal relationships have been distorted as the result of an erotic passion which has disregarded the code of conduct by which it should be regulated. Knighthood is seen here serving the interests of society at large, but there is also a specifically Arthurian dimension to Gawan's achievement, as the conquest of the castle leads to the four queens, prominent figures in the Arthurian world, being brought back to their family in the surprise reunion which Gawan subsequently stages at Joflanze.

Before he enters upon the adventure at Schastel Marveile, Gawan discovers from the ferryman (559,9–10) that Parzival had passed by the castle on the previous day (Ruh [114] suggests that Wolfram is in error and that it must have been at least a day earlier that Parzival was there [see also Nellmann 1994,719], but this does not materially affect the renewed synchronization of his movements with Gawan's). Plippalinot tells him that Parzival had, however, not learned about the adventure from him because he had not asked, adding "het ir selbe vrâgens niht erdâht. / nimmer wært irs innen brâht / von mir, waz hie mæres ist" (559,27–29= "If you had not thought to ask of your own accord, you would never have learned from me what's to do here"). The emphasis placed on questioning as a means of access to the adventure calls to mind the importance which a question has in the context of Parzival's relationship to Munsalvaesche, the grail castle. Whereas, at the time of his first visit to the grail castle, Parzival is unprepared for what awaits him there and fails to ask the question which would heal Anfortas and lead to his succeeding him as grail king, Gawan comes into the vicinity of Schastel Marveile armed with information which he proceeds to supplement by persistent questioning, to the extent even of bringing Bene to tears in the process, and in this way is able to approach the challenge of the castle aware of what has to be done. This contrast between Gawan and Parzival in terms of their prior knowledge of what is required of them and the use of questions is just one of several which can be drawn as a result of Wolfram's strategy of assimilating to one another the great challenges that confront them at Schastel Marveile and Munsalvaesche respectively. In both instances the lord of the castle where they have a task to perform has been rendered impotent by disobedience to the moral code which should govern his behavior — Clinschor by his adultery, Anfortas by his chivalric service to a lady, in defiance of the command that the lord of the grail should love only the woman chosen for him by God (478,13–16). Similarly, in each instance the protagonist is a kinsman of the leading members of the castle communities which await liberation from their suffering, and both castles possess a remarkable treasure — the grail at Munsalvaesche and Clinschor's magic pillar at Schastel Marveile. In essence, Parzival and Gawan are called upon to perform identical acts of deliverance, in which the dolorous consequences of disordered passion are to be overcome. But the differences between them are real: their spheres of activity are separate — it is no accident that Parzival, though he comes to Schastel Marveile before Gawan, does not even become aware of the challenge that it holds, nor that Gawan's quest for the grail remains a blind motif; and their challenges differ in nature — only Gawan's is a truly chivalric adventure, in which courage and prowess are tested to the limit in physical assaults, while Parzival has to wait upon God's grace to call him and enable him to ask the question which brings release to Anfortas and the grail community.

While the adventure at Schastel Marveile is reserved for Gawan alone as the leading Arthurian knight and represents his greatest chivalric achievement, it is above all with Orgeluse and the consequences of her history that Gawan is concerned throughout Books X–XIV. Orgeluse is one of Wolfram's most remarkable creations, radically different from the character in Chrétien on whom she is based, and in some respects a problematic figure for the modern interpreter (see Wynn

1976/77, Zimmermann 1972, and Bumke 1994, 109–113). More than any other woman in the work, Orgeluse acts independently, ruling over the duchy of Logroys after the death of her husband in her own right. She has an extraordinary beauty — second only to that of Parzival's wife Condwiramurs (508,22–23) — and exploits the power which this gives her over men to pursue her sole, all-consuming obsession in life, which is to take vengeance on Gramoflanz for the killing of her much-loved husband Cidegast. This killing had been motivated by Gramoflanz's desire to win Orgeluse for himself. The knights in her service keep a constant watch for Gramoflanz, but as often as they attack him, he succeeds in escaping. The effects of her obsessive pursuit of Gramoflanz are far-reaching, having caused the deaths of many fine men and extending even to the grail castle, for it was while serving for her love, contrary to God's ordinance for him, that Anfortas sustained the wound from which he and the community at Munsalvaesche still suffer. Only one knight has ever refused to enter her service — Parzival, who rejects the offer of her lands and person because, as she reports him saying, he has a wife who is fairer and whom he holds more dear and because he is seeking the grail (618,19–619,19). Orgeluse shares the fate of other women in *Parzival* whose husbands or lovers have been killed — Belacane, Herzeloyde, Sigune, to name but the most prominent of them — but her case differs from these, insofar as her husband was killed with the intention of supplanting him in her affections, and the fidelity (*triuwe*) which gave strength to her first love is transformed into a desire for revenge. It is with good reason that she has often been compared to Kriemhilde in the *Nibelungenlied*, whose life also comes to be dominated by the wish to avenge the death of her beloved husband. Although Orgeluse, unlike Kriemhilde, avoids overstepping the bounds of what is permissible to woman by taking revenge into her own hands, it is none the less evident in her too how the thwarting of an intense love can lead to severe distortion of the personality and can threaten the happiness and lives of other, innocent people, unless some means is found of breaking into the cycle of death and destruction which it sets in motion.

At an early stage in Orgeluse's appearance in the action the narrator urges the audience to reserve judgement of her conduct until they have learned "wiez umb ir herze stüende" (516,8= "the state of her heart"), but the history which explains this — as outlined above — is unknown both to the audience and to Gawan until after he has taken on the task of avenging the wrong done to her by Gramoflanz. At this juncture her attitude to Gawan undergoes a complete change: whereas she has treated him with nothing but disdain and mockery up to that point, she now throws herself submissively at his feet, asks forgiveness for her harsh behavior, declares faithful love for him, and explains her conduct as a means of testing his worthiness to be her lover and avenger (611,20–30; 614,1–17). However credible this change in her character may be (see Wynn 1976/77), the tragic past which she recounts by way of justification for her treatment of Gawan (612,21–27) provides a rationale for her earlier conduct, which at the time seemed capricious to the point of cruelty and left the audience uncertain as to how her character is to be read.

Gawan's first contact with Orgeluse occurs in circumstances which actually recall an incident from his past rather than hers. Attracted by the sight of a lady's horse and a battered shield which evoke thoughts in him of the Amazonian queen Camilla (another allusion to the story of Aeneas) and a possible erotic encounter (504,7–30), he finds a lady with a severely wounded knight lying in her lap (analogous to Parzival's meeting with Sigune, when she holds the dead Schionatulander in her lap). Although neither recognizes the other to begin with, the knight, Urjans, and Gawan have met before, at Arthur's court. There Urjans had been condemned to death for having raped a young lady, but after Gawan had pleaded for him — on the grounds that Urjans had surrendered to him when captured — and the young lady had been persuaded, with the help of Arthur's queen Ginover, that it was her beauty which had aroused his desire, the sentence was commuted to one of eating with the dogs (525,11–528,30). Gawan administers emergency treatment to the unrecognized Urjans, then goes in pursuit of the knight who had inflicted the wound on him — he is Lischoys Gwelljus, one of those who serve Orgeluse. This leads Gawan to the castle of Logroys, where he first sets eyes on Orgeluse. A little later, now in the company of Orgeluse, Gawan returns to Urjans, whom he assists further by binding to his wound a herb which he has found on the way. For this act of kindness he is ill-rewarded, for Urjans, who has in the meantime recognized Gawan, steals his horse, telling him that this is revenge for the disgrace he suffered at the Arthurian court. Gawan explains to Orgeluse the circumstances of his previous encounter with Urjans, and she immediately takes it upon herself to ensure that he is subjected to the penalty that he escaped at Arthur's court, sending word to Lischoys that he should intercept Urjans. She emphasizes that she does this not for Gawan's sake but for the sake of the lady who had been raped (529,2–16). From the fact that Lischoys appears shortly afterwards riding Gawan's horse it is clear that her commands have been carried out and likely that Urjans has been killed (see Mohr, "Zu den epischen Hintergründen," 178).

The episode with Urjans is of interest above all for its introduction of the motif of Gawan's healing skills (not normally the province of knights) and for the insight which it affords into Orgeluse's attitude to the issue of male violence directed against women. The healing of wounds inflicted in combat is a central issue in the Parzival story, where the application of the best medical remedies known to man has failed to bring any alleviation of the grail king's condition. In this portion of the Gawan story by contrast, the healing arts prove effective, not just here with Urjans, but also in the extended treatment that Gawan receives from Arnive following his conquest of Schastel Marveile, and it is no doubt legitimate to extend the notion of "Gawan the physician" metaphorically to his role as the healer of psychological wounds, above all in the case of Orgeluse, and of social wounds, as with the unnatural conditions that the prisoners of Schastel Marveile suffer under Clinschor (see the article of Bindschedler). As for Orgeluse's pursuit of justice for the victim of Urjans's violence, it is significant that she sees herself making good Arthur's failure (529,4–9) and implicitly rejects the mercy that had been shown to Urjans on the grounds of chivalric etiquette and the (ultimately misogynist) argument that the lady's beauty provoked the attack. In the light of her own experience (revealed of course only later), it is no surprise that she should identify with the lady in this case, but her determination to exact vengeance where others, including Ginover and the victim herself, have found it in themselves to exercise mercy signals an uncompromising nature.

Gawan's first sight of Orgeluse is in a context which is unusual for a woman of her obviously noble condition — alone, outside the castle, beside a spring — and, having had his earlier expectations of an erotic adventure disappointed, he is eager to seize to what appears to be a promising opportunity, addressing her with words that strain the limits of propriety in their sexual suggestiveness (509,1–9; 510,15–26). Orgeluse, however, is not a lady to be impressed by verbal assaults of this kind and immediately seizes the initiative in what becomes a sophisticated battle of words and wit that runs on throughout the experiences that they share on the first day of their acquaintance. Commanding the rhetoric of love discourse no less well than Gawan and prepared at times to descend into a crudeness of expression which seems incongruous in the mouth of a courtly lady, Orgeluse deflates his protestations of love and shows contempt for his offers of service to her, promising him only humiliation as reward. Yet, resistant as she seems to be to Gawan's every move, she avoids going so far as to dismiss him from her presence, and he appears helpless to avoid her spell, however demeaning her treatment of him may be.

At every opportunity which presents itself, she mocks him mercilessly and repeatedly casts doubt on his chivalric status, calling him at various points an "arzet" (516,30= "physician"), a "garzûn" (523,9= "unmounted page"), and a merchant (531,12–18), this last an echo of the aspersions cast on him by Obie in Book VII. Any discomfort which he suffers elicits only *Schadenfreude* on Orgeluse's part. When he is accosted by the hideous Malcreatiure, brother of the grail messenger Cundrie and a gift from Anfortas to Orgeluse, and is accused by him of unchivalrously abducting his lady, Gawan tries to respond with a suitably contemptuous gesture, grasping him by the hair and throwing him to the ground, but the hedgehog bristles which Malcreatiure has for hair cut his hand deeply, much to Orgeluse's delight: "des lachte diu frouwe: / si sprach 'vil gerne ich schouwe / iuch zwêne sus mit zornes site'" (521,15–17= "The lady laughed at this. She said, 'I love to see you two quarrelling like this'"). Scornful laughter is similarly her response when Gawan's horse is stolen and he has to make do with Malcreatiure's nag whose condition is so poor that he refrains from mounting it and leads it on foot instead (531,9). Most disturbingly, she deliberately leads Gawan into needless danger when she arranges for Lischoys to confront him in combat. For not only is Gawan endangered by having no other mount than the pitiable nag, but the combat also has no real justification, as the narrator points out on two occasions: "wer solte se drumbe prîsen, / daz di unwîsen / striten âne schulde, / niwan durch prîses hulde?" (538,1–4= "Who should praise them for fighting for no cause, other than that Fame should smile on them, rash men?"), and "âne nôt was ir gerich: / si möhtenz âne strîten lân" (542,16–17 "the punishment they meted out to one another was unnecessary: they could have let the matter rest without fighting"). Since Orgeluse does not wait to witness the outcome of the combat, Gawan does not even have the satisfaction of proving to her by his victory in this senseless encounter that he is capable of serving for love through deeds of chivalry (543,21–23).

The combat with Lischoys is the last major event in Gawan's first day with Orgeluse, and the narrator's critical comments prompt one to ask what is happening with him, for although Gawan clearly has no option but to defend himself once challenged by Lischoys, the fact remains that he has allowed himself to be drawn into acting irresponsibly and seemingly out of character — one thinks by contrast of his avoidance of unnecessary fighting in Book VI, when Parzival appeared outside Arthur's camp. During the course of the day he has been in situations in which he has been made to appear a ridiculous and comic figure — cutting his hand on Malcreatiure's hair, losing his horse to

Urjans, having to make do with a wretched nag — providing Orgeluse with ample opportunity to question his knightly status, and he has endured all this for the sake of remaining in her company. It looks possible that we may be witnessing a repeat of what happened at Schanpfanzun, when the prospect of a quick sexual conquest led him to lose control over events with consequent danger to his dignity and his life. In this light it appears ominous that when Gawan first set eyes on Orgeluse, she was described as "ein reizel minnen gir" (508,28= "a bait of love's desire"), recalling Liddamus's reference to Gawan being caught in a "klobe" ("fowling-stick") at Schanpfanzun.

On the other hand, there are hints that there may be more deliberation in his conduct than appearances suggest, for example, when he expresses himself confident that her present behavior towards him will change for the better:

> er sprach 'ist iu nu zornes gâch,
> dâ hœrt iedoch genâde nâch . . .
> die wîl mîn hant iu dienst tuot,
> unz ir gewinnet lônes muot' (515,17–22)

> (He said: 'Though you are swift with your anger now, you will show me favour in the end . . . Meanwhile I shall render you service till you feel inclined to reward me.').

These verses are almost immediately followed by the narrator's advice to the audience not to judge Orgeluse before they understand the state of her heart (516,3–14), the implication possibly being that intuitively Gawan has already recognized finer qualities of character in her than have yet emerged and is quite consciously tolerating her disrespectful treatment of him, in the belief that it represents only a storm which he can weather before reaching calmer waters. Furthermore, although Gawan's initial approach to Orgeluse is plainly that of the sexual adventurer, it becomes apparent by the end of the day that his interest is in something more than a casual liaison. During the combat with Lischoys the narrator refers to Gawan's "triuwe" (541,6= "fidelity") towards Orgeluse, and as he takes up lodgings for the night with Plippalinot after the combat, Gawan reveals to his host how deeply affected he has been by Orgeluse, speaking of his hope that she has such "triuwe" as will bring him happiness (547,28–30). A commitment to her at a deeper level is also suggested by the fact that he takes no advantage of the ferryman's daughter, Bene, although it is made obvious to him that there would be no objection to his doing so. For Wolfram *triuwe* is the essence of true love — "reht minne ist wâriu triuwe"

(532,10= "Benign love is true fidelity"), and it is clear that it is such love for Orgeluse which has taken root in Gawan's heart.

Gawan puts Orgeluse out of his mind on the next day and focuses on the adventure at Schastel Marveile, but thoughts of her assail him again immediately afterwards. The restlessness of his sleep that night is caused more by longing for Orgeluse than by the discomfort of his wounds, and the narrator details the extent to which members of Gawan's family have over the generations obeyed the commands of love and been acquainted with the anguish it causes, including in the roll-call of names that of Gawan's sister Itonje who bore King Gramoflanz a constant love (586,22–25) — this is the first allusion to an issue which will shortly preoccupy Gawan. In the meantime, it is Gawan in whom the lineage's submission to the power of love is manifest, as he espies Orgeluse approaching the castle with Florant von Itolac, another of the knights in her service. It is clearly Orgeluse's purpose to lure Gawan out of the castle into her company again and in this she is successful, but Wolfram does not attribute this unequivocally to the power of love, nor does he overlook the problematic nature of Gawan's decision to leave the castle. He presents Gawan as being in a dilemma as to what to do and lists the pros and cons (595,1–8). On the one hand, there is, first, what he regards as the "schande" (595,3= "affront") to him as lord of the castle represented by the knight "mit ûf gerihtem sper" (593,24= "with upraised lance") in his territory, which calls for a response (see 594,15–19) and, secondly, the promptings of his love for Orgeluse; on the other hand, as inhibiting factors, there are his still unhealed wounds and the fears of the ladies of the castle that if he ventures forth and does battle, their liberation from Clinschor's power will be short-lived (see 594,20–30). We are not told how Gawan decides between these conflicting considerations, nor how he reconciles his decision to ride out with the danger that that holds for the occupants of the castle. It is noteworthy that Wolfram introduces, alongside love, the new consideration of Gawan's lordship as a possible factor in prompting him to act in a way which is under the circumstances irresponsible and seemingly out of character. Wolfram alludes to Gawan's earlier combat with Lischoys in this scene (593,1–3), and just as that combat recalled, by way of contrast, Gawan's behavior in Book VI, so here too there are distinct echoes of the scene in which Parzival is spotted outside Arthur's camp "mit ûf gerihtem sper" (284,3), a posture which is interpreted as an affront to the court (284,21), leading to the assaults of Segramors and Keie upon him. In the present instance Gawan's response is no more reasonable than theirs on the earlier occasion.

Having overcome Florant in combat, Gawan rides away with Orgeluse, and matters move swiftly to a climax, as she offers him the opportunity to sue for her love if he fetches for her a garland from a certain tree (600,20–24). Gawan eagerly agrees to this, and she leads him to "Li gweiz prelljus" ("The Perilous Ford" — it is in fact a ravine through which the River Sabins flows), on the far side of which stands the tree in question, which she now tells him is tended by the man who robbed her of her happiness (601,26). With no more information than this to guide him, Gawan attempts the leap across the ravine. He fails and both he and his horse plunge into the river, but he is able to rescue the horse and scramble to safety on the far side. The bathetic effect of this near-debacle, enhanced by the narrator's debunking remark that he would not take Orgeluse's love on these terms (604,4–6), sets the tone for the following rather awkwardly motivated scene (Bumke 1991, 108–9) which on the one hand threatens to end in anticlimax, and on the other opens up a whole new dimension of complications which have scarcely yet been hinted at.

When Gawan breaks the garland from the tree, a knight appears (it is of course King Gramoflanz), dressed for hunting rather than combat, who explains that he will not challenge Gawan in spite of his having taken the garland because it is his custom never to fight fewer than two opponents at a time. Gramoflanz deduces from the state of Gawan's shield that he has overcome the adventure of Schastel Marveile, and this leads him to talk quite openly of his killing of Cidegast and of Orgeluse's hostility to him. He knows that she has sent Gawan to kill him in return for her love (this was not known to Gawan until now), but since he has come alone, there will be no contest — Gramoflanz rightly assumes that Gawan will not attack an unarmed man (607,25–30). Gramoflanz proceeds to seek the aid of Gawan, in his capacity as the new lord of Schastel Marveile, in the matter of his love for the daughter of King Lot, Itonje, to whom he ascribes any honor which he has earned since being rejected by Orgeluse (606,21–607,12). Although Itonje's captivity has meant that they have never seen one another, she has sent him tokens of her love, and he requests Gawan now to take to her a ring and assurances of his devotion. To this Gawan agrees, although it must already be apparent to him that there is a potential conflict of interests in this role of go-between, insofar as the woman he loves seeks the death of the man his sister loves. The two men are about to end their conversation at this point (if they do Orgeluse's objective will not have been achieved), when Gawan asks to be told Gramoflanz's name. In his reply Gramoflanz discloses that he is the son of Irot, who, he alleges, was slain by King Lot, and that if he ever fights against one man alone it will be Lot's son Gawan, whose fame as the leading knight of the Round Table is known to him (608,9–30). It is immediately clear to Gawan that each of the lovers — assuming Itonje does love Gramoflanz, as he claims — is guilty of treachery: Itonje in loving a man who accuses her father of murder and would kill her brother, Gramoflanz in blackening the name of the father of the woman he loves and seeking the death of her brother. Gawan reveals his own name and declares himself ready to defend the honor of Lot in a "teidinc" (611,5= "judicial combat"). (The charge against Lot is identical to the one levelled against Gawan by Kingrimursel; whether the allegation is unfounded in Lot's case, as it is in Gawan's, is not made clear, but in each instance the truth of the matter is to be established by a judicial combat [see 611,5–6 and 418,19–20].) The time and place are set by Gramoflanz — sixteen days hence at Joflanze — and it is agreed that each should bring a large company of ladies to witness the encounter, including on Gawan's side the former prisoners of Schastel Marveile and Arthur's court. With this they part, Orgeluse's objective having been thus unexpectedly realized after all, while Gawan finds himself in the position of being committed both to act as Gramoflanz's messenger of love to Itonje and to prepare himself for a duel with Gramoflanz to clear his father's name — and, as it appears, incidentally to avenge the wrong done to Orgeluse.

When Gawan leaps back over the ravine to Orgeluse bearing the garland, this means only one thing to her: that now at last revenge may be exacted for the killing of Cidegast. She falls at Gawan's feet, begs his forgiveness and declares her love. Gawan's response to this sudden transformation in Orgeluse is understandably cautious, given the many times she has made mock of him: "Dô sprach er 'frouwe, ist daz wâr / daz ir mich grüezet âne vâr, / sô nâhet ir dem prîse'" (612,1–3 "Then he said, 'My lady, if it is true that you greet me sincerely, then you are on the way to getting a good name'"). Rather than expressing delight at the change in her, however, he proceeds to speak of the high dignity of chivalry and how she has wronged it, and of his own reputation for chivalry and how she has impugned it. Giving her the garland, he roundly declares that she must never again insult knighthood and that if he is to be mocked by her then he would rather be without love. The controlled anger in these words betrays the smart that Gawan has felt at Orgeluse's persistent mockery and confirms the earlier suggestion that it was by a conscious act of will that he suppressed his sense of outrage at her conduct, in the confidence that it did not represent her true nature. Her present dramatic transformation now vindicates his patience, and her revelations concerning her past provide for him, as for the audience, a context in which her malicious behavior can be understood as the expression of an intense love which has been perverted by the destruction of its object and can as such be forgiven (614,26).

Confident that her cause now lies in competent hands, Orgeluse transfers her affection from Cidegast to Gawan, and she is as good as her word in granting him the reward of her love for having fetched the garland from Gramoflanz's tree. This happens at Schastel Marveile on the following night, coinciding with and matched by the restoration of the natural order of sexual relations among the occupants of the castle. Now she who had mocked Gawan's healing skills performs a healing role in respect of the wounds of love that he has suffered on her account (643,9–644,6). She is able to do this because her psychological wounds, inflicted by the disordered passion and the violence of Gramoflanz, have been healed by Gawan through his persistence with her, restoring the power of a benign love to her. Once more Gawan is seen to have fulfilled his role as "a catalyst of humaneness."

The consequences of Orgeluse's tragic history have, however, not yet been entirely dealt with. The love-making of Gawan and Orgeluse precedes the execution of her vengeance, a responsibility which he now assumes. Although Gawan crossed the ford *Li gweiz prelljus* ignorant of the fact that Orgeluse's wish was to see him committed to fighting Gramoflanz and although he commits himself to do so in order to defend his father's honor, he accepts without question the additional role of avenger which she has envisaged for him (614,6-25). Compassion for her grief on account of Cidegast, graphically described by her (612,21–613,30), and a sense of the injustice she has suffered no doubt play their part in this, but desire for her — so urgent in Gawan that he suggests that they make love on the spot (614,27–615,2) — is also clearly a motivating factor in his decision. Thus as love closes the door on one episode of suffering, it potentially helps to open the door on another, with Gawan's sister Itonje as the prime victim. Orgeluse may play no great part in the forefront of the action beyond this point, but through the unresolved matter of her vengeance she exercises a major influence on events — and it will not be forgotten that it was she who ensured that Urjans did not escape the penalty for his crime of violence against a woman.

The concluding stages of the Gawan story are centered on Joflanze, a location which signifies two things for Gawan: it is the place where he will reunite the four queens liberated from Schastel Marveile with the Arthurian court, and it is there also that he will fight Gramoflanz. These events should be the climaxes of the two main strands of action in which he has been involved since entering Logroys and Terre Marveile. With regard to the four queens, it is clear that it is Gawan's intention to spring a surprise on all concerned when he brings Arthur's mother, sister and nieces back to their family (see S. Johnson 1958, Poag 1977, and D. H. Green 1982, 165-175). This idea appears to have been conceived in the immediate aftermath of his victory in the adventure of Schastel Marveile, when he meets for the first time the four ladies whom he knows to be his kinswomen but does not identify himself to them (590,17-591,11); their failure to recognize him is adequately motivated by the length of time that they have been in captivity (see S. Johnson 1958 and D. H. Green 1982, 157). That the setting for this reunion should be Joflanze follows from the agreement to fight with Gramoflanz there and to invite the Arthurian court to be present.

The execution of Gawan's surprise is a masterpiece of organization on his part, though not entirely unproblematical in its effects. A letter is sent to Arthur appealing to him to be present at the combat with Gramoflanz on which Gawan's honor crucially depends (649,5-650,20), but it contains no word of his success at Schastel Marveile, for that might alert the court to what was in store for them, and the messenger bearing the letter is under strict instructions to keep Gawan's whereabouts secret (626,19-22; 647,24-26). A more sustained series of concealments is required to prevent the ladies in Schastel Marveile from learning of his identity and plan. Thus, as he and Orgeluse go to Schastel Marveile for the first time together, Gawan asks her to keep his name secret (620,1-12). The messenger by whom he sends the letter to Arthur is instructed to conceal his destination, which he succeeds in doing in spite of the enquiries of Arnive (626,24-29; 652,26-653,14). A particularly delicate situation arises when Gawan delivers to Itonje the ring sent her by Gramoflanz, for it obliges her to reveal the love which she has hitherto kept secret from all but Bene, who has previously acted as the lovers' intermediary. While this provides Gawan with the important confirmation that she reciprocates Gramoflanz's love, it involves her baring her heart to him in an especially intimate way, and yet for the sake of his surprise (and also to ensure that his combat with Gramoflanz should not be thwarted) he has to conceal their kinship from her. In this, the narrator suggests, he goes too far:

> ouch het er sich gesündet baz
> gein der einvaltigen magt
> diu im ir kumber hât geklagt;
> wander ir niht zuo gewuoc
> daz in unt si ein muoter truoc (636,6-10)

(Yet he was guilty of a greater fault towards the innocent girl who had told him of her troubles, for he did not mention to her that one mother had borne the two of them.)

When Arthur and his company camp for the night outside Schastel Marveile on their way to Joflanze, Gawan has to pretend that he does not know who they are (661,21–28), and he acts as though they might be a hostile force, against which the castle must be secured (663,9–14 and 20–30). It is noted that Arthur's men have already been involved in fighting, and the narrator reports that in passing through Logroys they have been engaged in battle by Orgeluse's knights (664,18–665,24); this elicits a further critical comment on Gawan's secretiveness:

> och solte mîn hêr Gâwân
> der herzogîn gekündet hân
> daz ein sîn helfære
> in ir lande wære:
> sô wære des strîtes niht geschehn (665,25–29)

(Truly, my lord Gawan ought to have informed the Duchess that an ally of his was in her territory. Then there would have been no fighting.)

Finally, Gawan has to arrange for the journey of his party to Joflanze and for their lodging, and for this purpose he takes into his confidence four of his knights, whom he appoints as his chamberlain, butler, steward, and marshal, thus filling the four main offices of a royal or princely court (Nellmann 1994,745). The marshal is instructed to go ahead to Joflanze and there to set up a camp for Gawan separate from Arthur's, while the other officers are to prepare for the march there in lavish style (666,23–667,26). With the stage thus set, Gawan makes his entry at Joflanze with his retinue of hundreds of knights and ladies from Schastel Marveile.

Compared with this careful orchestration of events, the surprise reunion is anti-climactic. In just seven verses Gawan identifies the four queens (672,8–14), and a further seven verses suffice to describe the scene of joy, the laughter and tears (672,15–21). No mention is made of Gawan's success at Schastel Marveile, no thanks given that the longstanding stain on the reputation of the Arthurian court has finally been removed. The only comment passed on the magnificence of Gawan's camp and retinue, evidence of his newly acquired lordship, comes from Keie, who observes that there had been no need to fear competition with Arthur and separate camps in the days of Lot (675,4–9). The criticism of Gawan's ambition implied here is immediately qualified by remarks on Keie's envious nature, but as was suggested earlier, his observations, however malicious, are often not without a grain of truth, and if this comment is taken together with the narrator's criticism of Gawan's secretiveness as it affects Itonje and the fighting in which Arthur has quite needlessly to engage, it is difficult to resist the suspicion that the motivation of Gawan's surprise and the ostentatious display of his wealth as lord of Schastel Marveile which accompanies it is being questioned in some measure. It may also be recalled that one of the reasons for Gawan feeling impelled to go out from Schastel Marveile to joust with Florant was the supposed affront to his authority as lord, even though to do so entailed serious risk for those he had just liberated. It appears that Gawan's success at Schastel Marveile and the new status it confers upon him have gone to his head and impaired his judgement; he has become over-eager to demonstrate his power, manipulating those around him in order to achieve a dramatic effect, which, in the event, falls flat and hardly justifies the cost to others that it has exacted. Keie's suggestion that Gawan's projection of himself at Joflanze is intended to rival Arthur or to be a declaration of independence from him no doubt overstates the case, but if there were any truth in it, then the folly of Gawan's aspiration would be only too apparent when it comes to the second matter which concerns him at Joflanze, the combat with Gramoflanz.

Up to the point of Gawan's arrival at Joflanze there appears to be little prospect that anything can prevent the trial by combat between him and Gramoflanz from taking place, with the tragic consequences for Itonje, of which neither man can have been ignorant from the start, whatever the outcome. As long as full awareness of the situation and its implications is restricted to them, no peaceable resolution seems possible. For they feel themselves to be under obligations which make it difficult, if not impossible, for either of them unilaterally to withdraw without loss of honor and, in Gawan's case, of love too. For Gawan it is a question of family honor — to clear his father's name — and of his obligation to avenge Orgeluse's wrong, while for Gramoflanz it is family honor — vengeance for his father's death — and personal honor — the theft of the garland from his tree — which are at stake.

What brings movement into this deadlocked situation is the chance intervention of Parzival, who arrives at Joflanze on the day appointed for the combat. For his own reasons, he has broken a garland from Gramoflanz's tree in order to be able to fight with him, and when Gawan rides out to exercise himself in advance of the encounter with Gramoflanz, he and Parzival, each thinking the other to be Gramoflanz, engage in combat. This combat between kinsmen, for Parzival the latest in a sequence of such incidents, but something entirely new for Gawan (and an indication that he is losing his grip on events) is halted when Parzival is clearly in the ascendancy. It is at this point that Bene becomes a key figure. She arrives on the scene with Gramoflanz, who has come thinking he will fight Gawan, and she discovers there that Gramoflanz's opponent is to be none other than the brother of Itonje. Having acted as the intermediary between Itonje and Gramoflanz, she knows of their love and is in a position to gauge the full extent of the tragedy that lies in store for Itonje if the combat takes place. She immediately turns on Gramoflanz, addressing him as "ir ungetriwer hunt!" (693,22= "You treacherous cur!") and "verfluochet man" (694,17= "cursed man"), and points out the contradiction in his position, which can only lead to the loss of Itonje's love, but he is unmoved by this. He asks her to assure Itonje of his devotion and, having agreed with Gawan upon a postponement of their duel to the following day, he departs. Aware that Bene's knowledge could jeopardize the combat and the fulfillment of his obligations, Gawan now takes her aside and instructs her not to tell Itonje that he and Gramoflanz are to fight (696,21–30). Her response pinpoints the problem precisely: whichever of the two dies in the combat, Itonje will be slain — "diu ist ze bêder sît erslagn" (697,5= "She is slain on either side"). But like Gramoflanz, Gawan is apparently unmoved by Bene's words, and the opportunity for reconsideration given to both men by her impassioned exposition of the tragic prospect for Itonje appears to have been wasted.

For a second time it is Parzival who brings about a further helpful delay and an important revelation. Having been re-introduced to the Arthurian company by Gawan after their combat — Gawan still performs this role in respect of the court — and having been re-admitted to membership of the Round Table, Parzival requests Gawan's permission to substitute for him in the combat with Gramoflanz on the following day (700,25–701,20). This is refused, but Parzival is undeterred, and the following morning sees him engaging Gramoflanz in combat, the latter thinking that he is fighting Gawan. In a reversal of the situation on the previous day, it is Gawan who arrives on the scene to find his adversary already exhausted from fighting with the wrong man. An agreement is quickly reached between Arthur and King Brandelidelin, Gramoflanz's uncle who is at Joflanze to support him, that the combat should be stopped, a foretaste of the co-operation between the uncles of Gawan and Gramoflanz which is to be of decisive importance in resolving the central problem at hand. At Gawan's instigation, the duel with Gramoflanz is postponed for a further day, but afterwards, talking with Arthur and Parzival, Gawan gives a sign that he would be glad not to have to fight with Gramoflanz at all (708,17–20).

There is no explicit indication of why Gawan's position has shifted; it is, however, likely that we are to understand that he was not as unmoved by the distress of Bene on account of his sister as he seemed to be at the time. Above all of importance is, however, that Arthur is aware that Gawan is no longer totally convinced of the necessity for his combat with Gramoflanz.

The signs of Bene's distress certainly do not leave Itonje unmoved (697,28–698,14). Whether it is as a result of inquiring into the cause of her distress or by some other means, we do not know, but the time gained by Parzival's second intervention allows word to reach Itonje that her brother and her beloved are to fight with one another (710,9–14). So extreme is her anguish that her grandmother and mother are alerted and learn of Itonje's love for Gramoflanz, kept secret from them until now. Arnive sends for Arthur and asks him to intervene. He speaks with Itonje, who sees Orgeluse as the villain of the piece for inciting her brother to kill her beloved; she misunderstands Gawan's position, being unaware of Gramoflanz's allegation against her father, and she thinks it is her brother's responsibility alone to halt the duel. Appealing to Arthur as her uncle, she pleads with him to prevent the combat (711,17–712,2). He can prevent it, he tells her, but he first needs to know whether Gramoflanz reciprocates her feelings; her love will have to play its part in staying his hand as well. Fortuitously messengers arrive bearing a letter from Gramoflanz to Itonje. Its contents convince Arthur of the sincerity of his love for her; it is clear what he must do: "ich wil den kampf undervarn" (716,9= "I will put a stop to this duel").

Called into action by the women in his family, aware of Gawan's reservations about the judicial combat, and with the happiness of a pair of young lovers to save, Arthur — "der wîse höfsche man" (717,1= "the wise, courteous man") — launches into a masterful and elegant display of diplomacy, the keynote of which is *suone* (reconciliation) in a spirit of love. He enlists the aid of Bene and the two young messengers from Gramoflanz to persuade their lord to visit his camp that day: Arthur wants Gramoflanz to meet Itonje, so that he comes directly under the influence of her love, but he suggests that they put it to Gramoflanz that he will be able to draw inspiration from the sight of Itonje for the combat on the morrow. In the meantime he will secure a truce from Orgeluse for the period of the visit (719,1–720,14). Gramoflanz accepts the invitation, anxious to see Itonje at last, and sets out with a small party which includes his uncle Brandelidelin. Orgeluse grants the truce, for the embraces of Gawan have mellowed her and compensated her for the loss of Cidegast, so that her hostility to Gramoflanz has all but been dispelled (723,1–10). Beacurs, the brother of Gawan and Itonje, escorts Gramoflanz into a pavilion in Arthur's camp, which he has packed with a hundred ladies, including Itonje. Gramoflanz is able to identify Itonje from the likeness to Beacurs. With Arthur's encouragement, the lovers exchange a kiss for all to see. Arthur takes Brandelidelin to a smaller tent a little distance away. To help the process along, drinks are served both in the pavilion and to the two kings. In private the two elder statesmen put their heads together: they quickly agree that Gramoflanz stands only to lose Itonje's love if he kills Gawan; they must prevent their nephews' combat, so that the love of Gramoflanz and Itonje may flourish; Itonje must command Gramoflanz to forgo the combat for the sake of her love; Arthur will help Gramoflanz gain the favor of Orgeluse, confident that Gawan has such influence with her now that she will leave the matter of her vengeance in their hands (726,8–727,16).

And that is precisely what happens. Arthur goes first to Gawan, with whose help Orgeluse's agreement to a "suone" (728,4) is secured. She makes two conditions: that Gawan should be willing for his part to forgo the combat, and that Gramoflanz should withdraw the accusation against Lot. Arthur conveys the terms to Gramoflanz, who, anxious to please Itonje in every way, renounces all hostility. Now Gawan and Orgeluse can join the main company for the final scene of reconciliation, marked by Gramoflanz kissing each of them. For Orgeluse this is understandably a poignant moment, as even now she still thinks of Cidegast and grieves for him; "welt ir, des jeht für triuwe" (729,24= "You may call that fidelity if you will"), says the narrator, leaving us with a final reminder of the force that animated Orgeluse's apparently relentless desire for vengeance, thoughts of which are now set aside in the interests of new love — hers and Gawan's, Itonje's and Gramoflanz's.

Marriage is the only fitting conclusion to this triumph of "liebe" ("affection/love") over "leit" ("sorrow") (728,24), and marriages there are in abundance, for "Artûs was frouwen milte" (730,11= "Arthur was generous in giving ladies away"): Itonje is given to Gramoflanz, Gawan's sister Cundrie to Lischoys, and Sangive to Florant; in addition, Orgeluse declares that Gawan has earned her love and is by right lord of her person and her lands (730,15–19). Of the leading actors in the final stage of the Gawan story, only Parzival is excluded from the general scene of connubial bliss; pining for his wife, he slips away to resume his quest — which is shortly to lead to a resolution too.

The events which pass at Joflanze have been well described as a "comedy of errors which so dangerously skirts the realm of tragedy" (D. H. Green 1982, 231). Indeed, as the plot unfolds, with incidents of mistaken identity, fortuitous arrivals, the meeting of separated lovers, and the redeeming of what seems to be a hopelessly entangled situation by the wisdom of an elder statesman, one does seem to be witnessing the denouement of a comedy. Characteristic of comedy in a more general sense is also the spirit that prevails at the end of the Gawan story, as hostilities give way to harmony on all sides, and love rules. Central to the problems and threatening a tragic outcome is the long-standing animosity of Gramoflanz and Orgeluse, which has spread like an infection to Itonje and Gawan, as they have aligned themselves with their partners in love, and which has even begun to affect the relationship between brother and sister, in Gawan's secretiveness towards Itonje and her misconception of his motives. Were the combat to take place, the malignant process would continue unabated, whichever way it was decided. This is avoided, however, because love exercises its power to induce a spirit of reconciliation — in Orgeluse through the love of Gawan, in Gramoflanz through the love of Itonje. As in the Bearosche episode, so here love works to overcome the problems that, in the form of Gramoflanz's destructive passion, it has created. And as on the earlier occasion, love's triumph is celebrated in marriage. Here not only is each pair of lovers united, but also, through the affinity created by marriage, all four principals are linked with one another: Gramoflanz becomes the brother-in-law of his erstwhile adversaries Gawan and Orgeluse, and Itonje becomes the sister-in-law of Orgeluse, whom she had seen as the instigator of Gawan's hostility to Gramoflanz.

If the story ends in comic vein and love has been able to spread its balm in this way, this is because of the role that Arthur plays. In the knowledge that Gawan would rather not defend his cause in judicial combat if there were some alternative, he has recourse to another legal means, namely "suone," by which the parties to conflict agree formally to renounce hostilities in favor of peace. The final scene of reconciliation is referred to as "dirre suone teidinc" (729,5= "the formal proceedings of this peacemaking"), and it replaces the "teidinc" — judicial combat — which Gawan and Gramoflanz had agreed upon. Peacemaking thus replaces armed conflict, allowing the past to be buried and not to dominate the present and the future. Arthur appears here as the *rex pacificus*, fulfilling one of the most sacred duties of kingship (see H. Brunner 69). He does so, even though he is in a foreign land, not his own jurisdiction, but he enjoys unquestioned authority in the matter as the uncle of Gawan and Itonje. The family dimension is altogether of importance for the resolution of the issue, the women in particular playing a vital role in prompting Arthur to act in the first place and in the marriage settlements. The fact that Arthur arranges three marriages has struck some commentators as comic exaggeration, but it is pertinent to note that the marriages of Florant to Arthur's daughter and of Lischoys to his niece help to secure the carefully crafted peace by binding to the Arthurian family also the two men who have been in the forefront of Orgeluse's attempts on Gramoflanz's life and who were as such abhorrent to Itonje (634,21–27). In his management of events at Joflanze, Arthur shows a shrewd understanding of human nature and a brilliant command of courtly and legal procedures to achieve an outcome which is manifestly in everyone's best interests.

Parzival for his part also contributes to the peaceful conclusion of events at Joflanze. His two interventions give rise to important revelations and buy time for those not immediately involved to get a grip on the situation. No personal merit accrues to him for this, as he is unaware of the situation into which he stumbles, and the combat which he fights with Gawan is a highly problematic example of a combat between kinsmen, which earns the narrator's censure (691,23). However, there is a sense in which Parzival, of all men, is fitted to have a salutary effect on events, for he is the only knight who has ever refused Orgeluse's invitation to enter her service, even though she offered him herself and her lands. Unlike Gawan and unlike Anfortas, who still has to endure the wound sustained in Orgeluse's service, Parzival was saved by his devotion to his wife and the quest for the grail from becoming caught up in the toils of the conflict between her and Gramoflanz. This means that he is available and able to perform a useful function at a critical juncture, that he can act as "the hand of God" (Poag 1977, 74) or as "an instrument of grace" (D. H. Green 1982,173) in steering the situation, however unwittingly, towards a resolution of Gawan's difficulties. Parzival's involvement in the process which brings an end to the Orgeluse-Gramoflanz conflict is followed very shortly by the healing of Anfortas, and it may be considered as a foreshadowing of the grace that is to be bestowed on Parzival in the healing power of his question that he has a hand in eradicating the baleful situation which led Orgeluse to draw Anfortas into her service. For Orgeluse the memory of Parzival's humiliating disdain of her love still rankles, and it causes her embarrassment when she is required by Gawan to welcome him (696,8–14), but, in a prefiguration of her willingness to be reconciled with Gramoflanz, she submits to Gawan's command to eat with Parzival (697,12–20). In due course she is overjoyed to learn that Anfortas is to be healed by Parzival (784,4–7), putting an end to what was for her a cause of grief no less painful than the loss of Cidegast (616,11–617,3). Parzival makes a contribution in another way, too, for the defeat which he single-handedly administers to Gramoflanz in combat cures him of his insistence that he will never fight with only one opponent (705,19–30). This lesson in humility has a bearing on Gramoflanz's readiness to seek a reconciliation with Orgeluse and prepares for his assumption of a place at the Round Table, where he will experience further the influence of its ethos, thus achieving what was Arthur's wish from the time that he heard of Gramoflanz's combat with Gawan, namely to tame his arrogance (650,13–20 — see H. Brunner 69).

From the vantage point of Joflanze, where Gawan's course comes full circle as he is re-united with the Arthurian court, we can look back on the Gawan story and attempt to pinpoint its principal themes. The world in which Gawan is seen to move, when he is away from the Arthurian milieu, is one characterized by severely disturbed personal and social relations. The principal cause of the dysfunctions is a failure to control the force of erotic love, unregulated sexual desire in short. It is this which is responsible for the warfare at Bearosche, for the murder and thirst for revenge of the Orgeluse-Gramoflanz conflict, and ultimately for the conditions which prevail at Schastel Marveile. A secondary factor is the failure of young lords to honor their commitments and to order properly their relations, particularly with the older generation of the nobility. This is seen above all in Vergulaht at Schanpfanzun but also in Meljanz at Bearosche.

In the course of his involvement in this world, where the Arthurian norms by which these things are better regulated do not hold sway, Gawan himself proves to be vulnerable to the forces of disorder with whose consequences he is confronted. Predisposed in this direction by the familial susceptibility to love, he is on occasion drawn by sexual desire into losing control over his destiny and over events (as seems to have been the case in the incidents in his past alluded to in Book VI). This is evident first at Schanpfanzun in his escapade with Antikonie, then more dangerously in his relationship with Orgeluse, where he in effect becomes part of the problem himself. Significant here is not so much her humiliating treatment of him — he has a sufficiently secure sense of his worth to be untouched by this and the insight to realize that it does not represent Orgeluse's true self — as the fact that he is led by desire for her into the role of avenger in a situation which threatens to result in tragedy for his sister. (Although the allegation against Lot adds the consideration of family honor to Gawan's motivation, it remains the case that it is the love of Orgeluse which has brought him to this pass.) While not a case of violence directed against an innocent person exactly, the end effect would be tantamount to that. In both these instances chivalric values are also adversely affected: his defense of Antikonie and himself is farcical, and each of the combats fought in the service of Orgeluse — against Lischoys, Florant, and Parzival — is made to seem questionable. Furthermore, as lord of Schastel Marveile, Gawan is motivated to display his power over people and resources in a way which leads Keie at least to suspect a wish to compete with Arthur and thus to alter the relationship with his lord and uncle, in a variation of the problem exemplified by Vergulaht and Meljanz.

Although there is a danger of Gawan becoming no better than those with whom he has to deal, this does not in fact happen, and his impact on the world in which he operates is ultimately to influence it for the good. A number of factors play a part in this. First, there is his chivalric prowess. Overall it is notable how infrequently chivalric action actually resolves problems in the Gawan story, but it is significant at Bearosche, insofar his capture of Meljanz creates circumstances in which a peaceful resolution can be reached, while at Schastel Marveile he is called upon to overcome a challenge of the highest order to his strength and courage. In this contest against evil, with its background of apostasy and heathen necromancy as well as of disordered passion, lines are drawn with a clarity which they do not have elsewhere, recalling accounts of religious warfare in the Chanson de Geste tradition and, within *Parzival* itself, the action of the knights at Munsalvaesche as protectors of the grail, though it is noteworthy that Gawan is not pitted directly against a human adversary in this context, so that the problems associated with the killing of a human opponent (for the grail knights fight to the death) are avoided. The task which Gawan has to perform at Schastel Marveile is one straightforwardly of liberation from the powers of darkness, and he comes there closest to fulfilling the role of a messianic deliverer and exponent of Christian chivalry. Secondly, there is his ability to work with and through other people and to activate the forces for good in them, chief among these forces being love and its power to heal. This is evident at its purest and most uncomplicated in an emotional sense in his co-operation with Obilot at Bearosche, where her love involves him in action which results in the restoration to the young lovers of their genuine feelings for one another. It is evident also in the effect which Gawan has on Orgeluse, removing the weight of her history from her and restoring her capacity for love, so that she in turn can heal the wounds inflicted on him by love and become a part of the healing process of peacemaking at Joflanze. In this situation, in which Gawan is immediately implicated, it falls, however, also to Arthur to stimulate the salutary effects of love in the interests of a settlement which works to the best advantage of all concerned. This includes Gawan himself, who is able to retain the love of Orgeluse, though Wolfram insures that he is in future shielded against the dangers which inhere in love by grounding his affection for Orgeluse in the quality of *triuwe* (fidelity) and, a rarity for the Gawan figure, leading him into the safe haven of marriage. Thirdly, there is his optimism. Gawan's confidence in the ultimately benign dispensation under which he lives, evident already in Book VI, never deserts him. In some situations, notably at Bearosche and in the Schastel Marveile adventure, this confidence takes an expressly religious form, as Gawan puts his trust in God. In other situations, this dimension is absent, but his conduct testifies to an underlying sense of assurance that events will finally turn out for the best. Thus, at Schanpfanzun, he maintains his composure in what is his greatest state of helplessness and relies on the good in others, possibly fostered by what he means to them, to overcome the forces of disorder and cynicism embodied in Vergulaht and Liddamus. Through all his initially difficult dealings with Orgeluse, he is buoyed up by the intuition that she cannot be what she seems and is vindicated in this belief. Finally, at Joflanze he is able to repose his trust in Arthur to insure that a humane resolution is reached, and he relinquishes any effort independently to influence events himself from the moment that he makes known to Arthur his reluctance to fight.

With Gawan's reincorporation into the Arthurian environment at Joflanze he comes again within the ordered ambit of the court and the chivalry of the Round Table and benefits from the benign influence which they exercise through the person of Arthur. Since leaving the court in Book VI, where the poise and peaceable self-control on which his reputation rested were most luminously demonstrated, Gawan has been engaged in a struggle with forces which are rampant in the world outside the court but also latent within him, the "glory of the Round Table." Maintenance of the humane and civilized values enshrined in the Arthurian ideal is a matter of constant effort, not only to combat the destructive forces outside but also to hold in check those which reside within. When Arthur steps in to assist Gawan at a point where he has reached an impasse and tragedy seems to be the inevitable outcome of the nexus of events in which he is caught up, we see the robustness of the court and its values and can appreciate the wisdom of an institution which keeps the king above the fray, free to act himself as "a catalyst of humaneness," when his knights, even his leading knight Gawan, become mired in the complexities of the world which represents their proper sphere of action.

In assessing finally the significance of the Gawan story within *Parzival* as a whole, it suffices to say that Wolfram did not devote such care to the elaboration of his adventures with a view to representing Gawan and Arthurian chivalry as inferior to Parzival and the chivalry of the grail with which he is associated. It is true that there is a moment in the darkest phase of the Gawan story when Parzival becomes constructively involved on Gawan's behalf and is able to do so because of his fidelity in marriage and his focus on the grail quest which kept him free of the influence of Orgeluse, but that same detachment from the affairs of the world led him to support the aggressor at Bearosche and to pass Schastel Marveile by without becoming aware of what needed to be done there. It is true that Parzival has the higher calling, for which his single-minded devotion to his wife and the grail fit him, but there are other demands to be satisfied as well, more mundane and messier no doubt, but none the less requiring a full-hearted commitment. Wolfram's imagination is more capacious than to insist on only one model of human conduct and one model of chivalry. In the Gawan story he exploits the opportunity to construct a figure whose presence repeatedly provides illuminating points of contrast with his hero, thereby helping to define him more clearly, and whose experiences as he moves through the world which is peculiarly his, with its diversity of human types and situations, contribute not a little to the sense that *Parzival* is a work of which (without any hint of the irony in Henry James's coining of the phrase) it can be said that "all human life is there."

SIDNEY JOHNSON

Doing his own Thing: Wolfram's Grail

WHEN PARZIVAL COMES TO THE GRAIL CASTLE FOR the first time in Book V, Wolfram interrupts his description of the banquet with the following words:

> man sagte mir, diz sag ouch ich
> ûf iwer iesliches eit,
> daz vorem grâle wære bereit
> (sol ich des iemen triegen,
> sô müezt ir mit mir liegen)
> swâ nâch jener bôt die hant,
> daz er al bereite vant
> spîse warm, spîse kalt,
> spîse niwe unt dar zuo alt,
> daz zam unt daz wilde. (238,8–17)

(I was told, and I'm telling you, too, on the oath of each and every one of you, that in front of the grail there was prepared [if I'm deceiving anyone in this regard, then you'll all be telling lies with me] whatever anyone stretched out his hand for. He found it readily available: warm food, cold food, new food and also old, domestic meat and game. — Translations are from Hatto.)

In saying this, Wolfram is implicitly acknowledging the skepticism of some in his audience and makes them all swear an oath so that, if he is lying, then they will all be lying along with him. He is, indeed, telling a fantastic story, but he does so with a convincing realism of detail, including, in effect, having the audience hold up its collective right hand and swear that the fantastic is true! Furthermore, as he has been describing the events at the grail castle, he deliberately leaves Parzival and his audience in the dark as to what it all means and why it is happening. In order for Parzival and the audience to get a full picture of the grail and its attendant circumstances, they must wait until Parzival meets his cousin Sigune the next day, but even that does very little to satisfy one's curiosity. Only in Book IX, finally, when Parzival meets his hermit uncle Trevrizent does Wolfram provide answers to Parzival's many unuttered questions and ours. But they are still not quite completely answered; more information comes ultimately in Book XVI. Wolfram excuses his delay in telling all by saying that his source, Kyot, told him to hold back "diu verholnen mære umben grâl" (452,30= "the concealed tale about the grail") until just the right time. With that, Wolfram may be following, wittingly or unwittingly, in the footsteps of his predecessor, Chrétien de Troyes, that Old French master of the Arthurian romance, who, especially in his *Perceval*, foreshadows Wolfram's narrative technique of concealing identity and not explaining events immediately. Unfortunately for us, perhaps for Wolfram too, Chrétien never did get around to explaining everything about his *graal*. His work remains a fragment.

We must, then, assemble all the facts that Wolfram gives us, scattered though they may be, to get a complete picture of his grail before we can consider the question of probable or even possible sources for Wolfram's grail. Instead of playing Wolfram's game and concealing our results until almost the end, we shall start right off by reviewing all the characteristics of Wolfram's grail and asserting that the most remarkable thing about it is that it is so very different from any other literary grail conception.

> Wolfram refers first to his grail as a "thing called the Gral," later a "stone" (235,23; 469,3).
>
> It has a name: "Lapsit exillîs." By virtue of this stone the Phoenix is burned to ashes and then reborn (469,7–14).
>
> Its origin is uncertain, but it was apparently already on the earth when God sent the neutral angels to it (454,24–30; 471,15–28).
>
> The grail family, headed by Titurel, was later appointed to guard the grail (455,17–22; 471,25–28; 474,10–13; 478,1–6).
>
> The grail provides food and drink for the people at the grail castle, Munsalvaesche, in the land of Terre de Salvæsche (238,8–239,7; 251,2–4).
>
> Anyone who is ill will be healed by seeing the grail and will not die for a week. At most, over time, one's hair will turn grey (469,14–28).
>
> It can only be carried by a pure virgin, i.e., it "allows itself to be carried" (235,25–30; 477,13–18; 809,9–14).
>
> A dove comes down from heaven every Good Friday with a communion wafer and renews the powers of the grail (469,29–470,20).

Only baptized Christians can see the grail; it is invisible to all others (810,7–13; 813,9–22).

Occasionally a written message appears on the grail, presumably from God, with directions or information for the people at the grail castle (470,23–40; 483,19–484,30; 781,15–30).

The grail is protected by the grail king and his family and by others who are summoned to serve the grail (473,5–11). The knights must observe the rule of chastity, though they may ride out in search of *aventiure*. These knights are called *templeise* (i.e., Knights Templar) and by defending the grail atone for any sins they may have committed (495,7–12; 468,23–30). Normally they are called to the grail as small children of noble birth, both boys and girls, from many countries, and they attain Paradise when they die. Only the grail king is allowed to marry (471,1–14; 494,5–6; 495,7–12).

It is generally believed that no one can find the grail without having been called (468,10–14; 798,24–30).

When a country is in need of a ruler, one is supplied by the grail, the maidens being sent out openly, and the men secretly with the condition that they not be asked where they come from (494,5–495,6; 818,24–819,8).

Connected with the grail and its characteristics is the story of the finding of information about the grail in Arabic in *Dôlet* (= presumably Toledo in Spain) and in Latin in *Anschouwe* (= Anjou) by the Provençal Kyot. He subsequently transmitted it to Wolfram in French. Wolfram claims that Kyot is his source. However, that need not concern us here, except to say that most scholars believe that despite what Wolfram says, his main source was the unfinished *Perceval ou Li contes del Graal* of Chrétien de Troyes, whom Wolfram mentions in his *Parzival* as an author, but not as his source. From time to time some scholars will attempt to justify the existence of a "Kyot" (the so-called "Kyot-Problem") or to suggest other sources for Wolfram's story.

Although the image of a cup or goblet with connections to Christian liturgy, i.e., the "Holy Grail," springs immediately to mind for most people who are more familiar with other grail stories and graphic, or even musical, representations, Wolfram's grail is quite definitely a stone. He uses the word *grâl* for it, which is very close to Chrétien's *graal*. The question is, of course, whether Wolfram knew what Chrétien was describing with the word. Chrétien uses *graal* as a generic term first, since he calls it *un graal*. It is clearly "*a* grail" here rather than "*the* Grail," although after the first mentioning of it, it is naturally referred to as "*the* Grail" in Chrétien's work. It appears to be some kind of bowl or serving platter, decorated with precious stones, with light emanating from it, and carried in the two hands of a lovely maiden (verses 3208–27 in F. Lecoy's edition). Etymologically the word *graal* is probably related to Greco-Roman *crater(a)*, a kind of vessel; more directly, perhaps, to Late Latin *gradale* = "by degrees" or "in stages." The word *gradale/graal* eventually does gain the meaning of "bowl" or "vessel" and occurs in a Latin chronicle by Helinand de Froidmont, a contemporary of Wolfram, but probably after Chrétien's time. He describes it as a "scutella lata et aliquantulum profunda" (= "a wide, flat dish and somewhat deep"), in other words a deep-dish serving platter in which rich foods are carried to the wealthy, one course after the other. He says later: "et dicitur vulgari nomine graalz" (= "and is called *graalz* in the vernacular" — *Patrologiae*, Migne ed., ccxii, col. 814–15).

Why Wolfram says at first "daz was ein dinc, daz hiez der Grâl" (235,23= "It was a thing that was called the Gral") and later has Trevrizent say that the Templars live from a stone named *lapsit exillis* (469,3–7) is not clear. If Chrétien was indeed his main source, was Wolfram perhaps puzzled by the word *graal* so that he calls it first "ein dinc"? To be sure, his knowledge of French was not faultless, but if he did not understand the word, he should have been able to guess what it meant from the context. If we look closely at Chrétien's text at the place where Perceval sees the *graal* for the first time (verses 3208–3233), we can ascertain the function of the *graal* and thereby have some idea of what it is, even without knowing its precise meaning. It is carried in the hands of a beautiful maiden in a procession, past Perceval and the Fisher King, after a bleeding lance and two candlesticks have gone by. It produces such a brilliant illumination that the candles lose their brightness. Another maiden follows, carrying a silver trencher. Then Chrétien says that the *graal* is made of gold and is adorned with many kinds of precious stones, and it is carried off with all the other objects into another chamber. One can easily guess that it is some kind of a bowl, but its contents are not mentioned. However, Chrétien does say that Perceval did not ask who was "served" from the *graal*, so that it would be difficult not to think of it as some kind of serving vessel. The *graal* is carried back and forth from the other chamber to the main hall between the courses of the sumptuous meal that is subsequently served, but in Perceval's conversation with his *germaine cousine* the next day there is no specific indication of the function of the *graal*. She merely asks whether he had seen it, and she laments the fact that he failed to ask any questions (verses 3569–78).

Eventually Perceval's hermit uncle explains what Perceval saw at the castle that night. He tells him that the person served by the *graal* is his (the hermit's) brother and that Perceval's mother was his sister. The rich Fisher King is the son of the king who is served by the *graal* in the adjoining chamber, therefore the Fisher King is Perceval's cousin. The hermit tells Perceval that the old king is not served pike, lamprey, or salmon; he is served with a consecrated wafer brought to him in the *graal*. He is so spiritual that he is sustained by the wafer which comes to him in the *graal* and that he has lived from that alone for fifteen years without leaving the room which Perceval saw the *graal* enter (verses 6199–6215). We must surely assume that Wolfram had read or heard all of what Chrétien had written before he started his own version of the story. Since Chrétien mentions what was *not* served in the *graal*, it seems almost impossible that Wolfram could have been unaware that the *graal* was indeed a serving dish.

It is generally assumed that Chrétien died about 1185, leaving his *Perceval* unfinished. Soon thereafter a series of four continuations arose over a period of forty years that attempted to bring it to a conclusion. Some scholars believe that Wolfram may have known at least the so-called "First Continuation," written by an anonymous poet perhaps shortly before 1200. If that dating is accurate, Wolfram could indeed have known it, since the time of composition of his *Parzival* is thought to be the first decade of the thirteenth century. If he did know it, he might well have assumed that it was part of Chrétien's tale. We should therefore ask whether anything in the description of the grail in the First Continuation could have influenced Wolfram's concept of the grail. Here it is Gauvain, rather than Perceval, who comes to the grail castle and sees the procession, in the course of which a beautiful maiden, weeping bitterly, holds aloft the *graal* for all to see, but it is called specifically "Le saint Graal" (= "the Holy Grail," verses 1362–66 in Roach's edition of *The Continuations*). A bit later she comes back with the *graal*, and mention is made of its many precious stones (verses 1405–07). The procession occurs three times during the evening, but Gauvain does not find out anything about the *graal*, and neither do we. Much later in the First Continuation Gauvain returns to the grail castle. Again the *graal* appears at the banquet, but this time no one is carrying it. It appears to float around by itself, dispensing food into large silver bowls, serving beautifully through the seven courses or more of the meal (verses 13281–13305). The contradictions here are very obvious. At the first visit a weeping maiden carries it; the second time it functions by itself as a waiter, providing food. On the first occasion it is called "Le saint Graal," but not the second time. Of course, calling it "the Holy Grail" could be the work of a later scribe under the influence of Robert de Boron's *Roman de L'Estoire dou Graal*, which we shall discuss below.

Of all the characteristics of Wolfram's grail that we listed initially, only one is to be found specifically in Chrétien: its ability to keep people who see it alive, and even that is somewhat different, for in Chrétien it is probably the consecrated wafer itself, served in the *graal*, a kind of ciborium, that does that. In Wolfram the wafer serves to renew annually the power of the grail which then keeps people alive. The fact that Wolfram says that the grail is a stone might possibly be derived from the precious stones which adorn it in Chrétien, but surely Wolfram knew enough French to recognize the difference between singular and plural forms in nouns, adjectives, and verbs. Perhaps the fact that Wolfram has the food which is provided by the grail served in golden bowls reflects the fact that Chrétien's *graal* is made "de fin or esmeré" (verse 3221= "of fine pure gold"), but Wolfram never does say that his grail is anything other than a stone. Similarly, the illumination that emanates from Chrétien's *graal* and causes the candles to lose their darkness as the moon and stars do at sunrise (verses 3214–17) may be reflected in the shining countenance of Repanse de Schoye, Wolfram's grail bearer, which makes everyone think that the sun is about to rise (235,15–24). However, it is only the simile itself that is the same, not the subjects of comparison. There is one similarity in the First Continuation on Gauvain's second visit to the grail castle: the *graal* floats around supplying food to the assembled company, and Wolfram's grail does feed everyone at Munsalvaesche, but in Wolfram the grail is stationary. Servants come to the grail to get whatever food and drink is requested.

It would seem then that Wolfram, although he undoubtedly knew Chrétien's work and quite possibly the First Continuation, was quite free in taking the very little that he did take directly and adapting it to his own purposes, thereby creating a completely new kind of grail. However, we cannot rule out the possibility that Wolfram may have had other sources for the characteristics that he ascribes to his grail. For example, he does give his grail a name, *lapsit exillîs*, and then goes on to say that the phoenix is burned to ashes by the power of the stone and then is regenerated from the ashes. It is tempting to read *lapis* (= stone) from *lapsit* and wonder whether Wolfram was thinking of the altar of the sun at Heliopolis in Egypt as a stone to which the young phoenix was said to fly with the ashes of his father and deposit them there. As for the name *lapsit exillîs* itself, there have been many attempts at finding just the right combination of the letters to produce a desired meaning, some quite ingenious. We are not even sure that the particular spelling in the Lachmann text among the several manuscript variants is the one originally intended by Wolfram. Or is the *Latin* expression just a case of hocus-pocus on Wolfram's part, something that sounds like Latin to impress a gullible audience and to amuse the savants among his listeners?

There can be no doubt that Wolfram's grail is connected with Christianity. The consecrated wafer that is brought by a dove every Good Friday, renewing the power of the grail; the fact that the grail cannot be seen by anyone who is not baptized; Parzival's coming to his uncle Trevrizent on Good Friday, confessing, and being given remission of his sins; and the fact that Parzival is allowed to come to the grail at all the first time would seem to be evidence of God's concern with the grail, not to mention its pre-history. But there are also other aspects of Christian tradition that have been considered as sources for the grail. One of these is Robert de Boron's *Roman de L'Estoire dou Graal*, a work that falls chronologically into the period of 1191–1202, about the time Wolfram was beginning to work on his *Parzival*. This seems to be the first work that clearly Christianizes the grail, that connects the story of the grail with Christ's crucifixion, and truly makes the grail the Holy Grail that then dominates in later grail stories.

For Robert the grail is the cup (*veissel*) that Christ used for the Last Supper (Nitze ed., verses 395ff.). It was given by a Jew to Pilate, who gave it to Joseph of Arimathea, who subsequently used it to catch the blood from Christ's wounds after the deposition. Joseph was then thrown into prison by the Jews, but the resurrected Christ brought the grail to Joseph in prison. There it shed light that illuminated the dungeon (verses 717–20). Many years later the emperor Vespasian, arriving in Jerusalem, freed Joseph, who had been kept alive, presumably by the grail, without food or drink. Joseph, his sister Enygeus, and her husband Hebron or Bron leave Judea and live with other Christians in a foreign land. When starvation threatens after some in the group are guilty of lechery, Joseph, obeying the Holy Spirit, sets up a recreation of the Last Supper by placing the grail on a table with a fish caught by Bron opposite it, and all who believe in the Holy Trinity are called to the table. Only they, not the sinners, enjoy great delight. As Robert says, "Car nus le Graal ne verra, / Ce croi je, qu'il ne li agree" ("For no one will see the grail, I believe, that it does not delight him" — verses 2660–1). Here the name *graal* is derived incorrectly from the verb *agreer*. The eucharistic aspect of the grail is its main characteristic in the *Estoire*, and it plays an important role in later versions in which the quest for the Holy Grail becomes paramount.

It would seem that there is so little here in common with Wolfram's grail that it is hardly possible to consider Robert de Boron as a source.

To be sure, it has two features that are also in Chrétien: the grail as a source of light and its ability to keep people alive, but we have already seen what Wolfram did with those. It is difficult, too, to find any connection between the fish on the table and the fact that Chrétien calls the grail king "le Riche Pecheor." Wolfram does have the grail king out fishing, but King Anfortas does that for relief from his wound. In Robert, the blood from Christ's wounds on the Cross is in part caused by the wound in his side from the lance thrust of the blind Roman centurion, Longinus, who then regains his sight when the blood spills out on his face, as the legend has it. The bleeding lance in Chrétien is thought by some to be a reflection of that story, but Robert's *Estoire* does not make a point of the Longinus role, so that there seems to be no connection to Chrétien there. In Chrétien, Perceval learns from his *germaine cousine* that the Fisher King was wounded in both thighs, but there is no explanation of why the lance bleeds, even though that is one of the two questions which Perceval failed to ask. In Wolfram, the lance does not bleed (but see Nellmann 1966). It is "bluotec" (255,11= "bloody"), and the steel point has just recently been thrust into Anfortas's wound so that the hot, poisoned tip will relieve the cold that Anfortas feels as the result of the position of Saturn in the heavens at that particular time (489,24–490,2). The lance is *not* a part of the grail procession in Wolfram. A page bounds into the hall carrying the bloody lance around all four sides and then exits before the procession begins. The purpose is undoubtedly to get Parzival to ask about it, but unfortunately he remains silent. Wolfram did know the Longinus legend. He refers to it in his *Willehalm* twice (Leitzmann ed., 68,17–25 and 303,24–27) and might be expected to have made the connection if indeed he had intended one in *Parzival*. (For an extensive study of the Longinus legend and its connection with the grail, see Burdach.)

Turning now from extant written sources that Wolfram could have known, we must consider the possibility that there may have been other writings available to him but now unknown to us. Such could be the case with the source that Wolfram claims as his own: Kyot, the Provençal. Attempts have been made to determine who Wolfram's Kyot might have been. The trouvère Guiot de Provins (southeast of Paris, ca. 1200) would seem to be a likely candidate, but then on the assumption that Wolfram had confused the city of Provins with the Provence, and there is no record of Guiot's having written anything of romance proportions. Another Guiot, the scribe who names himself in the manuscript of Chrétien's *Yvain* in a codex containing several of Chrétien's works, was also from Provins. Wolfram could possibly have mistaken him for the author, but Wolfram mentions Chrétien as an author who had not done justice to the story (827,3–4), adding that Kyot can well be angry about that. After all, he (Kyot) wrote the correct tale, and that is the one he (Wolfram) is retelling. Another possible Kyot is William of Tudela, a town in Navarre near the Aragonese border in Spain. His name could correspond to Catalan-Aragonese *Guillot*, a diminutive form of *Guillem*, and *Tudela* might be identified with *Dôlet*, usually thought to be Toledo (see H. and R. Kahane). This Kyot/William is the author of the first part of the *Chanson de la croisade albigeoise*, begun in the year 1210. Again, there is no record of William's ever having written about the grail, and we would have to assume personal acquaintance with him by Wolfram. Nevertheless, the geographical-cultural background might be significant in view of what Wolfram says of the origin of his story.

Since it has been impossible to find a specific Kyot who provided Wolfram with his "real" source, as opposed to Chrétien, despite the efforts of a number of scholars who still seem to hold on to the idea, (see, for example, Kolb, Ernst, and de Mandach), it is perhaps best to look at certain geographical areas where the background of Wolfram's Kyot might be found, namely the Arabic, Jewish, Christian scientific community in places like Toledo in Spain and recognize that Wolfram may well have had knowledge, however obtained, of astronomical-theological treatises from such areas. That still only pertains to his tale of the finding of the grail story, however, not necessarily to his conception of the grail itself. (For a very sensible review of the Kyot-problem, see Lofmark 1977.)

Getting away from the idea of attempting to identify Wolfram's Kyot, we can still find other theories of sources for Wolfram's grail. We have just mentioned the Catalonian-Aragonese areas of Spain and the adjoining Provence as a possible source, and we can add also possible influence of the Cathars or Albigensians in southern France, the heretical religious movement that was cruelly persecuted in a crusade led by Simon de Montfort, which ended in 1218 (see Rahn and Zeydel). However, if we go in the opposite direction, to the Celtic areas of Northern France and to Britain, we find a strong opinion that Wolfram's grail may have come from those areas where Arthurian legends in general are presumed to have originated. Yet almost all the evidence for this comes from manuscripts and works *after* Wolfram's day and requires the assumption that such evidence is a reflection of a now-lost *Ur-Parzival* or other stories that may have been the source not only for Chrétien, but also for Wolfram. Some have even argued that Wolfram mentions Chrétien so late (827,1 — the very last 30-line section) because he became acquainted with Chrétien's *Perceval* only when he was almost finished, after having followed some other source (presumably "Kyot"). This argument is strengthened too by Chrétien's remark in the introduction to his *Perceval* that Count Philip of Flanders had given him the book of the story of the grail ("ce est li contes del graal, / don li cuens li baille le livre" — verses 66-7) and commissioned him to put it into rhyme. Of course, we have no idea of what language that *livre* was written in — presumably it was written in prose, else why would the count have asked him to put it into verse? — but it may have been in Celtic, i.e., specifically Welsh or Irish, or possibly an Anglo-Norman adaptation of Celtic material. At least that is what proponents of the theory of Celtic origins for the grail story would maintain, and that would corroborate the idea that the Tristan-sources and Arthurian stories in general, the *matière de Bretagne*, originated in the area of the Britons on both sides of the Channel. Prominent among such scholars are Loomis, Nitze, Marx, and Frappier.

There is a strong similarity of motifs in the Welsh prose *Peredur* and in Chrétien and Wolfram. However, leaving aside all but those similarities involving the grail, we note that in *Peredur* there is no grail as such at the castle scene. A bleeding lance does appear, and the people in attendance there break out into loud laments at the sight of it, just as they do in Wolfram. Immediately following the lance two maidens bring in a dish with a man's head on it swimming in blood. The *Peredur* is generally considered to be a Welsh *mabinogi*, one of three folk tales (*mabinogion*), which are quite similar to Arthurian tales: *Gereint* (Chrétien's *Erec*), *Owein* (*Yvain*), and *Peredur* (*Perceval*). The oldest manuscripts of these tales are from the fourteenth century, but it is assumed that the originals were written down, probably from an earlier oral tradition, in the early thirteenth century. If that assumption is correct, then *Peredur* could have contributed to those features of Wolfram's *Parzival* that are not found in Chrétien (see the study of Goetinck). On the other hand, it is also possible that Chrétien's grail romance and particularly its continuations could have influenced the version of *Peredur* that we have. (For a recent English translation, see Wilhelm's edition.)

Another source for Welsh saga material is the OF prose romance *Perlesvaus*, a prose redaction dated to 1191–1212 of an earlier Welsh version. This undoubtedly shows influence of Chrétien, the Continuations, and Robert de Boron's Joseph of Arimathea-version, but some scholars maintain that Wolfram's *Parzival*, or rather his source itself derives from the Welsh sagas from which the *Perlesvaus* stems. Some of the features of the *Perlesvaus* seem to have similarities with Wolfram's grail. The author claims that a Latin book is his source and that the story of the grail was dictated by an angel to the historian Josephus. When Gauvain comes to the grail castle he finds twelve grey-haired knights over one hundred years old who look as if they were forty. Two damsels come from a chapel, one carrying the Holy Grail, the other the bleeding lance. Gauvain looks at the grail and thinks he sees a chalice within it, but there is none at that time; he looks at the lance and seems to see two angels who carry two candelabra of gold with lighted candles; the damsels go into another chapel, and when they return Gauvain thinks he sees three angels and in the midst of the grail the form of a child; Gauvain sees three drops of blood on the table, but he cannot pick them up; the two damsels come again, and Gauvain thinks that he sees three of them and that the grail is wholly up in the air; there appears aloft a man nailed to a cross with a spear fixed in his side. Gauvain fails to ask the question, as does Lancelet later. The similarity of motifs to those in Parzival's first visit to the grail castle is apparent, but hardly convincing as indications of sources for Wolfram's grail.

Roger Sherman Loomis, in his landmark study of 1926, goes even beyond Welsh sources. He sees a progression from the Irish mythical *echtra* (adventure tale) to Welsh *mabinogi* to French *contes* in a whole series of motifs, e.g., meat and drink come from a golden cup; a woman transformed from ugly to beautiful is reflected in the grail bearer and the Loathly Damsel (Wolfram's Repanse de Schoye and Cundrie la surziere); the question test, where the king and castle disappear when the question is asked incorrectly; the king, wounded in battle in the thigh, dispenses lavish hospitality; the Fisher King; the grey-haired knights in the castle seeming younger than their ages; the grail as a reflection of the original Irish cornucopia, which becomes a ciborium when the two meanings of Old French *cors* (= "horn" and "body") are mistakenly conflated into a ciborium which holds the body of Christ, i.e., the consecrated wafer. Again, there are many apparent similarities in motifs, but on the whole no fully persuasive evidence.

Oriental sources for Wolfram's grail have also been suggested as possibilities, especially for material or motifs that are not to be found in French literary works. Wolfram seems to have had considerable information about the Arab world, judging from the Arabic place names that occur in his works and the references to events there. Then, too, knowledge of the Crusades would certainly have been available from several quarters, yet the question of why Wolfram chose the Knights Templar as the name for his grail knights (i.e., *templeise*) has never been answered completely. The grail has been associated with various stones of the Orient since that is indeed one characteristic of Wolfram's grail that sets it apart from all others, but here again convincing real evidence is lacking. The same can be said also about Iranian and even Hebrew sources, and many of the arguments for Wolfram's knowledge of Orientalia are based on passages in *Parzival* or *Willehalm* that really do not concern the grail directly. No one would wish to deny that Wolfram was interested in unusual bits of information. His *Parzival* is peppered with references to wondrous things, e.g., the Arabic names of the planets that Cundrie lists when she calls Parzival to the grail, or the names of stones and their healing properties that Trevrizent mentions in describing the unsuccessful attempts to find a cure for Anfortas's wound. He obviously relished displaying his astonishing knowledge to his audience, while maintaining that he was just a poor, unlettered knight. And certainly many of the sources for Wolfram's knowledge have been identified, but does the fact that he happened to know the Arabic names of the planets or was acquainted with lapidaries help us in searching for the source(s) of his grail?

I am inclined to believe that there may have been tales based on the *matière de Bretagne* composed in Old French and circulating in northern France that Wolfram could have known aside from Chrétien's *Perceval*. However, it seems to me very difficult to ascertain the precise nature of such lost tales by working backwards, as it were, from later versions that we may happen to have. In doing so, we may be losing sight of the creative genius that is apparent in Wolfram's well-developed concept of the grail and how it fits into his monumental work as a whole. The study of possible sources for Wolfram's grail is a fascinating one, of which we have been able to give only a partial picture here. It is a study that has turned up at times tantalizing evidence, but very little that is completely satisfying.

Another aspect of Wolfram's grail is how it is to be understood in the light of the entire work. Here again, there are as many, if not more, contradictory opinions than there were among the studies of the source, but rather than examine different interpretations, let us look for general areas of agreement and see whether a composite picture of Wolfram's grail can be pieced together. Such a picture may not be completely satisfactory to everyone, but perhaps a minimal consensus can be reached.

As stated earlier, Wolfram's grail has very definite, undeniably Christian characteristics, even if it is not a chalice or ciborium. It gets its power from the holy wafer laid on it by the dove from heaven on Good Friday, Wolfram calls it "wunsch von pardîs" (235,21 = lit., "wish of Paradise"), and it feeds the grail company, which itself is a semi-monastic knightly religious order modeled after the historical Knights

Templar. The *templeise* are guaranteed remission of their sins and ultimately salvation. Wolfram says of it:

> wan der grâl was der sælden fruht,
> der werlde süeze ein sölh genuht,
> er wac vil nâch gelîche
> als man saget von himelrîche (238,21–24)

(for the Gral was the very fruit of bliss, a cornucopia of the sweets of this world and such that it scarcely fell short of the Heavenly Kingdom.)

The grail serves as a medium between God and man. The people there turn toward it and kneel in prayer, and God's answer may appear as an inscription on the grail, if, indeed, any answer at all is forthcoming. The grail can be seen only by the baptized, as we learn in the case of Feirefiz. It also provides water for the baptismal font. The dove descending from heaven is reminiscent of the appearance of the Holy Spirit "descending like a dove" at Christ's baptism by John the Baptist in all four gospels.

There will certainly be general agreement on the above as to the Christian aspects of the grail, and probably also on the following: Wolfram describes two contrasting worlds in his *Parzival*, the world of King Arthur, embodied most admirably by Gawan, and the world of the grail family, to be headed eventually by Parzival. Both worlds are idealized societies but differ in their basic conditions. King Arthur's knights are excellent, chivalrous knights who protect widows and orphans and help others in distress. Their exploits are performed in the course of unusually challenging adventures. They observe the chivalric code scrupulously and attempt to live up to all their obligations. Religion for them is not problematic. They attend mass before tournaments and perform their duties with the assurance that God will be on their side since they are standing up for what is right. This may not be expressed in so many words, but one gets a sense of conventional religiosity in their bearing and performance.

Parzival starts out wanting to be such a knight, a member of Arthur's *tavelrunde*. All his early efforts are aimed at that goal. Unfortunately, his striving involves him in the killing of a relative, and the robbery of the latter's armor, in the neglect of his mother, who dies of a broken heart after he leaves, and in mistaking the importance of form over substance, when he fails to ask the question at his first visit to the grail castle, although he feels sympathy with King Anfortas, who is in agony. It is not that Parzival has no compassion; he demonstrates that clearly in the case of Condwiramurs, Jeschute, and Sigune. However, at the moment of his greatest triumph, his joining the *tavelrunde*, he is denounced by Cundrie for his failure at the grail castle, and in a "feudal" way renounces his relationship to God, not realizing at this time that his membership in the grail family and his relationship to God are his greatest problems. Only once those are resolved, or at least revealed to him as such, by his uncle Trevrizent, is he in a position to be summoned to the grail as Anfortas's successor.

For Parzival, the recognition that he has a "higher" calling is paramount. This involves the admission and confession of his own sins and his acceptance of God's will in complete humility, casting aside his *superbia* and his reliance on the strength of his own right hand — not to be taken literally, of course, since he still continues to function as a knight, but with a different relationship to God. Christianity, then, is embedded in the grail family and its duty of guarding the grail. The failure of Anfortas lies in his disregard of his religious obligations when he rides out in the service of Orgeluse as her knight. Even though Anfortas as grail king would be allowed to marry, he apparently had no such intentions when serving for the reward of love. As Trevrizent tells Parzival: "Amor was sîn krîe. / Der ruoft ist zer dêmuot / iedoch niht vollechîchen guot" (478,30–479,2= "Amor was his battle cry, yet that shout is not quite right for humility"), with the result that he is wounded in the testicles by a poisoned heathen lance. Parzival himself comes very close to Anfortas's position when, after Cundrie's denunciation of him, he rejects God and advises Gawan to let the love of a proper lady protect him in battle (332,1–14). However, Parzival acts out of love for his *wife*, Condwiramurs, and is set on winning the grail by feats of arms, not on *aventiure* in the service of a lady. He must still learn not to rely solely on his own strength but to follow God's will in humility wherever it leads him.

The two worlds, that of Arthur and that of the grail, in Wolfram's *Parzival*, though different in their emphasis on Christianity, certainly underline the importance of religiosity in the work, the one by its virtual absence, the other by its essential presence through contrast. Given the constitutive role of the grail in *Parzival* then, it would seem that we should look at possible Biblical sources for the grail, not as a chalice, but rather as a stone or, by extension, a rock. Horgan points to the numerous references to God in the Old Testament as "Rock" or "Stone," citing, e.g., Deuteronomy 32:4, 15, 18, 30–31; Psalm 18 (17):2, and Isaiah 17:10; 26:4; 44:8. The expression "The stone that the builders rejected has become the cornerstone" in Psalm 118 (117) is combined in Romans 9:30–33 by St. Paul as both the stumbling block and the rejected stone that became the head of the corner and also in I Peter 2:4–8, where the faithful should emulate the Lord "like living stones." These words echo the words of Christ Himself in Luke 20:17–18, and Matthew 21:42–44. Horgan goes on further to quote St. Paul in I Corinthians 10:1–13, where he reports that the Israelites, baptized by Moses, "all ate the same spiritual food and all drank the same spiritual drink from the spiritual rock that followed them as they went, and that rock was Christ." This is a reference to Moses' water miracle in Numbers 20:6–13. Shortly after that passage in Numbers, the rebellious misbehavior of the Israelites in the desert is recorded. In 25:1–15 the debauchery of the Israelites with the daughters of Moab and the subsequent killing of an Israelite man and a Moabite woman who were killed together by Phineas's one spear-thrust through the groin is described. These details, Horgan argues, adumbrate both the provision of food by the grail and the wound of Anfortas as punishment for his sinful breaking of the rules for the grail king. Finally, the inscriptions that appear on the grail may be related to at least the Mosaic tablets, but also quite possibly to Revelation 2:14–17, where John refers to the hidden manna and a white stone that he will give to the church in Pergamum, a white stone on which is written a new name that no one knows except the one who receives it. As Horgan concludes:

> It seems to me that the Grail story identifies some section of Christian knighthood with the children of Israel in the wilderness. The Rock which is Christ is with them, sustaining them, mediating between them and the Father. But they are not to think on this account that their salvation is assured. If they defect from the life of election to which they have been called, and pursue merely erotic ends, they may expect to be punished, and to forfeit Divine favour. (360)

There is much more in Horgan's article, going into other aspects of *Parzival*, that does not seem particularly pertinent here. His argument appeals because it allows us to view Wolfram's grail as a stone on a Biblical basis without resorting to the Joseph of Arimathea-Longinus legend which Wolfram undoubtedly knew, but did not follow in his grail conception. It also does not rely on Irish-Welsh folklore about which we know only second or third hand, the original being something we must attempt to recreate. It eliminates the non-Christian, Arabic and Iranian sources, which may have been based on a stone, and concomitantly reveals Wolfram's Kyot as a delightfully enjoyable spoof by default. We can say that, in a sense, Wolfram has taken the basic idea of a stone or rock quite literally, has given it a concrete form, which is imbued with Christian characteristics, and has completed Chrétien's unfinished romance in a coherent, meaningful, and imaginative way.

Wherever he may have found his material — and there is no question that he had numerous sources — he has adapted it to the central idea of his grail.

Only one further element — another stone, to be sure — needs to be added to the basic ideology of Wolfram's grail: the concept of humility. Ranke (1946) takes up an earlier suggestion of Ehrismann that Wolfram's *lapsit exillîs* should be read as *lapis exilis*, where *exilis* has the meaning of "thin," or "inconspicuous" in the Latin version of the *Iter ad paradisum* of the medieval Alexander-saga. Ranke demonstrates conclusively that the grail was already on the earth when the neutral angels were sent to it to learn humility ("ûf die erden / zuo dem steine," 470,20–21). Whether the neutral angels were called back to heaven remains unknown, but we do know that a family of humans became the guardians of the grail. Alexander's messengers arrive at the gates of Paradise. They are given a precious stone and told to bring it to their leader. When he has recognized its significance, he will be healed of his ambitious striving. No one is able to explain that to him until an old Jew finally gives him the explanation: "lapis hic modicæ quantitatis est sed immensi ponderis" (= "this stone is modest in size but of immense weight"). Alexander has scales brought in and puts the stone in one pan and ever more gold in the other, but the stone balances the gold. However, when the old Jew covers the stone with some soil, its weight is so little that a mere feather can outweigh it. The stone is a symbol of transitoriness, and Alexander's realization of that causes a change in him, turning him from a world conqueror into a *rex justus*, and changing him from a ruler who suffers from overweening pride to a man of humility. Ranke suggests that the weight of Wolfram's grail — only a pure virgin can carry it — and the fact that it lacks the brilliance of Chrétien's graal are reflections of the humility theme. He then explains the function of humility in *Parzival*. It is the one thing above all else that Parzival must learn. His ambition made him center all his attention on becoming the perfect knight. When chastised by Cundrie, he persists in his belief that God has wronged him and proceeds to attempt to win the grail by his own strength, only to find that he cannot do it alone, that he must acknowledge his sinfulness first. This he does when he meets Trevrizent, who lectures him on the sin of pride and urges him to be humble. It is the lesson that the neutral angels were sent to learn at the grail — whether they did or not remains open — and the lesson that Anfortas learns so painfully when he puts his own erotic desire ahead of his duty as grail king. Instead of demanding that God recognize his worth as a knight, Parzival eventually humbly accepts his call to the grail kingship. He has learned humility. It is significant, Ranke believes, that the grail is called "wunsch von pardîs" ("wish of paradise") and that the stone in the Alexander-saga comes from Paradise.

Ranke's interpretation seems to fit very well, but not in every respect. Is Wolfram's grail a symbol of transitoriness? Hardly, but it is the center of a divinely ordained community which emphasizes spirituality in a world that otherwise is absorbed with personal ambition. And it provides rulers to lands lacking a king or queen, thereby underlining the sacerdotal mission of royalty at a time when that had been very much called into question during the investiture controversy. Wolfram's grail certainly is a stone, probably not the insignificant little stone of the Alexander story, though it may share some of its qualities. Is it the "stone" or "rock" of the Old Testament that gave food and drink to the Israelites in the wilderness? Is it Christ, the "rejected stone that has become the cornerstone" of the New Testament? Or is it the symbol of humility that Parzival must learn in the course of his spiritual development? Probably all of these things to a certain extent, but not exclusively. That is what makes Wolfram's grail unique and attests to his artistic genius.

*Parzival (on left, holding knife) is shown looking
at the grail, which is held by Repanse de Schoye.
Here it is a colored object of indistinct shape (a stone?).
(Parzival manuscript [thirteenth century] —
Bayerische Staatsbibliothek, Cgm.19, fol.50ᵛ.)*

On the left, Feirefiz receives baptism. The grail, held high by Repanse de Schoye, appears to be the same object as in the first illustration, but it is colored gold. On the right, Feirefiz seems to be chasing off a shadowy (beheaded?) figure, quite possibly one of his heathen gods. As on the left, Repanse holds forth the grail.
(Parzival manuscript [thirteenth century] —
Bayerische Staatsbibliothek, Cgm.19, fol.50ᵛ.)

Wolfram's Art of Narration

ADRIAN STEVENS

Fiction, Plot and Discourse: Wolfram's *Parzival* and its Narrative Sources

1

WHEN CHRÉTIEN DE TROYES WROTE HIS *Erec* (c. 1170), he not only created Arthurian romance as a literary genre, but introduced for the first time into twelfth-century Western Europe a form of vernacular narrative which was explicitly and self-consciously fictional (see Haug 1992,91–107 and 1995,31–44, and Grünkorn). In France and Norman England the rise of the new genre in response to the success of *Erec* and Chrétien's subsequent works was swift and spectacular (see Vinaver), while in Germany Hartmann's pioneering adaptations of Chrétien's *Erec* and *Yvain* were followed by Wolfram's radical reworking in *Parzival* of Chrétien's last, unfinished Arthurian narrative, *Li Contes del Graal*. To read *Parzival* within the context of the rise of Arthurian romance in Germany is to see Wolfram as a reader and interpreter of Chrétien, and to view *Parzival* as enacting an intensive narrative dialogue with *Li Contes del Graal* in the process of its construction as a work of fiction. In France Arthurian romance, apparently because its orally transmitted Celtic British sources were thought to lack any secure historical foundation, seems to have been regarded from the outset as a fictional genre enjoying a virtually uninhibited freedom to invent, expand, adapt, alter and rearrange narrative sequences at will. In the considered opinion of Jean Bodel, writing ca. 1200, stories derived from the Arthurian matter of Britain, although entertaining, were entirely devoid of historical substance ("Li conte de Bretaigne sont si vain et plaisant"), and it is significant that Chrétien in the prologue to his *Erec* makes no claim to be recording events that really happened. In ways that will have profound implications for Wolfram's self-presentation as the author-narrator of *Parzival*, Chrétien's legitimation of his project is done essentially in terms of literary innovation and crucially involves his art as a writer and creator of narrative. To understand the relationship between Wolfram and Chrétien and the affiliation of *Parzival* to the new narrative genre, it is necessary to say something about the way in which *Erec* is constituted as a work of fiction.

Chrétien's *Erec* prologue begins with the reflection that the worth of things which are commonly despised is often greater than is supposed. As a concrete example of this proverbial truth Chrétien cites the "conte d'aventure" (verse 13= "adventure story" — Fritz ed.), by which he means the story of Erec in particular and, by inference, all Arthurian stories deriving from the matter of Britain. The *Erec* prologue makes the bold and innovative claim that the true worth of Arthurian adventure stories can only be realized, and their status correspondingly enhanced, if they are translated into a literary form which will be perceived as both ambitious and prestigious. Chrétien indicates to his readers and listeners that he has set himself the task of accommodating the Erec story — "which those who try to live by storytelling customarily mangle and corrupt before kings and counts" (citing Carroll's translation in Chrétien, *Arthurian Romances*) — to a carefully articulated and meticulously executed literary narrative. If he succeeds in translating the story into a new and attractive form, he will not only rescue it from the low esteem in which it has previously been held, but at the same time offer a paradigmatic demonstration of the enormous but neglected potential of the Arthurian *conte d'aventure* as a genre. From Chrétien's perspective, what is needed to transform a generally despised Arthurian adventure story into an acclaimed literary text is first of all a clerical education. The ability to write literary narrative is the preserve in the twelfth century of the clerk. Chrétien's emphasis on learning and its practical use is an emphasis on his own book learning, which he presents as a fundamental prerequisite for the construction of *Erec*. When he pledges himself, "A bien dire et a bien aprendre" (verse 12= "to strive to speak well and to teach well"), he is signalling the intention of his text to accommodate to the vernacular the Latin-based criteria of literary composition propagated as exemplary by the schools. To speak well ("bien dire") is to exhibit mastery of rhetorical style in keeping with the commonplace definition of rhetoric as the *ars bene dicendi*. And to speak well and to instruct is to fulfil the traditional expectation, encapsulated in the axiom *prodesse et delectare*, that literature should please by virtue of its formal elegance, its facility in the use of rhetorical figures for stylistic embellishment, while proving also to be beneficial to its readers and listeners. But in the fundamental respect that it is his aim to construct a work of fiction by creating for the first time in *Erec* what he terms a "bele conjunture" (verse 14), Chrétien's literary program diverges from the prescriptive poetics of the schools and exceeds their descriptive capacity.

The precise meaning of the term *conjunture* or *conjointure,* which Chrétien appears to have introduced into twelfth-century French, has been endlessly debated. It has been suggested that Chrétien was alluding to Horace's term *junctura* (see Haug 1992, 102), but *junctura* in the *De arte poetica* has to do with arrangement in the context of rhetorical composition, and even if Chrétien was using Horace as an intertext, his *conjunture* clearly has a broader connotation than fine expression or diction. The primary association of *conjunture* or *conjointure* with *joindre* and *conjoindre* in Old French clearly implies a process of joining or fitting together a number of pieces, making a whole out of several parts (see Vinaver 33–52). What Chrétien proposes to join together is a "conte d'aventure" (verse 13= "an adventure story") which has previously been circulated in incomplete form in the renditions — presumably for the most part oral renditions, since there is no mention of a written source — of professional entertainers (see verse 22= "cil qui de conter vivre vuelent"). It is not clear whether the *ur-Erec* to which Chrétien is referring here is a single story that gets garbled in the retelling (see verse 21= "depecier et corrompre suelent"), or whether it consists of a bunch of episodic Erec stories which, in relation to the whole, are no more than disparate and fragmented parts, and to that extent corruptions of it. Either way, Chrétien is proposing to transform the hitherto despised genre of the adventure tale by taking it out of the hands of the professional storytellers and turning the orally transmitted and, as he sees it, crude and poorly constructed *ur-Erec* into a single rhetorically embellished and properly coordinated literary narrative, or what he describes as "une mout bele conjunture" (verse 14= "a beautifully ordered composition"). The polemical contrast on which the prologue turns is a contrast between the old *conte d'aventure* as the kind of unglamorous storytelling which has left the *ur-Erec* in disrepute, and the new *conte d'aventure* as an extended and rhetorically accomplished literary work of art calculated to promote through its transformation of the *ur-Erec* the revaluation of the entire narrative status of the matter of Britain.

If *Erec* cannot be defined solely in terms of Horace's *junctura*, it is because Chrétien presents the first Arthurian romance not simply as an illustration of the art of expression, an example of fine rhetorical writing, but as a literary construct in the strong sense that it is a fiction, a story which, because it has been joined together differently and therefore told differently from the *ur-Erec*, exists in the elevated and prestigious form in which Chrétien produces it only in his text. It is possible to get Chrétien's achievement and the nature of his literary ambition into clearer focus by employing the distinction first drawn by the Russian Formalists and subsequently elaborated by French structuralists between *fabula* and *sujet*, or fable and discourse. Roughly, fable is the set of events referred to by a narrative, whereas *sujet* is the ordering and presentation of those events effected through narrative discourse. Fable in the sense of "what really happened," the original or "true" story of events thought to precede any narrative realization of them, is an abstraction which readers derive from their interpretation of narrative discourse, understood as the articulation of the fable through the story actually available to them (see Brooks 3–36). The relationship of the *ur-Erec* to Chrétien's text is the relationship not of fable to story, but of story to story, of one narrative discourse to another. The original Erec *fabula* is, even for Chrétien, beyond recovery. It is not and cannot be identical with the stories told by the professional storytellers, since those stories are themselves, on Chrétien's account, corrupt and fragmentary. Although Chrétien implies that his story of Erec will be a whole story, it cannot be anything other than a story of his making, a fiction necessitated but also made possible by the poor transmission and corruption of the *fabula* over time. Chrétien can try to repair the loss by making his *Erec* into a whole rather than leaving it as a string of fragments; he can devise a *conjointure* that will fill the gaps left by incompetent storytellers and produce a rhetorically embellished and finely written narrative, but there is no original, no "true" history left for him to recover or repeat, and the relationship of his *conjointure* to the corrupted stories which retain such traces of the *fabula* as survive will remain a relationship of fictional discourse to fictional discourse.

If Chrétien's *conjointure* is seen as his reconstruction or reinvention of the Erec story as fictional discourse, it follows that that discourse comprises every aspect, both expressive and structural, of the narrative articulation of the work. Story as discourse is story as rhetorical construct, and as such it is story also as explanation and interpretation. "To narrate," according to Paul Ricoeur, "is already to explain" (178). There is, Ricoeur thinks, no first or original story, no *fabula*, merely retellings and reconstructions of it. With the problems of writing history in mind, he equates *fabula* with the events of which stories as histories are composed, and thinks of story always in its tangible form as discourse. Just as there is no one History, only histories, so there is no one Story, but only stories. Narrative, Ricoeur suggests, is best seen as a "redefining of what is already defined, a reinterpretation of what is already interpreted" (Clark 154). Whether fictional or historical, narrative is a medium not just for conveying information, but for conferring meaning on the events which it records. In answering the question "Why?" narrative at the same time answers the question "What?" To tell what happened is, as Ricoeur puts it, "to tell why it happened" (Ricoeur 152). If the question "What happened?" is conventionally linked in stories to an explanation of why it happened, this is because narrative is dependent on plot, and the function of plot in narrative is to connect and interrelate events in a form designed not only to record but to explain and interpret them (Ricoeur 152). Ricoeur speaks of plot connecting events within a story. "A story," as he puts it, "is *made out of* events to the extent that plot *makes* events *into* a story" (see Brooks 13–14). *Fabula* as event — what really happened — is only ever accessible through its interpretation in stories and the narrative discourse by which stories are constituted. Peter Brooks argues that it is impossible to think of story in its tangible form as narrative discourse without thinking of its relationship to plot. To speak of plot is, as Brooks points out, "to consider both story elements and their ordering," and plot becomes for him "the active interpretive work of discourse on story" (Brooks 13, 27). On this definition, what were in the *ur-Erec* simply fragments become in *Erec* elements of a new plot, parts meaningfully related by a *conjointure* or interpretive design which is itself a constitutive element of Chrétien's story as narrative discourse.

On the face of it, *Li Contes del Graal* is very unlike *Erec* in that it has a written source, but here, too, the relationship is, as between *Erec* and the *ur-Erec*, a relationship of story to story. Chrétien appears to deny this when he asserts in the prologue that it is his intention to offer no more than a rhymed version of a book containing the grail story which was given to him by his patron Philip of Alsace, count of Flanders, but as so often with Chrétien, things are not quite what they seem:

> Donc avra bien sauve sa peinne
> Crestïens qui antant et peinne
> A rimoier le meillor conte,
> Par le comandement le conte,
> Qui soit contez an cort real:
> Ce est li Contes del Graal,
> Dont li cuens li bailla le livre,
> S'orroiz comant il s'an delivre. (61–68 — Pickens ed.)

(Therefore Chrétien's efforts will not be in vain, since he strives and aims by command of the count to rhyme the best story that has ever been told in royal court: it is the Story of the Grail, whose book was given him by the count. Hear now how he acquits himself of it. — Kibler trans.)

The first impression is that the story of the grail is already recorded in an authoritative and unalterable form in the source, and that Chrétien's task of putting it into verse is little more than a technical exercise, but this is to overlook the rhyming pun on "le livre" and "s'an delivre" (verses 67–68). The phrase "s'an delivre" is normally assumed to refer to Chrétien's eagerness to obey Philip's command to rhyme his book, but syntactically it can also be taken to refer to "le livre." On this reading, Chrétien, in keeping with the standard meaning of Old French *delivrer*, is hinting at "delivering" or "liberating" himself from his source, and offering his own version of the grail story in place of Count Philip's book. Far from executing his commission by merely reproducing his patron's existing book, he is freeing himself from an old book in order to be able to present Count Philip with a new and different one. But for an author like Chrétien to free himself from an old book implies that he is asserting the right to alter and rewrite the story it tells, and to make such a far-reaching and radical change to a written source is implicitly to claim the liberty to write fiction. The rhyming of Philip's book would then involve Chrétien not simply in the production of a versified translation, but in the invention of the kind of narrative discourse which, as in *Erec* and his other romances, transforms the story which precedes it by imposing on it a new and different kind of *conjointure*.

2

Although Chrétien is his principal narrative source, Wolfram notoriously does his best to deny this and to obscure the relationship between *Parzival* and *Li Contes del Graal* (see Bumke 1991,156–167). Chrétien is not named until the very end of *Parzival,* and when Wolfram does finally acknowledge him, it is to suggest with polemical sarcasm that *Li Contes del Graal,* in neglecting to offer a complete account of the grail story, does it less than justice. There is evidence to suggest that Chrétien died before he could complete his last romance, but if Wolfram knew of this, he chose to ignore it, and to insinuate that *Parzival,* because it tells the whole of the grail story from start to finish, succeeds where Chrétien's narrative so conspicuously fails. But there is more at stake here than a simple insistence on the difference between *Parzival* and *Li Contes del Graal*: Wolfram proceeds to deny categorically any kind of close affiliation between his work and Chrétien's. He combines his dismissive reference to the incompleteness of *Li Contes del Graal* with a lengthy reminder of his claims in Book VIII (416,17–30) and Book IX (453,5–455,22) of *Parzival* to have taken as his source not Chrétien's text, but the full and authoritative version of the grail story supposedly written by a certain Kyot from Provence:

> Ob von Troys meister Cristjân
> disem mære hât unreht getân,
> daz mac wol zürnen Kyôt,
> der uns diu rehten mære enbôt.
> endehaft giht der Provenzâl,
> wie Herzeloyden kint den grâl
> erwarp, als im daz gordent was,
> dô in verworhte Anfortas.
> von Provenz in tiuschiu lant
> diu rehten mære uns sint gesant,
> und dirre âventiur endes zil.
> niht mêr dâ von nu sprechen wil
> ich Wolfram von Eschenbach,
> wan als dort der meister sprach.
> sîniu kint, sîn hôch geslehte
> hân ich iu benennet rehte,
> Parzivâls, den ich hân brâht
> dar sîn doch sælde het erdâht. (827,1–18)

(If Master Chrétien de Troyes failed to do justice to this story, Kyot has good reason to be angry, as he presented us with the correct version. The Provençal tells from beginning to end how Herzeloyde's son won the grail, as it was ordained that he should when Anfortas forfeited it. From Provence into our German lands the correct version has been sent to us, together with the proper conclusion to this story. I will tell no more of it here, I, Wolfram of Eschenbach, than what the master told of it there. His children and his high lineage I have correctly named for you [Parzival's, I mean] and I have brought him to the place which Fortune did after all intend for him. — Translations of *Parzival* are mine.)

Wolfram makes it plain that he finds Kyot's version superior to Chrétien's because it does not leave the grail story as a fragment, but tells it "endehaft" (827,5= "in its entirety"), from beginning to end. It is striking that the distinction Wolfram draws between the unfinished *Contes del Graal* and Kyot's completed grail story echoes Chrétien's polemical contrast between his *Erec* and the fragmentary *ur-Erec*. This is unlikely to be mere coincidence, as there is evidence to suggest that Wolfram knew Chrétien's *Erec*, and not just Hartmann's adaptation of it. Wolfram refers to Chrétien as "von Troys meister Cristjân" (827,1), and the only place in his entire work where Chrétien uses his full name is in the *Erec* prologue (see verse 9= "Crestïens de Troies"). In Book III of *Parzival*, Arthur's court is located at Nantes and not, as *Li Contes del Graal* has it, at Carduel (Chrétien's Carlisle, verse 336); but it is at Nantes that Arthur in Chrétien's *Erec* crowns the hero (verse 6554). And finally the place name Tenabroc, which occurs twice in *Parzival* (232,25 and 261,10), is found only in Chrétien's *Erec* (in the form *Danebroc*, verses 2127 and 2133, Chrétien's Edinburgh). If the *Erec* prologue is seen as an intertextual reference point for the epilogue of *Parzival*, then Wolfram's ironic suggestion is that the relationship between *Li Contes del Graal* and Kyot's grail story is not unlike that between *Erec* and the corrupted tales of Erec told by Chrétien's professional entertainers. According to Wolfram, not only is Kyot's grail narrative complete in the sense of being finished ("dirre âventiur endes zil," 827,11), it is also correct ("diu rehten mære," 827,10). The insinuation is that Chrétien's failure to provide a full and accurate rendering of the grail story is the direct result of his failure to follow Kyot, who consequently has every reason to be angry with him: "daz mac wol zürnen Kyôt" (827,3). Seen from this perspective, the crucial difference between *Parzival* and *Li Contes del Graal* is simply that Wolfram, in sharp contrast to Chrétien, has had the good sense to take Kyot as his source (see Lofmark 1977). But even as he asserts that in telling the grail story he has done no more than follow Kyot in preference to Chrétien, Wolfram shifts his ground, switching attention from the reproduction of Kyot's text to the production of his own. Just as Chrétien names himself as the author of his narrative at the end of the prologue to *Li Contes del Graal* (verse 62), so Wolfram in his epilogue demonstratively refers to himself as the author-narrator of *Parzival* ("ich Wolfram von Eschenbach," 827,13). Although he claims to be finishing his story at the point where Kyot finished his, Wolfram promptly goes on to emphasize that it is he who has finished recording Parzival's family history, so underlining his own role in (and responsibility for) the composition of *Parzival*.

A similar insistence by Wolfram on his own crucial importance as both narrator and originator is to be found in the short prologue to Book XV of *Parzival*, for which *Li Contes del Graal* no longer provides the source. Wolfram promises that he will at long last provide the missing conclusion to the grail story. The tacit allusion here is not to Kyot, but to Chrétien, and to the fact that Chrétien, to the annoyance of large numbers of readers and listeners, left *Li Contes del Graal* unfinished. The implied criticism of Chrétien is combined, just as it is in the epilogue of *Parzival*, with a self-dramatizing emphasis by Wolfram on his own enabling role as narrator. It is he, and he alone, Wolfram insists, who possesses the key that will at long last unlock the grail story by telling how it ends:

> Vil liut des hât verdrozzen,
> den diz mær was vor beslozzen:
> genuoge kundenz nie ervarn.
> nu wil ich daz niht langer sparn,
> ich tuonz iu kunt mit rehter sage,
> wande ich in dem munde trage
> daz slôz dirre âventiure,
> wie der süeze unt der gehiure
> Anfortas wart wol gesunt.(734,1–9)

(Many people have been annoyed because this part of the story has been locked away from them. A lot were never able to find out about it. Now I have no wish to withhold it any longer, but I shall make it known to you properly, since in my mouth I carry the lock to this tale of how gentle, handsome Anfortas was made well.)

If the key to the story is Wolfram's, and if the end as he tells it in *Parzival* is of his own making, then Kyot and Wolfram's pretended dependence on him are no more than fictions. Although Wolfram begins the final stage of his narrative with the phrase, "uns tuot diu âventiure kunt" (734,10= "the story informs us"), the self-dramatizing context undercuts any suggestion that he is merely reproducing an account already contained in a source. The consequences of this are momentous: if there is no Kyot, and no authoritative and independent history of the grail, then the only complete version of the story is the one given in *Parzival*, and that version, as Wolfram's invention, the *conjointure* which he constructs in the process of reworking *Li Contes del Graal*, is fiction.

It is precisely at points where he is inventing his own narrative entirely, or where he is departing radically from the story of events told by *Li Contes del Graal* that Wolfram signals the fictionality of his text (see Haug 1995, 109–124). It is a particular feature of the role which he creates for himself as the author-narrator of *Parzival* that he is at pains to subvert any simple belief on the part of his readers and listeners that his story has any secure or authenticated basis in recorded historical fact (see D. H. Green 1994, 249–264). Far from restricting himself to the kind of third-person narration that would have made *Parzival* history-like in the sense of appearing to be transparent on actual events, and far from attempting in any consistent way to sustain the illusion that he is merely translating or reproducing the story told by his source, Wolfram chooses in Book II to emphasize that the Gahmuret story, for which there is no parallel in Chrétien, is his own construction, the product of his freedom to invent and fashion his narrative as he thinks fit. He tells how, during the great tournament at Kanvoleis at which Gahmuret wins the hand of Herzeloyde, the aged king of Britain, Uther Pendragon, is unhorsed in a joust by the king of Aragon. Uther falls among flowers, but those flowers are, as Wolfram interrupts his narrative to point out, no more than his own authorial invention. Pointedly presenting himself as making rather than merely reporting events, he congratulates himself on his courtesy in allowing Uther to be unseated among flowers rather than making him tumble to the altogether less attractive ground trodden in everyday reality by peasants:

> wê wie gefüege ich doch pin,
> daz ich den werden Berteneis
> sô schône lege für Kanvoleis,
> dâ nie getrat vilânes fuoz
> (ob ichz iu rehte sagen muoz)
> noch lîhte nimmer dâ geschiht.(74,11–15)

(It just shows how courteous and considerate I am, that I should lay the noble Briton in such beauty outside Kanvoleis in a place never trodden by any peasant's foot and, if I am to be honest with you, likely always to remain that way.)

The intrusion by Wolfram as author-narrator into the narrative and his interruption of the third-person account of the joust are calculated to subvert the illusion of facticity, and to emphasize that what may look like a faithful report is in reality no more than a well contrived fiction. Only in fiction (and even there only if the storyteller is, like Wolfram, suitably well mannered and considerate) is it possible for elderly kings who participate unsuccessfully in tournaments to be fittingly unhorsed among flowers in meadows kept forever untrodden by the indecent feet of peasants. The text at this point signals clearly to its readers and listeners that the joust between Uther Pendragon and the king of Aragon, like the tournament at Kanvoleis at which it forms a part, never happened in the way in which it is told. *Parzival* at this point conspicuously advertises itself as the fictional construct of its author, who reveals his absolute discretion not only to decide what will happen to his characters, but just how it will be presented.

Another significant departure from Chrétien which explicitly involves the problem of narrative as fiction is Wolfram's description during Parzival's first visit to the grail castle of the miraculous feeding power of the grail. According to the account given by the hermit to Perceval in *Li Contes del Graal* (verses 6379–6397), the father of the

Fisher King is kept alive by the host brought to him in the grail; according to Wolfram, all those privileged to eat in the presence of the grail can miraculously obtain whatever kind of food they desire simply by stretching out their hands. In introducing his account of the feeding miracle, Wolfram claims merely to be repeating what his source has told him. But that source, as those readers and listeners familiar with the *Contes del Graal* will have recognized, is not Chrétien. This is very much Wolfram's invention, and as a fiction conspicuously lacking any basis either in his source or in reliably documented fact, it is open to the charge that it is a deception and a lie. What is at stake here is the whole complex issue of the truth of fiction, and it is important to notice the parallel between the phrase "man sagte mir" (238,8= "I was told"), used by Wolfram as author-narrator to refer to the account supposedly contained in his source, and the phrase "man saget von himelrîche" (238,24= "the stories told about heaven"). Wolfram points to a family resemblance between his story of the miraculous power of the grail to create food and the stories told about heaven. Nobody, neither he nor his audience, has ever seen anything like the grail or witnessed anything like its power to feed those admitted to its presence, but for his readers and listeners to disbelieve his story for that reason would be like disbelieving stories of heaven. The grail, like heaven, is invisible to Wolfram and to his audience alike, and to accept its miraculous power is as much an article of faith as it is to accept the stories told about heaven. The story of the grail and stories of heaven both point to a truth which transcends the mundane human criteria of observation and facticity conventionally associated with historical narrative.

Given his extraordinary eclecticism, the sheer breadth and diversity of his knowledge, it is likely that Wolfram will have been familiar in one form or another with Isidore of Seville's etymological definition of history as an eyewitness account of events. Konrad of Hirsau, summarizing Isidore, defines history as what has been seen ("res visa") and the historian as the writer who writes what he has seen ("rei visae scriptor"; cit. D. H. Green 1994, 238). On the basis of this definition, a commonplace throughout the Middle Ages, Wolfram's account of the grail can make no claim to being history, and its status, according to another of Isidore's endlessly recycled etymologies, can only be that of fiction (see D. H. Green 1994, 226–244). "Poets," as Isidore puts it, "have named fables from speaking [*a fando*], because they are not things that happened [*res factae*], but only fictions made by speaking [*sed tantum loquendo fictae*; cit. Irvine, 237]." Wolfram's account of the grail is a fiction made by speaking, but he nevertheless enters a very special kind of truth claim on its behalf. Given the inevitable shortage of eyewitnesses, heaven, like the grail in *Parzival*, may be fiction rather than history in the sense that the stories which describe it are not subject to conventional forms of verification, but for Wolfram as author-narrator and, he assumes, for the members of his audience, those stories remain true despite the fact that nobody can claim to have seen or experienced anything like the miraculous things which they depict. When Wolfram asks his audience to swear with him to the truth of a narrative which they — and he — have no means of verifying, he is asking them, contrary to the normal conventions of oath taking and eyewitness testimony, to swear to the truth of a fiction. If, as he encourages them to do, Wolfram's readers and listeners assent to the theory and practice of fiction adopted in *Parzival*, they will be conferring their approval on a type of narrative which seeks to justify itself on the grounds that it contrives, despite inventing things and so seeming to lie, to tell a special kind of truth.

3

It is now widely accepted that Kyot and his grail story constitute an elaborate literary hoax. No twelfth-century French version of the grail story written before *Li Contes del Graal* has survived; and despite Wolfram's assertion that Kyot is a "meister wol bekant" (453,11= "famous master"), there is no evidence other than *Parzival* itself to suggest that any Provençal author with a name resembling Guiot ever wrote a grail narrative in Old French (see Bumke 1991,164–167 and Grünkorn 98–101). Moreover, Wolfram's references to Kyot and his grail story are so casually self-contradictory that they seem almost designed to invite disbelief. Kyot is not introduced into *Parzival* until almost half way through the narrative. He does not make his first appearance until Book VIII, when Wolfram unexpectedly interrupts his account of Gawan's exploits in Schanpfanzun to announce that a Provençal named Kyot found a version of the grail story written in Arabic and translated it into French, and that *Parzival* itself is no more than a translation into German of Kyot's French translation of his "heathen" Arabic source:

> Kyôt ist ein Provenzâl,
> der dise âventiur von Parzivâl
> heidensch geschriben sach.
> swaz er en franzoys dâ von gesprach,
> bin ich niht der witze laz,
> daz sage ich tiuschen fürbaz.(416,25–30)

(Kyot is a Provençal, and he saw this story of Parzival written in a heathen language [i.e. Arabic]. What he said of it *en français*, if my wits are up to it, I will relate to you in German.)

But when Kyot's mysterious Arabic source makes a reappearance in Book IX of *Parzival* (453,11–14), its nature and status have changed, and it is no longer presented as a complete version of the grail story which Kyot has simply translated into French. When Kyot resurfaces, it is in Toledo in Spain, where he purportedly comes across a reference to the grail in the writings of an Arab astronomer named Flegetanis, who had miraculously read of it in the stars (454,17–30). Fantastical though this seems, it needs to be remembered that in the twelfth century Toledo was the most important European center for the translation of Arabic scientific texts into Latin, and that many of the identified medicinal and astronomical sources of *Parzival* derive from translations made in Toledo. Wolfram was clearly familiar with the massive influx of Arabic science into twelfth-century Latin culture, and was aware of the crucial part played by Toledo in its transmission and dissemination (see Groos 1995). But while it may appear that Wolfram is seeking to lend credibility to Kyot's alleged source by associating it with Arabic scientific writings found in Toledo, it is important to note that in this second, revised account of the sources of *Parzival*, the "heathen" astronomer Flegetanis's understanding of the grail is insufficient for him to write a narrative history of it in Arabic. In the new, expanded version of the Kyot story, Wolfram lays great stress on the fact that Kyot is a Christian, and he revokes his initial reference to a comprehensive grail narrative written in Arabic by emphasizing that only a Christian could have understood the mysteries of the grail and been able to recount them. The grail, Wolfram now insists, has its place in a realm well outside the scope of modern Arabic science:

> ez half daz im der touf was bî:
> anders wær diz mær noch unvernumn.
> kein heidensch list möht uns gefrumn
> ze künden umbes grâles art,
> wie man sîner tougen inne wart.(453,18–22)

(It helped him that he was baptized: otherwise this story would still be unknown. No heathen science could have helped us proclaim the nature of the grail, and how its mysteries came to be known.)

Wolfram decides in retrospect that it would be improper for Kyot to be seen to rely for a full treatment of the grail story exclusively on Arabic sources which as "heathen" works are blind to the truths of Christian revelation — like Flegetanis himself, who, for all his scientific learning, was tricked by the devil into worshipping a calf (453,23–455,1). Instead of simply finding and translating an Arabic text, Kyot is now obliged to search for a recorded version of the grail narrative in chronicles in the Christian West, in Britain, France and Ireland, until eventually he finds the history of the grail and its dynasty written in Latin, the official language of the Church, in a chronicle in Anjou (455,2–22). It is Kyot's French translation of this Latin chronicle, and not after all his translation of a "heathen" Arabic narrative ignorant of Christian revelation, that Wolfram belatedly claims as his source.

That Kyot finds the grail chronicle in Anjou is part of the elaborate *conjointure* that distinguishes *Parzival* from *Li Contes del Graal*. Anjou in terms of *Parzival* as fiction is the ancestral domain of Gahmuret, who briefly becomes its king after the death of his brother, although he never returns there to rule; and the counts of Anjou in historical reality were among the earliest families to promote the writing of genealogical narratives. The chronicle which Kyot discovers, and which is belatedly presented as the primary written source of *Parzival*, is described as a family history, a genealogical narrative of a type actually written in twelfth-century Anjou (see Duby 143–180). It is said to trace the lineage of Parzival through the families both of his father Gahmuret and of his mother Herzeloyde (55,17–56,26). The Angevin genealogy of Parzival begins with a fictional, not to say mythical ancestor Mazadan, the etymology of whose name, *Mac Adan*, designates him as a son (however remote) of Adam. On Parzival's mother's side, Kyot's chronicle shows the grail dynasty originating with Titurel, the grandfather of Herzeloyde and her brother Anfortas, Parzival's uncle. But all of this and more is known to Wolfram's readers and listeners long before any mention is made of Kyot. Sigune has already told Parzival during the course of their second encounter of his grail lineage, and of the fact that he is descended from the first grail king Titurel though his mother (251,2–20). And before Gahmuret leaves Belacane in the first Book, he writes her a letter in French into which he inserts, for her information and that of his son Feirefiz, a record of his Angevin lineage. Gahmuret traces his descent from his great-great-grandfather Mazadan and his wife, the fairy Terdelaschoye, and it subsequently emerges that it is because of "sîn art von der feien" (96,20= "his fairy ancestry"), which destines him to love and to desire love (96,21), that he finally agrees to marry Herzeloyde. Not only is he seemingly fated by his descent from Terdelaschoye to become a member by marriage of the grail family, but Gahmuret on his own account is related to Arthur through his great-grandfather Lazaliez, whose brother Brickus is the father of Uther Pendragon (Wolfram's Utepandragun; see 56,12) and therefore — although Gahmuret's letter does not specify this — the grandfather of Arthur.

The narrative articulation of Gahmuret and his lineage, for which *Li Contes del Graal* offers no model, are vital to Wolfram's design. By telling the story of the marriages between Gahmuret and Belacane, Gahmuret and Herzeloyde, and Feirefiz and Anfortas's sister Repanse de Schoye, Wolfram links the Angevin dynasty of Gahmuret both with the grail dynasty and with the royal dynasty of Belacane and Feirefiz in the East. The Eastern dynasty is converted to Christianity following the marriage of Feirefiz to Repanse de Schoye, Parzival's aunt, and the name Prester John, which they give to their son, is taken by all the Christian kings of India who succeed him (823,21–27). The theme of lineage itself forms part of an ambitious narrative of providential design, so that *Li Contes del Graal*, as Wolfram reworks and completes it, displacing Chrétien's fragmentary *conjointure* with his own, is transformed into a very different romance. When Wolfram in the epilogue to his work emphasizes that it is he who has provided a detailed specification of Parzival's genealogy and he who has brought his hero to the place reserved for him by Fortune (827,15–18), he is pointing to the extent to which his narrative and the discourse which characterizes it are his invention. Just as Chrétien openly proclaims his determination to redesign the *ur-Erec*, and obliquely asserts his right to change Count Philip's book, so Wolfram, as he alludes to the invention of his alternative and completed grail story, obliquely and retrospectively vindicates his right to change *Li Contes del Graal*. His text is no more a replica of Chrétien's text than *Li Contes del Graal* is a replica of Count Philip's book. For Wolfram as for Chrétien before him, to work within the generic form of Arthurian romance is consciously to write fiction, to enjoy the freedom to alter, to recast and to invent.

4

If the grail book given to Chrétien by Count Philip really did exist, Chrétien, as Per Nykrog remarks, took it to the grave with him, for it was unknown to any of the French authors who wrote continuations of *Li Contes del Graal* after Chrétien's death (Nykrog 179). In this it possesses a family resemblance not simply to Kyot's grail story, known only to Wolfram, but also to that unidentified "very ancient book written in the British language" on which Geoffrey of Monmouth claimed in 1136 to have based his *History of the Kings of Britain*, the first surviving narrative account of the life and deeds of Arthur. According to Geoffrey's own account, Walter, Archdeacon of Oxford, presented him with "a certain very ancient book written in the British language. This book, attractively composed to form a consecutive and orderly narrative, set out all the deeds of [the kings of Britain], from Brutus, the first king of the Britons, down to Cadwallader, the son of Cadwallo" (Thorpe trans., 51). Just as Kyot is said to provide a complete account of the grail story from start to finish, so Geoffrey's British source book is said to offer a truthful narrative of all the deeds of the early kings of Britain. But the differences between Geoffrey and Wolfram are as instructive as the similarities. Geoffrey is not concerned merely to underline the completeness of his account. He also describes Walter's book as being "attractively composed to form a consecutive and orderly narrative," implying that, in addition to its value as a chronicle, it meets the standards of rhetorical composition normally associated with the writing of narrative history in Latin. Since the Celtic vernacular literary culture of the early Middle Ages was essentially an oral culture, it is transparently improbable that Walter's ancient book in the British language, even if it did exist, would have been arranged and edited in the form of a Latin-style written history. Whatever British sources may have been available to Geoffrey, the attractive and orderly narrative discourse which he attributes to Walter's book has to be seen as his own invention, and not simply as the product of translation. The description of Walter's book emerges as an oblique characterization of Geoffrey's own work, and in this it resembles Wolfram's description of Kyot's grail story, but with the crucial difference that the *Parzival* narrative is famously neither consecutive nor orderly in the conventional sense predicated by Geoffrey.

Kyot's supposed French translation of the unidentified Latin family chronicle from Anjou does not conform to the style of narration associated by Geoffrey with Latin history writing, in which events are presented in the chronological order of their occurrence, and the deeds of kings connected, motivated and sequentially explained. But the Anjou chronicle as Kyot reads it does offer chronologically ordered accounts both of Parzival's Angevin lineage and of his grail lineage. The record of the Angevin dynasty begins with Mazadan and progresses through the lives of his descendants; and the record of the grail dynasty begins with Titurel, records the deeds of his son Frimutel, the accession of Anfortas and, it is to be inferred, the accession of Parzival (455,13–22). Even if, within the parameters of the framing fiction, the Angevin chronicle is Kyot's source, Kyot does not retain its reported presentation of persons and events. In terms of the Formalist distinction between fable and story, the relationship between Kyot's French grail story and its Latin source is a relationship of story to story, not of story to fable. If plot is the interpretation of story by discourse, then Kyot completely rewrites the Angevin chronicle, replacing its chronologically ordered narrative and the generically determined discourse which characterizes it with a very different narrative of his own, working in the process with a very different kind of discourse, and producing a very different kind of story. It is one of the most striking features of the *Parzival* narrative that, because it supposedly follows Kyot in telling the grail story it rejects the generic forms of connexity typical of medieval Latin history writing, ostentatiously choosing to withhold information and to delay explanations and in a manner designed to mystify and to promote suspense rather than to instruct by offering instant clarification.

In reality, the technique of creating suspense by withholding information is one of the central narrative features of *Li Contes del Graal*, and in this respect at least Wolfram's text imitates Chrétien's. But Wolfram, characteristically, refuses to acknowledge his debt to Chrétien. When he introduces the momentous encounter between Parzival and Trevrizent in Book IX, it is to Kyot, not to Chrétien, that Wolfram attributes his mystifying style of narration. He announces that Parzival and, equally importantly, the readers and listeners of his story, will at last receive a long delayed explanation of the grail and its secrets from Trevrizent (see D. H. Green 1982). But even as he makes this belated promise of disclosure, Wolfram defends himself against those members of his audience who have criticized him for withholding information about the grail, claiming that the delay was imposed at Kyot's explicit request, and that Kyot for his part only postponed revealing the secrets of the grail in obedience to an injunction contained in his own source:

> an dem ervert nu Parzivâl
> diu verholnen mære umben grâl.
> Swer mich dervon ê frâgte
> unt drumbe mich bâgte,
> ob ichs im niht sagte,
> umprîs der dran bejagte.
> mich batez helen Kyôt,
> wand im diu âventiure gebôt
> daz es immer man gedæhte,
> ê ez d'âventiure bræhte
> mit worten an der mære gruoz
> daz man dervon doch sprechen muoz.(452,29–453,10)

(From Trevrizent Parzival will now learn of things concerning the grail that have been kept secret. Those who asked me about all this before and reproached me when I would say nothing of it have brought shame on themselves. Kyot asked me to conceal it because his source told him that no mention should be made of it until the story itself came to address the matter at the point when it really ought to be discussed.)

That a Latin genealogical chronicle such as Wolfram belatedly identifies as Kyot's source would have violated the generically determined norm of presenting a chronologically ordered record, and even contained instructions to potential translators to respect and retain its non-sequential style of narration is transparently improbable. And Wolfram's subsequent description of the Angevin family history discovered by Kyot in any case has it proceeding conventionally according to chronology. Wolfram attributes to Kyot and to Kyot's source what is in fact the defining narrative form of *Li Contes del Graal*, so making Kyot's French version of the Grail story not radically different from Chrétien's, but on the contrary identical with it! But if Kyot's grail story is after all indistinguishable from Chrétien's, then Wolfram's convoluted double history of narrative mystification brought about by the need to delay disclosure of the secrets of the grail is, like the grail story itself, a fiction. Kyot and his sources are no more than a humorously contrived pointer to the differences between *Parzival* and *Li Contes del Graal*. They are not, as has been suggested, an attempt on the part of Wolfram to validate *Parzival* and lend it a bogus authenticity by pretending that it has an assured historical source (see Haug 1995 45–56, esp. 46). *Parzival*, for all that it may at times look like history, advertises itself repeatedly as a fictional construct. The casually self-contradictory references to Kyot invite the alert and competent interpreter to reflect that the source books so often invoked by the authors of courtly romances to authenticate their narratives as works of history may themselves be at best fictional and at worst simply fictitious. Wolfram humorously debunks the idea that written stories must be true just because they have been written, and at the same time he rejects any assumption that books, even books written in Latin and labelled as chronicles, necessarily constitute an unimpeachable historical source authority. It is precisely because he, like Chrétien, treats the grail story as fiction that Wolfram can allow himself the freedom to tell it by means of a highly complex and unconventional narrative structure far removed from the simple sequential plots that are a generic feature of Latin historical writing in the twelfth century. If Chrétien can liberate himself from Count Philip's book and Wolfram in his turn can free himself from *Li Contes del Graal* by changing, expanding and adapting it to his own different conception of the grail story, it is because neither he nor Chrétien has any need to contend with the burden of facticity which is a defining feature of all historical narrative. History as story may bear a family resemblance to fiction to the extent that it is, as Arthur Danto has argued, "a narrative structure imposed on events" (cited from Kermode 117). But although the same events can be (and in historical writing in practice are) accommodated to a wide variety of narrative discourses and plots, with the result that there is no one history, but a variety of histories, events as such cannot be changed or invented by authors wishing their narratives to be read as history. To that extent historical writing, whatever its particular narrative articulation, is more constrained than fictional writing. Wolfram is at liberty to change the events, characters, actions and situations narrated in *Le Conte du Graal* because he, like Chrétien, regards the grail story as fiction, not history.

5

At the end of the second Book of *Parzival*, immediately after he has finished the Gahmuret story, but just before he takes *Li Contes del Graal* as his main narrative source and embarks on the process of reworking it, Wolfram inserts a famous and much discussed digression in which he presents himself as a knight, and his narrative as a knight's tale:

> schildes ambet ist mîn art:
> swâ mîn ellen sî gespart,
> swelhiu mich minnet umbe sanc,
> sô dunket mich ir witze kranc.
> ob ich guotes wîbes minne ger,
> mag ich mit schilde und ouch mit sper
> verdienen niht ir minne solt,
> al dar nâch sî sie mir holt.
> vil hôhes topels er doch spilt,
> der an ritterschaft nâch minnen zilt.(115,11–20)

(The shield is my lineage: if I lack courage, and any lady loves me for my songs, I shall think her feeble minded. If I desire a noble woman's love and cannot win her love's reward with shield and spear, let her bestow her affections accordingly. Any man who aims for love through knightly deeds is playing for very high stakes indeed.)

Whatever the lost biographical context of these remarks, Wolfram in his role as the author-narrator of *Parzival* undertakes to speak plainly and unambiguously as a knight on behalf of knights and as a champion of knighthood. The reference to the women in his audience seeing and hearing him as he actually recites his work before them is a reminder that any fighting he will be doing in order to win their favor (and especially the favor of the woman he claims to love) will be literary rather than literal. He hopes to win love and esteem through his knight's tale, and he suggests, with ironic and self-deprecating humor, that the unusual business of being both an author and a knight is risky and dangerous. As Wolfram himself underlines by referring to Chrétien as a master or *magister* (see 827,1= "von Troys meister Cristjân"), Chrétien was a cleric, and *Li Contes del Graal* is very much a cleric's romance (see Stevens 1993). In offering his version of *Li Contes del Graal*, Wolfram is a knight taking on the dangerous risk of doing a cleric's work! It needs to be remembered that in the cultural context of the Germany of 1200, the writing of romances and the composition of literary texts was regarded essentially as the preserve of those who were clerics. The pointed references he makes in *Iwein* (Benecke ed., verses 21–30) and in *Der arme Heinrich* (Paul ed., verses 1–4) to the fact that he is a learned knight suggest that Hartmann von Aue, the first German author to rework Arthurian romances by Chrétien, regarded literate knights as very much an exception to the rule. Nevertheless, Hartmann, by turning Chrétien's clerical narratives into clerical narratives of his own in *Erec* and *Iwein*, had established something like a generic and compositional norm against which Wolfram knew he would be judged by the German literary public. The wealth of intertextual references in *Parzival* to *Erec* and *Iwein* clearly indicate Wolfram's assumption that his audiences were well acquainted with Hartmann's work and his awareness that he, simply by virtue of taking a romance by Chrétien as his source, would be compared as an author with his German predecessor. It is not for nothing that Wolfram stresses that he, unlike Hartmann, is a knight without the kind of Latin-based book learning that goes with a clerical education. Where Hartmann presents himself as a knight sufficiently educated to read — and to enjoy reading — books, Wolfram presents himself in explicit and deliberate contrast as a knight without clerical education whose tale proceeds without the support and guidance of books. Anybody who wishes him to continue his grail story must not, he insists, regard it as a book: "swer des von mir geruoche, / dern zels ze keinem buoche. / ine kan decheinen buochstap" (115,27–29= "Let anybody who wishes me to do this [i.e. continue with my story] not think of it as a book. I am quite unlettered). Although he defines himself as unlettered in the strong medieval sense of being an *illiteratus*, somebody without an intensive clerical training in Latin, it is likely that Wolfram was, to use Clanchy's term, practically literate (see Stevens 1993, 242), with some knowledge of Latin, able to read German and French, and perhaps even able, like Gahmuret in *Parzival*, to write in the vernacular. But what really matters is the narrative context of Wolfram's remarks. By emphasizing that he is a knight without clerical education, Wolfram is drawing a clear distinction between himself, Hartmann the clerical knight, and — just as he is about to use *Li Contes del Graal* as his source — between himself and Chrétien the paradigmatic clerical author. The fundamental difference between *Li Contes del Graal* and *Parzival* is best thought of as a difference between clerical and unclerical narrative, between the rhetorically accomplished discourse of Chrétien — the type of discourse to which he commits himself programmatically in his *Erec* prologue — and the chivalric discourse of the knight-author Wolfram. Wolfram's insistence that *Parzival* should not be thought of as a book is his way of underlining the fact that his narrative should not be judged by the literary criteria applicable to *Li Contes del Graal* or to Hartmann's *Erec* and *Iwein*.

It is to the difference between his own knightly discourse and the clerical discourse of his clerically educated precursors Hartmann and Chrétien that Wolfram obliquely alludes when he speaks of himself in his prologue of having to do the job of three authors all on his own:

> nu lât mîn eines wesen drî,
> der ieslîcher sunder phlege
> daz mîner künste widerwege:
> dar zuo gehôrte wilder *funt*,
> op si iu gerne tæten kunt
> daz ich iu eine künden wil.
> si heten arbeite vil.(4,2–8 — emphasis added)

(Even if the one of me became three, and that each of them individually had skills the equal of mine: it would still need a wild kind of *invention* for them to acquaint you with what I want to tell you all on my own. They really would have a struggle!)

In Middle High German, *funt* (or *vunt*) can be used to translate the Latin term *inventio*, associated since classical antiquity with rhetoric and poetics, and with the composition of literary texts (see Stevens 1994). As the art of memorizing, retrieving, repeating or adapting ideas and stylistic formulations derived from other authors and texts, invention in the context of Latin poetics promoted both stylistic fluency and a wide range of learned intertextual reference. But there is no equivalent, either in ancient or medieval Latin poetic sources, of Wolfram's phrase *wilder funt* (4,5). Although Wolfram makes the composition and completion of *Parzival* dependent on invention, and so seems to align it with an authoritative clerical literary paradigm, his authorial persona is not that of a clerk trained, like Chrétien and supposedly Kyot, in Latin and in the disciplines of grammar, rhetoric and dialectic which constitute the trivium. Wolfram engages in a sustained dialogue with clerical literary culture, but he repeatedly makes plain that he does not feel constrained by either its rhetorical or its ideological norms, and in his role as author-narrator he characteristically maintains a humorously subversive detachment from them. The phrase *wilder funt* (4,5) is a case in point. While the noun *funt* seems calculated in this context to evoke definitions of the art of invention derived from Latin texts, the adjective *wild*, which can be taken in the broad metaphorical sense of "untrained" or "unschooled," counteracts from the outset any suggestion of conformity to clerically mediated conventions of narrative composition. In the Foreword of his translation, A. T. Hatto draws attention to a salient feature of Wolfram's style: his tendency to work through "a succession of verse-sprung statements in which he leaves it to his audience to supply the logical nexus, as we often do in living speech." It is precisely Wolfram's seemingly artless and ungrammatical closeness to living speech which signals his general indifference to Latin-based notions of literariness, and it is this indifference that earns him his notorious exclusion from the competition for German poet laureate staged on the basis of clerical criteria of composition in the literary excursus of Gottfried's *Tristan* (see Thomas's article in this volume for a consideration of numerous aspects of Wolfram's style).

If plot is the interpretation of story through discourse, then the differences between the plot of *Parzival* and the plot of *Li Contes del Graal* are a function of the ways in which Wolfram's narrative discourse stands in both literary and ideological opposition to Chrétien's. The deletions, corrections and additions which Wolfram carries out in the course of remodelling Chrétien's text exemplify both his distinctive understanding of the grail story and its ideological motivation. In *Li Contes del Graal* chivalry, the pursuit of arms and knightly existence itself are characteristically viewed in a critical, even negative light (see Nykrog 179–221). The general theme of Chrétien's prologue is charity in the Christian sense of selfless love (see Busby 1993, 12–15), and the grail story as Chrétien tells it dwells insistently on the perceived absence of charity from a secular world seemingly dominated by the cruelty and violence of the knights who inhabit it. At the very beginning of *Li Contes del Graal*, in a passage which, significantly, is deleted by Wolfram, Perceval's mother tells her youngest and only surviving son of the disasters which have befallen both his family and his country. Her narrative links Perceval's family history to the early Arthurian section of Wace's *Brut*, itself an adaptation of Geoffrey of Monmouth's *History of the Kings of Britain* (see Busby 1993, 18). Depicting the anarchy which, according to Wace, reigned in Britain between the death of Uther Pendragon and the accession of Arthur, Perceval's mother tells him how his father, crippled by a wound through the thighs, and consequently unable to protect his lands and his inheritance, was forced to take refuge in the Waste Forest. Later Perceval's two brothers, knighted on the same day, were both killed in combat, and when the body of the elder was discovered, his eyes had been pecked out by crows and rooks. The mother's story of Perceval's family associates knighthood and fighting from the outset with cruelty, death and horror, and the subsequent narrative constantly returns to a grotesquely negative picture of chivalry (see Schmid). When Perceval kills the Red Knight, his javelin penetrates his eye and brain and — a detail which Wolfram omits — passes through the back of his neck amid a gush of blood and brains, so that his heart fails in agony (verses 1092–1099). When Perceval encounters his cousin (Wolfram's Sigune), the dead knight she is cradling in her arms has had his head cut off — again Wolfram omits the gruesome detail — , and the cousin herself is crying out for death to release her from her misery (verses 3394–3421).

If the women in *Li Contes del Graal* are typically the victims of knightly cruelty and aggression (see Nykrog 179–221), their situation in *Parzival* is much more complex. If they are victims, they are also instigators; they respond to the glamour of chivalry, and are excited and even sexually aroused by the prowess shown by knights who fight on their behalf (see Haug 1995, 125–139). Perceval's powerless crippled father is transformed by Wolfram into the charismatic and virile Gahmuret. When Gahmuret meets Belacane, she is grieving because she drove her lover Isenhart to fight to demonstrate the sincerity of his feelings for her. Isenhart, recklessly insisting on jousting without armor as proof of his courage and desire, is killed and Belacane, to her sorrow and remorse, is left a virgin (26,9–28,9). When Gahmuret fights for her and succeeds where Isenhart failed, Belacane herself relieves him of his armor and, anxious not to repeat the mistake she made with Isenhart and impatient to be rid of her virginity, she actively assumes the role of seductress and rushes Gahmuret into her bed, giving him no opportunity to rest, wash or even eat after his exploits in the field (44,18–30). As his cousin Kaylet puts it later, reflecting enviously on Gahmuret's good fortune, the ladies would have devoured the devil himself like sugar if he had fought as valiantly as Gahmuret (50,12–19)! When Gahmuret leaves her, Belacane dies of grief after giving birth to Feirefiz (750,24–26), yet consistently throughout the narrative all those who speak of Gahmuret do so in terms of unqualified admiration, including both Trevrizent and the two sons whose mothers he abandoned and who know him only by reputation (750,27–752,4). Nor is this all: desire, love, knightly combat and death are accepted in *Parzival* as being inseparably linked, part of a divine pattern which comprehends and affirms pain and joy as constitutive elements of the feudal chivalric world. Despite the grief endured by Belacane and by Herzeloyde as the price of falling in love with Gahmuret, it is part of the divine *conjointure* that their sons through their links with the grail should in their different ways triumphantly promote the Christian cause.

Parzival, no less than *Li Contes del Graal*, confronts the issue of knightly violence head on, but recontextualizes it in such a way as to confer on it an honorable place in the scheme of creation. Parzival's slaying of Ither is a crux. Whereas Chrétien emphasizes the brutality of Perceval's killing of the Red Knight, no special guilt attaches to it, and the hermit in *Li Contes del Graal* makes no reference to it. In Wolfram's reinterpretation of the story, Trevrizent sees the killing, because Parzival and Ither are related, as a symbolic re-enactment of Cain's murder of Abel (see Schmid 189–190). When Parzival and his brother Feirefiz fight each other at the beginning of Book XV, it appears that the sin of Cain is about to be repeated in an even more grievous form, but God intervenes, and at the stroke which stuns Feirefiz and brings him to his knees, Parzival's sword, taken from the corpse of Ither, breaks (744,10-18), so preventing him from killing his brother. But none of this is presented in any way as a straightforward condemnation of knighthood or of fighting. On the contrary, Wolfram in his role as knightly narrator repeatedly expresses his admiration for the two protagonists, for their courage and skill in combat, for their virtue, and for the whole practice and ideology of chivalry which they so conspicuously represent. As they are about to commence their fight, the brothers are described as "die lûtern truopheite vrî" (738,8= "pure and free of any blemish"), and this commendatory, even celebratory descriptive register is maintained throughout the ensuing scene. It is repeatedly emphasized that both Parzival and Feirefiz fight for the women they love, like their father Gahmuret before them, and like Isenhart, Schionatulander and so many other knights in *Parzival*, including Anfortas prior to his wound and even the hermit Trevrizent during his worldly career as a knight. For all that combat of the kind typified in the encounter between Parzival and Feirefiz is shown to involve the risk, even the probability of death and suffering, Wolfram as a knight describing knightly deeds finds nothing to fault and everything to admire about fighting in principle. What is wrong about the fight between Feirefiz and Parival is that it sets brother against brother, not that it involves fighting between knights or fighting for women. If Trevrizent regards the killing of Ither as a sin, Wolfram in his distinctly unclerical persona as narrator regards it as an act of "tumpheit" (744,18= "folly") — essentially a secular and social criterion of judgement, rather than a religious or theological one. Although Parzival, when he encounters Feirefiz, is under the protection of the grail, he is equally under the protection of the very human love of his wife Condwiramurs. Because he serves his wife, he is inspired to fight with all the courage and tenacity which are proper to a knight, and because he serves the grail, he will not be allowed to repeat the killing of Ither and re-enact the sin of Cain. The story, as Wolfram emphasizes once again, is totally under his control as narrator, and it is his intention to tell and interpret it in a way that will reconcile religious faith with the practice of chivalry:

> ich sorge des den ich hân brâht,
> wan daz ich trôstes hân gedâht,
> in süle des grâles kraft ernern.
> in sol ouch diu minne wern.(737,25–28)

(I am anxious for the man I have brought here [i.e. Parzival], but I have been consoled by the thought that the power of the grail must protect him. And love, too, must defend him.)

The human *conjointure* of Wolfram the knightly narrator is subsumed within the divine plot of God, the ultimate author, which comprehends the discourse of both spiritual and secular love, and allows each its valid place in knightly affairs. At the decisive moment in the fight, when God causes Parzival's sword to break, Parzival finds himself entirely at his brother's mercy, and then it is Feirefiz's consummate courtesy, his instinctive chivalry rather than any further explicit act of divine intervention which is responsible for his refusal to kill his defenseless brother and for his magnanimous decision to throw away his own sword so as not to have any unfair advantage should the fight be resumed (744,25–747,18). Knighthood as it is practiced by the exemplary figures who take center stage in *Parzival* is neither damned nor damnable, as the discourse, the *conjointure* of Wolfram the self-proclaimed knight-author is contrived to show.

NEIL THOMAS

Wolfram von Eschenbach: Modes of Narrative Presentation

SOMEWHAT ANALOGOUS TO THE WAY IN WHICH, at a later age, Goethe and Schiller were to draw on a common stock of expressions from the Lutheran Bible (a process which can give their writings occasional stylistic likenesses), medieval German narrative poets using the medium of rhymed couplets frequently drew on a restricted linguistic corpus known to language historians as the Middle High German literary language, or *Dichtersprache* (see C. Wells 116–122 and Paul 10–14). For that reason there often exist striking similarities of style and expression among a number of writers composing in the twelfth and early thirteenth centuries. Wolfram von Eschenbach, being a near-contemporary of Hartmann von Aue and Gottfried von Straßburg, also had some recourse to this poetic lingua franca of his age, and yet what is most immediately striking about Wolfram's narrator is the uniqueness of his style and narratorial self-(re)presentation. This uniqueness was a feature which the poet himself was keen to underline (particularly in his claim to illiteracy, which is discussed in the articles by Stevens and Classen in this volume).

We are of course not so fortunate as to have at our disposal such priceless critical tools as medieval equivalents of the correspondence between Goethe and Schiller, yet happily there do exist, embedded in a number of works as narratorial excursuses, contemporary testimonies by medieval poets as to both their own literary ambitions and to their opinions about other writers of their day (see Schweikle for a conspectus). One of the few contemporary references to Wolfram is made by Wirnt von Gravenberg:

> (. . .) her Wolfram
> ein wîse man von Eschenbach;
> sin herze ist ganzes sinnes dach;
> leien munt nie baz gesprach. (Kapteyn ed., 6344–6347)

(Sir Wolfram, the wise man of Eschenbach. His heart is the very epitome of reason. No layman's voice ever spoke better — Unless otherwise indicated, all translations are mine.)

We cannot be certain about what precise sense Wirnt von Gravenberg meant to attach to what he wrote in those verses of *Wigalois*. If he meant to give Wolfram a plaudit for his *style* (as opposed to the moral content of his work) then this would have been a minority verdict, both in his own age as in the modern period (in the foreword of his *editio princeps* of Wirnt's *Wigalois* [Berlin: G. Reimer, 1816], Benecke considered Wirnt the truest reflection of his older contemporary Hartmann von Aue, whose poetic sensibility shielded him from the "errors of Wolframian mannerism" ["Vor den Fehlern der Wolframschen Manier"]).

Wolfram's style is idiosyncratic (in a number of ways which will be explored below) and it certainly does not possess the clarity of the language of Hartmann or of Gottfried. A reading of Wirnt's own work (which mainly adheres to standard linguistic/stylistic forms of the *Dichtersprache*) makes it abundantly clear that he did not in the main follow the example of Wolfram but rather that of Hartmann. The praise of Wirnt might possibly then serve to obscure the polemical dimension of Wolfram's language, for from what we can infer from Wolfram's self-disclosures, he did not aspire to the idiomatic clarity of a Hartmann or the literary virtuosity of a Gottfried. In the following I shall be concerned both to illustrate something of the independent nature of Wolfram's style and to suggest reasons why he might have favored his particular repertoire of unorthodox registers and locutions.

The use of non-standard syntax, neologism, demotic registers and other studied linguistic peculiarities designed to shock and raise consciousness on behalf of one cause or another is a recurring feature of the German literary landscape of the post-1750 era — from Klopstock and the younger Goethe to the Expressionists and Celan. Wolfram's loudly trumpeted independence from canonical literary models and modes of expression can often give his verses a fresh sense of immediacy: his use of a variety of linguistic registers from "high" to "low" impressed Bakhtin as being the kind of realistic poetic signature which brings Wolfram's "romance" into close apposition with the modern novel (see Bakhtin 377). It is indeed difficult, as James Marchand put it in a special study of "Wolfram's bawdy" to "bowdlerise, ballhornize or lachmannize" the notorious passage in Book III where "poor Jeschute, who has practically no clothes on, and who has already been roughly handled by Parzival, worries about what is coming next." I quote Marchand further:

> Our text says. 'ir scham begunde switzen,' but the commentators, in typical 19th century German fashion, say that this means 'Sie schwitzte vor Schamhaftigkeit' (= 'she sweated with shame'). It may mean this, but its primary meaning is: 'Her pudendum (a meaning still attached to *Scham* in modern German) began to sweat.' (131)

The innuendo of a woman "sweating" more in sexual anticipation than from shame would inevitably have been clear to the often robust sense of humor of contemporary audiences (see the Introduction of D. S. Brewer, *Medieval Comic Tales*), however dubious and "politically incorrect" such a notion might be in the context of a sexual assault (albeit one by the naive and as yet unenlightened protagonist). It is fairly certain that such unvarnished descriptions would have been censored by more orthodox writers had they had the power to do so. Indeed, Wolfram's provocative scorn for the literary convention of decorum may have put him at odds on this issue with Gottfried von Straßburg, who in the near contemporary *Tristan* recommended the avoidance of general medical terms (let alone gynecological nomenclature) in a passage which contains a thinly veiled reproach to any poet who would overstep the mark in this regard (irrespective of whether we read these verses as an ad hominem criticism of Wolfram himself, or not):

> als verre als ichs bedenken kan,
> sô sol ich mich bewarn dar an,
> daz ich iu iemer wort gesage,
> daz iuwern ôren missehage
> und iuwerm herzen widerstê.
> ich spriche ouch deste minner ê
> von ieglîcher sache,
> ê ich iu daz mære mache
> unlîdic unde unsenfte bî
> mit rede, diu niht des hoves sî. (Marold ed., 7949–58)

(To the extent that I can bear this matter in mind I shall refrain from using any word which would be offensive to your ears or which would cause distress to your hearts. I would rather omit to mention some matter rather than make my story offensive to you through the use of words which do not properly belong to the Court.)

Wolfram's penchant for using "words not of the Court" probably represents on one level his attempt to lay down a marker of difference for himself which is strongly linked with his use of humor and irony. Humor and irony are omnipresent, often remarked features of his work which one suspects he uses sometimes with no grander intention than that of teasing liberal sympathies. Such is probably the case with Wolfram's description of the grotesque sexual encounter between Parzival and Jeschute cited above, and is certainly so in his rather "black" remarks about the emaciated inhabitants of the castle of Pelrapeire whose rations are depleted because of a long siege of the castle (184,1–26; on humor in *Parzival*, see Kant, Wehrli 1966, and the chapter on "Tote Witze" in Bertau; on irony see D. H. Green 1979 and Gaunt, especially the chapter "Irony, Medieval and Modern," 5–38). In the latter case we can be certain that he did not intend to be taken seriously in his remarks about the starving citizenry because he apologizes for what he later — after using similar humor to describe the paucity of the provisions which the hermit Trevrizent shares with Parzival — represents as being "mîn alt unvuoge" (487,12= "my old boorishness").

At the most basic level, Wolfram's impolite/humorous registers are trained on the somewhat easy target of the fastidiousness of the over-refined, the "Bigotterie der höfischen Gesellschaft" as it has been put (Bertau 89). In other passages, on the other hand, humor and irony are deployed to attack more sinister *idées reçues* of his society than those restricted to mere fastidiousness. This is a point which will be addressed further below, but before coming to that subject I wish to turn to another feature of Wolfram's language and style which incurred criticism both in his own time and thereafter: the charge of obscurity.

It may be that the above charge was being framed when, in another literary excursus, Gottfried von Straßburg, after conferring literary laurels on Hartmann von Aue for his "crystal-clear words" (*Tristan*, Marold ed., verse 4629) wrote aciduously of the work of a contemporary writer (unnamed but who may have been Wolfram) as being unclear and erratic (verses 4638–4690). Wolfram himself seems to concede the point about his having a rather convoluted style when he writes of his "crooked" German:

> mîn tiutsche ist etswâ doch sô krump,
> er mac mir lîhte sîn ze tump,
> den ichs niht gâhes bescheide:
> dâ sûme wir uns beide. (*Willehalm*, 237,11-14 — Leitzmann ed.)

(My German is so crooked as to fool anybody to whom I did not supply a speedy explanation — a process which holds us both up.)

He even seems to take a certain willful delight in obscurity when he writes in prefatory remarks to *Parzival* (which may conceivably have been intended as a counterblast to Gottfried's strictures) that his fleet metaphors will outstrip the wits of the unintelligent in his audience:

> diz vliegende bîspel
> ist tumben liuten gar ze snel,
> sine mugens niht erdenken:

> wand ez kan vor in wenken
> rehte alsam ein schellec hase. (1,15–19)

(This fleet image will far outpace people who are slow on the uptake: they won't see the point of it because it will pass them by like a hare in flight.)

Posterity has largely agreed with Wolfram's self-estimate, as noted above, and epithets used to characterize Wolfram's style in the post-Romantic era have traditionally been such as "dark" or "obscure." At the lexical level, the poet whom Gottfried apparently stigmatizes as a "wilderære" (*Tristan*, verse 4681= "jumbler" — Hatto trans.) does indeed, as Bakhtin observed, plunder a number of linguistic registers, so that alongside terms associated with the pre-romance vocabulary of the heroic epic, such as *recke* (hero), *ellen* (courage), *urliuge* (battle), *snel* (intrepid), *veige* ("doomed," a term redolent of notions of Germanic fatalism going back to the heroic age of the Migrations), we encounter a raft of more modern, imported Gallicisms such as *glævin* (lance, Old French *glävie*) or *kurteis* (Old French *cortois*). Alongside this mixing of linguistic levels there is also to be found elliptical or else periphrastic syntax. In describing Parzival's rustic youth we are told "er brach durch blates stimme en zwîc" (120, 13= "he broke off a twig for the sake of the leaf's voice"), by which is meant that he did so in order to whistle through the (cleft) leaf. The compressed nature of that phrase can be contrasted with a number of circumlocutions in describing the dramatis personae of the narrative. Parzival can be described variously as "He whom Herzeloyde bore" or "the child of the noble Gahmuret."

There are a further number of stylistic features which have traditionally been put down specifically to Wolfram's (claimed) illiteracy. These include the use of plural verbs with singular subjects (or vice versa), anacoluthon and the so-called *apo koinou* construction in which a single linguistic element has to serve different functions in separate clauses such as the following:

> gein strîter wolde füeren
> den helm er mit den snüeren
> eben ze sehne ructe. (260,13–15)

(Towards battle he wanted to take the helmet [*recte* "which"] he tightened with the straps [in order] to see clearly.)

Meanwhile, that which a hyper-literate age has dubbed abnormal word order (hyperbaton) — as in the following example where we have to wait seven lines before we get to know the object of the verb "bring" (i.e. the word "retinue") — has also been claimed as a quintessentially "illiterate" formulation:

> iu bringet ziwerm teile
> iwer œheim Artûs
> von einem lande daz alsus,
> Löver, ist genennet;
> habt ir die stat erkennet,
> Bems bi der Korchâ?
> diu massenie ist elliu dâ. (610,12–18)

(Arthur, your uncle will bring to you from the land called Löver — do you know that town, Bems on the Korka? — the retinue — it is all there.)

With reference to the above verses modern linguists would, I think, invoke the category of the "informal code" rather than that of illiteracy. In fact, the charge of "illiteracy" seems anachronistic. It should perhaps be borne in mind that written German from the medieval period up to the time of Luther reflected spoken norms and rhythms to an extent which is not now always easy to comprehend. The supremely literate (and polyglot) Luther, for instance, was accustomed to write largely as he thought and spoke, and it was only the various tides of linguistic prescriptivism which rolled in after the reformer's day (such as the Language Societies, and the stilted idiom of the Chanceries with its heavily Latinate style) which introduced the division between written and spoken codes with which we have had to become familiar today. In approaching Wolfram it is therefore necessary to attune our responses to a mode of "reading" which includes attentive listening — all the more so since, for the historical reasons alluded to above, this is a task which we have to perform scarcely more with him than with many of his literary contemporaries and successors up to the end of the sixteenth century. Wolfram's English translator, A. T. Hatto, puts the matter fairly in his Foreword:

> *Parzival* is definitely no book — and so the bare fact of translation has inevitably tidied (many passages) up. Thus the reader must imagine Wolfram to be in one sense rougher and less tidy than he appears in these pages. In another sense he is tidier than I could possibly render him, in that his compelling thought derives from his sappy and vigorous use of medieval German courtly couplets. (12)

The problems involved in reading Wolfram are real enough yet many older studies, especially those operating with the old model of the so-called *trobar clus*, a term that has been defined as "the awareness of a division in the audience between wise and foolish [and] the technique of gradually unfolding meaning through symbols or the complex interweaving of thoughts, to reveal difficult truths and to arrive at clear thinking" (Patterson 207) — the "dark style" supposedly mediated to

Wolfram by Provençal troubadours — may have represented Wolfram as being more difficult than he really is. This genetic theory, which postulates that the *trobar clus* (supposedly corresponding to the "Asiatic" style of Antiquity, in contradistinction to the limpid, Attic variety) was mediated to Wolfram via his claimed source "Kyot der Provenzale," has found little favor recently, not least because the reality of Kyot is now doubted (see also Lofmark 1972). Sacker made the important point that positivistic studies of the poet's style in *Parzival* made especially in the last century led in many cases to conclusions which "had little or no significance for the whole" (174–75). Kratz did a useful job in summarizing the evidence adduced in many of those earlier studies but this summary inevitably sometimes serves to underscore the gravamen of Sacker's stricture by perpetuating citations culled from the writings of nineteenth century scholars. I shall give two examples.

Kratz reports the use of litotes — where for instance Middle High German *selten* (seldom) or *lützel* (little) are used to convey an (unqualified) negative meaning — as being a particularly "Wolframian" stylistic feature (91). And yet this feature is commonly found in other courtly writers ca. 1200 where it counts simply as an alternative means of negation, not as a "quirky" self-conscious figure of speech (akin to the modern German and English *kaum*/scarcely, which fulfil precisely the same grammatical function). On the same page Kratz mentions Wolfram's supposed penchant for antiphrasis (expressing a positive verbal concept by using such a phrase as "he did not refrain from/forget to," followed by a verb), as in the sentence "Parzivâl des niht vergaz, / ern holte sînes bruoders swert" (754,22–23= "Parzival did not forget/omit to fetch his brother's sword"). But once again this is a common Middle High German construction, and by no means "crooked" or exclusively Wolframian.

The value of uncritically descriptive or else would-be genetic methods in explaining the poet's individual poetic voice may rightly be doubted. More productive than the stylistic surveys denounced by Sacker have been more recent studies involving the concepts of humor and irony (see L. P. Johnson 1968 and 1972 and D. H. Green 1979) and realism (Bakhtin, Stevens 1993, and Groos 1995). I therefore intend for the rest of my discussion to keep within the discursive parameters set by such modern scholars.

One of Wolfram's most trenchant jokes, suggesting almost inexhaustible seams of irony, is made in reference to King Arthur and the idealized setting in which he is conventionally placed in the romances:

> Artûs der meienbære man,
> swaz man ie von dem gesprach,
> zeinen pfinxten daz geschach,
> odr in der meien bluomenzît (281,16–19)

(Arthur the man of May. Whatever was ever told of him happened at Witsuntide or in the flowering time in May)

This parodying of an Arthurian fantasy realm with its fortunate immunity from the ravages of time and mutability probably represents an attack on the uncritical vogue for the fabulous king which had swept into Germany from France in the decades just before Wolfram began to compose, during which time the idealized king became, in Erich Köhler's phrase, "the creature of the feudal/courtly world." Such a credulity is then countered by the narrator's own program, which in this case is to present a more realistic and flawed king and court, an ambition which he encapsulates in the following cryptic terms: "diz mære ist hie vaste undersniten, / ez parriert sich mit snêwes siten" (281,21–22= "This story is to be of two sorts of fabric and snow will play a part in it"). This artfully mixed metaphor can be understood at a number of levels (secular poets were often keen to write in terms which could be decoded by analogy with the four-fold exegesis of Biblical literature — see Smalley). At the most literal it can mean that the asperities of the weather are to play a significant role in the narrative. This is most notably the case in the ninth Book, when the spiritually estranged Parzival is found riding aimlessly and disconsolately through the snow. Wolfram uses the technique of poetic fallacy to show the snow covering up the familiar footprints of the courtly world, leaving the protagonist in a terra incognita which he must chart with the compass of his own spiritual resources. (This in contradistinction to the peopled backdrop which Wolfram uses for his second hero, Gawan, in Books VII, VIII, X–XIII; Gawan is never "lost" in the same way as his knightly confrère or obliged to confront the same order of spiritual crisis [see Wynn 1984, 84–133, and McConnell's article in this volume, for an analysis of scenery and its symbolic significance].) At another level it might imply disbelief in the "Arthurian ideal" implied by other romances and the narrator's determination to relativize that ideal (as he does through the creation of an alternative grail realm to which the secular realm of King Arthur is made subordinate). It might further imply criticism of the arbitrary and unrealistic time scheme of his source text, Chrétien's *Contes del Graal*, which, as was worked out by Hermann Weigand (1969), does away with winter snow by having Pentecost recurring with preternatural swiftness. Such a barb implies Wolfram's desire for "at least an elementary form of realism, the recognition that Arthur's court must sometimes have been exposed to harsh climate and that there is only one Whitsun in any year" (D. H. Green 1979, 42). Dennis Green has pointed out yet a further level of irony here in that "it is dubious whether anyone before Weigand, let alone any medieval listeners, ever hit upon the idea of collating the poet's time references" (1979, 43; see also D. H. Green 1982) so that they could hardly see the full point of his barb, a fact which might have brought some secret mirth to Wolfram's soul.

The image of a solipsistic grin on the part of the narrator might here appear somewhat gratuitous, but at a deeper level the same critic has demonstrated that a vital part of the narrator's arsenal is precisely his capacity to keep both his audience and his hero in a baffled and questing state of mind. For long tracts of the narrative both we and the questing Parzival are made to remain in the dark about the location and nature of the quester's ultimate goal (see D. H. Green 1982). This is especially the case in the ninth Book (amplified seven-fold over Chrétien's account) where, unlike the situation in Chrétien where Perceval finds his way to the hermit counselor with ease — branches in the forest are tied back for him so that there is no possibility of his losing his way — Parzival is obliged to take various false paths (literally and figuratively) before reaching Trevrizent's cell. In this long and difficult journey (both for the quester and the audience) Wolfram makes few concessions to inattentive readers and indeed seems perfectly content to leave them by the wayside if necessary. When, for instance, the hermit asks Parzival in all innocence whether he might be Lähelin (474, 1), we have to be able to recall that the relatively minor character of Lähelin, introduced into the narrative much earlier and even then not overtly foregrounded, is the enemy of Parzival's dynasty, and that Parzival, although not factually Lähelin, has been guilty of homicide like his enemy (in his case for the killing of the knight Ither — see L. P. Johnson 1968).

Such attention to detail gives to Wolfram's narrative a particularly concrete texture, and the poet who appears to censure Chrétien for his arbitrary jumbling of the time frame is understandably vigilant to descriptions of time and space such as the seasons and the segmentation of the Church year in the liturgical calendar (see Groos 1975). Indeed, Wolfram makes some part of Parzival's sinfulness reside in the fact that he does not know what time of year it is within the Christian year when he meets the penitent pilgrims (Lord Kahenis and his family) who are obliged to tell him that it is in fact Good Friday. Further comparisons of the ninth Book of Parzival with the considerably briefer corresponding section of Chrétien would confirm how critical a part is played by dense allusiveness and dramatic irony in the creation of a fuller characterization than is to be found in the French source, but the limits of space demand that attention be given now to two further genres in which Wolfram chose to work, the lyric and the epic (Chanson de Geste).

The medieval lyric invariably stands out as the most stylized and "unrealistic" of medieval genres. The lyric tradition, which had its roots in French soil, typically contained largely stereotyped eulogies to highborn ladies. The tradition of *Hohe Minne* (literally high or exalted love) was swiftly brought to perfection and, arguably, to completion, in the last decades of the twelfth century by poets such as Reinmar, Heinrich von Morungen and others. Heinrich von Morungen in particular has some of the more haunting evocations in world literature of that "pleasurable pain" of sexual frustration in which the poet savors all the various permutations of love-longing to which the masochistic imagination can give rise. For the best-known of the medieval German lyric poets, Walther von der Vogelweide, such a lyric tradition ultimately proved limiting. Quickly forsaking the pose of chaste adoration from afar, Walther in his mature poetry proselytized for a more reciprocal form of love between the sexes (*ebene minne*), frequently subverting the conventions and limitations of the genre in poems laced with sexual innuendo. Wolfram, like Walther, (unsurprisingly, given his capacity to transform the genres in which he worked) also shows himself to be a critic rather than a continuator of the earlier poetic tradition in the sense that five of his seven extant lyrics were in the tradition of the Dawnsong, a genre which treats the theme not of mere sexual fantasizing but of (illicit) physical love. It should be noted that this genre, which came to be represented extensively in all the European vernaculars, was not well known in Germany in the first decades of the thirteenth century (see the large compilation in Hatto 1965; the erotic alba came to be a well-known European genre but the German lexicalisation for dawnsong, *tageliet*, is only found extensively in the second half of the thirteenth century).

The Dawnsong (which depicts a man and woman making love in constant fear of the dawn and hence of detection) gave Wolfram the opportunity to write affectingly straight erotic descriptions (far from any sniggering bawdy) as when he writes of his lovers "entwining their mouths, their breasts, their arms, their pure white legs," the evocation of unadorned physicality being linked to an equally raw description of their febrile emotional state:

Der tac mit kraft al durch diu venster dranc.
vil slôze sie besluzzen:
daz half niht: des wart in sorge kunt.
diu vriundîn den vriund vaste an sich twanc:
ir ougen diu beguzzen
ir beider wangel. sus sprach zim ir munt:
'zwei herze und einen lîp hân wir:
gar ungescheiden unser triuwe mit ein ander vert.
der grôzen liebe ich bin gar verhert,
wan sô dû kumes und ich zuo dir.'

Der trûric man nam urloup balde alsus:
ir liehten vel diu slehten
kômen nâher. sus der tac erschein:
weindiu ougen, süezer vrouwen kus.
sus kunden si dô vlehten
ir munde, ir brüste, ir arme, ir blankiu bein.
(Song One, Leitzmann, ed.)

(Day with all its might was thrusting through the windows. The lovers had locked up everywhere but it was no use and they were unable to remain strangers to sorrow. The female partner pressed her lover to herself closely. Her eyes covered both their cheeks with tears. Her lips spoke to him in the following words:

'We have two hearts and yet just one body. Our love for each other proceeds indissolubly. I am completely stripped of my supreme joy except at those times when you come to me and I to you.'

The sad man then took his leave in this way: their smooth, white skin came together. At that point the day appeared.

Tearful eyes — the kiss of a sweet woman. Well did they know how to intertwine mouths, breasts, arms and their pure white legs. [*Titurel and the Songs* — Gibbs/Johnson trans.])

Wolfram is particularly good at forging a suggestive linkage of the dangers and psychological trauma faced by the lovers with the intensity of their erotic passion, joining forces here with the perennial intuition that danger itself can whet the sexual appetite (this linkage was an empirically observable fact to Thucydides describing the sexual licence which prevailed at times of plague in Antiquity and was made intuitively by Shakespeare when he depicts bastards as being more vigorous than their legitimate brethren because of the dangerous conditions of their conception). The evocation of danger is supported by a group of images with a punitive and even sadistic semantic range. In the poem cited above the day is an unwelcome intruder who is heedless of the lovers' locks. In Song Three the day is imagined as having "claws thrusting through the clouds" — possibly like a griffon which threatens to part the lovers by violence: a striking metaphor for their perhaps only half-wakeful, dreamlike foreboding that they could be "torn apart" by society if their illicit liaison should become public knowledge (on the griffon image see Wack). In a paradoxical inversion of normal medieval preferences, daytime is shown to be inimical to the twilit world of illicit love whereas the night is welcomed by the couple whose love may not speak its name, a paradox which would have been even more strongly appreciated in the medieval era when the night, many centuries before it was to be hymned by the German Romantics, would have been regarded as a time of cold and of an all-enveloping darkness increasing the risk of assault. The phantasmagoric levels of imagery are an apt projection of the lovers' raw fears and hence an effective evocation of their claustrophobic, marginalized world in which their photophobia stands out as the clearest signal of their estrangement from the "straight" world.

An older generation of scholars found the term "realistic" problematical when applied to medieval literature, especially the lyric genre, but more recent critics (L. P. Johnson 1978, Wynn 1984) have contended otherwise, at least in the case of Wolfram's dawn songs. The former has argued that the physical topography of medieval castles, where bed chambers were often situated in towers and turrets patrolled by the watch, would have lent itself well to the idiosyncratic, quasi-"triangular" relationship between the lovers and the watchman found in Wolfram's lyric (where the watchman is typically in dialogue with and apparently in collusion with the lovers). Meanwhile, the latter, in suggesting that lyric poetry should be read properly, i.e. imaginatively, has suggested a number of plausible real-life scenarios which would fit well the data provided by the lyrics. Wolfram's powerfully imagined lyrics do indeed point to some realistic backdrop of experience and the tone of a sometimes brutal emotional realism is probably evidence of Wolfram polemically rejecting "the vapid purity of the average Minnelied" (L. P. Johnson 1978, 314). Support for this conclusion may be found in Wolfram's semi-lyric fragment *Titurel*, which contains essentially the *enfances* of the tragic lovers, Sigune and Schionatulander, expanded from *Parzival*. This elegiac narrative suggests the conclusion that it was the ill-judged sexual niggardliness of Sigune in refusing to give herself to her lover together with her insistence that he go on the ultimately fatal errand to fetch for her the setter's leash which led to Schionatulander's death.

Wolfram's aversion to polite fictions and euphemism in describing relations between the sexes is matched by an equally unsparing treatment of the wishful thinking lying behind the convention of euphemizing the issue of knightly homicide. This feature of his work has been fully studied with regard to *Parzival* (D. H. Green 1978) but it can also be well illustrated by reference to *Willehalm*, the Crusading epic based on the Old French *Bataille d'Aliscans* which Wolfram, at the behest of his patron, Hermann of Thuringia, adapted into German. There is abundant evidence that he did not find this commissioned work congenial since, although he keeps to the outlines of the French plot, he jettisons most of its ideological baggage, particularly the sectarian invective against the Saracen party so favored by the *Aliscans* poet. Wolfram conspicuously excises the language of hate of his source (the heathen foe in *Aliscans* are invariably "sons of whores" or "curs" — see the edition of Wienbeck) and at one point actively "deconstructs" Augustine's doctrine of the *bellum iustum* in the following lapidary *Sprachkritik*:

> dâ wart solh ritterschaft getân
> sol man ir geben rehtez wort,
> diu mac vür wâr wol heizen mort.
> (*Willehalm*, Leitzmann ed., 10,18–20)

(There [on the battlefield] such 'chivary' was performed that, if we were to call it by its proper name, that could [only] be 'slaughter.')

In articulating that conviction Wolfram regularly uses both narratorial excursuses and his central female character, Gyburg, to act as a mouthpiece to express sentiments bearing on the futility and waste of what would have been understood as legitimate crusading warfare by many of his peers. But in his concern to convey his moral he does not neglect to give full attention to a detailed depiction of battle scenes. Rather does he exploit such descriptions to convey the rigors and abominations of crusading warfare, using dramatic compression to give the sense of simultaneous battles going on in various theaters between the Christians and their religious foes, conflicts which eventually issue into a sense of "barely controlled confusion giving way to total chaos" (Gibbs 1976, 56). His skills in depicting battles are comparable in that regard to those of the anonymous poet of the *Nibelungenlied* (see *âventiure* 28–39) in that both narrators are able to give unsettling expression to the sense of engulfing chaos and tragic waste — with the important difference that the *Nibelungenlied* poet remains resolutely non-omniscient and non-judgmental in his stance, whereas Wolfram's shaft about crusading warfare being little more than slaughter lays the blame where he clearly believes it belongs, that is, in the court of any person who would sponsor "holy war." He thereby subverts the whole ideological *raison d'être* of the crusading genre, which may go a long way to explaining a key comic sequence found in *Parzival* which has sometimes been seen as being merely puckish but which may in fact be found to possess a profounder subtext. I refer to the ludicrous description of the baptism of Feirefiz, Parzival's pagan half-brother.

The conversion scene (Book XVI, sections 810–818) where Feirefiz volunteers for baptism not from burning spiritual conviction but rather in order to gain the hand of the beautiful grail bearer, Repanse de Schoye, is a piece of sublime comedy. Even if we accept that Feirefiz's sexual motivation might not have appeared so absurd to Wolfram's contemporaries as to us, given that many at the time might have taken more seriously Wolfram's somewhat pre-Freudian notions of woman (one thinks of Herzeloyde, Sigune, Gyburg as well as of Repanse; see Gibbs 1972 and in this volume) — whether seriously proposed or not — as the repository of a unique holiness, there is still a large residue of humor in the unvarnished sexual impetuosity of Feirefiz's wish to get his hands on the grail bearer at whatever cost. It is not even as if Feirefiz harbored a like kind of "affeccioun of holynesse" for Repanse as that held by Palamon and Arcite for Emily in Chaucer's Knight's Tale, both worshipping her from afar in their prison tower. Whereas Parzival and the old grail king, Anfortas, urge Feirefiz to take baptism in order to be able to see the grail (which must otherwise remain invisible to him in his pagan state), the latter is far more interested in whether this baptism might help him *in love* (813,24–814,3). He wonders further whether breaking a lance in combat (a further conventional route to the acquisition of love's guerdon — *minnelôn* — in the romances) might bring him his "baptism," at which point Parzival and Anfortas burst into broad peals of laughter (814,22–815,2). Meanwhile, the baptismal ceremony itself is preceded by the following dialogue between Parzival and his brother which, with perfect comic timing, yields Feirefiz's clinching *Pointe*:

> Parzivâl zuo sîm bruoder dô
> sprach 'wiltu die muomen mîn
> haben, al die gote dîn
> muostu durch si versprechen
> unt immer gerne rechen
> den widersatz des hôhsten gots
> und mit triwen schônen sîns gebots.'
> 'Swâ von ich sol die maget hân'
> sprach der heiden, 'diz wirt gar getân.' (816,24–817,2)

(Parzival then said to his brother: 'If you want to have my aunt [Repanse], you will have to renounce all your gods and always be ready to attack any who should oppose the Most High and keep loyally to his commandments.' 'Whatever I have to do for that maiden,' said the heathen, 'shall be performed to the letter and carried out by me with utter fidelity.')

Given that the comic treatment of this whole episode serves to deprive the ceremony of baptism of even the most minimal spiritual content, that ritual can seem little but a blasphemous parody of true baptism. "Baptism" here descends to the status of a merely arbitrary shibboleth, which must count as a provocation equally as audacious as the contention that the pagan Belacane was capable of achieving baptismal status merely through the possession of superlative (female) moral qualities (*kiusche*) or, alternatively, with the defiant statement of Gyburg in *Willehalm* that the Jewish ceremony of circumcision is functionally identical with baptism (Leitzmann ed., 307,23–24). Wolfram's humor in the baptism sequence seems to be not arbitrary and whimsical but rather serves to make vivid the kind of tolerant, even indifferentist notions which supply a deeper moral both to *Parzival* and to *Willehalm*. It is noteworthy that Wolfram did not, like other accounts such as the Third Continuation of Chrétien, elaborate his account of the "grail" realm by reference to standard ecclesiastical lore on the chalice used by Christ at the Last Supper. In fact, he indulged in much levity in his description of that mysterious vessel when, after having dangled the hyperbole of it being the "wunsch von pardîs" (235,21= "greatest conceivable boon of paradise") he descends to the bathos of describing it as "ein dinc, daz hiez der gral" (235,23= "a thing called the grail") with the function of serving food and drink. As James Poag once put it in an article which I believe fully had the measure of Wolfram's narrator:

> This version had changed Chrestien's Grail, a precious and luminous vessel, into an obscurely identified *dinc*, which functioned effectively as a sort of medieval wish-bone, dispensing treats for the tongue. Wolfram seems, with calculated malice, to have left his public hanging, uncertain as to what all these developments might mean. The German insists his way of narrating is like the string of a bow and propels 'adventure' directly towards a goal only, paradoxically, by bending. (1974,76)

Poag's final allusion here is to Wolfram's "bow metaphor" (241,1–30) where the narrator makes humorous references to his own digressiveness. What Poag calls Wolfram's "circuitousness and indirection" inevitably leaves us with a final mystery overhanging his "grail." Perhaps this was inevitable given the fact that the supposedly wondrous vessel appears to pall on Wolfram as he turns to what emerges as the *true* dénoument of his work: the reconciliation of Parzival with his long-lost pagan half-brother. The symbolism of Parzival choosing such an unlikely companion (given the degree of religious intolerance existing throughout the crusading age) to accompany him to the grail realm must have contained an enormous symbolic charge, particularly exciting in the early thirteenth century when a possible rapprochement between Christian and "heathen" was being seriously mooted by Christian intellectuals (see Siberry). It is likely that it was not the "grail" which finally interested Wolfram but the possibility of an (albeit vague and inchoate) ecumenical vision based loosely on the Prester John legend — the fabulous "priest-king" who was supposed by many of Wolfram's contemporaries to have ruled over an Oriental kingdom which included both Christian and non-Christian subjects (see Knefelkamp). The guiding spirit of Wolfram's work appears to have been not so much an orthodox body of Christian conceptions as, rather, lay conceptions regarding humane conduct here on earth. At any rate, the swift and unproblematical assimilation of the heathen Feirefiz, told with such profane brio, make it appear likely that Wolfram was moved more (using Lessing's distinction) by the spirit of "die Religion Christi" than by the precepts of the institutionalized "Christliche Religion."

Wolfram's humor and irony can often seem, like that of Chaucer or Shakespeare, of a rather variable standard. We will certainly never completely "plumb the depths of his irony" (to use Hatto's phrase with regard to Gottfried). Yet we can, I believe, understand enough of it to see that a considerable number of his more hard-hitting squibs are the result of strong and consistently held moral views. The directness of his writing and his willingness to confront and deftly pillory contemporary taboos indicate that he was aiming for an honest confrontation with his age. In this regard, he accepts neither literary/stylistic nor theological/ecclesiastical templates, his ideas being refracted not through other people's books and traditions but through his own powerful and often pungent use of the vernacular.

Cultural Contexts

BRIAN MURDOCH

Parzival and the Theology of Fallen Man

A LETTER SENT IN 1201 BY INNOCENT III TO the Archbishop of Arles on the subject of baptism summarizes with admirable lucidity the view of sin at the time of Wolfram:

> Dicimus distinguendum, quod peccatum est duplex: originale scilicet et actuale; originale, quod absque consensu contrahitur, et actuale, quod committitur cum consensu. Originale igitur, quod sine consensu contrahitur, sine consensu per vim remittitur sacramenti; actuale vero, quod cum consensu contrahitur, sine consensu minime relaxatur... Poena originalis peccati est carentia visionis Dei, actualis vero poena peccati est gehennae perpetuae cruciatus
> (*Enchiridion Symbolorum* — Denzinger ed., 180, Nr. 410)
>
> (We make a distinction, because sin is twofold, original or actual; original sin is contracted without consent, actual sin is committed with consent. Thus original sin, since it is contracted without consent, can be removed without consent by the force of the sacrament; actual sin, which is contracted with consent, cannot be remitted without effort... The penalty of original sin is the loss of the sight of God, and in truth the penalty for actual sin is the torment of everlasting hell — Translations are mine unless otherwise indicated.)

Sin in mankind, then, is of two kinds, original sin and committed sin; the first can be wiped out by the sacraments, notably by the primary sacrament of baptism; the second requires effort if it is to be cancelled. Original sin is the sin of Adam, who, having committed the first sin (*peccatum originans*, in German *Ursünde*), passed on to all his progeny a propensity to sin (*peccatum originale*, in German the inherited sin, *Erbsünde*), a doctrine given support by the Latin reading (though not the Greek — see Tennant and Wiles 95) of Romans 5, 12, referring to Adam, "in quo omnes peccaverunt" (= "in whom all sinned" — biblical citations are from the Vulgate). This transference of sin has various ramifications: it is passed on by sexual concupiscence — biblical support is provided by Psalm 50, 7 — and it is itself part of the punishment for the first sin (see Murdoch 1978, 86f. and Tobin 87). Its manifestations are not only ignorance of God's will, but above all the impossibility of not sinning, a *non posse non peccare*, which found its clearest expression in the writings of Augustine (see Tobin). That the sin of Adam is central to the interpretation of *Parzival* is made clear in the ninth Book, in which there are frequent references to Adam (discussed by Singer 374–412), especially in a much-cited passage addressed to Parzival himself (on which see Schwietering 373 and Schmid 189):

> Von Adâmes künne
> huop sich riwe unde wünne,
> sît er uns sippe lougent niht,
> den ieslîch engel ob im siht,
> unt daz diu sippe ist sünden wagen,
> sô daz wir sünde müezen tragen. (465,1–6)

(With Adam's race there began both sorrow and joy, for he whom all angels see above them does not deny our consanguinity, and his lineage is a vehicle of sin; so that we, too, have to bear our load of it. — Translations of *Parzival* are from Hatto)

At the center of medieval (and not only medieval) Christian theology is the divine economy of fall and redemption. Lucifer rebelled against God, was ejected from heaven with his followers and banished to the infernal regions. The place of the fallen angels was to be taken by man, who is in some theological writings the reason for Lucifer's rebellion, after he refused to bow down to a later creation (see Hatto 1980, 414 and Salmon). Adam and Eve shared paradise, but were tempted by the snake, usually interpreted as a disguised devil, to break what is on the face of it a fairly minor prohibition, although it is the breaking of God's commandment that is at issue, not the nature of the commandment as such. Having succumbed to the blandishments of the devil and been interrogated by God, the protoplasts were in their turn expelled from paradise, but already then were given an indication that they might return. In the tradition of biblical interpretation this is based usually on what is seen as a prophecy in Genesis 3, 15: that the woman's heel shall bruise the head of the snake is seen as the crushing of the devil by the child of Mary. In a different, but extremely widespread medieval tradition, Adam and Eve attempt to return to paradise by penance, and their son, Seth, receives a more direct promise of the redemption by the sacrifice of Christ. The incarnation therefore makes the apparent misfortune of the fall and the resultant propensity in mankind towards sin into something positive. By placing mankind *sub gratia*, the redemption negates the original sin inherited from Adam through baptism, and offers the possibility of release from other sins through penance. It is, therefore, in the words of the *Exsultet*, the celebrated and familiar chant culminating in the lighting of the Paschal Candle on Holy Saturday, a *felix culpa* (see Tax 1965, 461). The redemption offers a possibility of the return to paradise after all.

The narrative of Adam's sin operates on different levels and consequently has a variety of different reflections in literature. It is, in the historical sense, a specific event in the lives of the progenitors of all humans, so that the taint of the original act of disobedience is literally passed on to all the descendants. In typological terms it foreshadows the redemption, in that Christ's act of complete obedience cancels the sin of the first couple and — again underlined in the liturgy — the tree of the cross cancels the effect of the tree of knowledge. At the same time, however, the story serves as a model or as an image, a warning of how not to behave if God's grace is to be granted. Mankind must take care not to behave like Adam, although all share in Adam's sin. The so-called Vienna (or Old German) *Genesis*, an eleventh-century poetical reworking of the biblical Genesis, makes the polyvalence of the narrative clear in the poet's summary:

> Wer mach sín so herte,
> daz ín nine steche an daz herze
> daz durch so bosen strít
> den Adam héte unt sin wib
> al man chunne
> sol darben solehere wunne.
> Da bi megen wir nemen pilede
> daz wir nechomen hin ze himile,
> unz wir die sunde nieht begeben . . .
> (verses 1001–9 — Dollmayr, ed.)

(Who could be so hard that his heart would not be pained by the fact that through this wicked conflict that Adam and his wife had with God, all mankind should have lost such joy. We should take this as an image, showing that we shall not get to heaven until we give up sin . . .)

Just before this summarizing excursus, the poet has told of how Adam and Eve did not show proper contrition, in spite of being given many opportunities by God to do so, and hence were expelled from paradise, although the poet later reminds the audience that a redemption will come "ze bezzereme zite" (verse 1040= "at a better time").

The narrative of the fall and the broad theological outlines of its interpretation with the integrated concept of the redemption provide a direct and indirect formative structure for much medieval literature, with the different interpretative levels existing side-by-side. Adam's conflict with God becomes a paradigmatic narrative model which focuses upon a given postlapsarian individual, the hero who is burdened, like Adam and because of Adam, by original sin and by the propensity to sin, and therefore in need of redemptive grace for the former and penance for the latter. Normally the text invites reference to the complex of the fall by direct biblical citation — the name "Adam" occurs, for example, around a dozen times in *Parzival* — whilst other key phrases might trigger off the allusion (Sacker 46–63).

The story of Adam is first developed in an essentially literary manner in the many apocryphal lives of Adam and Eve extant in Greek, Latin, German and most other European vernaculars (see Murdoch 1975 and 1991), where the biblical loss of paradise is followed by the attempt to regain what was lost. The same notion of falling from and returning to God lies behind *Parzival* as it does behind the two works of Hartmann von Aue most closely related to it, *Der arme Heinrich* and *Gregorius*. The three works — which have been compared and contrasted on a number of occasions (most notably by Ranke 1952,26–29) — need to be considered closely together. Wolfram invites not only direct links with Adam and the biblical story, but (in one specific reference and in various less obvious places) with Hartmann, and Wolfram-criticism has long debated the precise relationship between the two writers, seeing *Gregorius* in particular both as a precursor of and as an antithesis to *Parzival* (Wand, 181f., refers to Cormeau/Störmer on the one side and Wapnewski 1955 on the other). In fact, Hartmann's *Gregorius* is extremely close to Wolfram's work. It is of incidental interest, further, that the theology of the fall and the redemption should have informed specifically *literary* works by major writers in classical Middle High German around 1200, where in the earlier period we may point to numerous works dealing *directly* with the divine economy, such as *Ezzos Gesang*, the *Anegenge*, the *Summa Theologiae* and others, the same being true of the post-classical period with writers such as Heinrich Hesler, Tilo von Kulm, Johannes von Frankenstein, Gundacker von Judenburg, Heinrich von Neustadt, and works like the *Erlösung* or *Der saelden hort* (see Wiedmer 152f.).

Parzival is not just "Adâmes künne" (= "Adam's race"), but the mirror and repetition of Adam, who, even though cleansed of original sin at baptism and thus given a chance to regain paradise, nevertheless lapses, and requires a renewal of faith, and penance before he can achieve his rightful end, the grail crown. This may be taken, of course, as the ultimate goal of the human quest, the heavenly crown. The message of *Parzival* is that in spite of the sinfulness of man and the inevitability of sin, the acquisition of a crown (and the readmission of Adam into the lost paradise) is indeed possible. Adam lived before the law — *ante legem*; Moses brought the law, after which man lived under that law, *sub lege*, until the incarnation, the redemption and the provision of grace, so that events thereafter happen *sub gratia*, under the grace of God. The literary hero effectively becomes Adam *sub gratia*, and the story of Parzival himself mirrors that human quest, which requires the progression from *tumpheit* (= *ignorance*, which can be justified by age and inexperience, or can be reprehensible as such), to awareness of error, to amendment and renewal (see Haas) until circumstances permit the regaining of paradise. The whole narrative mirrors not only the tale of Adam, but the divine economy as such, as Parzival moves through the stages of lawlessness to formal instruction and then to grace.

Parallels between Wolfram's work and theological writings have been discussed with reference to the Bible (for example, by Duckworth 1980) and to commentaries on the theology of original sin, such as those of Augustine (by Wapnewski). But it is instructive to consider also works that address in a more general sense the lapse of faith in God, and in this context attention may usefully be paid to a work on that general theme called *De lapsis* by Cyprian of Carthage, who wrote in the middle of the third century, and whose theme overlaps very much with the *Parzival* story. Cyprian considers in detail those who lapse from the faith and effectively deny God, but who then return, and although the book is concerned essentially with the treatment of those who had lapsed from the faith in the face of the Decian persecutions in Cyprian's own time, the general implications of the work were recognized early, and it had considerable influence throughout the Middle Ages and well into the humanist period. This is attested by the large number of extant manuscripts, and the book was frequently cited, although whether Wolfram knew it directly or indirectly is a matter of conjecture.

In Wolfram's narrative the parallels with Adam become clear at an early stage. Parzival grows up in idyllic surroundings, but in isolation from the world, and his only religious instruction from his mother is a description of God as one who is shining, and who offers help against the devil. It is notable that when Parzival first encounters the world outside, in the shape of a group of knights, he is actually linked with Adam:

> Dô lac diu gotes kunst an im.
> von der âventiure ich daz nim,
> diu mich mit wârheit des beschiet.

>   nie mannes varwe baz geriet
>   vor im sît Adâmes zît. (123,13–17)

(He bore the marks of God's own handiwork. I have it from my source, which told me the truth of the matter, that from Adam's day till then none turned out better for looks than he.)

It is true that phrases like "sît Adâmes zît" might in some contexts represent no more than a simple circumlocution for "a very long time indeed," but the position of the young Parzival is of itself Adamic as he makes his way into the world outside for the first time. He is aware of God (see Dahlgrün) but is in a state of ignorance otherwise. Some less overt parallels with Adam are apparent already, however, with Parzival's parents. Adam's paradisiacal marriage was intended to be chaste (see Grimm), but after the fall sexuality provided the basis for original sin, a point made in such influential works such as Augustine's *On Genesis against the Manichaeans* (Migne, *Patrologia Latina* 34, 187) and in later, widely-disseminated encyclopedic texts like Honorius's *Elucidarium* (Migne, *Patrologia Latina* 172, 1118). Herzeloyde's first marriage, Parzival is told by Trevrizent, was also a chaste one, to King Castis (whose name makes its own point), but it is that to the more worldly Gahmuret from which Parzival himself is born.

There are strong parallels between the narrative of the fall and Hartmann von Aue's *Gregorius*, and numerous comparisons between *Gregorius* and *Parzival* suggest themselves. The conception of Gregorius is incestuous, and he is born of a noble but sheltered brother and sister. This is a reflection of Adam and Eve, who are also of the same flesh. There is, of course, no incest in *Parzival*; but there are echoes of this motif (perhaps alluding deliberately to Hartmann) both in Herzeloyde's words on the child of Gahmuret: "[ich] bin sîn muoter und sîn wîp" (109,25= "I am his mother and his bride"), and in her thoughts after Parzival is born: "si dûht, si hete Gahmureten / wider an ir arm erbeten" (113,13f.= "It was as though her prayers had restored Gahmuret to her arms again"). The first passage echoes closely *Gregorius*, in which the eponymous hero's mother confesses to him "ich bin iuwer muoter und iuwer wip" (verse 2604= "I am your mother and your wife" — Paul ed.).

When the young Parzival begins his journey into the world away from his mother, with only a vague notion of God and dazzled by knighthood, he is ignorant of a great many things, including his and man's propensity to sin. Dressed like a fool, even later on beneath his armor, he is in the first stage of his journey into life quite literally lawless in formal theological terms: he is *ante legem*. Not until his encounter with Gurnemanz does he acquire knowledge of the Church — God's law — and its spiritual benefits. This is the first stage of his education:

> dô gienc der helt mit witzen kranc
> dâ man got und dem wirte sanc.
> der wirt zer messe in lêrte
> daz noch die sælde mêrte,
> opfern und segnen sich,
> und gein dem tiuvel kêrn gerich. (169,15–20)

(Our simple warrior went to where Mass was sung and for his lordship. At Mass the latter taught him something that would still increase one's blessings today: to make his offering and cross himself, and so punish the devil.)

Gurnemanz is now able to provide further advice to the young man. This advice has been the subject of detailed scrutiny, most recently and especially clearly by David Wells, who not only relates it to the formal teaching in schools of Cato's *Distichs*, but links it with the advice of the abbot in Hartmann's *Gregorius* (verses 1432–78). Gurnemanz's advice is more detailed than that given earlier by Herzeloyde to her son, as indeed it must be, as Parzival is now older. That he continues to make mistakes even when following intrinsically good and certainly wellmeant advice indicates simply how difficult it is for man not to err. In the apocryphal lives of Adam, the protoplasts undertake a penance, each standing in a river and fasting. Eve is tricked out of this by the devil when he claims to be an angel. This time Adam recognizes him, and the point is, of course, that the devil — or a wrong action — has to be (and potentially *is*) recognizable. A vivid illustration in a fifteenth century manuscript shows the devil disguised as an angel but with his cloven hoofs showing, tempting Eve to fall a second time (see Halford 20). In medieval illustrations of the temptation in the desert, the devil is also disguised as a friar (albeit again with cloven hoofs), although Christ recognizes him (Murdoch 1974, 162–4). Parzival, though given instruction, also fails to recognize the truth of a situation, either when in the third Book he fails to see that the river he wishes to cross is dark not because it is deep, but because it is overshadowed, or with far greater significance, when he fails to grasp what is going on at Munsalvaesche. That Parzival's sins are in the main sins of ignorance or omission does not, of course, exculpate him, but this does reinforce the existential *non posse non peccare* of fallen man.

The topos of the *patria paradisi*, from which man is an exile, is known in German from the time of Otfried von Weissenburg onwards (see Gruenter), and Adam is in medieval German literature frequently "der ellende" (= "the exile") trying to return to his true homeland of paradise. The irony of Parzival's case is that the hero is permitted to see, but cannot yet gain access to his own intended paradise, the grail kingdom. Although Parzival fails to ask the fisher king the question that will complete the action, he does at least see (though he does not fully comprehend) the grail, the description of which in the fifth Book makes very clear the link with paradise. Feirefiz, later on, will not even be able to see it until he is baptized, but to those who are baptized, the possibility of regaining paradise is literally visible. The grail, borne by Repanse de Schoye, *is* paradise, it is the ultimate goal:

> ûf einem grüenen achmardî
> truoc si den wunsch von pardîs,
> bêde wurzeln unde rîs.
> daz was ein dinc, daz hiez der Grâl,
> erden wunsches überwal. (235,20-4)

(Upon a green achmardi she bore the consummation of heart's desire, its root and its blossoming — a thing called "The Gral," paradisal, transcending all earthly perfection!)

The grail, we are told later, produces food and gives life, much as paradise did for unfallen man. Fallen man, represented at this point by Parzival, can be aware of it, but cannot grasp it. There is a parallel once more in the apocryphal lives of Adam and Eve, in which Seth returns to paradise to try and obtain the oil of mercy which will help the dying Adam. Seth sees through the gate of paradise a tree which contains a baby in its crown (in some versions he sees the Virgin carrying the child). The child is, of course, the future savior, but for Seth at this point the scene is enigmatic. As an Old Testament figure, Seth cannot understand the implications. There will be a redemption, but it is still in the future, and mankind (of which Seth is the representative as the son of Adam) will not understand until the proper time.

It is inappropriate to speculate further here on the *precise* nature of the grail, literature on which ranges from Jessie Weston's influential *From Ritual to Romance* in 1920 to more recent interpretations of the name *lapsit exillis*, which is given later in *Parzival* (see Sidney Johnson's article in this volume). The attendant symbolism of the grail as it is presented to the as yet uncomprehending Parzival is complex, but in any case, the youthful Parzival does not ask the question that will indicate his own *caritas* and thus redeem Anfortas and himself (see Willson). Gurnemanz had, however, warned him against asking questions, and we are reminded too that he is still very young (244,9). It is after this point that Parzival's actual lapse — his conflict with God (the Vienna *Genesis* uses the word *strît* in a corresponding context) — occurs, when Sigune points out to him the enormity of his failure to act appropriately. The precise nature of Parzival's sin is far less relevant than his response to sinfulness as such. That response is to distance himself from God, to become one of those who have fallen away from God in the sense of Cyprian's *De lapsis*, as well as being merely a member of fallen humanity, and it is from this point that he must make his way back to Munsalvaesche, which can, of course, (also) be interpreted as *mons salvationis*, the hill of the redemption, on which the Rood-tree negated the effect of the tree of knowledge. After he has been reviled by Cundrie, Parzival utters his celebrated overt rejection of God (332,1–18), but for all that, God is still kept as part of the picture by the narrator, who allows other characters to commend the Red Knight to God and has him do the same for others.

Parzival does not return to God until the ninth Book. In the biblical narrative of Adam and Eve, after the transgression, the protoplasts hide themselves from God, who then calls to Adam with the words "ubi es?" (= "where art thou?"). Commentators point out that this is not divine ignorance (see Augustine's *Literal Interpretation of Genesis* in Migne, *Patrologia Latina* 34, 449), but rather an admonition and a chance to repent. Gregory the Great's literal exegesis in the *Moral Interpretations of the Book of Job* (Migne, *Patrologia Latina* 75, 558) tells us that God has called Adam to repent. Isidore, finally, in his *Questions on the Old Testament* offers a more generally moralizing view (much repeated by Carolingian commentators and after), referring to the way in which God offers the possibility of repentance to all men with a citation of Ezechiel 33, 11:

> Hic ostendit quod si quis a fide vel bonis operibus a mendacia sua desideriaque latuntur, non despicit illos Deus, sed adhuc ut redeant ad poenitentiam vocat, quia non vult mortem peccatoris . . . Ergo non est desperandum quibuslibet peccatoribus, dum et ipsi impii ad spem indulgentiae provocatur.
> (Migne, *Patrologia Latina* 83,220; see Murdoch 1972, 119–29)
>
> (This shows us that if anyone is led astray from faith or good works by lies or desires, God does not despise such people, but calls them back to penance, because He does not desire the death of the sinner . . . Thus no sinner should despair, since even these wicked people are prompted back to the hope of grace.)

Parzival is not Adam, but he *is* Adam's kin. Although he does not hear a direct call from God asking where he is, Wolfram has an extended and (in the context of the work as a whole) unusual opening to the ninth

Book in which he depicts his audience as asking the spirit of the story where Parzival is, and also whether Parzival "von jâmer sî erlôst?" (433,28= "has been redeemed from his sorrows?"). The choice of the verb *erlôst* (= redeemed) is not insignificant. It is echoed later in the same Book (488,4–13) when Parzival himself confesses that he remained silent at Munsalvaesche (see Duckworth 1980, 153).

Even if God does not speak directly to Parzival, as He does to Adam, the repetition of the story of the fall is made clear by the parallels between what follows and the interrogation by God in Genesis. In the opening part of the ninth Book questions are put to Parzival by a sequence of representatives: Sigune, Kahenis and Trevrizent himself. God's words to Adam were concerned not only with his deliberate hiding from God, but also with his reasons for covering up the nakedness of his lost paradisiacal innocence. Here, too, the questions directed at Parzival concern why he is covering himself. Kahenis and his family are not naked (since this is a post-lapsarian world), but they are barefoot and Kahenis is not in armor. Hence they are critical, as is Trevrizent later, of the fact that Parzival appears in full armor on Good Friday. Indeed, throughout the ninth Book Parzival gradually reveals himself as one who has been hiding from God, although unlike Adam, he does express contrition for doing so, rather than adopt the *defensionis audacia* (= audacious defense) attributed to Adam by the exegetes when he shifted the blame onto Eve. Parzival has in the past indeed tried to place the blame on others, more specifically on the advice given by Herzeloyde and Gurnemanz in 330,1–6 (see Sacker 46–63 and von Simson 219). But he does not do so now.

It has been noted that the spiritual guidance offered to Parzival in the ninth Book to help him to cope with sin comes from three separate sources, Sigune, Kahenis and then Trevrizent, none of whom is part of the theological establishment (see Schröder 1952). Sigune, though a kind of anchorite, "hôrte selten messe" (435,24= "never heard Mass"), Kahenis is a pilgrim, and Trevrizent, who explains the grail and the story of man's salvation to Parzival, granting absolution and imposing penance, is not a priest. This may be a deliberate attempt on Wolfram's part to keep outside the sphere of orthodox religion, and there has been some debate, much of it inconclusive and not particularly helpful, on possible links with Catharism. However, lay confession was not necessarily condemned in the twelfth century (see Wapnewski 179 and Wessels 234–6), and in other contexts the same imposition of religious rites outside the priesthood is actually necessary, most notably in the case of Adam once again, who imposes penance upon Eve and himself in the apocryphal Adam-literature. Adam does penance himself in the

Jordan as an antitype of Christ's baptism, which was itself performed by a hermit, John the Baptist (see Murdoch 1991).

Parzival's first encounter with penance is by observation in the encounter with Kahenis and his wife and daughters, poorly clad in the snow on their way to confession. Parzival is unaware that it is Good Friday, and Kahenis stresses the paradox of rejoicing and sorrowing — "des al diu werlt sich freun mac / und dâ bî mit angest siufzec sîn" (448,8f.= "in which the whole world can rejoice and at the same time mourn in anguish"). Easter, the time of renewal, commemorates the turning point of the divine economy of human history, and it is — as has frequently been noted — the most significant of the liturgical calendar-references in the work (see Weigand 1969, Groos 1975, and Tax 1965). Parzival reiterates his lapse from God, but this is countered by Kahenis with a stress on God's *triuwe*, His loyalty to man. Parzival is advised to do penance and to seek absolution from Trevrizent.

Wolfram makes very clear that at this point Parzival begins to think about his creator properly for the first time. The passage, a little over halfway through Wolfram's poem as a whole, is a striking one:

>   alrêrste er dô gedâhte,
>   wer al die werlt volbrâhte,
>   an sînen schephære,
>   wie gewaltec der wære.
>   er sprach: 'waz ob got helfe phligt,
>   diu mînem trûren an gesigt?
>   wart ab er ie ritter holt,
>   gedient ie ritter sînen solt,
>   ode mac schilt unde swert
>   sîner helfe sîn sô wert,
>   und rehtiu manlîchiu wer,
>   daz sîn helfe mich vor sorgen *ner*,
>   ist hiut sîn helflîcher tac,
>   sô helfe er, ob er helfen mac.'
>   (451,9–21 — emphasis added)

(Only now did he ponder Who had brought the world into being, only now think of his Creator and how mighty He must be. 'What if God has such power to succour as would overcome my sorrow?' he asked himself. 'If He ever favoured a knight, and if any knight ever earned His reward or if shield and sword and true manly ardour can ever be so worthy of His help that he could save me from my cares, and if this is His Helpful Day, then let Him help me, if help He can!')

The italicized form of the verb *nêren* in this passage is also significant. It can mean "heal" or "cure," and is applied also to Christ as the savior;

the whole complex of the vocabulary of soteriology is used regularly in this context (see Murdoch 1978 and Haage on genuine medical aspects), and the verb can in Old High German even gloss *absolvere*. Equally significant is the link with the Psalms of the Good Friday services, most notably Psalm 21, which is echoed by Christ Himself on the cross. In the relevant verses the Psalmist sees himself as a outcast from men, without help:

> Deus meus respice in me: quare me dereliquisti? longe a salute mea verba delictorum meorum.
>
> (Oh God, my God look upon me; why hast thou forsaken me? Far from my salvation are the words of my sins.)

and then later:

> Tu autem Domine ne elongaveris auxilium tuum a me
>
> (But thou, O Lord, remove not thy help to a distance from me)

The notion of divine help is, of course, constantly present in the Psalms (see Tax 1965, 456, S. Johnson 1970, 110–13, and Duckworth 1980, 280).

Parzival, then, begins to think in appropriate terms of his Creator and submits himself to the will of God. Moreover, when Parzival meets Trevrizent he announces himself (456,30) with the liturgical "peccavi" (= "I have sinned"). That he has lapsed from Christian practice is made clear in his admission that he has not visited a church for a long period. He does not really know the full extent of his sins, but becoming aware is the first necessary move from the fallen state to that of grace. Cyprian of Carthage makes a significant point in this regard in his work *De lapsis*:

> Si cladis causa cognoscitur, et medella vulneris invenitur. Dominus probari familiam suam voluit. (Bénevot ed., 8f.)
>
> (If we know what made us fall, we can learn how to heal our wounds. The maker wanted his household to be tested — Bénevot trans.)

Trevrizent first of all gives a brief account of the history of the fall, of Lucifer first, then of Adam and Eve, Eve having fallen "dazs ir schepfære überhôrte" (463,21= "by not listening to her maker"). This is all reminiscent of Parzival's own case. Trevrizent names and then explains the nature of the grail to Parzival, again with reference to paradise, and there is an allusion to the role of the grail both in reviving the phoenix and rejuvenating men as well. Both allusions belong to the broader medieval paradise tradition: "selhe kraft dem menschen gît der stein, / daz im fleisch unde bein / jugent enpfæht al sunder twâl" (469,25–7=

"Such powers does the stone confer on mortal men that their flesh and bones are soon made young again"). The paradise-description of Avitus describes how the phoenix is made young again in paradise, and the application to man in general is a commonplace. There is a significant example in the paradisiacal vision of Hartmann von Aue's maiden in his poem *Der arme Heinrich*: "da enwirt von jâren niemen alt / der alte wirt junger" (verse 784f.= "nobody ages there, the old become young" — Paul ed.)

Trevrizent then refers to a visitor to the grail castle who came but went away without asking any questions, a passage crucial in the evaluation of Parzival's sin, the precise nature of which has often been the subject of detailed literary speculation. One interpretation sees the sin at the grail castle as pride (Groos 1975,55), but an even simpler view commends itself: Parzival is guilty at best of a sin of omission, just as in Hartmann von Aue's works Heinrich's sin is that of failing to acknowledge God and Gregorius's sin of incest with his mother is of such bizarre improbability that he would have been unlikely to have foreseen it. All these mirror man's propensity to incur sin whether it is deserved or not. In Parzival's case the one real sin, perhaps, is his anger during his visit to the grail castle, which is manifested in his treatment of the jester. The link between anger and self-centeredness is made clear in theological treatises. A late medieval homiletic handbook, the *Fasisculus Morum* (ed. Wenzel), includes lack of pity under the heading of the signs of anger, and cites Augustine's repeated statement: "non meretur misericordiam qui eam proximo negat" (= "he deserves no mercy who denies it to his neighbour"). Augustine makes this and similar comments in several works (Wenzel's edition 118f. cites Migne, *Patrologia Latina* 38, 395).

Though he does not know yet with whom he is speaking, Trevrizent states that Parzival carried off a burden of sin, and it was in such terms that Parzival introduced himself to the hermit. Once it emerges that Parzival was the unfortunate visitor to the grail castle, Trevrizent warns him about the extent of his penance: "dune solt och niht ze sêre klagn. / du solt in rehten mâzen / klagen und klagen lâzen" (489,2–4= "You must not grieve to excess, but grieve and cease grieving in measure"). The roughly contemporary *Penitential* of Alain of Lille makes the same point — "temperandæ ergo sunt poenitentia" (= "penances are to be moderated") — adding that a penance that cannot be carried out is of questionable value. Appropriate penances include, however, "oblationes, orationes, peregrinationes" (= "sacrifice, prayers and pilgrimages" [Migne, *Patrologia Latina* 210, 293]; see Murdoch 1991, 220). It is indeed a kind of pilgrimage which Parzival now undertakes by way of showing his contrition, the validity of which Trevrizent (like a priest) says that he will guarantee, although he urges Parzival at the end of Book IX to make confession to a consecrated priest. At the same time we are reminded again of the divine economy:

> 'du muost zen pfaffen haben muot.
> swaz dîn ouge ûf erden siht,
> daz glîchet sich dem priester niht.
> sîn munt die marter sprichet,
> diu unser flust zebrichet:
> ouch grîfet sîn gewîhtiu hant
> an daz hœheste pfant
> daz ie für schult gesetzet wart.' (502,12–19)

('Place your trust in the clergy. Nothing you see on earth is like a priest. His lips pronounce the Passion that nullifies our damnation. Into his consecrated hand he takes the highest Pledge ever given for debt.')

Parzival's only real sin is his lapse from God, and that both stems from and is parallel with the sin of Adam, the *lapsus*. The other listed sins all stem from ignorance, and can be atoned for and indeed remedied. Ignorance, moreover, is one of the penalties of original sin (see Swinburne and Dimler), something with which Adam's children are born.

Parzival's penance takes the form of a pilgrimage, and once this is completed, he can be actively redeemed, and in token of that, be given a second chance to pose the question that saves his uncle and gains the grail crown. Parzival continues his wanderings until he is forgiven, first by Cundrie, and then formally in the grail castle. Cundrie tells Parzival towards the end of Book XV:

> 'du hetes junge sorge erzogn:
> die hât kumendiu freude an dir betrogn.
> du hâst der sêle ruowe erstriten
> und des lîbes freude in sorge erbiten.' (782, 27–30)

('You raised a brood of cares in tender years; but the happiness which is on its way to you has dashed their expectations. You have won through to peace of soul and outlived cares to have joy of your body.')

The curing of Anfortas as an expression of *caritas* confirms the resolution of Parzival's state. Having demonstrated the two precepts of the New Testament and shown love for God and for his neighbor, he is able to cancel the old Adam once and for all, something which is a possibility for all men since the redemption (see Tax, "Biblical Typology," 14). When Parzival asks the question of Anfortas he weeps tears of contrition (795,20–29 — see Duckworth 1980, 281), and the actual moment of achieving grail kingship links the reward of the earthly paradise with the notion of the heavenly crown. The baptism of Feirefiz is now given prominence, and although the scene has been criticized (by Sacker 164 and Kratz 541), the fact that there is a detailed baptism presented to us at this stage is of considerable importance as a reminder of the new baptism called for by Cyprian, and the Easter renewal which Parzival has now undergone. Baptism is referred back to Christ and also Adam by the priest who explains it to Feirefiz (817,22–4) and the details now given of the blessing of the water once more recall the Holy Saturday liturgy (on the importance of this see Couratin 198–214). Adult baptism also requires the formal renunciation of other gods (see Schröder 1952,57–62 and Blamires 459).

Parzival submits himself completely to the will of God in Book IX when he tells his horse to take him wherever God wishes: "nu genc nâch der gotes kür" (452,9= "Now go where God chooses"). This resignation to God's will is the essential theological underpinning of *Parzival*, and its basis is expressed particularly well by Cyprian. The final paragraph of Cyprian's work on those who lapse is worth quoting *in extenso* for its signal relevance to Parzival:

> Si precem toto corde quis faciat, si veris paenitentiae lamentis et lacrimis ingemescat, si ad veniam delicti sui Dominum iustis et continuis operibus inflectat, misereri talium potest qui et misericordiam suam protulit dicens: 'cum conversus gemueris tunc salvaberis et scies ubi fueris' [. . .] Repetet certamen suum miles, iterabit aciem, provocabit hostem et quidem factus ad proelium fortior per dolorem. Qui sic Deo satisfecerit, qui paenitentia facti sui, qui pudore delicti plus et virtutis et fidei de ipso lapsus sui dolore conceperit, exauditus et adiutus a Domino, quam contristaverat nuper laetam faciet ecclesiam, nec iam solam Dei veniam merebitur sed coronam.
>
> (Bénevot ed., 52–4)

> (To him who prays with all his heart, to him who mourns with tears and sighs of true repentance, to him who by good works of persevering charity pleads to the Lord for mercy on his sin, to such He can extend mercy, since he has shown the mercy of His heart when he said 'When thou shalt return and mourn, then shalt thou be saved; and thou shalt know where thou once wast . . . ' A soldier once more he will return to the fray, he will engage anew and challenge the enemy — and will do so with all the more courage for his remorse. He who has made such satisfaction to God, he who by his repentance and shame for his sin, draws from the bitterness of his fall a fresh fund of valour and loyalty, shall by the help he has won from the Lord rejoice the heart of the church whom he has so lately pained; he will earn not merely God's forgiveness, but His crown. — Bénevot trans.)

The quotation from Isaiah 30, 15 differs slightly from that in the Latin Vulgate, which has *quiescatis* (= rest) rather than *gemueris* (= mourn), but Cyprian's version and military parallel fits well with Parzival's special case. Cyprian's work expands, although in fact it does not cite, the biblical Epistle of James, which also has a reference to the heavenly crown (James 1, 12; see Duckworth 1980, 59–69). The effect of other sections of that Epistle have been the subject of detailed consideration, but Cyprian's work has not. Cyprian's final reference to a crown, here intended as the heavenly crown, might equally well apply to that of the lapsed and then restored grail king, a soldier who now realizes where he once was, and who returns with renewed courage to overcome sin. A final comment from Cyprian on the achievement of the heavenly crown, which could be the grail crown, is of special significance:

> Nam cum corona de Dei dignatione descendat, nec possit accipi nisi fuerit hora sumenda.

> (The crown is bestowed at God's good pleasure and is not received until the appointed hour.)

W. H. JACKSON

Tournaments and Battles in *Parzival*

MILITARY EQUIPMENT, MILITARY ENCOUNTERS, and military values play a leading part in Wolfram's *Parzival*. A wide range of military activities figures in the work, from a novice's training through to collective battles and potentially mortal single combats. Moreover, military life is shown in *Parzival* from an inside perspective, and this marks an important shift in the cultural history of romance. The early romances of the twelfth century were clerical in authorship, and Chrétien de Troyes still maintains a certain clerical detachment from the chivalric world in his grail romance, but Wolfram presents himself as a knightly narrator, one whose "office is the shield" (*Parzival*, 115,11) and who speaks from within the dominant military class. This narrative perspective is particularly significant for an understanding of *Parzival* because the narrator has an unusually high profile in this work, and his knightly status links him to the main male characters in his fictive world. It is characteristic of Wolfram's approach that, in his adaptation of Chrétien's *Perceval*, he reduces Chrétien's references to church institutions and shows far greater interest than the French poet in details of military life, which he views from the dual perspective of an author who has intimate knowledge of chivalric practices and of the contemporary literary scene. (On the sociological and stylistic implications of the shift from Chrétien's clerical to Wolfram's knightly narration, see Jaeger 242–43, Stevens 1993, and Stevens and Thomas in this volume.)

The present contribution will discuss military equipment and military encounters in *Parzival* in a technical sense and with regard to their social and ethical dimensions, for the military, the social and the ethical were intimately connected in the secular culture of the medieval German aristocracy. In a few cases the discussed equipment and military encounters will be illustrated by reproductions from the Manesse Codex which are located at the end of this article. It is important to recognize that the illustrations in this manuscript date from about a century after Wolfram's *Parzival*, and they contain features that only emerged after Wolfram's time. Much that was new about chivalric equipment in *Parzival* is already well-established or further developed in the Manesse Codex (e.g., the shields in the codex are smaller, the horse covers more elaborate and heraldry more complex than in Wolfram's day). Nevertheless, the illustrations preserve the main basic features of knightly equipment in *Parzival*: mail hauberk with coif and chausses, helm with decoration, shield, surcoat and horse cover with matching devices, and lance and sword as the weapons of mounted knightly combat. The military power and festive colorfulness of the illustrations in the codex also match the celebratory strand in Wolfram's literary presentation of chivalry.

Warfare in Wolfram's day

Before turning to the work itself it may be useful to look at some features of warfare in the historical reality of Wolfram's time so as to place his work in context and to avoid the misunderstandings that can arise from projecting later concepts and conditions of warfare back onto the period around 1200.

First it should be emphasized that warfare was different in its political and social dimensions in the Middle Ages from the twentieth century in Europe. Whereas today the right to use armed force lies with the state, not the individual (save in certain limited situations such as self-defense), the bearing of arms was a hereditary right of the medieval aristocracy. In the German empire, as in many other parts of Europe, individuals still had the right to settle disputes by military means, in the process of feud, in the thirteenth century and later. Alongside the armed feud, settlements by amicable procedures and peaceful legal processes had long existed throughout Europe (see Bossy 287–92); and whilst armed feuds were still widely practiced in Germany in the twelfth and thirteenth centuries, the non-violent forms of conflict resolution were gaining ground at this time, not least in the peace movements emanating from the church and from secular authorities (discussed by Gernhuber). Thus when Wolfram was working on *Parzival* the proper use of armed force was a subject of debate, change, and difference of view, and this was a matter of immediate concern to the actual life of the sword-bearing class to which Wolfram assigns himself as narrator. Moreover, it would be misleading to see the aristocracy's right of arms and the practice of the feud as "anarchy," since these were part of a complex and living network of customary rights that permeated the social mentality and underpinned forms of communal order in a way that cannot fully be understood by reference to the relation of the individual and the state in the modern world. (On the legal, social and political dimensions of the feud see O. Brunner 1–110.)

With regard to military techniques, medieval warfare knew considerable variety according to terrain, strength of forces and military objectives. However, medieval strategy does seem "to have been dominated by two general principles: fear of the pitched battle, of the confrontation in open country, and what one might call the 'siege mentality'" (Contamine 219), that is to say the tendency to respond to attack by withdrawing into the most easily defensible stronghold, with the consequence that warfare was often local and involved devastation of lands, pillaging, ambushes, sallies and sieges rather than large-scale pitched battles. Pitched battles were nevertheless of great political and military importance when they did occur.

Medieval war was diverse also in the intensity of fighting and the number of casualties. War seems to have been most fiercely fought when religious differences were involved; for instance the crusading historian William of Tyre wrote that "war is waged differently and less vigorously between men who hold the same law and faith" (cit. Bradbury 297). Even within Christendom wars varied widely in intensity. In local feuds the aim was often less to kill the enemy than to exercise pressure in the direction of a negotiated settlement, for example by taking a leading member of the enemy's family captive. Moreover, in the twelfth and thirteenth centuries the defensive armor of the knight was sufficiently effective to keep casualties often surprisingly low; for instance the author of the Welf chronicle records that, during a feud between Duke Welf VII and Count Palatine Hugo of Tübingen in 1164 the two sides fought for two hours with only one casualty, "for all were so well protected by their armour, that it was easier to take them prisoner than to kill them" (*Historia Welforum*, König ed., 64). The harshness of warfare in Christendom should not be underplayed, but the effectiveness of defensive armor and the political and material usefulness of taking prisoners were pragmatic factors that held the death count down — at least for the aristocratic combatants.

In military personnel and equipment, old and new overlapped in Wolfram's day. The leading personnel were the heavily armored, mounted knights who fought with the ancient weapon of the sword and the newer weapon of the couched lance, that is, the lance held under the arm. The use of the couched lance allowed the weight of the charging horse to be brought to bear in mounted shock combat, and this combat in turn exercised a major, though not unchallenged, influence on the battlefield from the twelfth century until the end of the Middle Ages. Evidence as to the degree of discipline shown in medieval warfare is patchy. However, against older views of the lack of coordination in knightly warfare recent scholars have emphasized the importance of disciplined group fighting (see Verbruggen 72–97 and Jones 1989), even though some accounts do suggest that at times individuals or groups were indeed more concerned with the pursuit of booty or personal glory than with the implementation of an overall strategy (see Contamine 229).

The interweaving of the military into the fabric of everyday social life is shown in the dual, military and social value of the word *ritter* (= knight) which during the twelfth century acquired connotations of social, aristocratic preeminence beside its original professional military and feudal sense of "mounted warrior" in the service of a lord. Finally, besides the knights, military personnel in Wolfram's day included a whole range of sub-knightly figures (mounted sergeants, foot soldiers, archers, crossbowmen, siege engineers) whose activities and equipment are rarely described in detail in the sources, but whose importance was if anything increasing as the knights became a more restricted military and social élite from the late twelfth century onwards. (On knights in Germany in the twelfth and thirteenth centuries see Bumke 1977, Arnold, and Jackson, *Chivalry* 37–83; on military equipment in general see Schultz 1889, Boeheim, Blair, Gamber, Bumke 1986, 210–40, Nicolle, and DeVries.)

The military equipment of knights in *Parzival*

The figure of the knight commands far more interest than any other military phenomenon in *Parzival*, and Wolfram's concern with the military aspect of chivalry is communicated in descriptions of knightly equipment and the many references to individual items of it that occur throughout the text. Three general points deserve special note in this connection. First, references to chivalric equipment go well beyond Chrétien's *Perceval*, and well beyond what is strictly necessary for reasons of the action. They form a stylistic recognition of the social prestige of chivalry that doubtless met an audience taste. Second, the terms for this equipment are partly native German, partly borrowings from French, and this juxtaposition reflects the mixture of indigenous German components and modern imports from France in the material and the literary culture of the German aristocracy around 1200. Finally, although the action of *Parzival* is located in a distant past, the knightly equipment that figures in the text represents the latest in technical developments in Wolfram's day. (On the terms for individual items of knightly equipment in *Parzival,* see the useful commentaries by Zimmermann 1974, Noltze, and especially Nellmann 1994; on borrowing from French see Vorderstemann.)

The military equipment of the knight comprises in *Parzival* the offensive weapons lance and sword and, as defensive arms, the hauberk or shirt of chain mail (*halsperc*; the word *harnasch* is also used to designate either the equipment as a whole or the hauberk), with attached mail coif or hood (*hersenier/hèrsenier*), mail chausses (*hosen*), helm, and shield. These items formed the basic equipment of knights for around two centuries from the late eleventh century onwards until the widespread adoption of plate armor. However, within this general pattern there were many developments in equipment during the twelfth and early thirteenth centuries in the direction of a more complete covering of the body, a greater complexity of items, the emergence of small-scale plates, the introduction of horse armor and an increase in decoration. All these developments are reflected in Wolfram's *Parzival.*

Several small pieces of armor in *Parzival* show the tendency towards complexity and more complete protection. Two provide additional face protection. The ventail (*fintâle* 44,4; 575,19; also 260,12; 256,9) was a mail flap that was attached to the coif and could be fastened across the mouth. Wolfram is perhaps the first German author to use the word, though the item itself had been in use for some time. The *barbier(e)* (155,7; 265,29; 598,1) was a face-guard in the form of a plate with ventilation holes and slits for the eyes that was attached to the front of the helm. The item was introduced around 1180 and only came into general use in the first decade of the thirteenth century (see Blair 30). The earliest German attestation of this face-guard is an equestrian seal of Leopold VI of Austria in 1197 (see Bumke 1986, 214), and again Wolfram is perhaps the first German author to use the word (both these face pieces also appear in the *Lanzelet* of Ulrich von Zatzikhoven). Reinforcing plates attached to the knees, usually called *poleyns* by historians of armor, seem to have been a development of the early thirteenth century, and Wolfram is the first German author to mention them, as *schinnelier* (155,23) or *schillier* (261,18). The early stages of reinforced plate to protect the chest are obscure, but it appears often in thirteenth century German texts, as *plate* (Schultz, II, 47–48) and the one occurrence of the word in *Parzival* (261,26) is very early.

The surcoat (*wâpenroc*), a long, flowing fabric gown, usually sleeveless and worn over the hauberk, appeared soon after the middle of the twelfth century in Germany, and cloth horse covers (*decke, kover-*

tiure) are also recorded from the late twelfth century. Both these items appear frequently in *Parzival*. Protective armor for the warhorse in the shape of a mail cover is recorded in historical sources from the 1180s onwards (see Jackson, *Chivalry* 44), and *Parzival* is one of the earliest German texts to mention this feature (36,23; 261,13).

The decorative tendency emerges in Wolfram's treatment of helms and heraldry. As changes in helmet design covered more of the face from about 1180 onwards it became customary to wear a crest on top of the helm, presumably to help identify the wearer. Crests appear in German literature before the end of the twelfth century, and *Parzival* is the first work to present fully developed decoration of the helm (36,16; 39,16; 262,6 — see Bumke 1986, 216–17). In the same period the practice grew of decorating the rest of the knight's equipment with colorful matching emblems which could be applied to shields, surcoats and horse covers. This marks an important stage in the history of heraldry, and yet again Wolfram reflects the latest trends by introducing heraldic elements independently of Chrétien, for instance the emblem of the anchor on Gahmuret's equipment (14,12–28) and the dragon on that of Orilus (262,1–13 — see Timpson 91).

Defensive armor and offensive weapons appear in a variety of situations in *Parzival*, which will be discussed in a sequence leading from training and friendly display through the tournament to serious warfare and potentially mortal combats. This range corresponds to some extent to the complex role of arms in the real life of Wolfram's day, but while Wolfram draws on contemporary reality in his accounts of military activity he also subjects this activity to considerable literary stylization, and it is important for an understanding of his work to assess the balance and interplay of realism and stylization in the presentation of military encounters.

Training and the *buhurt*

The armor and weapons of the knight had become so complex by Wolfram's day that they could not be used effectively without training. The young Parzival's inability even to unlace the dead Ither's helm and knee guards (155,21ff.) marks with dark humor the cultural gap between Parzival's rustic upbringing and the world of chivalry, and his subsequent instruction at the hands of Gurnemanz (173,11–175,9) is a key stage in his mastery of the techniques of combat. Effective use of the couched lance called for particular skill, and Gurnemanz's military instruction focuses on this aspect, as Parzival learns how to hold the shield properly, how to accelerate from gallop to full tilt by applying pressure with spurs and thighs, and how to lower and aim his lance and position his shield correctly against his opponent's thrust. In jousting, the combatants usually aimed at one of two targets: the four nails visible in the opponent's shield, or the opponent's neck or face (see Schultz, II, 128–29 and Bumke 1986, 228–29). Both targets figure in *Parzival* (174,28; 444,18–20; 597,28–598,9; 739,3–6). Wolfram also frequently mentions the acceleration from gallop to full tilt which provides maximum force in jousting (37,21–23; 173,29–174,3; 262,1–22; 444,11–14), and the terms he uses for "gallop" (*walap*) and "full tilt" (*poinder, rabbîn*) are typical recent chivalric borrowings from French, with *poinder* first being attested in *Parzival*. Wolfram's jousting terminology indeed typifies general features of his treatment of military chivalry: modernity, technical knowledge and insider interest.

Jousting involved strength and considerable skill in controlling many physical variables in man and horse and, from a moving platform, focusing energy on one small point, the tip of the lance that was directed against a small area of a moving target — and this in an action that could lead to serious injury or even death. Wolfram's account of Parzival's learning to joust indicates that this form of combat was recognized as an acquired technique, a matter of *kunst* (173,20; 173,27; 175,9), not brute violence. However, Parzival also acquires a mastery of the joust with remarkable speed, which the narrator attributes specifically to his inheritance of his father Gahmuret's qualities (174,24). At the corresponding point, Chrétien speaks more generally of Perceval's success coming to him "by nature" (verses 1480–84 — Hilka ed.). In both works, the hero's prowess results from a combination of individual effort and inborn aptitude, and Wolfram lays a particular emphasis on the transmission of qualities from father to son in such a way as to provide ideological support to the aristocratic family structures that play such an important part in his work.

The topic of training and practice leads on to the role of the *buhurt*. The *buhurt* was a normal pastime for the knighthood of the twelfth and thirteenth centuries. It was a form of friendly exercise in riding skills and carrying arms in which groups of mounted knights rode against each other in jostling and charging movements that involved lance play or shield-clashing actions. Such maneuvers ranged from informal training sessions to more highly organized accompaniments of aristocratic festivities such as weddings and knighting ceremonies. The *buhurt* is never described in *Parzival*, but is mentioned several times as something that the audience takes for granted. The main features of the exercise in Wolfram's romance are its connection with social joy (242,4–5; 777,24) and its demonstration of equestrian skill, *kunst*

(623,5; 624,18; 777,23). The *buhurt* shows how intimately military display was woven into the fabric of aristocratic life in Wolfram's day, and in terms of narrative mood in *Parzival*, Wolfram plays on his audience's familiarity with the *buhurt* as a pastime of German knights so as to evoke the somber mood of the grail castle by referring to the absence of such joyful display there (242,4–5). (On the *buhurt* in general see Bumke 1986, 357–60 and Jackson, "Lance and Shield.")

The tournament

Tournaments emerged during the twelfth century, first in France and then spreading to other areas, as a form of mounted military encounter that combined elements of sport and war. Tournaments were prearranged encounters of knights who wore full battle armor and fought in groups with lance and sword; prisoners were taken and had to buy themselves free, and horses were taken as booty; and the tournament was banned by the church as a useless threat to body and soul. Tournaments also had elements of sport in that they were distinct from the blood enmity of feud; each side had a safe base to retire to; squires were used to drag horses off the field, but basically the tournament was a limited encounter of mounted knights in a supposedly friendly contest. Tournaments were thus far more serious matters than the more frequent *buhurt*, but more limited in damage potential than serious warfare. (On the tournament in general see the edition of Fleckenstein 1985, Bumke 1986, 342–79, and Barber/Barker 1989.)

Tourneying is a familiar activity of the knights in *Parzival*. Gahmuret insists on permission to tourney once a month (97,8) as a condition of marrying Herzeloyde, and he visits eighteen such events before seeking "harder," more serious battles overseas (101,21–102,20). Trevrizent, in his youthful service of a woman, preferred "wild adventures" to tourneying (495,15–21). Parzival undertakes many tournaments with his men as the young married lord of Brobarz (222,20–23), and towards the end of the work his prowess is marked by the list of his victories in "tourneying" (772,1–25). With this literary presentation of tourneying as a praiseworthy activity of young lords, Wolfram's grail romance forms part of a broader strand of discussion about the relation of chivalric enterprise and lordly duties in the literature and life of the aristocracy in the decades around 1200.

There is only one actual description of a tournament in *Parzival*, that called by Queen Herzeloyde of Waleis at her capital, Kanvoleis. However, this event is independent of Chrétien, it is one of the longest accounts of passages of arms in the work, and much about it matches the historical record for the early, warlike tourneys of the twelfth century. The tourney is called in advance (60,9–11), it is attended by knights from various lands, including British, Irish, French, and Brabanters (85,16–19), and the fighting takes place on a field beside the town, close enough to be watched by ladies in the palace (69,21–23). The combatants wear full battle armor, use lance and sword, and form two sides with different bases, the "inners" and the "outers" (79,8). (On the tournament at Kanvoleis see also Czerwinski 35–44.)

Feirefiz testifies to the importance of the lance when he speaks, towards the end of the romance, of "five lance-strokes" in tourneying (812,9–16). There is some debate about the precise meaning of Feirefiz's terms (see Nellmann 1994,781 and Barber/Barker 1989,197), but it seems clear that he refers to a head-on group charge (*zem puneiz*), a charge from the side (*ze triviers*), a joust one to one (*ze rehter tjost*), pursuit of the opponent (*zer volge*) and possibly to a tactic of awaiting the opponent's attack (*zentmuoten*). However, in the real tourneys of Wolfram's day sword fighting was also an essential feature, and Wolfram's literary account shows groups involved in both kinds of fighting. Knights enter the field in squadrons (*rotten*) under a leader and with standards as rallying signs (72,17–21). The fighting includes concerted lance charges by groups (78,4) and the characteristic cavalry tactic of charging through the opponent's ranks in order to break them up (72,2–8). Another typical tournament situation is the mêlée of combatants when the groups intermingle (69,11) in a combination of lance and sword fighting. A characteristic example of the tactics involved in the mêlée involves Lambekin, duke of Brabant, and Utepandragun, king of Britain (King Arthur's father). Each of these leaders is unhorsed in a lance charge, and then protected from capture by his men who gather around their unseated leader and shield him with their swords (73,29–74,19).

Captives and booty are taken in the fighting. At the end of the day Gahmuret has four captive kings in his pavilion (83,8), not to speak of the lesser men who have been taken, and whereas captives were a valuable source of ransom in real tournaments, Gahmuret shows his courtesy, his *zuht*, by releasing his captives without any statement of conditions (100,19–20). Booty is taken especially in the form of the horses of unseated opponents, which Gahmuret gives away in an act of generosity (72,13–16). The knightly combatants at the tournament cover a considerable social range, from kings down to knights of modest means, *armman* (70,8). Far from involving all participants in a state of social equality, the tournament reflects the hierarchical difference between great lords and lesser knights that was a major feature of German society in the twelfth and thirteenth centuries (see Bumke 1977, 130–48 and Jackson, *Chivalry*, 37–83), and the narrator's reference to the brave deeds of the lesser knights is typical of a note of sympathy for this level of society in *Parzival*. Squires, or *knappen* (69,13), are also mentioned on the tournament field, and Wolfram's audience would recognize these squires at work in the reference to knights being bruised with cudgels, *kiulen* (75,7), for this sub-knightly weapon was a characteristic piece of equipment used by squires to help their masters subdue opponents in tournaments.

It is clear that the tournament at Kanvoleis is, like real warfare, a form of group fighting. Moreover, whilst this event falls short of real warfare in its range and intensity, it is still a serious test of military strength and skill and a toughly fought encounter. Indeed the fighting risks getting out of control as tempers rise, agreements are forgotten and the participants set about each other in some earnest (78,5–12). This too has parallels in real life, for quarrelling and the breakdown of control were recurrent problems in the history of war games throughout the Middle Ages (see Barber/Barker 1989, 146–49 and Jackson 1995).

However, there is also much literary stylization in Wolfram's account of the tournament, not least in the way in which the narrative focuses on Gahmuret, who appears ironically as an unwilling victor. It is a poetic fantasy to have a queen offering her person and her lands as prize to the victor in a tournament, as Herzeloyde does at Kanvoleis (60,15–17), and this motif is treated with characteristically Wolframesque twists. For one thing, the fighting that takes place was supposed to have been merely a *vesperíe* (68,24), a warming up session before the tourney proper, but it turned so fierce that further tourneying was cancelled (86,21–24). Furthermore, as the victor in the tournament, Gahmuret finds himself caught between three women, all queens, and all with a claim on him: the beautiful mooress Belacane, queen of Zazamanc, his wife; Ampflise, queen of France, whom he served in the tournament; and Herzeloyde, queen of Waleis, whose hand is the prize at the tournament. Gahmuret tries to wriggle out of the obligation to marry Herzeloyde on the grounds that after all, it had only been a *vesperíe* and not a proper tourney (95,13–16), but the matter is put to an arbiter who reaches the decision that any man who fought in the passages of arms must accept the queen's hand if he is deemed to have performed better than anyone else (96,2–5). Thus an element of humor is brought into the narrative as the valiant Gahmuret, having left one queen, finds himself drawn into marriage with another, who uses precisely the custom of the tournament, at which

Gahmuret excels in a military sense, to take the great knight as her husband, almost against his will (though Gahmuret quickly comes to terms with the situation).

At a more serious level the tournament at Kanvoleis has the crucial narrative function of bringing together the pair who will produce the story's hero, Parzival. The tournament also allusively points forward in the narrative by being divided into two sides largely according to whether the participants or their kin appear as future friends or enemies of Parzival and Gawan (see Bumke 1991, 55–56). Finally, the tournament scene is rich in intertextual references to other courtly romances, with figures from the Tristan material and the Arthurian world appearing as participants, so that this event gives a certain historical perspective and depth to the narrative by sketching the father-generation of Parzival and by introducing figures from other romances as if they were part of a historically real world (see Draesner 177–84).

Collective warfare

Collective warfare plays a far smaller part in *Parzival* than in Wolfram's later epic, *Willehalm*, which treats war between Christians and Saracens. Over a third of the narrative in *Willehalm* is devoted to mass battles, which Wolfram treats with considerable skill and originality in his portrayal of tactics, and studies of warfare and battle descriptions in German literature of the twelfth and thirteenth centuries have rightly devoted more attention to *Willehalm* than to *Parzival*. However, collective warfare also plays a larger part in *Parzival* than it does in the Arthurian romances of Hartmann von Aue, and three situations of serious warfare are directly described in Wolfram's grail romance, one involving each of the three knightly protagonists. The circumstances leading up to warfare, the actual engagements, and the settlements that follow the hostilities are dominant narrative complexes in Books I, IV, and VII: in Book I Gahmuret becomes involved in the war around Patelamunt, in Book IV Parzival fights at Pelrapeire, and in Book VII Gawan fights at Bearosche. The encounter at Patelamunt has no equivalent in Chrétien's romance, and Wolfram also shows much independence in his handling of the other two engagements. All three situations show considerable literary stylization, for instance in the way that each arises from some disturbance in the relation between man and woman and has a strong focus on the hero knight who appears as a charismatic rescuer; and all three also show important features of serious warfare as it was conducted in the historical reality of the twelfth and thirteenth centuries. In addition the narrator brings brief accounts of collective military engagements that happen off-stage: the battle in which Gahmuret is killed (105,25–106,28) and the skirmish involving the forces of Arthur and Orgeluse (664,17–665,24; 673,2–24). (On battle descriptions in *Willehalm* see Pütz 90–160, Schäfer-Maulbetsch 111–36, 216–52, 576–722, Czerwinski 11–35, and Jones 1988; on such descriptions in romances, including *Parzival*, see Czerwinski 101–43.)

The engagements at Patelamunt, Pelrapeire and Bearosche all fit into one of the main military paradigms of Wolfram's day: the defense of a stronghold, with an attacking army trying to take the fortified place into which a defending army has withdrawn. Wolfram presents his protagonists in a favorable light by having them join forces with the defenders of the strongholds, and he draws the audience into an inside view of the three encounters by introducing each one through the perspective of the knightly protagonist, whose eyes light upon military features of the scene. On entering Patelamunt, Gahmuret sees the battered shields and wounded men and horses that speak of battle (19,20–20,3); when Perceval enters Belrepeire in Chrétien's romance the narrator describes the damage that has been done to church property and to nuns and monks (verses 1756–1765 — Hilka ed.), but Wolfram characteristically makes the perspective more military and subjective by omitting these references to church matters and having Parzival see a crowd of armed men and the town's fortifications (183,4–27); similarly when Gawan approaches Bearosche, it is an army that he sees, with its banners, painted lances and camp-followers (338,21–341,30).

The seriousness of the engagements is shown in the fact that, unlike the tournament at Kanvoleis, they result in deaths, although these deaths are referred to remarkably briefly (for example 19,26–30; 182,7–12; 194,21–25; 205,9–16; 386,15–18), and this is a matter to which we shall return later. In the encounter at Bearosche, Wolfram changes what was a tournament in Chrétien into a serious act of war in which a king attacks the town of his vassal, though there are echoes of Chrétien's portrayal in Wolfram's use of the word *turnei* (386,28; 387,30). All three encounters involve sizeable armies, which are especially large in the war in Zazamanc, where divisions are numbered in thousands of knights (47,12; 48,23) and come from various parts of Asia and Europe. The armies in *Parzival* show a mixture of family and feudal relations and mercenary service that is typical of the composition of real armies in the twelfth and thirteenth centuries. For combat purposes the armies are divided into smaller units of groups around a leader (*schar*, *rotten*), and standards and banners (*vanen*, *baniere*), and battle-cries (*krîe*) are used as means of recognition. It is typical of Wolfram's interest in military matters that banners and battle-cries, which had important tactical functions in medieval warfare, appear in unusually differentiated forms in his works (Zimmermann 1974,21–22, and 27–30).

The military operations at Patelamunt and at Pelrapeire are the culmination of long campaigns in which the attacking armies have burned and ravaged the lands of the defending party (16,14–18; 194,14–17) in a way that is typical of feud warfare in Wolfram's day, so that in each case the defending queen has been forced to withdraw into her fortified capital as a last line of defense. Truces in which military activities were suspended for an agreed period of time were a familiar feature of medieval sieges (Bradbury 310–11), and a day's truce at Patelamunt allows the burgrave to take Gahmuret on a tour of inspection of the sixteen city gates, each of which is defended by a prince who undertakes sallies with the men under his banner (31,17–19), and to inform Gahumuret about the military situation, for example about the importance of the defenders having taken a noble count captive whom they are holding as a bargaining counter — though they have rarely had such good fortune (31,20–26). These are credible features of collective operations around a beleaguered city. However, the resolution of the conflict at Patelamunt is highly stylized in the direction of a celebration of individual chivalry, for on the actual day of fighting that leads to the raising of the siege there is no portrayal of group fighting, instead the description focuses on Gahmuret's winning the day by undertaking jousts with leading men from the attacking forces (36,9–42,6). Battle descriptions in courtly literature in general are characterized by a tension between two potentially contradictory tendencies: the portrayal of conflict as disciplined collective action and the accentuation of special individuals, and this tension seems particularly marked in Wolfram's account of the military operations in Zazamanc (see also Czerwinski 143–150).

The hero still plays the decisive part in the battles at Pelrapeire and Bearosche, for at Bearosche it is Gawan's prowess, especially his capturing of the attacking King Meljanz (385,23–26), that provides the military basis for a settlement of the dispute, whilst at Pelrapeire it is Parzival's victory over the attacking King Clamide in a formal single combat that raises the siege and finally secures peace (213,11–28). However, more attention is also paid to group fighting in these two encounters than was the case at Patelamunt. At Pelrapeire, Parzival is shown leading the army of the city in close-contact fighting against Clamide's men outside the city gates (207,7–208,20). The defenders of Pelrapeire here work their way through the besiegers' army, killing the enemy's standard-bearer, who dies beside the king. The standard-bearer's proximity to the military leader in battle reflects his tactical function as a rallying point. The death of the standard-bearer is a sign of collective danger, Clamide is forced to call off the assault (208,15–20), and the narrator recognizes the importance of the collective effort by crediting the victory to the army of the city as a whole (208,21–22).

At Bearosche the main day of fighting is vividly described as a battle outside the city, with individual squadrons rallied by war-cries and standards, and the two sides so closely interlocked in a mêlée that at times manoeuvering is hardly possible (380,1–387,30). The interdependence of individual and group in the conflict is expressed for instance in the way in which Duke Kardefablet's men protect him with hard sword-fighting, to the accompaniment of war-cries, when he has been unhorsed (381,11–20) and Gawan leads a charge with his company and his host's banner to provide further cover for his exposed ally (381,21–27). Indeed the battle at Bearosche and the tournament at Kanvoleis form the longest and liveliest accounts of combat in *Parzival*.

The descriptions of the battles at Pelrapeire and Bearosche also differ from that at Patelamunt by bringing non-knightly combatants into view and presenting more detail about the tactics of siege warfare. With the list of armed men whom Parzival sees when he enters Pelrapeire (183,6–18) Wolfram includes in his romance in a passage independent of Chrétien the main non-knightly components of a typical defending force in a siege of the period around 1200. The only category of these men to be given a laudatory adjective — *küen* (= bold) — are men-at-arms or sergeants (*sarjande*). Such men are distinct from knights, but they are also mentioned with respect elsewhere in *Parzival*. On one occasion they are explicitly described as foot soldiers, *sarjande ad piet* (386,12), elsewhere the reference to their wearing armor (210,15; 214,22; 666,20; 681,21) may indicate a mounted function; in historical sources mounted sergeants first appear beside knights in the late twelfth century and references become more frequent in the early thirteenth century (Smail 107).

Beside the sergeants, Parzival also sees slingmen (*slingaere*), fighters called *patelierre*, archers (*schützen*), and merchants (*koufman*). The meaning of the word *patelierre* is obscure. It appears only in Wolfram's works and seems not to be a regular military term. Slingmen and especially archers were widely used in siege warfare, and the use of the pejorative adjective "arc" (183,9= "vile") to describe the archers conveys the prejudice of knighthood against the wielders of long-distance weapons (Hatto 1940 and 1945). The weapons carried by the merchants, axes (*hâschen*) and javelins (*gabilôt*), are also non-chivalric weapons — earlier the narrator has described it as a matter for particular grief that Ither was killed not in fair knightly combat, but by a javelin (159,5–12). The arming of merchants matches other military details (for instance Condwiramurs's comment that Clamide has ravaged her entire kingdom save for her capital city [194,14–17] and that half or more of her army has already been lost in the war [194,21–25]) to indicate that Condwiramurs's forces are in dire straits and have to call on their last resources; and this military extremity makes Parzival's achievement in rescuing the situation all the more impressive.

Pelrapeire is in an advanced state of siege when Parzival arrives, some of its inhabitants dying of starvation (190,29–30), and Wolfram exploits this situation to bring a brief but evocatively detailed account of defensive and offensive siege weapons which is again independent of Chrétien (205,17–206,4). The besiegers have brought various siege engines (*antwerc*) to bear, and Wolfram specifies these as siege towers or belfries (*ebenhœhe*), mangonels (*mangen*), hedgehogs (*igel*) and cats (*katzen*). Siege towers were normally several stories high and had the purpose of bringing attackers (for instance archers) close to the fortress walls; mangonels were stone-throwing engines; hedgehogs were probably a kind of battering ram; and cats were protective roofs on wheels that could be used to cover mining or battering operations. Two major tactics against siege engines were for the defenders to damage or destroy the engines by fire or by battering, and Wolfram describes how the defenders in Pelrapeire prepared spiked tree trunks that could be let down onto the attackers (205,20–24), and how they went on to destroy the siege-engines by using Greek fire (205,27–206,4). In this passage Wolfram thus sketches in the fictive world of his romance some of the main offensive and defensive tactics that were used in the real sieges of the twelfth and thirteenth centuries, including those conducted by German emperors and princes — indeed the basic techniques of siege warfare long predate the high Middle Ages and go back to Roman antiquity. (On siege tactics and weapons see Schultz 363–455 and Bradbury 241–95.)

The military situation that Gawan finds at Bearosche is different from that encountered by Parzival at Pelrapeire, for the dispute at Bearosche is of recent date, and the armies are only beginning to gather. Through Gawan's eyes, Wolfram not only evokes the magnificence of King Poydiconjunz's army as it marches on Bearosche, but also brings a non-idealizing description of the baggage-train and the camp followers: heavily laden mules and carts followed by a rabble of sutlers, camp women and vagabonds (341,11–30) such as frequently accompanied medieval armies in historical reality but are rarely mentioned in poetic literature. As well as knights, the attackers and defenders at Bearosche use men-at-arms, *sarjande* (351,10; 386,7; 386,12), the defenders man their battlements with crossbowmen (351,29), and the attackers use *turkople* (351,12; 386,9) in the actual battle. Turcopoles were lightly armed, mounted men, predominantly archers, with whom the Christian armies came into contact on crusades in the Middle East. The Frankish knights were not expert in this type of combat and they often drafted turcopoles for use on crusade, but they seem not to have been used in Europe (see Zimmermann 1974,93–96). Their introduction as mounted archers in *Parzival* probably reflects Wolfram's knowledge of crusading warfare, and it introduces an element of the threateningly exotic to the attacking forces as the turcopoles cause the defenders of Bearosche much harm with their arrowfire (386,4–9). The crossbow was particularly despised and feared by knights and it is characteristic of Wolfram's aristocratic perspective that he devotes far less space in his battle description to these archers than to the knights who fight with lance and sword. (On turcopoles in history see Smail 112 and Contamine 64, 70, 115.)

Wolfram also brings realistic details of military fortification when he tells of the army in Bearosche making last-minute supplementary defenses in the form of twelve redoubts (*zingel*), each of which was furnished with three barbicans for mounted sorties (376,10–14). The German word *barbigân* is another military term borrowed from French that is first attested in *Parzival*, and Wolfram's eye for the realities of fortification is shown in the way he refers to Gawan dragging his key captive into a barbican (385,23–26) and much later in the romance to the barbicans at Orgeluse's fortress (664,11; 673,9).

The military situations at Pelarapeire and Bearosche also bring illuminating insights into the role of the ruler as commander and into questions of tactics and discipline in combat. At Pelrapeire this dimension bears upon the destiny of Parzival himself. As Arthur Groos has observed (1995,104), Parzival's adventures culminate in kingship, and this destiny is foreshadowed when Wolfram diverges from Chrétien in his account of the events at Pelrapeire to have Parzival show his qualities as a ruler by organizing the purchase and distribution of provisions for the good of his people. So too in the battle Parzival demonstrates the authority that belongs to good generalship when he forbids his men to kill enemy knights who have been incapacitated and instead has them taken prisoner (207,17–26). Moreover, the good treatment he shows to the captives has a positive tactical consequence since it shows the besieged forces to be in good shape when the captives are released on parole to report back to the enemy (208,23–209,14).

In the encounter at Bearosche tactics and discipline are at issue in two exchanges of direct speech, one from each of the two sides in the conflict (354,28–356,25; 359,1–360,5). On Gawan's arrival at Bearosche the innocent Lyppaut has reluctantly walled up the gates of the town against the hostility of his own young king, and the scene looks set for a long siege. However, after the arrival of reinforcements Lyppaut takes counsel from men of good judgement who advise that they should change tactics, open the gates and take on Meljanz's two armies in a battle on open ground (*veltstrît*) rather than wait to be forced out by a long siege (355,26–356,25). Nor is this thoughtless battlelust on the defenders' part, for they base their advice on an assessment of the military strengths and weaknesses of the opposing forces, on the psychological point that their youthful king might moderate his anger if he is allowed to show his military prowess, and on the tactical consideration that the seizing of a hostage is always likely to encourage a settlement. The course of events shows the wisdom of this advice, particularly since Gawan's capture of King Meljanz creates the conditions in which a happy settlement can be made of a situation which could easily have led to a long-lasting feud.

The exchange on the other side (359,1–360,5) involves the question of military discipline and the pursuit of individual glory. The preservation of military discipline, for instance in insuring well timed attacks, was a major problem in medieval armies, where overall command was often difficult to exercise against individual magnates who might be intent on pursuing their own interests, and criticism of knights whose undisciplined attacks damage the larger military cause is a recurrent theme in accounts of warfare in historical sources of the twelfth century. Rahewin for instance records that in the summer of 1158, on Frederick Barbarossa's campaign in Italy, a number of nobles and knights from the imperial army, "laudis avidi" (= "avid for glory"), launched an undisciplined attack which resulted in deaths and captivities without any military gain, and which provoked a stern warning from the emperor himself that no attacks were to be undertaken without the direct command of a general (see Otto von Freising and Rahewin's *Gesta Frederici*). Similarly in *Parzival*, when Arthur's court is travelling in dangerous territory, the king forbids his knights to undertake jousts without his permission (280,18–281,8), and before Bearosche the aged, grizzled warrior leader Poydiconjunz accuses Duke Astor of Lanverunz of having acted out of vainglory ("durch rüemen") when he took his men into combat without waiting for his commander (358,21–359,14). In fact Astor defends himself with some reason

(359,16–30), but the exchange shows the precarious relation of individual and collective action in knightly warfare.

Finally Wolfram makes explicit links between the military operations at Pelrapeire and Bearosche and the present-day German world of his audience. The food situation in Pelrapeire prompts the narrator to refer humorously to "my lord the Count of Wertheim" (184,4), to fritters (*kraphen*) from Trühending (184,24–25), to his own modest circumstances (184,27–185,8), and to his willingness to serve as a mercenary when new provisions arrive (201,5–7). At Bearosche the surcoats of knights are brighter than taffeta from Regensburg (377,30), and the marching of Poydiconjunz's mighty army prompts comparisons with the Black Forest (379,6) and the vineyards of Erfurt which have been trampled under horses' hoofs (379,16–20). The reference to the vineyards of Erfurt must allude to the war between the Hohenstaufen King Philip and Landgrave Hermann of Thuringia, when Philip was trapped in Erfurt by the besieging forces of Hermann and his allies in summer 1203 (see Zimmermann 1974,253–256 and Bumke 1991,20–21). It seems likely that Wolfram had direct experience of this campaign, and it is possible that he was processing some of this experience in his account of the events at Bearosche. A further pointer in this direction is the fact that Wolfram devotes far more attention than Chrétien does to the relation between king and vassal in this episode, which was a matter of immediate political interest to a German aristocratic public at this time of troubled relations between crown and princes.

There is considerable stylization in Wolfram's presentation of collective warfare, and the evidence is too thin to allow a detailed reading of his military situations in terms of specific campaigns in historical reality. It does seem clear, however, that the presentation of warfare in *Parzival* opens the narrative to the real world around the German poet and his audience (see Mohr 1957,279), and contributes to the sense of an unusually wide-ranging "dialogue with the feudal world" (Stevens 1993, 244), that is one of the main qualities of Wolfram's work.

Single combat

Whereas mass battles play a major part in heroic epics, crusading epics and epics based on classical material, they are infrequent in Arthurian romance, and single combats form the main military encounters in this new genre of the twelfth century. In *Parzival* too, the most frequent type of military encounter is the single combat between two fully armed and mounted knights. Even in the collective military encounters, all of which figure in the first half of the work, attention focusses on the individual protagonist; and single combats form one of the most important compositional and thematic constituents of the work as a whole (though none is described at so great a length in its military aspect as the tournament at Kanvoleis or the battle at Bearosche).

The single combats in *Parzival* follow a basic pattern which corresponds to such combats in other romances of the late twelfth and thirteenth centuries and which is filled out to various degrees in individual situations (210,5–215,18; 260,22–266,2; 284,1–295,30; 444,1–445,12; 537,1–543,26; 597,16–598,13; 679,1–680,30/688,11–690,2; 703,30–704,19/706,5–707,13; 738,21–745,12). The combats begin with the most modern and spectacular passage of arms, a lance joust or series of jousts in which a number of lances may be broken and one or both opponents unseated. The joust is followed by sword fighting on foot or on horseback. The narrator's comment in Hartmann's *Iwein* (verses 7116–24 — Benecke ed.) that it is boorish for knights to use the sword whilst still mounted is an extreme idealization, for it was normal for knights to use the sword on horseback in warfare and in tournaments. In some cases wrestling forms a third and final phase. The encounter between Parzival and Duke Orilus (260,22–266,2) is one of the most extensively described single combats in the work and it illustrates all three phases, with Parzival finally overcoming Orilus by dragging him out of the saddle and forcing him into submission with a bear hug so powerful that it forces blood through Orilus's face-guard. (On knightly single combat see Bumke 1986,227–36.)

All the individual phases of knightly single combat had practical usefulness in collective warfare — recent work has shown that jousting, for instance, continued to be a practical training for warfare as late as the fifteenth century (see Vale 78, 118, 128). Nevertheless the single combats in *Parzival* are very different from serious warfare in their overall ritual. They are stylized cultural products which answered thematic and compositional requirements of a new kind of literature and which had a powerful ideological function in articulating and reflecting upon the self-consciousness of the secular aristocracy. The image of the knight riding alone and fully armed in pursuit of *aventiure* and engaging in potentially mortal combat with opponents he meets by chance is a literary motif. In real life, the equipment of the knight was so complex by the late twelfth century that he needed one or more squires, at least two horses for himself, and a further baggage horse or mule for the transport of arms and armor (see Fleckenstein 1977,103); and combat usually took place within the collective framework of tournaments or warfare.

The actual conduct of fighting also sets knightly single combat apart from serious warfare in that in single combat the participants often seem more concerned with honor than with victory. A classic example of this is Parzival's climactic fight against his own half-brother, when Feirefiz ceases fighting after Parzival's sword has broken because he says that it would bring him no honor to fight against a disadvantaged opponent (744,25–745,8). This combat was memorable enough to be portrayed in the illustrated Munich manuscript of Parzival a few decades after Wolfram's composition (see Schirok 1985, 10), and to be referred to as a model of chivalric fair play over two hundred years later in Hermann von Sachsenheim's *Die Mörin* (verses 4110–19 — Schlosser ed.).

The knightly combats in *Parzival* are also characterized by the avoidance of death, as the victor accepts the defeated opponent's surrender, his promise of *sicherheit*, rather than killing him as was more frequent in older epic traditions. The granting of quarter is sufficiently important in *Parzival* for the narrator to give it a place in Gurnemanz's teachings (171,25–30), to show Parzival consciously implementing this injunction in his combat with Clamide (213,29–214,2), and to refer recurrently to the benign practice throughout the romance. It is, however, important for an understanding of the ethical values of the military aristocracy in *Parzival* to note that whereas Chrétien has Perceval's mentor advocate the showing of mercy to a defeated opponent without formulating a reservation (verses 1639–1647 — Hilka ed.), Wolfram's Gurnemanz urges Parzival to accept a defeated opponent's submission and allow him to live, but with the qualification: "ern hab iu sölhiu leit / getân diu herzen kumber wesn" (171,28–29= "unless he has done you mortal wrong"). The "mercy" that Gurnemanz advocates is thus not the absolute Christian mercy that involves forgiveness even of an enemy, but a limited virtue that retains for the aristocracy the crucial right of retribution for a wrong done, even to the point of exacting blood vengeance.

It is a characteristic of the grail knights in particular that they do not grant quarter (492,8–10). Wolfram's description of the grail knights, the *templeise* (e.g. 444,23), is reminiscent in some ways of the Knights Templar (see Nellmann 1994,660–61), and it is likely that their refusal of quarter is a feature drawn from the harsh reality of crusading warfare. However, it is a norm of Arthurian romance for the knightly hero to show quarter, and this is the dominant pattern in *Parzival*, as all the leading knightly figures (Gahmuret, Parzival, Gawan, Feirefiz) are characterized as men who show mercy in single combat and in battle. (On the theme of *sicherheit* in *Parzival*, see D. H. Green 1978,26–30, 39–41.)

In the real wars and tournaments of the period around 1200 mercy was often shown with the pragmatic material purpose of exacting a ransom from the defeated enemy, but the granting of pardon has a more ideal, or socially and personally more constructive dimension in Wolfram's work. For instance Parzival makes it a condition of his granting pardon to Orilus that Orilus restores good marital relations with Jeschute (267,25–268,2); and as a condition of his pardon Clamide (who has earlier oppressed Condwiramurs) is sent to Arthur's court, where peace is made between Clamide and Arthur and where Clamide is betrothed to Cunneware (214,28ff.; 217,19ff.; 326,30–327,30). These two cases typify a strand of wish-fulfillment in *Parzival* in which chivalric combat leads to the restoration of personal and social harmony and to an enlargement of the aristocratic community symbolized in love and marriage.

The literary image of aristocratic knights fighting in single combat with the noble close-encounter weapons of lance and sword, removed from the vicissitudes of real collective warfare with its siege-engines and crossbowmen, and demonstrating martial and moral qualities, clearly answered the wish of an aristocratic audience for an idealized literary demonstration of its own privileged position. Indeed, the literary single combats of romance had a far-reaching influence on the aristocracy's self-presentation in military sports from the thirteenth century onwards throughout Western Europe in the practice of Round Table tournaments in which nobles and leading members of the urban patriciate undertook individual jousts in imitation of the Arthurian knights of literature. In Germany figures and motifs from the Parzival story appear especially in Ulrich von Lichtenstein's account of his journeying in the persona of King Arthur in 1240 and in a jousting festivity with the name of a grail that was organized by the Magdeburg patrician Brun von Schönebeck probably between 1270 and 1280. These chivalric events are parallels in the history of sport and festival to the celebration of knighthood in literature, as displays of military prowess that enacted culturally the claim of the aristocracy to social eminence. (On Round Table tournaments and the Magdeburg grail festivity see Schirok 1982, 152–57 and Barber/Barker 1989, 50–56.)

However, in Wolfram's *Parzival* the laudatory tone is also accompanied by a strand of reservation about aspects of military chivalry. This topic can be considered in a brief closing discussion of some ethical features of the use of armed force in the work.

The ethics of force in *Parzival*

In view of the considerable attention that has been paid by scholars to the moral and religious dimensions of Wolfram's *Parzival*, it is worth emphasizing that military prowess is highly valued in the text as a personal quality of the leading male characters, all of whom are, or have been, active knights. All the main areas of society represented in the work — the Orient, the Western world, the grail realm — place a high value on military competence. When Parzival himself is first introduced the narrator immediately draws attention to his having the quality of steel in battle (4,14–17). Parzival is so large that his birth almost costs his mother her life (112,5–8), he has exceptional physical strength as a youth (120,7–10), and once this strength is backed up by the skill in arms that he quickly acquires under Gurnemanz's tuition (173,27–175,9), his outstanding quality as a fighting man remains a fundamental characteristic throughout the work. Controversial as the grounds might be on which Parzival attains the grail, it constitutes a positive sanctioning of the profession of arms that God calls such a man to the grail kingship. Parzival, when he travels from Arthur's court to the grail kingdom in the closing stages of the work, is not transported into a metaphysical realm in which military prowess is no longer valued, but rather the narrator affirms this prowess in the vignette of Anfortas, Feirefiz and Parzival sitting in the presence of the grail as three of the best and bravest knights who ever bore arms:

> dâ sâzen dem grâle bî
> der aller besten rîter drî,
> die dô der schilde pflâgen:
> wan si getorstenz wâgen. (815,17–20)

It is true that Trevrizent, brother of Anfortas and uncle to Parzival, has given up chivalry in favor of the life of a hermit in order to atone for his sins (251,12–15; 823,19–22), but this does not imply a general moral rejection of military life, rather it is part of the pluralism of values, the variety of ways to fulfillment that characterizes the spiritual world of Wolfram's *Parzival*, as at the end of the work Trevrizent's withdrawal from chivalry stands side by side with Loherangrin's winning praise by his chivalry in the service of the grail and as ruler over Brabant (823,27; 826,6–8). (On the high evaluation of military prowess see Jones 1972 and Hasty 1994; on pluralism see Groos 1995,17–21 and often.)

However, Wolfram's grail romance also touches on darker sides of the use of force and the first point to consider in this connection is the role of killing in *Parzival*. The possibility of inflicting or suffering death was (and is) an ever-present feature of military life, the treatment of which in Wolfram's *Parzival* has elicited widely differing reactions from critics, ranging from the view that homicide is a problematical theme that shows chivalry in a critical light (see D. H. Green 1978), or shows a profound ambivalence in the proximity of guilt and merit at the very center of Wolfram's ideal of chivalry (see Ortmann 705), to the view that Wolfram presents death as an occupational hazard of military life without necessarily implying criticism of knighthood (see Hasty 1994 16–17). What is clear is that Wolfram shows a certain reticence on the subject of killing, for even in collective battles he refers to deaths only briefly or indirectly, and in the whole work only one act of killing is actually described in a single combat: Parzival's killing of Ither (Mohr, "Zu den epischen Hintergründen," 178).

This one act of killing has an important place in the narrative in that it is the means whereby the young Parzival becomes a knight. Moreover, Wolfram gives this act a greater prominence than it has in Chrétien and a different moral interpretation, for whereas the killing is not regarded as a crime in Chrétien's text, Wolfram has Trevrizent describe it as one of Parzival's great sins (499,20). Mohr is surely right to connect this new interpretation of Parzival's killing of Ither with the knightly perspective that characterizes Wolfram's narrative (1970, 347–48; see also Groos 1995,84–85). Indeed, the apparently contradictory features of Wolfram's general reticence about killing in combat and his foregrounding of Parzival's achieving knightly arms by an act of homicide are really the two sides of one coin, both conveying, in different ways, the knightly narrator's uneasiness about the ultimate danger of the military profession.

In passages of overt didacticism, in the presentation of character, in the theme of single combat, and elsewhere in the large-scale conduct of the narrative Wolfram also weaves a thread of discourse which indicates that military prowess is not in itself sufficient to guarantee exemplary status for the individual or to maintain social harmony without other ethical qualities and other forms of human interaction. A full treatment of this discourse would go well beyond the present contribution, but a schematic account of its range is necessary for a cultural placing of the theme of armed force in *Parzival*.

At the level of overt didacticism Parzival's military prowess is placed within the framework of an enhanced awareness of social ethics and religious spirituality in his conversations with the mentor figures Gurnemanz and Trevrizent (170,7–173,6;456,5–501,18). The civilizing dimension of these two conversations is signalled by metaphor and symbolic ritual which indicate a dual process of refining an inborn wildness and also stripping away acquired guilt, as Gurnemanz's advice is presented as a process of "taming a wild spirit" (170, 8) and Trevrizent's religious teachings are preceded by Parzival's taking off his armor — the armor he stripped from Ither's corpse — to reveal a clear shining skin (459,9–13).

In the presentation of character the limitations of military force are indicated in figures whose strength and prowess are accompanied by ethical deficiency. Meljacanz for instance is presented as a formidable and courageous warrior who is resolute in his pursuit of combat, *riterschaft* (344,2), but he is also a rapist (343,27–30), and the sympathetic, courtly squire who tells Gawan about him comments: "ine hôrte man geprîsen nie, / was sîn ellen âne fuoge" (344,8= "I never heard any man praised whose courage was not paired with decency"). The squire's words clearly show that the term *riterschaft* does not necessarily have moral connotations in Wolfram's usage, and can still mean simply, and without any idealization "military combat of the knight." Moreover, the squire echoes and intensifies the metaphor of wildness used to describe Parzival's untamed spirit by commenting that Meljacanz's warrior boldness is animal in quality, he is like a sow defending her young (344,6–7), and such a merely military prowess does not merit praise.

Ethically well above Meljacanz's level but still showing behavioral flaws in their pursuit of arms are three knights defeated in single combat by Gawan or Parzival in the later stages of the work. Lischoys Gwelljus is too proud to surrender to Gawan, and when Gawan allows him to live nonetheless Lischoys misuses his opponent's magnanimity by seizing his sword and starting the fight afresh (537,1–543,26); Florant, a princely knight in Orgeluse's service, is so confident in his jousting ability that he disdains use of the sword (596,16–30); and King Gramoflanz in his arrogance (*hôchvart*) normally insists on fighting at least two opponents at once (604,12–18). These three figures are part of a strand in Wolfram's *Parzival* that touches (not without irony and humor) on the problematics of knightly combats concerned solely with the accretion of personal glory (see D. H. Green 1978,62–66 and Bumke 1991, 102, 108, 118).

The limitations of military force are indicated in the large-scale project of the narrative in that it is a moral issue — Parzival's failure to ask the question that would have released Anfortas from his suffering — rather than a military matter on which the story hinges. In a typically Wolframesque way, this marking of the existential limitations of military force is echoed in a humorous manner and from within the realm of grail knighthood when Feirefiz, eager to be baptized in order to win

Repanse de Schoye, asks whether baptism can be won by fighting, to which Parzival and Anfortas smile (814,25–815,2). Finally, throughout the work the scenes of battle and combat are bedded into lengthy scenes of peace-making in which reconciliations are effected between enemies or passages of arms avoided by negotiations which often lead to the resolution of conflict by marriage. Leading examples of this tendency are the new, complex reconciliation scenes in which Gawan helps restore harmony between estranged lovers and between lord and vassal at Bearosche in the seventh Book (see Zimmermann 1974,7) and Arthur conducts the negotiations which lead to peace between Orgeluse and Gramoflanz and an avoidance of combat between Gawan and Gramoflanz in Book XIV.

In terms of literary genre the military dimension links *Parzival* to heroic literature, whilst the reconciliatory strand of the narrative has affinities with comedy. In terms of social ethics, the reconciliation scenes point to a world in which peaceful social interactions are highly valued beside military prowess, and this raises again the question of a historical placing of the work. The right and the ability of individuals to use military force was an important basis of feudal society, and the carrying of arms was a mark of the social prestige of aristocracy in Wolfram's day: professional function and social prestige are inextricably bound up in the narrator's commitment to *schildes ambet* in *Parzival* (115,11). At the same time social and political developments, not least the emergence of larger territorial lordships and the stabilizing of knightly and noble families along dynastic lines and by the heritability of feudal holdings, were lending socio-political and material force to the peace movements which had been largely ecclesiastical in origin, and in the increasingly complex situation produced by these developments, non-violent forms of interaction gained in prestige alongside the continuing cultivation of armed force in the culture of the lay aristocracy.

Arno Borst has written aptly of the period from 1100 to 1250 as a key period of transition between a largely untrammelled nobility and the power of the state (229). In terms of Norbert Elias's model of the process of civilization, this period saw the beginnings of the gradual transformation of the early medieval warrior to the courtier of the seventeenth and eighteenth centuries, though Elias rightly emphasizes in the second volume of his study that the knight of the twelfth century was still primarily a warrior (351–369). With its high evaluation of individual military prowess and of peaceful social interaction, Wolfram's *Parzival* gives literary form to both poles of the tension indicated by Borst and Elias within aristocratic society. Indeed, Wolfram's concern with the use of armed force contributes essentially to the richness and the immediacy of his grail romance precisely because it represents not a fixed and theoretical moral program, but a dynamic literary processing of the complex and changing cultural situation of the lay aristocracy by a narrator who speaks from inside the knightly world.

Wolfram is shown fully armed, with a pointed lance of battle, as a mark of his military profession. There is, however, no evidence to suggest that the axes on shield and helmet were a device of Wolfram's family in real life. (Manesse Codex, Heidelberg cpg 848, 149ʳ)

This illustration shows lances being broken and a participant unseated in a joust, as happen often in Parzival. *The three stunted points (the "coronal") on the tip of the lance were a development of the second half of the thirteenth century for jousts of peace. However, the illustration gives a vivid impression of the skill and physical force that were involved in jousting from its earliest time onward. (Manesse Codex, Heidelberg cpg 848, 61ʳ)*

Knights using swords in a tournament mêlée, watched by spectators. The participants grip their opponents' heads in a wrestling hold, and two of the knights have already lost their helmets and are almost defenseless. The illustration captures something of the roughness of the early tournament as Wolfram describes the event at Kanvoleis. (*Manesse Codex, Heidelberg cpg 848, 17ʳ*)

A scene of siege and the storming of a castle. The use of crossbows, stones, fire and axes matches Wolfram's siege descriptions. It is worth noting that the archers, whilst wearing mail protection, do not have the aristocratic helm and surcoat that is worn by the knightly figure who defends the castle with lance and sword. (Manesse Codex, Heidelberg cpg 848, 229ᵛ)

ALBRECHT CLASSEN

Reading, Writing, and Learning in Wolfram von Eschenbach's *Parzival*

AT THE END OF THE SECOND BOOK OF HIS famous treatise *The Art of Courtly Love*, Andreas Capellanus, royal cleric at the court of Paris at the end of the twelfth century, includes a brief Arthurian novella in which the male protagonist wins a hunting hawk from King Arthur after overcoming many difficulties during his quest for the love of his lady. King Arthur is so impressed by the protagonist's accomplishments that he not only lets him take the bird, but also presents him with a parchment on which all the rules of love are copied, saying, "You should take it with you and make these rules known to all lovers" (Parry trans.,184). Later, having returned home, the young Breton carefully studies these rules, and when his lady has accepted him as her lover and also familiarized herself with the teachings on love, she calls together a court of knights and ladies, instructs them about love according to these rules, and then hands over a written copy of them to each, thus disseminating this knowledge throughout the world. Although written in Latin around 1180–90 and probably intended for a learned, clerical audience, Andreas's treatise quickly became one of the most influential sources for vernacular courtly literature (see Karnein). As a text that is, in many respects, representative of late twelfth and thirteenth century courtly culture, Andreas's treatise presents with this novella a significant scenario of reading in which both courtly ladies and knights, all interested in the pursuit of love, are involved in reading and writing (see Allen 59–78). Reading is depicted here not just as a pastime, but rather as a detailed and extensive examination of the various meanings in a text. In Andreas's instructions on the art of love, reading is of central importance, indeed, it might be regarded as indispensable to the fulfillment of love. *The Art of Courtly Love* tells its readers surprisingly little in concrete terms about how to accomplish love and what forms courtly love should take (e.g., whether it should be adulterous — see Benton 30f. and Baldwin 16–25), but by employing self-contradiction, ambiguity, irony, and satire, Andreas forces his audience to develop a sharp sense for reading and the power of the written word, implying that the true lover must also be a good writer and especially a good reader. Thus, rather than illuminating us about what courtly love means in concrete terms (see Classen 1994), Andreas utilizes the theme of courtly love in order to emphasize reading as an epistemological process.

Wolfram von Eschenbach, renowned during his lifetime and today as one of the greatest medieval writers (see Wynn 1994), seems remote from the standpoint of Andreas. In the often cited words at the end of the second Book of his *Parzival*, the narrator Wolfram tells us "ine kan decheinen buochstap" (115,27= "I don't know a single letter of the alphabet") and that book learning will be of no help in understanding his story. In his typically ironic fashion, Wolfram sneers at those writers who derive their material from reading older texts, saying of his work:

> ê man si hete für ein buoch,
> ich wære ê nacket âne tuoch,
> sô ich in dem bade sæze,
> ob ichs questen niht vergæze. (116,1–4)

(Rather than have anybody think it is a book, I would sit naked without a towel, the way I would sit in the bath — if I didn't forget the bouquet of twigs — trans. Passage).

In another of his works, *Willehalm* (ca. 1218), Wolfram again stresses his illiteracy, charging that other authors simply derive their knowledge from books, whereas he has obtained it both from God and his own mind:

> mîn sin dich kreftec merket.
> swaz an den buochen stêt geschriben,
> des bin ich künstelôs beliben:
> niht anders ich gelêret bin,
> wan hân ich kunst, die gît mir sin.
> (2,18–22 — Leitzmann ed.)

(My mind feels the force of Thy Presence. / I have remained ignorant of what is written in books / and I am tutored in this way alone: if I have any skill, / it comes from my mind — Gibbs/Johnson trans.).

There cannot be any question about the deliberate ambivalence of such statements, for Wolfram displays throughout his work an extensive exposure to the clerical world of book learning and a knowledge of occult sciences (see Ruh 52f. and Groos 1995, chapters 7 and 8). Scholars have argued much about whether the author is being serious or facetious when he claims to be illiterate, but the truth might well lie in the middle, between the extremes of oral narrative traditions on the one hand and clerical literary culture on the other (see Scholz 199-202 and D. H. Green 1994, 190–194). Wolfram even implies both means of experiencing his text — reading and listening — in a single statement, when he submits his work to the judgment of women at the end of the sixth Book in this way:

> Nu weiz ich, swelch sinnec wîp,
> ob si hât getriwen lîp,
> diu diz mære geschriben siht,
> daz si mir mit wârheit giht,
> ich kunde wîben sprechen baz
> denne als ich sanc gein einer maz. (337,1–6)

(Now I know that any reasonable woman who sees this story written, if she is also true of heart, will own to me in truth that I can speak better of women than I did in the songs I sang to one.)

This playful, but deliberate dialectic of reading and listening is a major theme in *Parzival* that needs to be placed in relation to contemporary attitudes towards both of these ways of knowing. Andreas Capellanus is only one important voice among many medieval authors, among them philosophers and theologians, who argued strongly in favor of the idea of the book, and of close and careful reading, and who suggested that only a true reader would be capable of reaching higher levels of divine wisdom (see Classen 1996). Countless examples show that the idea of the book and of reading played an increasingly significant role both in the world of learning and in the public domain of law and government during the period of time that is often referred to as the "Twelfth-Century Renaissance" (see Clanchy and Haskins). Thomas of Celano (ca. 1200-ca.1255) includes, in his *Dies irae*, a reference to the Book of Judgment, or the Book of the Apocalypse, stressing that all human deeds are recorded on parchment and form part of a universal book, and in his *Vita* of St. Francis of Assisi, Thomas refers to the saints as having stated that every piece of written text forms part of the name of God. Hildebert of Lavardin (ca. 1056–1133) advises his audience in a sermon to write life's teachings into one's heart and to prepare the heart for God's teachings in the same way a craftsman would prepare parchment and binding to make a book. Alain of Lille (ca.1128–1202) metamorphosed the entire world into a book which the devout Christian had to read in order to understand God. According to Bernard Silvestris, writing around 1150, human history consists of nothing but pages in a book, and the true believer only has to turn his eyes towards heaven and study the pictures in that divine book to be illuminated about God's creation (see Curtius 315–20). The mystic Mechthild von Magdeburg stresses that in order to be properly understood, her text needs to be read nine times. Although her book is a material object, Mechthild depicts God as the source and the sense behind it (in what is, by the way, the first known significant text in the German vernacular by a woman author, *Das fließende Licht der Gottheit* [*The Flowing Light of the Godhead*]):

> This book is threefold / And describes only Me [i.e., God]. / The parchment which surrounds it / Describes My pure, white, and righteous humanity / Which suffered death for your sake. / The words which describe My marvelous Divinity / Flow hourly into your soul from My divine mouth. / The voice of the words describes My living spirit / And fulfills in itself the right truth" (Galvani trans., 56).

Increased book production and a new prominence of images of the book in illuminated manuscripts and stained glass as well as in sculpture and other art forms draw attention to the increasing importance of reading in the changing world of the twelfth and thirteenth centuries. According to Hugh of St. Victor (1097–1141), as Ivan Illich has argued, "Learning and, specifically, reading, are both simply forms of a search for Christ the Remedy, Christ the Example and Form which fallen humanity, which has lost it, hopes to recover" (cit. Illich 10; see also Camille 1985, 26–49, and Coleman). In 1286 the Bishop of Mende, Guillaume Durandus (ca. 1230–1296), energetically advocated the book as an essential vehicle for spiritual inspiration and learning, "because the apostles were perfectly taught of Christ, therefore the books, which are the emblems of this perfect knowledge, are open" (Camille 1989, 111). At least since the early twelfth century Christian theologians all over Europe defended the book as the single most important witness of Christ's coming and the promise of salvation, as it invited not only factual, but also allegorical and anagogical interpretation in contrast to the Jewish literal reading of the Old Testament "according to the letter" (Camille 1989, 115; see also the article of Hausherr). From the old cathedral schools to the new universities, the book embodies the spirit of an age. In the courtly romances, as we shall see, the significance of the book and of learning is expressed by the innovative portrayal of literary characters as readers and writers (see Scholz and Gellrich 51–93), and by the metaphorical understanding of ritualized events and sacred objects — in our case most notably Wolfram's grail — as special kinds of texts that have to be properly "read" and understood if the truth is to be known.

When Wolfram proudly announces his illiteracy (115,27), he would seem to be at odds with most of the authors of his day. Closer scrutiny of these words and of Wolfram's work as a whole suggests a different relationship to the spirit of the times. As is often pointed out, Wolfram's claim to be illiterate has a parallel in Psalms 70/71,15 ("quoniam non cognovi litteraturam" [= "because I cannot read written texts or numbers"]) and thus seems to be indebted to the clerical culture he seems to be rejecting. It is more than likely that Wolfram gained his knowledge of the grail romance not from oral sources, but from a manuscript, Chrétien's *Perceval*. Wolfram therefore read French, even if he frequently seems to misunderstand Chrétien's version and to err in his translation of it into German (although even this alleged shortcoming could have been more a deliberate ironic strategy than an actual failure on his part [Ruh 61–69 and Wynn 1994,189]). Apart from Chrétien's *Perceval*, Wolfram may have relied on other French sources and, as has recently been suggested by Bumke, on Celtic texts (1991,156–161). The wide range of source materials employed by Wolfram also suggests that he was a well-read person with a good command of Latin. Most notably, Wolfram reveals concrete and detailed knowledge in areas such as astronomy, lapidary and other occult sciences, theology, anthropology, and geography (see Bumke 1991,7–9).

This knowledge is exemplified by Wolfram's portrayal of the grail messenger Cundrie, who possesses thorough expertise in most of these areas of learning and also easily handles foreign languages such as French, Arabic, and Latin (see strophes 312 and 782). The fact that Cundrie is a *surziere* (= sorceress) and portrayed as extremely ugly may correspond to a patriarchal view of learned women as monstrous aberrations, but it need not be seen as an indictment of learnedness per se. Dallapiazza argues convincingly that Cundrie's physical appearance forces the spectator to penetrate the external cover and to "read" the inner truth of her person (419–421). Groos suggests that Wolfram's text reflects in the figure of Cundrie the power struggle between clerical and lay culture, as the latter was "appropriating contemporary Latin discourse on science and religion for vernacular narrative" (1995,169; see also Wehrli 1975,189–201). This struggle would only be possible if the lay audience had access to books and had mastered the basics of reading and writing, as Scholz has convincingly demonstrated for the German language area. In light of this we begin to understand why Wolfram insists so vehemently on being illiterate, for literacy was traditionally the exclusive domain of the cathedral schools and monasteries. Wolfram's claim serves to distance him from clerical circles and to associate him with a secular class of learned people. Although not a member of the traditional intellectual clerical establishment, Wolfram insists on having and conveying profound knowledge with his grail romance. About a century and a half later Boccaccio (1313–1375) takes a position very similar to that of Wolfram by rejecting the epistemological primacy of theology and arguing that secular poetry is not simply fiction (i.e. a lie), but rather that it also reveals, in its own way, fundamental truths (see the edition of Hardison et al.).

Another significant reader is Trevrizent, who teaches his nephew Parzival the essential lessons of the Christian religion and who, in a priestly fashion, gives Parzival "absolution" for his sins and takes these sins upon himself so that he can atone for them in his nephew's place. Trevrizent is described as a deeply learned man who studies books (459,20–22). Although Trevrizent has not received a clerical training and used to be a knight himself, he points out how much his books have helped him to achieve an understanding of God:

> doch ich ein leie wære,
> der wâren buoche mære
> kund ich lesen unde schrîben,
> wie der mensche sol belîben
> mit dienste gein des helfe grôz,
> den der stæten helfe nie verdrôz
> für der sêle senken. (462,11–17)

(Though I was but a layman, I could read the Scriptures and set forth in writing how man should be steadfast in serving Him Whose help is great and Who never wearies in helping the soul that may be lost.)

Trevrizent obviously perceives written documents — here the Scriptures — and, even more important, the ability to read them, as fundamental in the search for the ultimate truth. We have seen that very significant figures connected in different ways to the grail place a very high value on reading in the pursuit of knowledge. We have been able to surmise that Wolfram was very learned and able to read — despite his statements to the contrary — and we have yet to consider that he may assign a role to himself in his romance — that of a reader in pursuit of the truth among books — which is very similar to that of Trevrizent.

Perhaps the most significant instance of reading occurs when the narrator Wolfram explains how he gained knowledge of the grail adventure and the grail family. The first to discover the truth about the grail, Wolfram tells us in the ninth Book, was a man called Kyot (see 453,1ff.) who revealed it to Wolfram but also asked him to keep it hidden until the right time had come. Kyot is portrayed as a highly learned master who studied in Toledo and came across heathen writings containing "dirre âventiure gestifte" (453,14= "the first source of this adventure"). He could not, however, decipher the document until he had learned to read and write, "ân den list von nigrômanzî" (453,17= "without the art of black magic"). Whereas Kyot was a Christian, the author of the original account, Flegetanis, was not. Despite this, Wolfram is filled with respect for this mysterious heathen scholar, who was

> geborn von Salmôn,
> ûz israhêlscher sippe erzilt
> von alter her, unz unser schilt
> der touf wart fürz hellfiur (453,26–29)

(descended from Solomon and born of a family which had long been Israelite until baptism became our shield against the fire of Hell).

Flegetanis's greatest accomplishment was, as the narrator implies, the composition of the adventure of the grail, and noteworthy in Wolfram's description of the transmission of the grail story is that Flegetanis was not only able to read written words, but also the "script" of the heavens, which is to say the stars:

> Flegetânîs der heiden sach,
> dâ von er blûwecliche sprach,
> im gestirn mit sînen ougen
> verholenbæriu tougen.
> er jach, ez hiez ein dinc der grâl:
> des namen las er sunder twâl
> inme gestirne, wie der hiez. (454,17–23)

(Flegetanis the heathen saw with his own eyes in the constellations things he was shy to talk about, hidden mysteries. He said there was a thing called the Grail whose name he had read clearly in the constellations.)

In this way Flegetanis learned that the grail had been handed over to mankind by angels and that Christians had it in their guardianship (454,24–30), but the heathen scholar's written account of this remained secret until the next reader, Kyot, discovered it. Even as Wolfram elsewhere characterizes himself as illiterate, in his account of the transmission of the grail story he appears to advocate literacy as the way to obtain knowledge: basing himself on the written account of Flegetanis, Kyot discovers and researches the history of the grail family from the patriarch Mazadan to Parzival "in latînschen buochen" (455,4) and then in "der lande chrônica / ze Britâne unt anderswâ" (455,9–10= "chronicles of the lands, in Britain and elsewhere"). Although the narrator Wolfram does not explain how *he* got hold of Kyot's texts, the importance placed by Wolfram on writing and reading suggests that he must have *read* them. Even if the whole story about the genesis and transmission of the grail story is completely fictitious, the logic of this fiction seems to require Wolfram to adopt the role of a reader, despite his repeated, but probably facetious insistence on his illiteracy. To the extent that he portrays himself as the final link in the written transmission of the grail story, Wolfram is perhaps not so distant after all from his famous literary contemporary and rival Gottfried von Straßburg, who similarly claims to have learned about his story, *Tristan* (ca. 1210), by reading numerous sources before discovering what he regards as the definitive version of the Tristan-story (that of Thomas of Britain):

> sus treib ich manege suoche,
> unz ich an eime buoche
> alle sîne jehe gelas,
> wie dirre âventiure was.
> waz aber mîn lesen dô wære
> von disem senemære,
> daz lege ich mîner willekür
> allen edelen herzen vür,
> daz sî dâ mite unmüezic wesen:
> ez ist in sêre guot gelesen.
>
> (163–172 — Marold ed.)

(Thus I made many researches till I had read in a book all that he says happened in this story. And now I freely offer the fruits of my reading of this love-tale to all noble hearts to distract them. They will find it very good reading. — Hatto trans.)

It is consistent with Wolfram's probable position between orality and literacy that the most important kind of "reading" that takes place in *Parzival* is a metaphorical reading of signs, and not a literal reading of letters. The first such reading of signs occurs during Parzival's first visit to Munsalvaesche as a foolish young man who witnesses the appearance of the grail and marvels at the miraculous objects placed before him. Unfortunately, because of Gurnemanz's council not to ask too many questions (171,17), Parzival does not understand the spectacle displayed in the hall — the "text" as we might call it — although he beholds the bleeding lance, the general mourning and grief, and, above all, the wealth and wonders. The presentation of the grail and the lance, among other objects, is intended to make the guest wonder about this marvelous place and ask the redeeming question. But the staging is overdone, the splendid pages of this mysterious "book" overwhelm the "reader," and he fails to respond to the message contained in the pages that are opened for him.

This metaphorical understanding of the mysterious objects at the grail castle as a kind of text is consistent with the presentation of sacred objects in the church, where paintings and stained glass, along with theatrical performances of biblical events such as the Passion, functioned as substitutes for the actual text of the Bible. The splendor of high medieval church decorations was not only a form of propaganda, but also an effort to provide the unlearned flock with appropriate "reading material" (see Dinzelbacher 78f.). Understanding the grail as a kind of text is also consistent with the nature of the grail as described to Parzival by Trevrizent, which is as a kind of book for the grail community. In it the names of those who are supposed to join this community are inscribed:

> zende an des steines drum
> von karacten ein epitafum
> sagt sînen namen und sînen art,
> swer dar tuon sol die sælden vart.
> ez sî von meiden ode von knaben,
> die schrift darf niemen danne schaben:
> sô man den namen gelesen hât,
> vor ir ougen si zergât. (470,23–30)

(On the stone, around the edge, appear letters inscribed, giving the name and lineage of each one, maid or body, who is to take this blessed journey. No one needs to rub out the inscription, for once he has read the name, it fades away before his eyes.)

Wolfram here depicts a religious covenant between God and mankind in the form of the grail as a written text. To continue with this covenant, the grail community needs to read God's messages and adhere to His commands. If we turn to another of Wolfram's works, the *Titurel* fragments (ca. 1220), we find indications that Wolfram understands the grail as a kind of text that is comparable to the Ten Commandments, which were first communicated to Moses orally but then copied down by him (Exodus, 24:4). Whereas the Tables of the Ten Commandments are "the work of God, the writing was the writing of God, graven upon the tables" (Exodus, 32:16), in *Titurel* Wolfram shows us — here in the words of the former grail king Titurel, who remains a mysterious presence at the grail castle in *Parzival* — that the grail family, like the Israelites, is also instructed by holy texts in stone:

> dô ich den grâl emphienc von der botschefte,
> die mir der engel hêre her enbôt mit sîner hôhen krefte,

dâ vant ich geschriben al mîn orden.
vor mir was diu gâbe nie menschlîcher hende worden.
(strophe 6 — Leitzmann ed.)

(When I received the Grail by the authority bestowed upon me by the holy angel with his mighty power, I found all my commandments written on it. This gift had never passed into human hands until it came into mine. — trans. Gibbs/Johnson)

It is clear, then, that the grail is a kind of text, and that those who are called upon to protect God's holiest of objects on earth must be able to read.

The grail first appears to the uninitiated Parzival as illuminations of a sacred book appear to the illiterate person. He sees and is fascinated by the ornate "letters," but is unable to grasp their meaning. We might say that it is only after Parzival has received the education as a knight and Christian which he needs to assume the throne at Munsalvaesche that he is able to understand the meaning of this special text. With actions that are reminiscent of the liturgy, Parzival kneels before the grail, prays, and then performs the act of "redemption" by posing the long awaited question to his uncle: "œheim, waz wirret dier?" (795,29= "Uncle, what is it that troubles you?"). As if to stress the importance of a knowledge that can be obtained only from books, Wolfram has preceded this happy outcome of Parzival's quest with a detailed and lengthy list of precious stones doubtless obtained from a book on lapidary science (791,1–30). Once Parzival has asked the question, his ascension to the throne of the grail kingdom is marked by one of the final significant pronouncements of the grail as a written text:

da ergienc dô dehein ander wal,
wan die diu schrift ame grâl
hete ze hêrren in benant:
Parzivâl wart schiere bekant
ze künige unt ze hêrren dâ. (796,17–21)

(The election was made of none other than the writing upon the Grail had named for its Lord, and Parzival was forthwith proclaimed there King and Lord.)

Beyond these examples of literal and metaphorical reading in Wolfram's text, we also observe many characters in Wolfram's text, with Parzival himself being the notable exception, who are remarkable writers. Parzival's father Gahmuret, for example, writes a letter in French to his first wife, the black queen Belacane (see Mielke on the role of black women in medieval German literature), which explains to her the reasons for his secret departure at the end of the first Book. Although he loves her, as he writes in this letter, it is knighthood that entices him away from her, despite his declaration: "frouwe, wiltu toufen dich, / du maht ouch noch erwerben mich" (65,23–4= "Lady, if you will receive baptism, you may yet win me back"). Gahmuret, however, will never return, for he will later meet Herzeloyde and die in battle somewhere in the Orient. His letter to Belacane, which seems to anticipate his early demise, or at least the fact that he will never return to her ("und hân doch immer nâch dir pîn" [55,27= "I would yearn for you eternally"]) serves as a kind of birth certificate and family tree for his future son, Feirefiz, who will never meet his father and hence must be informed about his family background via this written document: "wizzen sol der sun mîn, / sîn an der hiez Gandîn: / der lac an rîterschefte tôt" (56,5–7= "My son should know that his grandfather was named Gandin and that he died from knightly deeds"). Only a close reading of all the events surrounding Gahmuret's departure reveals that he deceptively uses the religious difference between himself and Belacane as a pretense for his escape from their marriage, and upon reading his letter Belacane immediately contradicts Gahmuret's reason for his departure by stating: "ich mich gerne toufen solte / unde leben swie er wolte" (57,7–8= "I would gladly agree to be baptized and live as he desired") and thus refutes his insinuation of their incompatibility on religious grounds. Belacane hereby demonstrates that her intellectual skills closely match those of Gahmuret as she is in full command of French and able to read his letter (see the article of Camargo). Gahmuret's letter is clearly a bittersweet, passionate farewell, but also a very sophisticated epistolary document that reflects the literary accomplishments of twelfth-century laity.

Another written document that matches the literary quality of Gahmuret's letter is his epitaph at the end of the second Book, which glorifies his fighting abilities, his dedication to chivalric virtues, and stresses that he was loved both by Christians and Saracens. Although, as we have seen, Gahmuret had asserted in his letter that Belacane's heathendom was his reason for his leaving her, the epitaph emphasizes that "sîn tot tet Sarrazînen wê" (108,22= "his death was a grief to Saracens"), a people with whom he had spent a large portion of his adult life. On the other hand, the epitaph's claim, "er leit durch wîp vil schärpfen pîn" (108,20= "for women's sake he endured sharp pain") sounds rather dubious in light of what he did to both his first and his second wife, impregnating them and then abandoning them for the sake of chivalry. Consequently, this epitaph, also a masterpiece of writing, sheds significant light both on the knight and the writer Gahmuret, inviting posterity to learn about him by reading a document in which the knight's whole life passes before our eyes in a few lines. Both the letter and the epitaph hide as much as they reveal about this admired man. His beliefs remain very uncertain in both texts, as he clearly expresses his love for Belacane, yet leaves her because of religious differences. His Christianity is stressed — "er truoc den touf und kristen ê" (108,21= "he was baptized and supported the Christian law") — but it is said of him that he lost his life for the sake of the heathen Baruc (108,10f.). Finally, we learn: "er hete der valscheit an gesigt" (108,27= "Over treachery he triumphed"), but we feel very much reminded of his seemingly treacherous treatment of Belacane, who would have gladly agreed to be baptized and live as Gahmuret desired (see Mielke 103f.). The glowing way in which Gahmuret is put forward in this epitaph might be considered a reflection of the rhetorical skill of its unnamed author.

Gawan's expertise in writing is demonstrated by his letter to King Arthur and Queen Ginover at the end of the twelfth Book (625,16–30), which asks them to bring their retinue of knights and ladies to Joflanze, where he is to face the formidable Gramoflanz in combat. He masters the standard forms of polite epistolary expressions: "al den werden er enbôt / sîn dienst unt sînes kampfes nôt" (626,7–9= "To all the noble company he pledged his service and told them of the peril of his combat"), but also employs the epistolary form to impart crucial information about the importance of the presence of Arthur and his retinue at this combat for Gawan's reputation. It is again interesting, and perhaps indicative of the proximity of orality and literacy in the transmission of information, to observe that the dress, comportment, and words of the squire as he delivers the letter — non-written information that Wolfram describes in great detail (644,12–650,30) — seems to insure that the addressees pay close attention to the full significance of the message. As important as the non-written codes may be in this case, this letter proves to be a key instrument in the communication among significant members of the Arthurian court and indicates that literacy is indispensable to its integrity.

Besides Gahmuret and Gawan, other writers in *Parzival* are the French queen Ampflise, who sends a love letter to Gahmuret (76,23–77,18), Gramoflanz, who declares his love for Itonje (715,1–30), and Feirefiz, who informs his waiting army to send gifts which he wants to distribute among all members of Arthur's court (785,27–30; see Groos 1995,31f.). It is clear that the traditional intellectual wall separating clerics from lay authors was no longer in place at the beginning of the thirteenth century. The court literature of this time reflects a world in which orality certainly continues to dominate, but where literacy has become a much more significant medium of religious and secular knowledge. The community of writers and readers at the various courts that is mentioned by Andreas Capellanus was not therefore simply a literary device made up by a cleric who was addressing an exclusively clerical audience.

As important as written texts are in *Parzival*, it is clear that Wolfram was fully aware of the catastrophic consequences of misreading, false reading, or simply fragmented reading. As Wolfram seems to imply with the magpie imagery of his prologue, most things appear simple on the surface, but quickly reveal a disturbing complexity and ambiguity when they are studied more closely. The happy ending of *Parzival* is due at least in part to the ultimately successful attempt to understand a text: as we have seen, the hero ultimately understands the true significance of the grail. A darker hue of the magpie's plumage dominates in the later *Titurel* fragments. Although Sigune demonstrates that she is not only literate, but also capable of reading a story about two lovers that is embossed on a dog leash with jewels, she reads the narrative very hastily and ignores the initial warning, which also happens to be the dog's name: "hüete der verte" (Leitzmann ed., 143,4= "Keep on the trail!"). In her eagerness to find out more about what happened to the lovers, she unties the knot in the leash so that she can continue reading, and thus allows the dog to escape. This mistake is the beginning of her life-long misery for she does not "keep on the trail," but rather forces Schionatulander to pursue the dog into the wilderness and fetch it for her so that she can finish reading, and Schionatulander dies in his attempt to recover the dog and leash. In the end Sigune has lost both the text and her lover, and she even gives up her kingdom as she withdraws from worldly life in order to mourn the death of her lover. It is in this situation of mourning that she is already being portrayed in the presumably earlier *Parzival*.

In all of his narrative works it is evident that Wolfram was a witness to the rise of literacy among laity at the end of the twelfth century. He fully grasped its far-reaching epistemological significance in his subtle but powerful narrative references to reading and writing. He did not disregard oral narrative traditions, indeed he even claimed to be part of them, but he also allowed the written document to assume a divine function, fully in agreement with contemporary interpretations of the metaphor of the book as a representation of God's creation. True readers are the only ones who can, according to Wolfram, reach the grail, achieve salvation (see Curtius 315ff. and Sturges). In this respect we can identify *Parzival* as a challenge to the Church's claim on absolute authority derived from God, because the knights and ladies here appear, by virtue of their contact with the grail, not only as good readers and writers, but also as worldly clerics who know as much about God as the traditional ones because they have access to books, are learned, know how to read and write, and can communicate in many different languages.

In a way that is similar to Wolfram's conception of the grail as a divine book and the grail community as a reading community, Dante (1265–1321), some ninety years later, conceived of the book as a mirror of one's life and as a reflector of things divine when he composed his *Vita Nuova*: "In the book of my memory, after the first pages, which are almost blank, there is a section with the heading *Incipit vita nova*. Beneath this heading I find the words which it is my intention to copy into this smaller book, or if not all, at least their meaning" (Reynolds trans., 29). Dante turns more to his own self, his personal life, and metamorphoses it into a book, but both Wolfram and Dante fully grasped the significance of the book as the ultimate catalyst for self experience and the experience of God, the original creator and scribe.

WINDER MCCONNELL

Otherworlds, Alchemy, Pythagoras, and Jung: Symbols of Transformation in *Parzival*

IN HIS TIMELY AND HIGHLY SIGNIFICANT WORK, *The Western Canon*, Harold Bloom cites only one Arthurian romance from the German High Middle Ages in Appendix A: "The Theocratic Age," namely, Wolfram von Eschenbach's *Parzival* (500). There is a compelling reason to include it among the works which, in Bloom's opinion, constitute an integral part of Western culture. By no means limited to the historical parameters of the High Middle Ages, Wolfram's romance presents, in many respects, the predicament of modern man, of man at any time in any historical context. It depicts him at his best and at his worst, but the vision that it ultimately holds out for him is one of hope and salvation, one in which (perhaps in contrast to the view that Wolfram's and Gottfried von Straßburg's ethics and aesthetics were diametrically opposed to one another) the intent is ultimately to address, and perhaps even *accept*, the duality of good and evil, of joy and suffering, to establish or re-establish a balance of both within the Arthurian world, in particular, and the cosmos in general.

If one were to employ the catchword "relevant" so popular over the past three decades, then the presence of the Parzival figure in the person of Luke Skywalker in the recently revived *Star Wars* trilogy directed by George Lucas should underscore to anyone familiar with the medieval legend just how vital both the character of Parzival and his "development" have remained throughout the ages. (For George Lucas, who had more than a nodding acquaintanceship with Joseph Campbell, it could scarcely have been otherwise!) As was the case with his medieval precursor, Luke Skywalker has his encounter with the "other," both in a physical and metaphysical sense, in a process of maturation which involves encounters with indispensable mentors of both sexes, otherworlds, periods of depression and desperation, doubt, and ultimate triumph. Both *Parzival* and *Star Wars* are, to use C. G. Jung's term, "visionary" works of art, based on "primordial experiences" that "rend from top to bottom the curtain upon which is painted the picture of an ordered world, and allow a glimpse into the unfathomable abyss of the unborn and of things yet to be" (Jung 1972,90–91).

Part of what might be called the hero's maturation process, in terms of analytical psychology his "process of individuation," is the passage through uncivilized (here: uncourtly) geography with which he is unfamiliar and which presents him with formidable obstacles to his further development. These may take the form of external adversaries such as knightly opponents, as well as life-threatening encounters with beasts of prey, giants, dragons, and other mythological creatures, but they may also consist of internal demons, repressed or denied elements of the hero's own psyche which need to be recognized, combatted, and defeated before the hero can proceed on his ultimate journey. Overcoming them is part of the archetypal quest faced by the hero. The geographical setting for such encounters is normally far removed from the (Arthurian) court: traditionally, the forest, an enchanted castle, or an island (often at the periphery of the then known world). Wolfram's *Parzival* abounds in such "otherworldly" landscapes. The entry into or sojourn of the hero in the physical otherworld corresponds to a psychic transformation of great significance for his process of individuation.

It is important to understand from the outset what is meant by the concept of the otherworld with respect to *Parzival*. One could argue that, in the medieval imagination at least, the entire Arthurian world constituted something of an "otherworld," a mythical or semi-mythical realm unfettered by either historical time or place, a stark contrast to the reality of the time. Unlike works such as *Herzog Ernst*, *Kudrun*, and the *Nibelungenlied*, the major otherworldly landscapes in *Parzival* are not "located" in distant lands, far apart from the primary area of events. Prudence must be exercised with regard to the term "located," as otherworlds, whether of a benevolent or of a malevolent nature, are rarely phenomena which can be geographically "fixed." Within the romances themselves, Arthur's world, or court, appears to be consistently on the move, setting it apart from places such as Graharz and Pelrapeire, and according it a certain affinity to Schastel Marveile or Munsalvaesche. All of these "otherworlds" are, above all, places of formation or transformation of the hero, where the given expectations and patterns of the rest of courtly society either do not exist, have been suspended, destroyed, or, as in the case of Arthur's court, are elevated (sometimes unjustifiably) to utopian levels. The otherworld may thus be inherently positive in nature, a veritable *locus amoenus* — which is not to suggest, however, that it is entirely unproblematical — or it may be the antithesis of the latter, a haven for every conceivable force that stands in an adversarial relationship to the court. Above all, the otherworld should be seen as representing something far removed from "normalcy" as understood by both the protagonist and his medieval audience. My own thoughts on the matter of the otherworld and its importance in *Parzival* as well as other works of medieval literature owe much to the work of C. G. Jung, Mircea Eliade, and Ernst Dick, whose article "*Katabasis* and the Grail Epic: Wolfram von Eschenbach's *Parzival*" (1978), remains an indispensable resource for scholars concerned with this topos in *Parzival*. The current study differs from Dick's focus in that I am less concerned with the topography of the journeys to the otherworld than with the make-up and (symbolic) nature of otherworldly realms per se, in particular as the latter pertain to what I believe was Wolfram's extensive knowledge of alchemy and numerology.

The realistic and the fantastic commingle in Wolfram's *Parzival*, especially with respect to the movement of the two major protagonists, Parzival and Gawan, between the courtly world and the non-courtly sphere. Even when places do not appear to have any equivalent in historical geography — such as the kingdom of Zazamanc and the town of Patelamunt in the first of the two Gahmuret Books — a realistic description of events which transpire there is provided by Wolfram, who appears eager to delight his readers with the exotic nature of its inhabitants. Yet, the common denominator, knighthood, links such unfamiliar "otherworlds" as Baghdad, Patelamunt, and Zazamanc with European knightly culture: "Knighthood . . . is practiced everywhere, and by stressing that point the hero pays high tribute to his own cherished social class" (Mustard/Passage trans., xlv–xlvi). Among the Moors of Baghdad, Gahmuret appears as much at home as he would have been among his fellow Angevins, and his subsequent offer of service to Belacane is quite in keeping with the dictates of feudal society in western Europe. Even the forest of Azagouc, in which Belacane's suitor, Isenhart, together with his challenger from Patelamunt, Prothizilas, meets his death, is described in the most succinct and matter-of-fact manner: "dâ grôz schade in niht vermeit. / zem fôrest in Azagouc" (27,28–29= "in the forest of Azagouc he found no mock death" [Mustard/Passage trans.]). There is nothing here of the image of the forest as one of those geographical locations "on the extreme fringes of society," in contrast to the "organized world" (Le Goff 1988, 56 and 58). Patelamunt is also clearly a place where East and West, more precisely, Christian and Moor, come together in a symbolic way. Apart from the subsequent liaison between Gahmuret and Belacane, the issue of whose union is the bi-racial Feirefiz, Belacane's dead suitor, Isenhart, is the son of the maternal uncle of the king of Scots. This is, perhaps, to be viewed as indicative of Wolfram's relatively high level of tolerance towards the "other" (Bertau 241–258) — it may also be indicative of his constant endeavor to integrate opposites — and Belacane's court is certainly the equivalent of anything to be found in the West.

While I have concentrated in the following on the forest of Soltane (which may be considered by some as less in keeping with the epithet "otherworldly"), Munsalvaesche, and Schastel Marveile, these are by no means the only landscapes with otherworldly features in *Parzival*. Ernst Dick has already demonstrated those properties for Trevrizent's realm as it appears to us in the ninth Book, and much could be said in this regard concerning various other terrains in the work with their waterfalls, rivers, ravines, enchanted gardens, caves, and forests. A systematic investigation of all the otherworldly landscapes in *Parzival* remains a most worthwhile desideratum.

Herzeloyde's decision to retire to the clearing in the forest of Soltane is motivated by her intent to remove Parzival as much as possible from the milieu of the knight. It has been discussed at length by previous scholars and need not be dealt with again here. We are more concerned with the alienation of Herzeloyde herself from courtly society and the nature of the locale to which she removes herself and her son (117,4–9). With the death of Gahmuret, Herzeloyde's bond to courtly society is irrevocably destroyed. She will never return: "frou Herzeloyd diu rîche / ir drîer lande wart ein gast" (116,28–29= "Lady Herzeloyde, the mighty, became a stranger to her three kingdoms"). Yet, in the context of this alienation, the narrator praises her sincerity, her lack of falsity: "der valsch sô gar an ir verswant, / ouge noch ôre in nie dâ vant" (117,1f.= "Falsity had so utterly vanished from her heart that neither eye nor ear could detect it"). The move to Soltane is prompted, however, by the extreme, one might say absolute, sorrow that she perceives following the death of her husband. As the one locale which represents the antithesis of courtly society, the forest may be seen, paradoxically, not as a place of foreboding, but rather of refuge: "si brâhte dar durch flühtesal / des werden Gahmuretes kint" (117,14–15= "And there, for refuge, she brought noble Gahmuret's child"). The sojourn in Soltane comes at the conclusion of Herzeloyde's life, whereas it represents the place where Parzival spends his first, formative years. It is a topsy-turvy world deliberately deprived, by Herzeloyde, of the essentials of courtly existence (see Schröder 1963,13). The forest bestows upon Parzival the status of an outsider (see Stauffer 105).

Uninitiated into the ways of the court and its decorum, but quite at home in the ways of nature and himself the apogee of natural spontaneity, Parzival becomes the conveyor of chaos in the world outside the forest. His is a state of less than benign ignorance. Herzeloyde's actions in the forest appear to go beyond "protecting" her child from knighthood. Although it might be assumed that her association of the birds' singing with her son's unhappiness causes her to order her retainers to capture and kill the culprits (119,2–4), there is the enigmatic statement by the narrator to the effect that she does not seem to understand precisely *why* she is directing her hatred against the birds: "sine wesse um waz" (118,30= "without quite knowing why"). As her subsequent comment to Parzival demonstrates ("wes wende ich sîn gebôt, / der doch ist der hœhste got?" [119,13–14= "Why should I alter His commandment Who is, after all, Supreme God?"]), Herzeloyde appears to comprehend that her behavior represents a transgression against the natural and sacred order of things. It is intriguing that Herzeloyde recognizes that her instructions to have the birds killed are ill-conceived. But was not her decision to have Parzival removed to Soltane an equally questionable act that must be interpreted as a violation of the natural *ordo*? The Soltane episode is ultimately characterized by spiritual or psychological chaos, with Herzeloyde acting as both the confused — consider again 117,5: "ir was gelîch naht unt der tac" (= "To her night and day were the same") — and the confuser, as she provides Parzival with fragmentary information that predetermines his naive identification of the material and transitory (Karnahkarnanz and his vassals) with the transcendent and eternal (God). His "natural" development as a member of chivalrous society outside the otherworldly atmosphere of Soltane is impeded by a more primal "naturalness," although the time spent by Parzival as a "country bumpkin" may also be viewed as a necessary prerequisite to his ascension to the grail throne (on the contradictions involved in the Soltane episode, see Schröder 1963, 15). Parzival receives information, regarding both the world and the nature of God, which is without a proper contextual basis and which must inevitably lead to confused behavior when he attempts to "re-enter" courtly society. At the same time, Soltane is the place of Parzival's first exposure to a mentor, in the person of his mother; but it is in a thoroughly unenlightened state that he leaves the forest, and one of the consequences of his having been raised there, without the benefit of courtly breeding, combined with his ignorance and youthful zeal (as well as his purely "natural" spontaneity), is the chaos which subsequently erupts in the Arthurian world.

One final point may be made about the sojourn in Soltane which is of considerable relevance for the later psychic development of Parzival. His early years spent in Soltane are devoid of a masculine-feminine balance. The "quest" for the grail, with which he is most understandably and justifiably associated, is chronologically, at least, secondary to his subconscious quest for his father — who is, of course, totally missing, even in surrogate form, during the time he spends in Soltane — and later on to his desire, prominent after his marriage to Condwiramurs, to return to his mother (which may be seen to take on symbolic realization through his final return to the grail). In the case of the former, the initial surrogate father-figure is Arthur, but Gurnemanz, Anfortas, and Trevrizent also have contributions to make as "foster-fathers" to Parzival, with the first two providing secular, physical guidance or encouragement, the latter two being concerned with his spiritual well-being. It is, perhaps, no coincidence that these father-figures constitute a tetralogy. Wolfram, as we shall observe, makes copious use of the number four and multiples of four throughout his romance, undoubtedly because he was fully aware of the symbolic significance that the numeral represents and its consequent relevance for the major theme of his work. Paralleling them on the feminine side are the four most significant women in Parzival's life: Herzeloyde, Condwiramurs, Sigune, and Cundrie. Here, too, the tetralogy consists of two women who are primarily concerned with the secular world (Herzeloyde, despite her denial of Parzival's innate knightly qualities, and Condwiramurs), and two who are indispensable to his spiritual development (Sigune and Cundrie). When he departs Soltane, Parzival cuts himself off forever from his physical mother, who embodies aspects of both the Great Mother and the Terrible Mother (see Neumann and Jung 1989), but much of his time thereafter will also be spent attempting to re-establish the connection to the feminine. Underlying his movement through time and space in the period to follow (which often appears to be timeless) is a psychological striving for wholeness and unity, ultimately culminating in his accession to the grail kingship.

Of the various otherworldly landscapes in *Parzival*, Munsalvaesche and Schastel Marveile constitute two of the most prominent and enigmatic. While Munsalvaesche, as the host castle of the grail, is most assuredly to be regarded as ultimately positive in nature, Schastel Marveile constitutes a negative pole that requires either dissolution or re-integration into courtly society. Both worlds have overseers who are sexually incapacitated, both appear to lack any firm anchorage in a geographical sense, a state of disorder reigns within each sphere that also has an influence on the Arthurian world at large. That "disorder" can be traced in each instance to the sexual indiscretions or improprieties of the respective rulers of these domains: Anfortas and Clinschor. Munsalvaesche and Schastel Marveile have become wastelands, as the landscape around the former, in particular, underscores, yet both offer the heroes Parzival and Gawan the opportunity to restore harmony not only within the otherworlds themselves, but also within courtly society in general.

Parzival departs from Condwiramurs and Pelrapeire ostensibly to see how his mother is faring and to seek "âventiure" for the sake of his wife (223,17–25). Herzeloyde is dead, however, and so Parzival's search for his mother takes on a metaphysical hew. Now ruler of Brobarz and savior/defender of the people of Pelrapeire, his attention turns from the assertion of his masculinity to the cultivation of his feminine side. This will prove more arduous in the long run than his development as a warrior and knight, which came to him quite naturally, after some refining by Gurnemanz. The path that he takes now is one he must take alone ("von allen sînen mannen / schiet er al eine dannen" [223,29–30= "From all his vassals he then took his leave and rode away alone"]), and it is one with which he is completely unfamiliar, as the lack of guidance he provides his mount underscores: "mit gewalt den zoum daz ros / truog über ronen und durchez mos: / wandez wîste niemens hant" (224,19–21= "The horse pulled the dragging reins over fallen trees and through marshy land, for no one's hand guided it"). While the experiences of Parzival in Pelrapeire and his marriage to Condwiramurs may appear, on the surface, to have provided him with a central axis, he is, in essence, quite lost, a novice on the path of individuation. Parzival gives himself over to being guided, and enters a realm which no longer adheres to the norms of time and space:

> uns tuot diu âventiure bekant
> daz er bî dem tage reit,
> ein vogel hetes arbeit,
> solt erz allez hân erflogen. (224,22–25)

(The story tells us that on that day he rode so far that a bird could only with difficulty have flown all that way.)

This move from Brobarz to the area of Munsalvaesche effectively transports Parzival from the anchor of a court, replete with obligations incumbent upon him as a ruler and husband to Condwiramurs, to the ethereal regions of the grail otherworld. As Emma Jung and Marie-Louise von Franz have stated: " . . . it seems legitimate to treat the whole episode as a dream or as a descent into the collective unconscious" (Jung/von Franz 69). While Parzival may have left Condwiramurs to search out his mother, it is not she, at least not in person, whom he finds in this part of the romance, but rather father-figures, who are, in fact, related to him through his mother: Anfortas, his uncle, and Frimutel, his grandfather.

The grail world is imbued with diverse and rich forms of symbolism, but those associated with the idea of wholeness/unity are particularly striking. Ernst Dick's depiction of the realm of the grail as "a symbolic center" (Dick 71) is supported not only by the thematic "polarity of life and death" (Dick 70) to be discerned there, but also by symbols of wholeness and unity which abound in the description Wolfram provides of the area and its remarkable rituals. Similarly, Jung and von Franz underscore the significance of Anfortas's world as a "projection of the Self as an inner centre, extending far beyond the ego, which expresses wholeness and harmony and from which radiate healing, integrating influences" (333). When Parzival first encounters the grail king on the lake, Anfortas is wearing a remarkable hat: "sîn huot was pfâwîn" (225,12= "His hat was trimmed with peacock feathers"). Peacock feathers, specifically, the multi-colored spectrum which they present when unfolded, are a symbolic manifestation of completeness: "The peacock's tail, in particular, appears in the eighty-fourth emblem of the *Ars Symbolica* of Bosch as a symbol for the blending together of all colours and for the idea of totality" (Cirlot 251). Anfortas is not the only one in *Parzival* whose hat is adorned with peacock feathers. Cundrie sports the latest fashion from London when she arrives at Arthur's court to admonish Parzival and the Round Table: "von Lunders ein pfæwîn huot, / gefurriert mit einem blîalt / (der huot was niwe, diu snuor niht alt)" (313,10–12= "A hat from London, trimmed with peacock plumes and lined with cloth of gold — the hat was new and the tie ribbon was not old"). When Gawan encounters King Gramoflanz in the twelfth Book, the latter is also wearing a hat of peacock feathers: "phæwîn von Sinzester / ein huot ûf sîme houbte was" (605,8–9= "The hat on his head was of peacock plumes from Sinzester"). Similar images of totality abound throughout Wolfram's tale. This color symbolism is complemented by number symbolism: the grail castle is separated from the rest of mankind by a circumference of thirty miles (225,20–21), i.e., 3 x 10, both integers underscoring unity and the divine. This number is repeated in 231,25 to describe the number of lands which could not have produced as many tears as those wept by the grail company when the lance is carried into the Great Hall by a squire. It is especially in the Great Hall of Munsalvaesche that such number symbolism is in evidence: a hundred (10 x 10) chandeliers are alight with candles (229,24), a hundred couches have been set up

(229,28), and a hundred blankets adorn them (229,30), with a carpet (a total of one hundred) before each couch (230,2). They can accommodate four knights apiece (230,1), making a total of four hundred and permitting an association with the number of women captives referred to in Schastel Marveile. The number four is the number in the Middle Ages most often used to denote completeness or unity. Referring to the work of Ludwig Paneth, Cirlot observes that "*Four*, as a kind of double division (two and two), no longer signifies separation (like the number two) but the orderly arrangement of what is separate. Hence, it is a symbol of order in space and, by analogy, of every other well-ordered structure" (Cirlot 235). The Great Hall also contains three great fireplaces — three being symbolic of "spiritual synthesis ... the solution of the conflict posed by dualism" (Cirlot 232).

In the grail procession, described in remarkable detail, the countess of Tenabroc and her companion, along with an unnamed duchess and her companion, appear to form a natural grouping of four: "die nigen alle viere ... / und wâren alle wol gevar. / den vieren was gelîch ir wât" (233,5-11= "They bowed, all four ... all four dressed alike and fair to see"). Furthermore, the accent is on four and two in the description of the ladies who follow them: "nû seht wâ sich niht versûmet hât / ander frouwen vierstunt zwuo" (233,12f.= "But look how quickly they have been joined by more ladies, four times two"). Four of them are carrying candles (233,15), while the second group of four carries a brilliant hyacinth (233,17ff.). All eight women bow graciously to their host, following which the narrator again comments on the activity of four of them who then rejoin the other quartet:

> viere die taveln legten
> ûf helfenbein wîz als ein snê,
> stollen die dâ kômen ê.
> Mit zuht si kunden wider gên,
> zuo den êrsten vieren stên. (233,28–234,2)

(Four laid the table top on the snow-white ivory of the stools placed there before, and stepped back decorously to stand with the first four.)

They are followed by four maidens holding candles (234,28), and after them there approach two princesses, the daughters of foreign counts, who carry two magnificent knives (234,16ff.). The procession is rounded out by six more ladies (235,8) and finally by Repanse de Schoye who enters the hall carrying the grail (235,25f.). She assumes a position between two flanking groups of twelve ladies apiece. The grail procession is thus described in precise mathematical terms, whereby four, or multiples of four, are predominant. The entire ritual is dominated by the feminine element. A more passive role is assumed by the knights in attendance, but here once again the number four — or derivatives thereof — are strikingly present. We are told that for every four knights there is a steward and a page carrying a white towel (236,25ff.), that one hundred tables are brought into the hall at each of which four knights can sit (237,1–4), that there are four squires assigned to each table (237,14) — two to sit and carve the meal, two to bring food and drink to the knights — that four carts bring vessels of gold to every knight present (237,22ff.), and that four knights are delegated, in each case, to place vessels upon each of the (one hundred) tables (237,26f.), and that there is one clerk for each knight engaged in the task (237,28). Finally, one hundred squires present bread to those seated at the tables (238,3f.). In addition, the bleeding spear that had earlier been carried into the Great Hall by a squire is drawn around the four walls (231,27ff.). All of this acquires yet greater significance when one considers how the numbers four and ten are symbolically linked:

> *Ten*: Symbolic, in decimal systems, of the return to unity. In the *Tetractys* (whose triangle of points — four, three, two, one — adds up to ten) it is related to four. Symbolic also of spiritual achievement, as well as of unity in its function as an even (or ambivalent) number or as the beginning of a new, multiple series. According to some theories, ten symbolizes the totality of the universe — both metaphysical and material — since it raises all things to unity. From ancient oriental thought through the Pythagorean school and right up to St. Jerome, it was known as the number of perfection. (Cirlot 234; see also Heninger 84)

Against this backdrop, the preponderance of the numbers four and one hundred (i.e., 10 x 10) in the descriptions of the grail castle and Schastel Marveile is hardly coincidental. With the ritual bearing of the lance around the Great Hall, the reader is presented with the symbolically weighty image of a circle being described within a square, assuming, of course, that the squire does not stop at each corner to effect a 90° turn. This might be seen as the converse of the age-old problem of squaring the circle, something which had fascinated geometricians from earliest times and which had also occupied Pythagoras and his followers. Here, however, the square is circularized, which "becomes an effort to make continuous what is discontinuous, an effort to raise the physical to the level of perfection" (Heninger 114). This symbolic transformation of the physical to the transcendental is further bolstered by the possibility that the bleeding lance carried by the squire was regarded as analogous to the lance of Longinus, believed found by crusaders during the siege of Antioch in 1098 (Jung/von Franz 87).

The preponderance of the number four (and its derivatives) as well as the number one hundred (and derivatives) cannot help but remind us of Pythagorean mathematics and the significance of the former as representing "the extended universe" and with the square root of the latter, the decad, "which exhausts the possibilities of physical extension . . . equivalent to perfection" (Heninger 84). Moreover, " . . . we have a notion of cosmos conceived as a derivative of the number 4, and the physical universe is described as an organism composed of four elements" (Heninger 79). Wolfram's use of numbers is clearly sophisticated (note the intricacy of the design techniques elucidated by Hart in his article) and harks back, I suspect, to Pythagorean principles on numbers, specifically, "the belief that numbers are the ultimate constituents of reality" (Heninger 71). Moreover, "[t]he contemplation of numbers provides a means of rising from the temporal world to participation in the divine, the ulterior motive for study in Pythagoras's school" (Heninger 76). Extremely important for our evaluation of the significance of numbers in *Parzival* is Heninger's comment: "While [Pythagorean metaphysics] posits a dualism, a world of forms and a world of matter, it nonetheless effectively interrelates them . . . . Numbers have existence in both worlds, embrace both worlds, allow interaction between both worlds" (77–78). Wolfram's particular fascination throughout his romance with the number four (and its cognates and derivatives) can be understood against the backdrop of its Pythagorean significance (see Heninger 79).

Wolfram deviates from his predecessor Chrétien when he describes the grail itself as a stone instead of a vessel (as is also the case in the *Chronicle of Helinandus* [1204], while Heinrich von dem Türlin describes it as a reliquary casket in his *Krône* [composed around 1215–1220]). This, however, only becomes clear later in Trevrizent's spiritual mentoring of Parzival:

> si lebent von einem steine:
> des geslähte ist vil reine.
> hât ir des niht erkennet,
> der wirt iu hie genennet.
> er heizet lapsit exillîs. (469,3–7)

(They live from a stone of purest kind. If you do not know it, it shall here be named to you. It is called *lapsit exillîs*.)

The fifteenth-century *Rosarium philosophorum* refers to verses ostensibly to be attributed to Arnold of Villanova who is believed to have died about 1312: "Hic lapis exilis extat precio quoque vilis / Spernitur a stultis, amatur plus ab edoctis" (Jung/von Franz 149= "This insignificant stone is indeed of trifling value; It is despised by fools, the more cherished by the wise"; see also Jung, *Psychology and Alchemy* 180, note 125). Wolfram and Arnold appear to have shared similar astrological and alchemical ideas that were current during the High Middle Ages. While the grail is also portrayed in other strands of the tradition as a vessel (or as a goblet, as in the film, *Indiana Jones and the Last Crusade*), it is noteworthy that Wolfram chose to depict it as a stone, thus making the link to alchemy and to alchemical symbolism that also abounds in the description of Gawan's adventures in the description of Schastel Marveile all the more compelling.

It might be suggested that Parzival's trip to Munsalvaesche is comparable to the κατάβασις experienced by Aeneas in the Sixth Book of Virgil's poem, or that of Heracles, Odysseus, and Orpheus to the Underworld. In a sense, Munsalvaesche embodies aspects of the land of the dead, as the sexual wound endured by Anfortas symbolizes an end to all productivity while the grail king languishes in a state of limbo awaiting the arrival of the savior who will restore life and vitality to the realm. Despite the display of obvious glamour that characterizes the grail procession, the castle itself is located in a veritable wasteland. There is, however, a major difference to be noted between Parzival's sojourn at Munsalvaesche and the journey to the World of Shades undertaken by his illustrious classical forebears. Parzival remains but an observer, he does not return to the world outside the grail castle enlightened and in a position to assist in its improvement. Given his "negligence" in not asking the question of Anfortas, Parzival actually creates further suffering at Munsalvaesche and brings disgrace upon both himself and the Arthurian court. The κατάβασις of Parzival is to be understood more in terms of a disjointed "landscape of the mind," and it begins *after* he has left Munsalvaesche and culminates in his denial of God subsequent to the invective to which he is subjected from Cundrie at the court of Arthur. He does not emerge from his self-made psychological wasteland until long after his meeting with Trevrizent in Book IX. In contrast to otherworldly journeys such as that of Aeneas to the Underworld to consult with his dead father Anchises, or that of Gilgamesh to his ancestor Utnapishtim for the sake of gathering information, Parzival, it should be remembered, does not *consciously* participate in any quest at this time. He "stumbles" upon the grail realm, and although it is the grail which predetermines the role Parzival is eventually to assume, he himself has, as yet, no awareness of the significance of these surroundings. In contradistinction to the classical questers, Parzival learns virtually nothing at Munsalvaesche, either with respect to the functioning of the grail or the relationship that the grail society has to the world outside. What he learns about Munsalvaesche and Anfortas is gained from sources outside the immediate grail boundaries (although Cundrie clearly has a connection to Munsalvaesche in her capacity as intermediary between the grail castle, the Arthurian court, and Schastel Marveile) and it is knowledge which is indispensable to him if he is to return to Munsalvaesche.

Gawan's adventures have, perhaps understandably, been eclipsed in scholarship by the attention accorded Parzival and his maturation process from naive youth to king of the grail (see, for example, Dick 74). Gawan never faces, of course, the spiritual vacuum encountered by his cousin, nor has he any integral role to play in the grail quest. Yet he does, through his successes at Schastel Marveile, complement the role played by Parzival at Munsalvaesche in the restoration of harmony and the (re-)affirmation of the universal principle of unity and wholeness even if, as Dick correctly points out, the "universal aspect of Clinschor's magic power (658,26–30) is obviously not being transferred to [him]" (74).

Schastel Marveile has all of the outer trappings of an otherworldly realm: to reach it, Gawan has to pass through a great forest and be ferried across a river (after having defeated Lischoys Gwelljus). From the ferryman he learns that the entire surrounding land is one of wondrous adventure:

> ez ist iu lîhte unbekant:
> gar âventiure ist al diz lant:
> sus wert ez naht und ouch den tac. (548,9–11)

> (It is perhaps unknown to you that this whole country here is a land of fantastic adventure.)

Intriguingly, however, this is not a place where questions about the wondrous castle and the ladies who can be seen therein are welcomed, as the ferryman's daughter, Bene, makes abundantly clear to Gawan: "do erschrac daz juncfreuwelîn, / si sprach 'hêr, nu vrâgt es niht: / ... / lâtz iu von mir niht swære, / und vrâget ander mære'" (555,2–3; 7–8= "The girl started with alarm. 'Sir, do not ask! ... Do not be offended at me. Ask me something else'"). Her reaction is duplicated by her father, Plippalinot, when Gawan pursues his inquiry: "der wirt want sîne hende: / dô sprach er: 'vrâgets niht durch got: / hêr, dâ ist nôt ob aller nôt'" (556,14–16= "The host wrung his hands. 'For God's sake! do not ask!' he said. 'Sir, *there* is misery beyond misery!'"). It is the ferryman who initially provides the designations of the land ("Terre Marveile," 557,6), the castle ("Schastel Marveile," 557,9), and the remarkable bed to be found inside ("Lît Marveile," 557,7). He serves as both narrator to the reader and guide to Gawan with his detailed report of the circumstances prevailing at Schastel Marveile. This is also the juncture at which the paths of Parzival and Gawan cross, the grail king designate having ridden through on the previous day, but without any knowledge of the presence of Schastel Marveile (559,9ff.)! Plippalinot functions as sometime gatekeeper to the otherworld, an initiate who is quite familiar with the castle and its surroundings, but whose very knowledge of the place precludes his willingness to impart that information to anyone other than the most resolute knight. As such, he serves as a mentor to Gawan prior to the latter's adventure in Schastel Marveile, a notable contrast to the situation that prevailed with Parzival in Book V when the latter entered the grail world in a state of complete unpreparedness.

Having left his horse with the tradesman before the entrance to the Castle of Wonders, Gawan proceeds toward the Great Hall, the roof of which is described as follows: "dô Gâwân den palas sach, / dem was alumbe sîn dach / rehte als pfâwîn gevider gar" (565,7-10= "when Gawan saw the great hall, its roof was just like peacocks' plumes"), which reminds the reader of the description of Anfortas's hat in 225,12. Moreover, the brilliance of the roof appears to be of a permanent nature as "weder regen noch der snê / entet des daches blicke wê" (565,11-12= "neither rain nor snow could damage the roof's brilliance at all"). Prior to entering Schastel Marveile, Gawan has thus been confronted with a symbol of renewal and unity: "The peacock is an old emblem of rebirth and resurrection, quite frequently found on Christian sarcophagi" (Jung, *Archetypes* 375-376). There is thus an early symbolic link to be noted between Schastel Marveile and the properties of the grail at Munsalvaesche. This connection may be much more significant than has hitherto been perceived. Let us return for a moment to the term — "lapsit exillîs" (469,7) — used by Trevrizent to describe the grail in Book IX. While the corrupt Latin form "lapsit exillîs" has given rise to much speculation as to its ultimate meaning (Mustard/Passage trans., 251, fn. 11; Jung/von Franz 142-160; Jung, *Psychology and Alchemy* 180, fn. 125), there may be a compelling reason to assume that Wolfram most likely meant "lapis" when he wrote "lapsit." Jung has referred to the role played by the peacock as "an ancient Christian symbol of resurrection" and in alchemy as a "symbol of renewal and resurrection, and more especially as a synonym for the lapis . . . . The exquisite display of colours in the peacock's fan heralds the imminent synthesis of all qualities and elements, which are united in the 'rotundity' of the philosophical stone" (1977, 290; see also the chapter "The Lapis-Christ Parallel" in Jung's *Psychology and Alchemy* 345–431).

The "tests" to which Gawan is subjected in Schastel Marveile have direct links to alchemy. In one of the chambers adjacent to the Great Hall, Gawan encounters the Lit Marveile (566,14), which deftly moves out of his way with every step he takes. Whether one views the Lit Marveile as a test designed to determine Gawan's ability to "ride one's own unconscious, desirous impulsiveness" (Sussman 154) or simply as evidence of Clinschor's skill in combining "magic and technology" to produce, in conjunction with the remarkably smooth floor on which it stands, a "masterpiece[] of construction" (Maksymiuk 111), it is impossible to conceive of the bed as lacking symbolic significance. The marvelous bed and the lion — which Gawan will also subsequently engage in combat — are linked in legend and alchemy (see Jung/von Franz 391), both of them possibly representing unbridled passion that needs to be tamed for the sake of balance and harmony. We note, however, that the bed, in its effort to dislodge Gawan, who has jumped onto it and landed in the middle, systematically, and at a terrible speed that is coupled with incredible force and resonance, slams against all four walls of the chamber, behavior that is analogous to the "bucking bronco" of the modern-day rodeo. Gawan attempts to "tame" the bed in what is described as a series of jousts ("sus reit er manegen poynder grôz" [567,19= "In this fashion he rode the bed to joust after joust"]), but ultimately places all of his faith and trust in God's hands:

> Er lac, unde liez es walten
> den der helfe hât behalten
> und den der helfe nie verdrôz,
> swer in sînem kumber grôz
> helfe an in versuochen kan. (568,1–5)

(He lay there and let Him take charge of it Who has help to bestow, and Who never failed to grant help to one who in great need seeks help from Him.)

In stark contrast to Parzival — and in defiance of the advice given by the latter to put his faith in women when going into battle (332,9ff.) — Gawan turns without hesitation to God when in dire peril. The reaction (or response) is immediate, and the bed, which appears to be multi-colored like the roof of the Great Hall (see 568,18), comes to a complete rest in the center of the floor, with Gawan still in the middle of it. We have in this image of the center another symbol of the movement "from the exterior to the interior, from form to contemplation, from multiplicity to unity, from space to spacelessness, from time to timelessness . . . " (Cirlot 40).

When Gawan is assailed by gravel stones and arrows — some of which do manage to penetrate his shield and armor wounding him — these missiles may also be regarded as symbolic of unbridled passion (see Jung/von Franz 233), something which Gawan must overcome if he is to find a reliable center. The arrows, in particular, are reminiscent of the *tela passionis* associated with Mercury with which he is purported to have pierced Adam (see Jung, *Psychology and Alchemy* 256, fig. 131): "In the alchemical hierarchy of gods Mercurius comes lowest as *prima materia* and highest as *lapis philosophorum*" (Jung, *Psychology and Alchemy* 66–67). Viewed from a symbolic/psychological perspective then, Gawan's trials at Schastel Marveile have as much to do with effecting a spiritual transformation within his psyche as they do with his breaking the spell of Clinschor's castle and freeing its female and male captives. Again, on this plane, Gawan's subconscious search for a center and for totality demonstrates a closer affinity between his "quest" and that of Parzival than we are normally inclined to admit. That Parzival's function within the work is considered to be more important than that of Gawan is based on our own ideas of the significance of gradation in the Middle Ages, but there is no indication within the romance itself that Wolfram intended to emphasize a *process of gradation* with respect to the paths taken by Parzival and Gawan. It should be remembered at this time that the amount of space devoted by Wolfram to Gawan in *Parzival* encompasses, in the aggregate, nearly the same number of verses that are accorded the title hero.

In his fight against the lion, Gawan defends himself with acumen, slicing off one of the beast's legs while another is stuck fast in Gawan's shield, and finally piercing the lion's heart with his sword. The narrator's comment on this reads: "Gâwân het die grôze nôt / mit strîte überwunden" (572,22–23= "Gawan had now fought and overcome the supreme danger"). Jung refers to the familiarity of later alchemists with "the slaying . . . of a lion, which took the form of his having all four paws cut off" (Jung 1984,126), and, while the latter reference is to the alchemists of the fifteenth and sixteenth centuries, Emma Jung and Marie-Louise von Franz clearly associate Gawan's confrontation with the lion, regarded as "an outbreak of animal greediness and overwhelming passion," with alchemical concepts contemporary with Wolfram's age (231).

Of all the wonders associated with Schastel Marveile, none is perhaps as intriguing as the "clâriu sûl" (589,5= "shining pillar") which the hero comes upon while on a "tour" of the castle following a night of recovery from his wounds. This pillar was brought by Clinschor to Schastel Marveile from the land of Feirefiz and is thoroughly magical in nature: "ez was geworht mit liste" (589,17= "it had been wrought by sorcery"). Gawan's attention is drawn initially to the properties of the column, in which he is able to view — or so it appears to him — all of the surrounding lands and the activities of various individuals. This *speculum mundi* requires an explanation, which Gawan requests from Queen Arnive. He learns from her that its major property is that of light: " . . . hêrre, dirre stein / bî tage und alle nähte schein" (592,1–2= "Sir, this stone has cast its glow, by day and all the nights"). (Once again the reader is reminded of the prominence of light at Munsalvaesche, primarily exuding from the candles carried by the maidens but also from the radiance of Repanse de Schoye; in Chrétien's version, the light emanating from the grail itself tends to outshine the light of the candles.) Within a radius of six miles it "records" all events, a veritable medieval surveillance system! Here, however, Gawan is distracted from Arnive's account by the appearance in the column of riders and, following a brief explanation from Arnive as to their identity (Orgeluse and the Turkoite Florant), he rushes off to do combat with the knight.

In Chrétien's *Perceval*, the marvelous pillar, designed and constructed, along with the castle, by Merlin, was depicted as a tethering post, but only the most noble knight could tie up his horse there. The pillar may originally have had a structural function similar to that of the grail in the sense that only one individual was predestined to have full access to it. In Wolfram's *Parzival*, on the other hand, Gawan is as dependent upon Arnive for a (limited) explanation of the column's origins as Parzival is on Trevrizent for an exegesis of the grail, but this is broken off once Gawan becomes distracted by the appearance of Orgeluse and Florant. The reader is also deprived of any further elucidation of the significance of the column and is left to draw his own conclusions as to its ultimate role within the work. Stolen from Secundille, queen of India and wife of Feirefiz, the pillar thus originated (along with Cundrie and her brother Malcreatiure) in a land on the periphery of the world. Given its peculiar properties of "surveillance," one could agree with Linda Sussman that "[t]he 'seeing' pillar in the Castle of Wonders extends Gawan's powers of perception; in possession of it, he will, from now on, always have a much broader view than was possible in the past" (Sussman 166). The pillar, as a source and conveyor of historical, temporal knowledge, is complementary to the grail as a transmitter of spiritual, transcendental knowledge.

Wolfram is undoubtedly one of the most complex and one of the most erudite writers of his time. His rendition of *Parzival* is testimony not solely to the master storyteller, but also to his wide-ranging knowledge of contemporary physical and metaphysical phenomena. Nothing of significance in thirteenth-century Europe appears to have escaped Wolfram's attention and with each new reading, one detects yet another fascinating detail which contributes to our understanding of this most visionary of works. Many questions remain open. To what extent was Wolfram involved with Catharism? What was his actual relationship to the community of alchemists? Was he, in fact, the skilled mathematical designer that Thomas Hart suggests? Perhaps our best approach to Wolfram von Eschenbach and, in particular, his *Parzival*, should be guided by an avoidance of any tendency to underestimate the artist's interest in and comprehension of what might nowadays be considered merely the "esoteric."

Commenting on Goethe's (and perhaps the world's) most famous drama, Carl Gustav Jung maintained that

> ... *Faust* is an alchemical drama from beginning to end, although the educated man of today has only the haziest notion of this. Our conscious mind is far from understanding everything, but the unconscious always keeps an eye on the "age-old, sacred things," however strange they may be, and reminds us of them at a suitable opportunity. (*Psychology and Alchemy* 67)

What Jung said of *Faust* can be paraphrased to fit the medieval work: "*Parzival* is an alchemical *romance* from beginning to end." Once again, the words — and advice — of Karl Bertau in his introduction are especially appropriate: "Bei Wolfram geht keine Einzelheit verloren, jede spiegelt sich in schier unendlichen Variationen ihrer Wiederkehr. Wer etwas bloß so liest, ohne etwas bestimmtes wissen zu wollen, der braucht überhaupt nicht zu lesen und kann seine Zeit besser verwenden" (Bertau 12= "Wolfram does not lose track of a single detail. Each one is revisited, reflected in an infinite number of variations. Whoever reads this without wanting to know something in particular does not need to be reading at all and can spend time better with something else"). Even long-term readers who have gained an appreciation for Wolfram's multifaceted game-playing will readily admit that much remains to be uncovered among the 24,810 verses of *Parzival*.

Wolfram is a master in the application of mathematical principles and numerical symbolism that evinces, as we have seen, familiarity with the theories of Pythagoras, to whom he refers in 773,25f. ("der wîse Pictagoras, / der ein astronomierre was" [= "the wise Pictagoras, who was an astronomer"), and his statement that Pythagoras was the wisest man one has seen since Adam's time ("unt sô wîse âne strît, / niemen sît Adâmes zît / möhte im glîchen sin getragen" [773,27–29= "and without doubt so wise that no one since Adam's time can be compared to him") has prompted Wilhelm Deinert to consider the possibility that Wolfram effectively substitutes Pythagoras for Solomon as the world's wisest man, thereby casting the heathen philosopher as a spiritual predecessor of the keepers of the grail (122–127). As well as the tenets of medieval alchemy, Wolfram has presented in *Parzival* a metaphor for the synthesis of opposites, a vision of the ultimate unity of the secular and the transcendental. While we are inclined to speak in terms of "gradation" with regard to the courtly world (as represented by Gawan) and the grail World (Parzival), the consistent link that is maintained between both should always be kept in mind (Munsalvaesche's providing warrior-rulers to lands in need of leadership and its sending out of maidens to suitable mates; the grail's "calling" of knights from the courtly, Arthurian realm to its company, as well as its acceptance of qualified maidens [see 494, 1ff.]). Above all, the final scenes in the romance graphically underscore Wolfram's intent to portray an image of wholeness and a resolution of binary tension. All worlds come together in the festival organized by Gawan: Schastel Marveile, freed from its spell, the Arthurian court with its long-absent male and female figures re-integrated into society — underscored by the marriages of Itonje to Gramoflanz, Cundrie (Gawan's sister) to Lischoys, and Sangive to Florant — the grail world, on the threshold of having its balance and harmony restored by a mature and enlightened Parzival, and the "peripheral" world of Feirefiz, assimilated through marriage into the grail realm. If one were to select a single phrase that might best describe the situation with regard to both Munsalvaesche and Schastel Marveile, as well as Arthur's court, at the conclusion of *Parzival*, an appropriate choice would be "transformation through integration." This phenomenon of transformation pertains not only to individuals such as Parzival and Feirefiz, as well as Gawan, now more firmly "rooted" with his exorcising and acquisition of Clinschor's kingdom and a wife in the person of Orgeluse. It also involves more than groups of people such as the female and male captives of Schastel Marveile, but rather encompasses entire societies. The "transformation" is from a fragmented, disjointed, disharmonious, binary existence to one characterized by balance, integration of the masculine and feminine elements, and restoration of harmony in both the individual and collective psyche. In the realization of this ideal, both Parzival and Gawan have pivotal roles to play. While the one is characterized more by the temporal, the other by the atemporal, the ultimate image imparted to the reader is less that of a superior existence contrasted with the mundaneness and unpredictability of the everyday world than a mutual interdependence of all worlds set against the backdrop of the heroes' processes of individuation.

WILL HASTY

At the Limits of Chivalry in Wolfram's *Parzival*: An Arthurian Perspective

1

AUTHORS OF THE FIRST ARTHURIAN ROMANCES SUCH as Chrétien de Troyes and his German successors Hartmann von Aue and Wolfram von Eschenbach participated in a complex convergence of oral and written narrative traditions and socio-cultural values and interests, during the period from the late eleventh to the early thirteenth century, that generated what has come to be known as the Arthurian tradition. Perhaps the most significant early document of this convergence is the *Historia regum Brittaniae* (ca.1136) of Geoffrey of Monmouth. In this pseudo-history consisting of diverse historical and legendary elements, Geoffrey purports to relate the history of the British monarchy over a period of some two thousand years, from the fall of Troy to the death of the last British king in 542, at which time the Angles and Saxons began to reign in Britain. It is in Geoffrey's *Historia* that we first find the figure of King Arthur connected to the courtly/chivalric way of life at medieval courts. Geoffrey tells us that Arthur developed a code of courtliness that inspired imitation in faraway kingdoms and that even men of noblest birth thought nothing of themselves unless they wore their arms and dressed in the same way as Arthur's knights (222). After serious military challenges to its integrity have been overcome, Arthur's courtly/chivalric order is depicted by Geoffrey in terms of its sophistication of taste and dress and in terms of a regulation of aggression in the relationship between the sexes that will have a much more prominent position in the later romances in the form of love service, what Wolfram will later call "ritterschaft nâch minnen zilt" (*Parzival*, 115,20= "love through chivalric exploits"):

> Indeed, by this time, Britain had reached such a standard of sophistication that it excelled all other kingdoms in its general affluence, the richness of its decorations, and the courteous behavior of its inhabitants. Every knight in the country who was in any way famed for his bravery wore livery and arms showing his own distinctive colour; and women of fashion often displayed the same colours. They scorned to give their love to any man who had not proved himself three times in battle. In this way the womenfolk became chaste and more virtuous and for their love the knights were ever more daring. (229)

Geoffrey's *Historia*, which reached wider European audiences by way of vernacular reworkings such as Wace's *Roman de Brut* (1155), seems to set the stage for the King Arthur of the later romances. Geoffrey casts Arthur as the sponsor of a brief period of harmonious order against the backdrop of an otherwise depraved and turbulent British history, while the romances of authors like Chrétien, Hartmann von Aue, and Wolfram tend to juxtapose Arthur and his court to a similarly chaotic, but largely timeless wilderness region inhabited by strange beings and objects that alternately threaten and entice, and inevitably provoke some kind of chivalric response on the part of Arthur's knights. In Geoffrey's "history" and in the romances, King Arthur is the centerpoint of an exclusive, opulent, and idealized chivalric order, in which aggression — effectively managed and directed externally (toward Gaul and Rome during the highest point of Arthur's fame in Geoffrey's text; toward the various challenges posed by that wilderness realm in the romances) — is not internally debilitating.

As noteworthy as similarities such as these is the manner in which the medieval narratives about Arthur are connected to the aristocratic values and interests of the patrons who sponsored their production and the audiences who read or heard them. Henry II of England (Fletcher 186) was among the first in a long line of political leaders extending at least as far as John F. Kennedy who seem to have derived some propagandistic benefit from their association with King Arthur's courtly/chivalric order. The frequent portrayals of courtly sophistication, etiquette, and opulence in the romances no doubt held a more general appeal for medieval audiences that would have been flattered to see in these portrayals an image — however idealized (see the introduction of Bumke's *Höfische Kultur*) — of themselves, while the depictions of chivalric deeds-of-arms would have appealed to the basically military self-understanding of the lay nobility. Beyond this, it may be possible to perceive in depictions of Arthur's relatively peaceful courtly/chivalric order a literary articulation of a broader regulation of aggression in the High Middle Ages, which may be related to the new social situation at the larger courts discussed in the study of Elias, or to the attempt on the part of the Church beginning around 1000 (with the *pax dei*) and subsequently on the part of lay authorities (e.g., the *Reichslandfrieden* of 1235) to control the disruptive effects of feuding. While the courtly/chivalric order of Arthur and his knights can be seen as a highly idealized literary construct or as a kind of myth in its own right, it may nevertheless be assumed that literary representations of the courtly/chivalric order of Arthur articulate, at least to some extent, the values and interests of historical courts in the High Middle Ages (see Bayer 340, Jan-Dirk Müller 1980, 11, Wenzel 1980, 342, and Haferland 1988,12).

As central as it is in the romances, the courtly/chivalric order of King Arthur is nevertheless juxtaposed in myriad ways to non-Arthurian alternatives that are no less significant, for it is out of the friction occurring between the Arthurian courtly/chivalric order and more or less desirable alternatives beyond the reaches of the good king's "civilization" that most Arthurian narratives are generated. These alternatives are generally connected in the romances to that primordial wilderness region beyond the court, characteristic of which is a convergence of beings, objects, and events mythical and religious. The possibilities of the wilds are experienced — by Arthur's knights and presumably also by the audiences of the Arthurian works — both positively as alluring alternative modes of being or as opportunities for reflection about, criticism of, or emancipation from a constrictive, unjust social conformity; and negatively as chaotic, turbulent, or destructive disruptions of a more or less stable, more or less ideal social order.

A striking example of a positive portrayal of the more purely mythic alternative possibilities represented by regions beyond Arthur's courtly/chivalric order is contained in Marie de France's *Lanval*, in which the young knight Lanval is virtually liberated from the court of Arthur, where he has endured the king's arbitrary and unjust treatment of him and the false accusations of the queen, when he rides off with his fabulously beautiful otherworldly lady to *Avalun*. A different tack is taken in the French Vulgate Cycle and in the *Prose Tristan*, composed in the first half of the thirteenth century, in which Morgen le Fay, who like the otherworldly lady of *Lanval* also maintains associations with the mythical otherworld of Avalon, is more negatively cast as a villainess who unsuccessfully attempts to seduce Lancelot and to expose his affair with Guenevere, in order to bring down Arthur's chivalric order.

The quest for the grail is the most memorable way in which Arthur's courtly/chivalric order engages a religious alternative mode of being beyond its limits. If the court of Arthur represents an initial ordering of chaotic aspects of the primordial wilderness — an ordering that already understands itself as divinely instituted — , then the demands of the quest for the grail — particularly the asceticism, demonization of sexual desire, and the transformation of the generally messy business of fighting into a neat allegorical representation of the victory of good over evil, which is visible in the adventures of Galahad, Perceval, and Bors as set down in *La Queste del Saint Graal* of the Vulgate Cycle — seem to require an even "higher" and exclusive level of ordering.

Whether construed psychologically in terms of the engagement of a courtly/chivalric ego with the unconscious mind as represented by the wilderness beyond the court (for very different psychological studies along these lines, see Bertau, especially chapters 3 and 4, Steiner, and Jung/von Franz), or in terms of the values of specific communities in the treatment of the limits of chivalry, for example of monastic (possibly Cistercian, according to Barber 1973, 81–82) values in *La Queste del Saint Graal*, it is clear that the relationship between Arthur's courtly/chivalric order and the alternative possibilities of the wilds is not just a literary, but also a cultural issue, demonstrative in different ways of what Kaiser has called the "Bruchstellen und Dissonanzen" (7= "breaks and dissonances") of courtly culture.

If we turn now to Wolfram's *Parzival* as a specific example of the Arthurian tradition as outlined above, we observe that the courtly/chivalric order of Arthur and the mythic/religious alternative possibilities of the wilds seem to be cast as specific responses to an "existential" limit that is experienced frequently and at crucial moments in Wolfram's narrative: in the events described in the first three Books alone, Wolfram's audience learns of the chivalric deaths of Parzival's great grandfather Addanz, his grandfather Gandin, his uncle Galoes, his father Gahmuret, Schionatulander, Ither, Schentaflurs, Lascoyt, and Gurzgri, to name only some of the most significant knightly fatalities; Gahmuret's adventures begin with the death of Gandin, the departure of Herzeloyde into the wilderness is largely motivated by the death of Gahmuret, Parzival becomes a knight by killing the Red Knight Ither, and the suffering of the grail court seems inextricable from the "living death" of Anfortas (see 230,20: "er lebte niht wan töude" [= "he was more dead than alive"]). The weight given to chivalric death and its effects, particularly in the adventures of the title hero and the events pertaining to them, suggests that this problem, this existential limit of chivalry, is one of the central concerns of Wolfram's text (the issue of chivalric death also presents itself in the adventures of Gawan, although perhaps not with the same degree of urgency). The ways in which courtly/chivalric, mythic, and religious elements stand in relation to this limit suggest that Wolfram's text occupies a unique position among medieval Arthurian romances as a staunchly chivalric version of the quest for the grail that nevertheless accommodates the disruptive effects of the alternative possibilities of the wilderness beyond.

2

Wolfram portrays himself as a staunch advocate of courtly/chivalric order in ways that distinguish his *Parzival* from the works of his influential predecessors Chrétien de Troyes and Hartmann von Aue. Perhaps most striking is the forceful way in which the narrator Wolfram puts himself forward as a knight in the famous "self-defense" at the end of Book II, where he warns his audience in a characteristically provocative tone — similar to the one he uses when addressing Hartmann on behalf of his hero (143,21–144,4) — that he places at least as much value on his chivalric as on his literary qualifications (115,11–20). While there has been much debate about how literally his advocation of fighting has to be taken, there is no compelling reason to doubt Wolfram when he says that if he desires a lady's love, he will win it with lance and sword, however obscure other parts of this "self-defense" may be (Boigs has recently argued that the self-defense is not a literary-theoretical reflection, but rather a reference to Wolfram's personal situation). Given that Wolfram puts himself forward as a knight, who considers that it is appropriate to win the love of ladies with chivalric deeds and not just with song, it is not surprising that he remains the staunch supporter of characters such as Gahmuret and his hero Parzival, whose chivalric values and priorities — which are basically those of the Arthurian court depicted in his romance — he seems to share.

Further evidence for the strongly chivalric orientation of Wolfram is the detailed knowledge he shows about the different aspects of medieval warfare, ranging from armor and siege engines to strategic thinking (see Jackson in this volume). In the numerous detailed depictions of warfare and jousting, and also in his portrayals of the etiquette and pageantry of courtly life — what Hatto in the introduction of his translation of *Parzival* calls "the style of life which Wolfram knew at the German courts of the very brilliant Hohenstauffen period" (8–9), Wolfram achieved within the more or less restrictive generic devices at his disposal what is arguably the most transparently historical Arthurian text of his time (see Gürttler 164, Jones 1972, 70, and H. Brunner).

The manner in which the narrator Wolfram seems to respond in the "self-defense" to adverse circumstances (i.e., the disfavor in which he is held because of his unspecified transgression against a lady) with forceful self-assertion and an advocation of deeds of arms, is consistent with the manner in which his chivalric protagonists respond to adversity in their lives. The first example of this is the story of Gahmuret with which Wolfram's tale begins. As a consequence of the chivalric death of Gandin, the status of the members of Gandin's family in the kingdom of Anjou has to be redefined according to the customary practice of primogeniture. The youngest son Gahmuret suddenly finds himself without the material support necessary for the political and social status he has heretofore enjoyed, and it is clear that his elder brother Galoes's offer to accept him as a member of his household (*ingesinde* [= inmate]), is not an acceptable option for Gahmuret, who somewhat contemptuously equates the status of *ingesinde* with *gemach* (7,22= idle comfort). Gahmuret turns down the kind offer of his brother and rides away into distant lands in hopes that his own valor will win him the love of a lady (8,1–11), an action that is patently Arthurian in its value, even if Arthur's court does not appear in the narrative until after Gahmuret's death. Chivalric self-assertion (that of Gahmuret) thus presents itself as the appropriate and honorable response to death in chivalric self-assertion (that of Gandin). Only a single verse suggests that Gahmuret, in his haste to address his own situation with chivalric action, appreciates the seemingly paradoxical nature of his course of action; that he may be setting out along the same road that led to the death of his father: "ôwe war jaget mich mîn gelust" (9,26= "Oh where is my ambition taking me?"). But this verse is surrounded by others that are suggestive not of a critical attitude toward the aggressive chivalric orientation, but rather of something closer to the opposite: the "unverzaget mannes muot" (1,5= "steadfast masculine courage") of a knight who is aware that he must exert himself, must risk life and limb in the pursuit of love, honor, and fortune, if he is physically able (see 9,23: "mîn herze iedoch nâch hoehe strebet" [= but my heart is set on the heights!] and 9,27: "ich solz versuochen ob ich mac" [= I shall attempt it if I can]). Gahmuret here seems to evince the chivalric posture very aptly described by Martin Jones: "the knight must affirm his calling when the realities of his life seem to suggest that he should despair of it" (1972,70).

The manner in which Gahmuret's son Parzival responds to the limits of chivalry can be seen most clearly at the end of Book VI, when he is being feted by the Arthurian court for the honor his chivalric deeds have brought to it. If Wolfram's audience does not know or suspect this already, it is about to discover that the heights to which Parzival has already taken chivalry — inextricable from his departure from his mother in order to become a knight at Arthur's court, his killing of Arthur's political rival Ither in order to obtain armor, and his steadfast adherence to the chivalric council of Gurnemanz during his initial visit to the grail court — also have an*other* significance that pertains not to the honor and glory that chivalry accrues, but rather to the pain it causes. Cundrie la surziere, who spoils this celebration of Parzival's chivalric exploits when she lambastes him for his failure to ask the Question, is noteworthy among many figures connected to the wilderness beyond the courtly/chivalric world of King Arthur who make us aware of other manners of experiencing the limits of chivalry. Parzival's response to this lambasting, however inculpatory from a religious standpoint, can nonetheless be regarded in terms of a consistent adherence to the aggressive self-assertion that has characterized his actions to this point and that is the most important and necessary aspect of the chivalric life. When Gawan expresses hope that God will be on Parzival's side in his future challenges, Parzival responds with his notorious and much cited declaration of enmity towards God (332,1–14), in which he revokes his service from God, resolves to bear any enmity God may have toward him, and councils his chivalric comrade to let love service — that same essentially Arthurian principle advocated by the narrator Wolfram and by Parzival's father Gahmuret — be his guiding principle.

What from a Christian perspective is another step into sin (see Wapnewski 87), may be seen from a courtly/chivalric one as the appropriately aggressive response to a challenge or provocation. Confronted by what he perceives as the unjustified enmity of God, Parzival responds with *zorn* (= anger). *Zorn* is defined in a recent article by Swisher as "an expression of strife that is directed outwardly in the form of an attitude and preparedness to do battle" [393]). Parzival's experience of the "limits of chivalry" is not one of critical self-reflection, but rather of renewed vigorous self-assertion. Despite some evidence of a softening of his position during the coming adventures, which might be seen as indicative of an inner, spiritual transformation or development, Parzival continues to act in a way that is consistent with the aggressive posture he manifests here, not to mention with Gahmuret's and the narrator Wolfram's advocation of deeds of arms in the service of ladies. In the "schildes ambet umben gral" (333,27) that begins at this point, Parzival's wife Condwiramurs is placed on the same level with the grail (Huby 267), which suggests that the quintessentially Arthurian courtly/chivalric value of "ritterschaft nâch minnen zilt" (115,20) is being taken to another level. From the moment he leaves Arthur's court, until he rides up to Munsalvaesche to take possession of the grail — which is to say *after* his sojourn with Trevrizent, Parzival continues to fight.

Fighting at the limits of chivalry, Parzival experiences the stiffest opposition not from chivalric opponents (whose names are ceremoniously pronounced later on at Arthur's court [771,23–772,30]), but in the powers of an inscrutable deity who seems to withhold His favor by preventing him from finding his way back to the grail. Despite this formidable opposition, Parzival's attitude does not seem to change much. Even Book IX, in which the spiritual transformation of Parzival presumably occurs, contains passages that are consistent with the aggressive posture Parzival manifests more openly elsewhere. A spiritual transformation is first suggested shortly after Parzival has parted company with the grey knight and his daughters, on account of the hatred he continues to harbor against the God they love (450,18–19), when Parzival begins to experience remorse and to ponder the greatness of God (451,8–12). Following immediately upon these thoughts about the power of the creator are words that seem somewhat more suggestive of the aggressive attitude of an angry knight than the contrite attitude of a repentant heart: "ist hiut sîn helflîcher tac, / sô helfe er, ob er helfen mac." (451,21f.= "if this is His Helpful Day, then let Him help, if help He can!"). Parzival's use of the third person imperative (see Paul 372) in the final verse of this passage is at the very least suggestive of impatience, if not of ongoing anger, about his having to continue on this day of all days, a day on which God is reputed to show His favor, to go without it, despite the illustrious deeds of arms that he has performed. The concentration of passages such as these, the first consistent with a more strictly religious, the second with a somewhat more aggressively chivalric feudal approach, suggests the occasional proximity in Wolfram's work of orientations that ordinarily run in different directions. Such a narrative juxtaposition might be construed in terms of individual development or transformation (i.e., Parzival is becoming more multi-faceted, the structure of his psyche more complex), but this does not detract from the ongoing compelling logic of the basic orientations, here chivalric aggression (i.e., *zorn*) and religious contrition.

The aggressive, self-assertive attitude characteristic of the chivalric orientation continues to manifest itself until Parzival has finally achieved the "thing" for which he has been fighting, at which time the limits of chivalry and love service have seemingly been redefined. Parzival's continued aggression is especially evident in his attitude toward Cundrie when she makes her second appearance at Arthur's court in Book XV to call him to Munsalvaesche. When the grail messenger falls at Parzival's feet and begs for his forgiveness, Parzival's initial response indicates the continuation of the anger that has been the driving force in him: "Parzivâl truoc ûf si haz" (779,29= "Parzival nursed great resentment toward her"). At the prodding of his courtly friends Arthur and Feirefiz, Parzival agrees to forgive Cundrie, but it is difficult to avoid seeing in his ongoing enmity toward her a continuing anger against the inscrutable power that has so long kept him away from the grail. Any doubt about the unwavering chivalric orientation of Parzival, and the consistently aggressive and angry self-assertion it has involved, seems to be dispelled in the final Book when Trevrizent pronounces that Parzival's approach, to his great wonderment, has been successful:

> Trevrizent ze Parzivâle sprach
> 'groezer wunder selten ie geschach,
> sît ir ab got erzürnet hât
> daz sîn endelôsiu Trinitât
> iwers willen werhaft worden ist.' (798,1–5)

(Trevrizent told Parzival . . . 'A greater marvel never occurred, in that, after all, with your defiance you have wrung the concession from God that His everlasting Trinity has given you your wish.')

Trevrizent's words have far-reaching implications. They can clearly be taken as an acknowledgement (albeit on the part of an obviously fallible individual) that Parzival has imposed his chivalric will on God, that his sinful anger (see the discussion of Trevrizent below) has been the key to his achieving the grail (see Swisher 407–8). At the very least, they support the idea that Parzival's aggressively chivalric approach does not ever really change. This idea is put forward in the assessment of Huby, who maintains that Parzival's approach does not change the slightest bit, that he fights as stubbornly and victoriously between Book IX and XIV as during the four and a half years of his revolt against God. Huby makes another point that is of great significance for our assessment of Parzival's courtly/chivalric orientation: "Der Artushof ist ihm wie früher der absolute Bezugspunkt" (267= "The court of Arthur remains as before the absolute point of reference"). While the courtly/chivalric orientation in *Parzival* as outlined here may be somewhat difficult to reconcile with critical assessments positing an inner transformation or development in the hero as he moves beyond the immaturity or sinfulness of his initial aggressive approach, it is nevertheless consistent with the logic of chivalric action — Knapp calls this the "Automatismus von Bewährung und Erfolg" (351= "the automatic relationship between persistent endeavor and success") — that is visible in most Arthurian narratives. Seen in Arthurian terms, Parzival does not give up on the values of *minne* and *âventiure*, but rather seems to take them to another level.

3

As in most Arthurian narratives we find also in Wolfram's text a wilderness "alternative" to the courtly/chivalric world that is largely characterized by a convergence of mythic and religious elements. The first alternative space in Wolfram's text, the Orient of Gahmuret's adventures that presents itself upon the death of his father, is more like a projection of the courtly/chivalric world than a mythic/religious alternative to it, although the fabulous wealth and the unusual characteristics of the marvelous figures (e.g., the Baruc) and events that it contains seem "otherworldly" in many respects. Perhaps in keeping with Gahmuret's own "art von der feien" (96,20= "fairy blood"), the Oriental space of his adventures is what Kunitzsch calls "ein Land der Phantasie und der Wunder" (110= "a land of fantasy and wonders"). In Wolfram's highly sympathetic depictions of its different characteristics, for example those of Belacane ("Gahmureten dûhte sân, / swie si wære ein heidenin, / mit triwen wîplîcher sin / in wîbes herze nie geslouf" [28,10–13= "It seemed to Gahmuret that although she was an infidel, a more affectionate spirit of womanliness had never stolen over a woman's heart"]), we see important indications of Wolfram's knowledge about and tolerance for very different ways of life. If Wolfram's Orient, which adds significant new terrain to Arthurian romance (Wynn 1984,341), can be regarded as an "alternative" space at all, the possibilities it affords are not so different from the one in which Gandin was killed that Gahmuret is able to avoid suffering the same fate.

Upon the death of Gahmuret the wilderness first appears in which most of the remaining action of Wolfram's work takes place, which includes the *waste* of Herzeloyde, the grail court, and the grotto of Trevrizent. Particularly noteworthy about the numerous and diverse mythic elements in Wolfram's depiction of this space — which distinguish *Parzival* from the more starkly Christian accentuation of Chrétien's *Perceval* and the association of the grail with the legend of Joseph of Arimathea in the *L'Estoire dou Graal* (ca.1191–1202) of Robert de Boron — is the concern with regeneration, the natural cycle of barrenness and fertility. This concern is visible not only in the elements of Irish and Welsh myths that *Parzival* shares with other medieval Arthurian works, but also at another, "deeper" level in archetypal images that find symbolic expression in the myths and folklore of peoples around the world. A characteristic both of the otherworlds in Irish and Welsh myths (M. Green 87–88) and of the primary processes as understood in psychoanalysis (Bertau 112) is the suspension of normal spatial and temporal frames of reference, and such a suspension is suggested by Herzeloyde's words and actions even before she leaves her regal life of power at the beginning of the third Book for the solitude and isolation of the wilds, where night for her will be the same as day (117,5). In her laments over the death of her husband Gahmuret, which has just been reported to her, Herzeloyde blurs the distinctions between wife/mother and husband/son (109,19–25 and 112, 13–14), seemingly becoming herself something purely feminine and — as suggested by her "baptism" of the newborn Parzival with the milk from her "soft white breasts" — manifesting a very physical, if not erotic spirituality. Seen in terms of individual characterization, this blurring suggests Herzeloyde is losing her powers of reasoning (see Yeandle 1981,10); seen in terms of the Arthurian tradition more generally, it may be that Herzeloyde is reverting to an identifiably mythic type.

Herzeloyde puts forward the Virgin as the model for her actions (113,17–26), but she is in many respects similar to other "otherworldly" figures in the Arthurian tradition such as the lady of Marie de France's Lanval, who takes a very active and sexual role in choosing her knight, in bestowing her favor and wealth upon him and in challenging his position in the courtly/chivalric order of Arthur. In much the same way Herzeloyde has actively pursued Gahmuret (to satisfy her erotic desire, according to Lewis 470), and now challenges the courtly/chivalric order (even if it is not yet explicitly that of Arthur) by taking Parzival with her to what might be considered her wilderness "otherworld." The immediate model for Herzeloyde is Chrétien's *veve fame de la gaste forest* (= Widow lady of the Waste Forest), but Herzeloyde seems to have another, more distant Arthurian relative in Perceval's aunt as described in *La Queste del Saint Graal*, who was once known as *la reine de la Terre Gaste* (= the queen of the Waste Land). Although Perceval's aunt is here a religious eremite, who informs Perceval of the death of his mother and of the ascetic demands of the quest for the grail, she later comes to be numbered by Malory — who took the *Queste* as the source of his grail story — among the three queens who accompany King Arthur back to "the vale of Avylyon" after his fateful battle with Mordred:

> Thus of Arthur I fynde no more wrytten in bokis that bene auctorysed, nothir more of the verry sertaynté of hys deth harde I never rede, but thus was he lad away in a shyp wherein were three quenys; that one was kynge Arthur syster, quene Morgan le Fay, the tother was the

quene of North Galis, and the thirde was the quene of the Waste Londis. (III,1242)

If we take a broad Arthurian view, Herzeloyde thus seems in many respects similar to a group of female characters that includes otherworldly figures such as the lady of Lanval, Morgen le Fay, and the "quene of the Waste Londis." Other significant characters somewhat closer to Wolfram, such as the lady of Mabonagrin in Hartmann's *Erec* and the Laudine figure in Hartmann's *Iwein* (both based, of course, on characters in the corresponding romances of Chrétien de Troyes), also manifest otherworldly characteristics (particularly the unusual features of their domains — the magical garden and fountain respectively — and the wish to lure or keep their knights away from life in the "real world," i.e., from chivalric pursuits). While it is difficult to establish with certainty the relationship between female figures such as these in the Arthurian tradition and the otherworldly goddesses, sprites, and nymphs of Irish and Welsh myths (a relationship is assumed especially in the case of Morgen le Fay — see Lacy, ed. 329), both groups demonstrate similar ambivalent characteristics: they are by turns dangerous and desirable, implicated alternately in fighting, death, sexuality, and fertility (on the Celtic goddesses see M. Green 40–45).

At another level Herzeloyde might also be seen as a symbolic expression of the Archetypal Feminine, which elsewhere finds symbolic expression in figurines of the mother goddess, or *magna mater* — "standing pregnant, squatting as though in childbirth, holding an infant to her breast, clutching her breasts with her two hands" (Campbell 140) — that bear striking resemblance to some of Herzeloyde's memorable poses upon the birth of Parzival. After the death of her husband, Herzeloyde seems herself to become in the form of her wilderness existence a site of regeneration, of ends (Gahmuret) and beginnings (Parzival): "si vreute sich ir suns geburt: / ir schimph ertranc in riwen furt" (114,3–4= "She rejoiced in the birth of her son, yet her gay spirit was drowned at sorrow's ford"). The complexity of the Herzeloyde figure may be due at least in part to mythic aspects it seems to contain, which would have contributed to making her an enigmatic, and sometimes objectionable figure (see Lewis 474).

Herzeloyde's characteristics as nourisher and the wilderness location of her alternative existence prefigure the grail court to which she is related (it is interesting to note here that the *magna mater* was in ancient times represented by a sacred stone, said to have fallen from the heavens, in which were concentrated all the vital forces of mother earth — see Willoughby 115). The grail court is organized around an object that nourishes and otherwise sustains a vast number of people (a mythic feature of the grail that takes Wolfram beyond Chrétien), and which is also located in the wilds ("mount savage" or "wild mountain" according to Hatto 1980, 431). Another important similarity pertains to the limits of chivalry: in the same way that Herzeloyde mourns the chivalric death of her husband Gahmuret, the grail court laments and mourns the "living death" of its king Anfortas (230,20), whose wound might be considered a symbol of the destructive aspects of chivalry more generally. Herzeloyde's *waste* and the grail court both combine the suspension of courtly/chivalric "business as usual" ("dâ was bûhurdieren vermiten" [227,11= "there was no vying at the bohort there"]) with lamentation ("in was wol herzen jâmer kunt" [227,16= "they had come to know heartfelt grief"]) in a manner that is characteristic of the wasteland theme (discussed by Weston 12–21, Loomis 1991, 74–81, and Darrah 54–55). Perhaps the best-known example of this theme is Malory's tale of the Dolorous Stroke (based on the thirteenth century *Suite du Merlin*), in which Pellam is wounded by Balin with the lance of Longeus (Longinus): "and grete pité hit was of hys hurte, for thorow that stroke hit turned to grete dole, tray and tene" (I, 86). The presence in Wolfram's work of elements suggestive of the wasteland theme (not to mention the life-sustaining powers of Wolfram's grail) draws attention again to the mythic concern with regeneration, in the case of the grail court to the replacement of an impotent king (Anfortas, who has been wounded in the scrotum) by a virile and potent young ruler (Parzival), upon which the fertility and happiness of the entire kingdom is based. It thus seems that the story of successful chivalric endeavor converges with and is supported by a more archaic mythic structure.

How the mythic elements not contained in Chrétien's *Perceval* reached Wolfram's *Parzival* is a matter of speculation. Previous scholars have discussed the possibility that Wolfram may have known other oral or written narratives (see Bumke 1991,156–67), and such narratives may have contained them. At one point Wolfram refers to a Shrovetide tradition involving the "koufwîp ze Tolenstein" (409,8f.= "huckstresses at Dollenstein"), and it is tempting to consider that his artistry may have been shaped by what Jessie Weston called "Folk practice" (i.e., the continuation of pagan nature rituals in the form of popular traditions). If we look at mythic elements in terms of their psychological significance, then they might be related to an unconscious creative potential in Wolfram: perhaps the author was psychologically disposed to the production of "wild" narratives (Erich Neumann sees creativity as one of the fundamental aspects of the Archetypal Feminine underlying the *magna mater* — see especially chapter 5). However we view them with respect to their points of origin and broader significance, elements associable with the mythic concern with regeneration have clearly helped to shape the people who inhabit Wolfram's wilderness and the events that occur in it. Such elements seem to have provided formative possibilities for Wolfram's deeply spiritual, but not always very straightforwardly Christian depiction of the ways in which people, particularly women figures, deal with the challenges posed by a way of life in which love is bound to combat, and hence to death. The "closeness of the relationship between the sacred and the profane, the spiritual and the mundane, the supernatural and earthly worlds" (M. Green 9) characteristic of the pagan universe as recalled in myths seems to be compatible with the unorthodox spiritual extension of a worldly, even carnal *minne* that is visible when Herzeloyde holds her son (who seems to her to be her husband) to her breast (113,11–14) and "baptizes" him with her milk; and possibly even, in a different way, in the lamentations of the much more overtly Christian Sigune over the body of her dead lover:

> 'ich hete kranke sinne,
> daz ich im niht minne gap:
> des hât der sorgen urhap
> mir freude verschrôten:
> nu minne i'n alsô tôten.' (141,20–24)

('Where were my poor wits, that I denied him enjoyment of love? From this prime source of grief my happiness is slashed to shreds and now I love him dead.')

The last of the three significant wilderness spaces in the adventures of Parzival, the grotto of the hermit Trevrizent, is the most overtly Christian, and it is generally seen by scholars as the space in which the inner transformation occurs in Parzival that later allows him to win the grail. Whereas the mythic elements seem to demonstrate a concern with regeneration, a transformation grounded in nature, Trevrizent and his hermitic existence might be seen as representative of a specifically Christian version of transformation involving the achievement of a pure form of spirituality above and beyond the limitations and temptations of the natural world. This version of transformation based on transcendence has generally been connected in the Christian tradition with a distrust of, if not contempt for, the world and the senses that is most manifestly expressed in asceticism. Of the myriad religious elements in *Parzival*, asceticism in the interest of transcendence might be regarded as the clearest religious alternative to the sensual worldliness of the courtly/chivalric orientation.

An ascetic aspect is clear in Trevrizent's grotto existence, which has come about as a consequence of the damaging effects of chivalry, in this case the wound — the living death — of Anfortas:

> mîne venje viel ich nider:
> dâ lobet ich der gotes kraft,
> daz ich deheine rîterschaft
> getæte nimmer mêre,
> daz got durch sîn êre
> mînem bruoder hulfe von der nôt.
> ich verswuor ouch fleisch, wîn unde brôt,
> unt dar nâch al daz trüege bluot
> daz ichs nimmer mêr gewünne muot.

(I fell on my knees in prayer and vowed to Almighty God that I would practise chivalry no more, in the hope that to His own glory He would help my brother in his need. I also foreswore meat, bread and wine, and indeed promised that I would never again relish anything else that had blood.)

The ascetic characteristics of Trevrizent's response to the limits of chivalry, which are later made more pronounced when he withdraws from Munsalvaesche to the hermitic existence of his grotto, might be seen as a more extreme and patently Christian monastic version of the greater degree of self-control that is already required at the grail court. In the case of combat such self-control might be seen in the vow of the grail knights to grant no quarter in penance for their sins (492,8–10), the effect of which is to make combat "absolute" and thus perhaps to disconnect it from its gratifying but sinful groundedness in worldly [i.e., Arthurian] honor, fame, and love. The grail's interdiction against the Arthurian brand of love service (495,7–8) also seems to have a distinctly ascetic quality.

The ascetic characteristics of his grotto existence permit us to view Trevrizent as occupying a position similar to that of the monks and eremites in *La Queste del Saint Graal*, who invariably interpret the significance of the adventures of Bors, Perceval, and Galahad allegorically in terms of the struggle of good against evil. It must be recognized, though, that Trevrizent — like almost every one of the significant figures in *Parzival* — is a complex individual, a mixture of chivalric and religious values, who accepts the chivalric logic of Parzival's quarrel with God (by defending God against Parzival's accusations and by maintaining that God *must* help anyone who trusts in him; 461,27–462,1), even as he is highly critical of the pridefulness of Parzival's aggressive chivalric approach. In this complexity Trevrizent is very unlike the one-dimensional spiritual commentators of the *Queste*.

In Trevrizent's ascetic characteristics and the demands they seem to make, which may be the most purely Christian and least courtly/chivalric aspect of Wolfram's romance, we seem to see an articulation of the Christian moral consciousness as defined by John Casey:

> Pride, the desire for honour, and still more wealth and beauty, have nothing to do with Christian goodness. Even those active virtues (so admired by Hume and Gibbon) which make a man formidable, great, a valuable member of a city state, have always met with an equivocal response from the Christian tradition. Meekness, humility, a conviction that human corruption cannot be overcome by human effort, a rejection of the world and its pomps, are at the centre of the Christian moral consciousness. (v–vi)

Trevrizent seems to express such a moral consciousness when he links Parzival's anger — his *zorn* against God (discussed above) — with the pride of Lucifer (463,1–5), and when he later responds to Parzival's chivalric advocation of the value of combat with a description of the attitude of humility that is appropriate for the grail court:

> 'ir müest aldâ vor hôchvart
> mit senften willen sîn bewart.
> iuch verleit lîcht iwer jugent
> daz ir der kiusche bræchet tugent.
> hôchvart ie seic unde viel' (472,13–17)

> ('There of all places you would have to guard against arrogance by cultivating meekness of spirit . . . You could be misled by youthfulness into breaches of self-control. — Pride goes before a fall!')

The importance of such a moral consciousness for the successful culmination of Parzival's adventures and hence of Wolfram's romance is difficult to determine. We have observed that Parzival's behavior after the sojourn with Trevrizent is not fundamentally different from his behavior before. It may be that we have to construe Parzival's fighting itself — the long years of wandering and struggling — as a specifically chivalric version of asceticism (compare Jones 1972,69–70), but outside of Trevrizent's grotto, Wolfram's work never really advocates anything close to "meekness, humility, a conviction that human corruption cannot be overcome by human effort." If we are to view divine action in *Parzival* as occurring at a level that is clearly and entirely beyond that of Parzival's chivalric aggression (i.e., beyond the courtly/chivalric God who enjoys watching a good fight, as in Hartmann's *Iwein* [verses 1020–22 — Benecke ed.]), it seems necessary to consider that two very different, if not contradictory paradigms have been juxtaposed in Wolfram's romance: according to one, Parzival fights his way to the grail by overcoming all opposition and relying on little else but "unverzaget mannes muot" (1,5= "the courage of a steadfast man"); according to the other, Parzival receives the grail by recognizing the sin into which he has fallen and by trusting in God (see 456,29–30 and 741,26 — and Murdoch's article in this volume).

4

Whether seen as sacred or profane, as a religious kingdom on earth or as a mythic otherworld, the wilderness of Parzival's adventures that is organized around the grail kingdom seems to present itself above all as a space of profound psychological and spiritual reflection. In these wilderness spaces, and in the relatively complex figures who occupy them (who for the most part seem quite a bit more complex than the hero himself), we seem among other things to witness different ways of coming to grips with the damaging effects of chivalry, but in ways that are as demonstrative of a continuation of worldly, courtly/chivalric concerns as of a qualification or criticism of them. If it is possible at all to speak of the multifarious mythic/religious elements in the wilderness of Parzival's adventures as a coherent alternative to the courtly/chivalric orientation, then it might be appropriate to speak of a juxtaposition of worldly and spiritual values, as represented by the Arthurian court and the Grail court respectively, rather than of a subordination of the former to the latter in the adventures (or "development") of Parzival. Perhaps it is in this way, as an increase in the complexity of the manner in which the world is being experienced, rather than as a progression or development of Parzival beyond the courtly/chivalric life, that we have to understand the balance between divine favor and "der werlde hulde" (827,22= "The good-will and respect of one's fellows") that Wolfram has achieved at the end of his work.

We have seen that death in the chivalric pursuit of love, honor, and fame, and the manner in which people come to grips with this limit, seems to be one of the central concerns of Wolfram's *Parzival*. This is indicated by the importance of the death of Gandin (for initiating the adventures of Gahmuret), the death of Gahmuret (for leading by way of Herzeloyde's *waste* to the unusual beginning point of the adventures of Parzival and thereby contributing to their extraordinary impetus and trajectory), the death of Ither (for establishing specifically Christian parameters for an understanding of chivalric death in terms of sin), and of the "living death" of Anfortas (which, with its mythic and Christian implications, marks the narrative beginning and end of Parzival's fighting for the grail). The concern with mortality in chivalry, its centrality and frequency in comparison to the earlier Arthurian romances of Chrétien and Hartmann, is one of the many ways that Wolfram's romance seems to take the measure of human life, although it must be observed that these, in their sum total, involve at least as much joy and happiness as grief and suffering.

The very different ways in which people come to grips with the damaging effects of chivalry are at the heart of Wolfram's interweaving of courtly/chivalric, mythic, and religious elements on an unprecedented scale in the High Middle Ages. Wolfram's Arthurian "tapestry" is, to use the current terms, very diverse and inclusive: it pursues, as we have seen, a staunchly chivalric agenda (much more so than the *Perceval* of Chrétien), even as it accommodates with sympathy and reverence mythic and religious figures and elements that seem, at least in some of their manifestations, to stand in the way of this agenda. *Parzival* has therefore to be distinguished from the grail quest as described in *La Queste del Saint Graal*, upon which part of Malory's influential Arthuriad was based. Wolfram's work, in which the different elements seem to be juxtaposed and in which courtly/chivalric values remain pronounced from beginning to end, can be read as an ideological counterpoint to the ascetic and sometimes misogynistic spirit of the *Queste*, which was composed in all likelihood in a Cistercian context a few decades later. In the first, the (sinful) contingencies of involvement in worldly life are accepted, even as a variety of more or less orthodox spiritual/psychological experiences are explored; in the latter these contingencies are overcome altogether in the extreme self-abnegation and rejection of flesh, world, and woman that is required by a single, exclusive, and predominantly masculine religiosity. The sinful Lancelot and his chosen son Galahad of the *Queste* are not divided in the person of Wolfram's Parzival, who wins the grail without renouncing his very worldly, courtly/chivalric orientation.

In the twentieth century, as in the Middle Ages, the Arthurian tradition has continued to appeal to international audiences, and the aspects that have been under discussion here are still pertinent to this popularity. The courtly/chivalric orientation, although no longer the representation — however conventional or idealized — of a way of life, has shown itself to be adaptable to the representation of many different social situations and conceptions of social order, ranging from the moral quandaries of Arthur in the novels of T. H. White composed at the outset of World War II, to the "politically correct" Camelot in the recent film *First Knight* (1995), to the overtly Arthurian imagery of recent television advertisements for the United States Marine Corps.

What Richard Barber calls "the Search for the Spiritual" in his discussion of the Arthurian tradition in the nineteenth century (1961,146–178) involves a fascinated preoccupation on the part of modern authors and audiences with its mythic and religious elements, which have lost none of their ability to resonate today in a cultural situation characterized by an intense interest in myth, not just in the fantasy of popular culture, but in highbrow literature as well (see Agena). Read against this contemporary cultural backdrop, Wolfram's *Parzival* speaks to us as a unique medieval work that combines pride in one's community and tolerance for the rich complexity and diversity of life.

The Modern Reception of Wolfram's *Parzival*

ULRICH MÜLLER

Wolfram, Wagner, and the Germans

IT IS CHARACTERISTIC OF MANY, MAYBE EVEN all, cultural and political communities to create an individual identity by "separating" one's own community from others. Stories which embody religion and history play an important role in this respect, as for example, those told in the Homeric myths of the ancient Greeks or those told in the *Mahabharata* and the *Ramayana* which are important to the Hindus of India to the present day. The European countries that increasingly saw themselves as nation states since the late eighteenth century also endeavored, especially during the course of the nineteenth century, to define their national identity through their history and epic myths. The search for an identity grounded in a national past was particularly pronounced in those areas which — in contrast to France, England, and Russia — did not have the political identity for which their inhabitants strove: the Balkans, the non-German parts of the Danubian monarchy, divided Poland, Italy, Greece, and German-speaking central Europe (I use "German" to mean the German language; a political meaning will be indicated). In their cultural life the German-speaking peoples of the early nineteenth century, politically disunited and powerless, escaped into the past, especially to the glorious time of the Hohenstaufen dynasty in the twelfth and thirteenth centuries, which was used to legitimate the longing for a national unity that could not be realized in the present. The story of Siegfried, the Nibelungs and the Burgundians, published in full in 1782 for the first time by the Swiss Christoph Heinrich Myller, gradually became something like a German national myth. Initially meeting with great resistance, the *Nibelungenlied* was strongly promoted during the Napoleonic occupation and the (so-called) "Wars of Liberation." This epic obtained a significance it never had during the high and late Middle Ages and which would have puzzled medieval readers or listeners: it became the German national epic with the claim of a rank equal, if not somewhat superior, to Homer, Virgil, Dante, and the French *Chanson de Roland*.

There was little room next to this German national epic of the Nibelungs for stories about Arthur, Parzival, the grail quest, Tristan, and the knights of the Round Table. Despite the influence of English and American translations and movies, the popularity of the tales of King Arthur, Guinevere, Lancelot, and the other Knights of the Round Table in the English-speaking world has not been matched in German speaking countries. This has, in my opinion, different but closely related reasons: 1) the difficulty of "exporting" the British national understanding and meaning of the legend of King Arthur, 2) the specific fixations of German-speaking peoples on other myths or legends of the Middle Ages, and 3) the dominating influence of Richard Wagner on the total German artistic reception of medieval literature. The only medieval vernacular narratives that have really played an important cultural role in German-speaking countries since their rediscovery in the eighteenth century are those Richard Wagner converted into his operas *Tannhäuser* (1845), *Tristan und Isolde* (1865), *Der Ring des Nibelungen* (1869, 1870, 1876), and *Parsifal* (1882). All of the operas and music dramas which Wagner completed are bound up with the Middle Ages. This is true, in the widest sense, even of *Die Feen* (written 1833/1834), *Rienzi* (1842), and *Der fliegende Holländer* (1843), as well as of the world of Hans Sachs and the Mastersingers as depicted in *Die Meistersinger von Nürnberg* (1868).

Wagner's "Bühnenweihfestspiel" (= Sacred Stage Festival Play) *Parsifal*, premiering at the Bayreuth Festspielhaus in 1882, was of critical importance in shaping the modern German reception of the Arthurian tradition, since it practically cemented the uniquely German "reception of King Arthur without King Arthur." Since the revival of interest in the Arthurian tradition in the early nineteenth century, German-speaking artists and authors have concentrated not on the king of the Round Table and his court at Camelot, but rather on the story of Parzival; that is, his ultimately successful search for the grail, as well as on the events surrounding his son Loherangrin (Lohengrin). For his treatment of these stories, Wagner's main source was Wolfram von Eschenbach's *Parzival*. Some explanations are necessary about the different spellings of the protagonist's name: Wolfram's source, *Li contes del Graal* of Chrétien de Troyes, uses the name "Perceval" (in the mss. also spelled and named "Percheval", "Perchevax," etc.), as do Chrétien's French continuators and the later French grail tradition. Already in the Middle Ages, but not by Chrétien, the name is etymologically defined as "Perce-val" = "penetrate the valley" (other forms of the name fit this pattern as well: "Perce-vaux" = "penetrate the valleys," "Perce-forest" = "penetrate the forest," etc.). However, these meanings were of no consequence either in the French version of Chrétien or later for Wolfram. The hero's name in the manuscripts of Wolfram's poem is "Parzival" (with the *z* sounding like English *ts* and the *v* like *f*). In verse 140,17, Wolfram's Sigune says to Parzival: "du heizest Parzivâl / der nam ist rehte enmitten durch" ("your name is Parzival / the name means 'through the middle'"). This explanation of the significance of the name Parzival is similar to the above mentioned French definition. In the following verse, Wolfram links the meaning of the name to the pain Parzival caused his mother by leaving her: "grôz liebe ier solch herzen furch / mit dîner muoter triuwe" (140, 18f.= "Great love plowed just such a furrow through your mother's heart" — here Hatto's translation). Other than that, as in the French versions, the meaning of the name is of no importance for Wolfram. Wagner mentions "Parzival" as king of the grail and Lohengrin's father in his romantic opera *Lohengrin*. Creating his music drama *Parsifal* he concentrates entirely on the figure of the Seeker of the grail, first calling him "Parzival," but then later deciding to use the spelling "Parsifal." This name is derived from an etymology (Arabic "fal parsi" = "pure fool"), conceived by the German historian and journalist Joseph Görres, which was later shown to be incorrect, although Wagner employed Görres's etymology in his libretto in spite of this, explaining that there would probably be no specialists of Arabic philology among his audiences.

Although the legends of Arthur, and of Parzival and the grail, were known to educated Germans at the end of the eighteenth and beginning of the nineteenth centuries by means of French and English versions, anyone interested in Wolfram's epic would have had to find a library which owned a copy of the late-medieval printing of *Parzival* published by Johann Mentelin in Strasbourg in 1477. The first modern printing of Wolfram's poem, together with many other Middle High German epics, was a transliteration edited by the above mentioned Swiss Myller. However, there was generally little interest in Myller's publication of these medieval works. King Frederick II. of Prussia ("The Great"), to whom Myller dedicated a copy of his edition, responded politely, but stressed that these old poems had no value for him. The Wolfram edition by Karl Lachmann (1833), and particularly the translations of San Marte, whose pen name was Alfred Schulz, in 1836 (*Parcival. Rittergedicht von Wolfram von Eschenbach. Aus dem Mittelhochdeutschen zum ersten Male übersetzt*, 2 vols [Magdeburg: Creutzsche Buchhandlung]) and in 1841 and of Karl Simrock in 1842 (*Parzival und Titurel. Rittergedichte von Wolfram von Eschenbach. Übersetzt und erläutert*, 2 vols [Stuttgart: Cotta]) are responsible for first stimulating interest in the Parzival legend. Richard Wagner, who had been working with the grail material since 1845 (for his "romantic opera" *Lohengrin*), was the crucial station of reception: he influenced and left a mark on the creative reception and interpretation of medieval narratives that is hard to overestimate.

Between 1843 and 1845, while he was working on *Tannhäuser* and preparing for its first performance at the Royal Opera House in Dresden, where he held the post of Court Kapellmeister, Wagner's thoughts were more or less simultaneously occupied with almost all of his later medieval sources and subjects, an occupation that became more intense during his visit to the health resort of Marienbad in the summer of 1845. The thoroughness with which he proceeded is clear from the books in his so-called "Dresden library," which Wagner first began to assemble in 1842 and which he was obliged to leave behind in 1849 when he fled Saxony because of his revolutionary activities (see von Westernhagen). After many vicissitudes, this collection, largely complete and undamaged, was bequeathed to the National Archives in Bayreuth in 1971. In addition to a number of modern works, it contains mainly texts, translations and scholarly works dealing with the literature of classical antiquity and, more especially, of the Middle Ages. The completeness and excellence of the collection would have been the envy of virtually every philologist of Wagner's day.

It is not possible to gain a reliable picture of the medieval legends and romances on the basis of Wagner's works. Wagner himself, of course, claimed that he had, so to speak, distilled and depicted the essential meaning of each of the medieval tales which form the basis of his music dramas. But the composer is mistaken here, which is not unusual, since artists are notoriously unreliable judges of their own works. Wagner's reworking of his medieval sources can generally be addressed in the form of four observations, which also involve the relationship between Wolfram's *Parzival* and Richard Wagner's *Lohengrin* and *Parsifal*. First, with regard to the content of his medieval sources and the use to which he puts them, Wagner evolves in the direction of an increasingly drastic reduction of the source material. Whereas, initially, the story taken over from the medieval source may even be expanded in various ways, Wagner later leaves more and more out, concentrating instead upon individual sections of the action. Second, parallel to the above mentioned reduction of the source material is an increasing tendency on Wagner's part to alter the message of his medieval source until he finally turns the message upside-down. Third, as to the relationship between narrative content and the message of the piece, it can be observed that the story in question, as presented on stage, tends increasingly to assume the form of a programmatical statement: a dramatic narrative develops into the dramatico-theatrical proclamation of one particular message. It follows from this that specifically medieval features thereby disappear increasingly from the later music dramas and that Wagner's new message gains in importance. The fourth and final thesis regarding Wagner and his medieval sources is sort of a résumé combining the three above: The so-called "romantic operas" *Tannhäuser* and *Lohengrin*, on the one hand, and the so-called "music dramas" *Tristan* and *Parsifal*, on the other, form well-structured pairs of opposites in terms of their relationship to their medieval sources, and hence also in terms of the relative predominance of the plot or message (conceived between 1842 and 1852, the text of the *Ring* occupies a position midway between these extremes).

An expansion of the source material is visible in Wagner's earlier "romantic operas" about Tannhäuser and Lohengrin. Wagner's principal source for *Lohengrin* was the final section of Wolfram von Eschenbach's *Parzival*, where the entire story of Loherangrin is told in a few lines at the end of the romance, together with a later anonymous strophic poem edited and published by Joseph Görres in 1813 under the title *Lohengrin, ein altteutsches Gedicht* (Heidelberg: Mohr, 1813). Here the figure of Lohengrin is linked with both the Wartburg Song Contest and the figure of Wolfram. Wagner uses the medieval story of Loherangrin (Parzival's son), the duchess of Brabant and the forbidden question she asks, skillfully tightening up the plot and embellishing it with one of the more impressive scenes from the *Nibelungenlied*. This scene, which occupies almost the whole of the second act of *Lohengrin*, revolves around the quarrel between the figures of Kriemhilde and Brunhilde as transferred to Elsa, duchess of Brabant, and her opponent Ortrud. In his *Lohengrin* (as well as previously in *Tannhäuser*), Wagner has turned the original story-line into a dramatically viable stage action by adding something extra to the existing medieval source and in this way producing a dramatically effective second act.

The situation is completely different in the case of the later music dramas *Tristan und Isolde* and *Parsifal*. The primary sources here were the epic poems of Gottfried von Straßburg and Wolfram von Eschenbach respectively, both available to Wagner in extensively annotated translations, of the latter by San Marte 1836 and Karl Simrock 1842, of the former by Hermann Kurtz (*Tristan und Isolde. Gedicht von Gottfried von Straßburg* [Stuttgart: Rieger, 1844]). On both occasions Wagner cut the action decisively, not to say drastically, in the case of *Parsifal* in an even radical way. Wolfram's *Parzival* — to quote the Foreword of Hatto's translation — "is the retelling and ending by one genius, Wolfram von Eschenbach [. . .], of the unfinished romance of another, the *Perceval* of Chrétien de Troyes" (7). Wolfram's narrative follows Chrétien's, but he alters so much, both on the large scale and in the details, that his *Parzival* is a new, independent work, and cannot be described as a free rendering of the original, still less as a translation. Wolfram — unlike Chrétien — depicts a whole cosmos: his romance embraces three generations and gives the impression of containing vast numbers of characters, including — as in the romance of Chrétien — no less than two heroes, Parzival and Gawan. Of this, all that remains in Wagner's music drama are Parzival, his mother Herzeloyde (at least in the form of a retrospective), the wounded grail-king, the Castle of the grail, Parzival's failure to ask about the reason of the king's suffering, and the final act of redemption. Wagner uses the names Gurnemanz and Clinschor (Klingsor) from Wolfram's epic in his music drama, but both figures have been extensively modified by him, while the character and history of Wagner's Kundry are largely new. Only a few basic structures and themes, together with the names of characters, have been retained by Wagner, although Wolfram's poem is still clearly recognizable as the source of the relevant action.

With respect to Wagner's increasing tendency to alter, if not invert, the message of his medieval source, we observe that the medieval storyline of *Tannhäuser*, the errant and penitent knight, and of *Lohengrin*, the son of the grail-king, were retained in Wagner's "romantic operas" of the forties. In *Lohengrin* the crucial themes remain, namely the knight's celestial origins, the forbidden question (which in Wolfram's *Parzival* had been intended as a cryptic contrast to the question the hero is required to ask the ailing grail-king Anfortas), and an ending which involves no act of redemption for the characters concerned. Exactly the opposite is to be found in the later music dramas *Tristan und Isolde* and *Parsifal*: in both cases, Wagner criticized and even condemned his sources (see Wagner's letter to Mathilde Wesendonck, cited below). Wolfram's comprehensive, world-affirming fairy-tale romance is transformed by Wagner into a philosophical music drama which, with the aid of the persuasive arts of music and drama, and of ideas found in Buddhism and in the philosophy of Arthur Schopenhauer (see Ulrich Müller 1980 and Marianne Wynn 1983), proclaims a gospel of asceticism and world-denial that represents the triumph of conservatism over progress.

Tannhäuser and *Lohengrin*, and even substantial parts of the *Ring of the Nibelung*, exist primarily by virtue of their plot as presented on stage. From the *Ring* onwards there is an increase in the number of passages in which events are not simply presented, but in which past actions are retold, reflected upon, or interpreted. Here the great narrations, monologues and dialogues in *Tristan* and *Parsifal* spring to mind, the scenes in which, according to popular belief, "nothing happens" on the stage, at least at first glance. Parallel to the increasing tendentiousness of Wagner's later works, arguments as to how they should be interpreted — between Wagnerians on the one hand and anti-Wagnerians on the other — have grown ever more intense and even bitter as the years have gone by. Despite the vitriol in many scholarly assessments of Wagner, *Tristan*, *Parsifal*, and parts of the *Ring* affect their listeners' lives deeply and challenge them to adopt a philosophical or even a religious stance towards these works. This development in the direction of a programmatic statement culminates in the responses evoked and provoked by *Parsifal*, which Wagner himself called a *Bühnenweihfestspiel* (= Sacred Stage Festival Play): this work claimed, not unjustifiably, to embody a message that almost amounts to an ersatz-religion.

Among the most controversial aspects of *Parsifal*, according to scholars like Theodor W. Adorno, Hartmut Zelinsky, Richard Gutman, and Marc A. Weiner, is that it contains anti-Semitic aspects. While such accusations have provoked heated discussions, no convincing examples have been found in the libretto or music to back up them up (compare Katz and Kühnel). On the other hand, it is undeniable that Wagner's subjective and emotionally laden anti-Semitism, as it can be found in his notorious essay "Judentum in der Musik" (published in slightly different versions in 1850 and 1869), often played an important underlying role in the later interpretation of *Parsifal* by fanatical and conservative Wagnerians.

Much of what has been said above about the later development of Wagner's treatment of his sources — particularly the tendencies to reduce the scope of his medieval sources and to change their message — is exemplified by a long letter Wagner wrote on 29–30 May 1859 to his confidante Mathilde Wesendonck in Zurich, in which Wagner criticizes Wolfram's poem from a decidedly personal standpoint and draws a contrast between the medieval author's universal romance and his own conception of a three-part (i.e. three-act) philosophical drama. Important for our understanding of this letter is that Wagner had found, in the second volume of San Marte's translation, a lengthy excursus on the "legend of the Holy Grail" that summarized the current state of knowledge. It was presumably from here that Wagner took the idea that the grail (to quote from *Lohengrin*) was "a vessel of miraculous blessings," rather than Wolfram's stone.

Because of the light it sheds on Wagner's regard for and treatment of Wolfram's *Parzival*, this letter is cited at length (the italicized words were underscored by Wagner himself):

It has again dawned upon me of late that this [*Parzival*] would again be a fundamental evil task. Looked at closely, it is Anfortas who is in the centre of attention and principal subject. Of course, it is not at all a bad story. Consider, in heaven's name, all that goes on there! It suddenly became dreadfully clear to me: it is my third-act Tristan inconceivably intensified. With the spear-wound and perhaps another wound, too — in his heart — , the wretched man knows of no other longing in his terrible pain than the longing to die; in order to attain this supreme solace, he demands repeatedly to be allowed a glimpse of the Grail in the hope that it might at least close his wounds, for everything else is useless, nothing — nothing can help him: — but the Grail can give him one thing only, which is precisely that he *cannot* die; its very sight increases his torments by conferring immortality upon them. The Grail, according to my own interpretation, is the goblet used at the Last Supper in which Joseph of Arimathia caught the Saviour's blood on the Cross. What terrible significance the connection between Anfortas and this miraculous chalice now acquires; *he*, infected by the same wound as was dealt him by a rival's spear in a passionate love intrigue, — his only solace lies in the benediction of the blood that once flowed from the Saviour's own, similar, spear-wound as He languished upon the Cross, world-renouncing, world-redeeming and world-suffering! Blood for blood, wound for wound — but what a gulf between the blood of the one and that of the other, between the one wound and the other! [. . .] And you expect me to carry through something like this? and set it to music, into the bargain? — No thank you very much! I leave that to anyone who has a mind for such things; *I* shall do all to keep my distance from it! — Let someone do it who will carry it through à la Wolfram; it will then cause little offence, and in the end may perhaps sound like something, maybe even something quite pretty. But *I* take such things far too seriously. Yet just look at the extent to which Master Wolfram has made light of it, by contrast! That he has understood absolutely nothing of the actual content is of no great matter. He tacks one event on to the next, one adventure to another, links together the Grail motif with all manner of strange and curious episodes and images, gropes around and leaves any serious reader wondering whatever his intention can have been? To which he is bound to reply that he himself in fact knows no more about what he is doing than the priest understands the Christianity that he serves up at the altar without knowing what is involved. — That's how it is. Wolfram is a thoroughly immature phenomenon, although it must be said that his barbaric and utterly confused age is largely to blame for this, fluctuating as it did between early Christianity and a more modern political economy. Nothing could ever come to fruition at such a period; poetic profundity was immediately submerged in insubstantial caprice. I almost agree with Frederick the Great who, on being presented with a copy of Wolfram, told the publisher not to bother him with such stuff! — Indeed it is sufficient to have given new life to such a subject on the basis of the genuine feature of the legend, as I have now done with the Grail legend, and then to take a quick look at how such a poet as Wolfram has depicted the very same thing — as I have now done by leafing through your book [i.e., a new copy of the translation of Wolfram's *Parzival* that Mathilde Wesendonck had sent to Wagner — Wagner had left behind his own copy in the "Dresdner Bibliothek"] — in order to be utterly repelled by the poet's incompetence. (The same thing happened to me with Gottfried v. Straßburg in the context of Tristan.) Consider only this one point, that, of all the interpretations to which the Grail has been subjected in the various legends, this superficial 'deep thinker' should have chosen the most meaningless of all. That this miraculous object should be a precious stone is a feature which, admittedly, can be traced to the earliest sources, namely the Arabic texts of Spanish Moors. One notices, unfortunately, that all our Christian legends have a foreign, pagan origin. As they gazed on in amazement, the early Christians learned, namely, that the Moors in the Caaba at Mecca (deriving from the pre-Muhammedan religion) venerated a stone (a sunstone — or a meteoric stone — but at all events one that had fallen from heaven). However, the legends of its miraculous power were soon interpreted by the Christians after their own fashion, by associating the sacred objects with Christian myth, a process which, in turn, was made easier by the fact that an old legend existed in southern France telling how Joseph of Arimathia had once fled there with the sacred chalice that had been used at the Last Supper, a version entirely consonant with the early Christian church's enthusiasm for relics. Only now did sense and reason enter into it, and I feel a very real admiration and sense of rapture at this splendid feature of Christian mythogenesis, which invented the most profound symbol that could ever have been invented as the content of the physical-spiritual kernel of any religion [. . .] — And all of this has been so senselessly misinterpreted by our poet, who took only the inferior French chivalric romances as his subject-matter and repeated them like a parrot! You can infer from this what the rest must be like! Only individual descriptions are in any way attractive, but this is the forte of all medieval poets, for whom the predominant mood is a finely felt pictoriality. But each work *as a whole* always remains confused and silly. I should have to make a completely fresh start with Parzival! For Wolfram hadn't the first idea of what he was doing: his (scil. Parzival's) despair in God is stupid and unmotivated, and his conversion is even more unsatisfactory. The thing about the 'question' is that it is *so* utterly preposterous and totally meaningless. I should simply have to invent everything here. And there is a further difficulty with Parzival. He is indispensably necessary as the redeemer whom Anfortas longs for: but if Anfortas is placed in his true and appropriate light, he will become of such immense tragic interest that it will be almost impossible to introduce a second focus of attention, and yet this focus of attention must centre upon Parzival if the latter is not simply to enter at the end as a deus ex machina who leaves us completely cold. Thus Parzival's development and the profound sublimity of his purification, although entirely predestined by his thoughtful and deeply compassionate nature, must again be brought into the foreground. But I cannot choose to work on such a broad scale as Wolfram was able to do: I have to compress everything into *three* climactic situations of violent intensity, so that the work's profound and ramified content emerges clearly and distinctly; for *my* art consists in working and representing things in *this* way. And — am I to undertake such a task? God forbid! Today I take my leave of this insane project . . . (*Selected Letters of Richard Wagner*, trans. Stewart Spencer [London: Dent, 1987], 458–460).

This letter provides glimpses into the early conceptual stages of *Parsifal* and indicates how it will deal with the "flaws" Wagner sees in his medieval source. The result will be a work which, as Peter Wapnewski has written, "In its hostility to the senses and to women, [. . .] is a profoundly inhuman spectacle, glorifying a barren masculine world whose ideals are a combination of militarism and monasticism" (1992, 91). However, this negative assessment is followed by words that must also be kept in mind: "its dramaturgic structure is admirable, and the music amazing. Even the fiercest critics of Wagner as a person have paid tribute to the music of *Parsifal* — from Hanslick (who liked the Flower Maidens) and Nietzsche to Debussy and Adorno." The leading modern French composer Pierre Boulez, who during his revolutionary days in 1968 declared that all opera-houses representing bourgeois culture should be burnt down, conducted — several years later — Wagner-operas at the Bayreuth Festspielhaus, and the first of all was *Parsifal*.

Before proceeding to the twentieth century, another important artistic rendering of Wolfram's *Parzival* from the early nineteenth century must be mentioned. Literary scholars have been well aware that the Prussian officer and writer Friedrich Baron de la Motte Fouqué (1777–1843), descendant of Huguenot emigrants from France, was not only a best selling Romantic author for several years (*Der Held des Nordens* [1808–1810], *Undine* [1811], *Der Zauberring* [1813]), but that he also later wrote the first significant retelling of Wolfram's *Parzi-*

val of the 19th century: *Der Parcival. Rittergedicht* (1831–32). Nearly nobody was familiar with this first version of *Parzival* in modern German, because Fouqué, who had become totally out-of-date, could not find a publisher for his manuscript of roughly 500 pages. Finally, in January 1997, Fouqué's *Parcival* was edited by Tilman Spreckelsen, Peter Henning Hischer, Frank Rainer Max, and Ursula Rautenberg (Hildesheim-Zürich-New York: Olms, 1997), and now we have easy access to a nearly forgotten piece of German literature from the late Romantic period.

Fouqué follows Wolfram's story-line rather closely, but he uses an entirely different technique of writing, combining elements of epic, dramatic and lyric poetry, using mostly verses of different meters, with and without rhyme, but also sometimes employing prose. Fictitious dialogues between "Meister Friedrich" (i.e., the author himself) and "Meister Wolfram" (i.e. the author of his medieval source), regularly interrupt and comment on the story, thus creating a chain of intermezzi which gives structure to the endless stream of scenes retelling the medieval legend of Parcival, Gawan, and the grail. Fouqué's *Parcival* was so old-fashioned in its time that it is understandable that no publisher wanted to take the risk to print this huge piece of literature. The whole work is conservative in its message, antiquated in its highly stylized language, and subjective and emotional in its organization of the narration. But it might be fascinating for post-modern readers of the nineties, and not only in my opinion: it was Arno Schmidt, eccentric author of *Zettels Traum* and well-known rediscoverer of many interesting, but forgotten pieces of German literature, who valued Fouqué's *Parcival* highly and praised it lavishly in his Fouqué-biography of 1958. Even if it took more than 150 years before it appeared as a printed book, the modern German reception of Wolfram's *Parzival* began with a hidden treasure, something like a veiled grail.

It was the combination of Wagner and Wagnerism which dominated the entire twentieth-century reception of the story of Parzival and the grail in German-speaking countries. Parzival became here somewhat like a medieval brother of Faust, the prototype of a searcher spending his life on a quest. This tradition is found not only in literature, for example in the neo-romantic Parzival novel of Albrecht Schaeffer (*Parzival. Ein Versroman in drei Kreisen* [Leipzig: Insel, 1922]), but it is also perceptible in Rudolf Steiner's anthroposophistic interpretations as well as in the depth-psychological interpretations of the C. G. Jung school: Jung's wife Emma and Marie-Louise von Franz interpreted the grail story as being a symbolic-mystical "experience of God." The grail itself is related to the alchemist's mystical vessel and therefore to Jung's "anima," which, according to his teachings, is the functioning feminine component contained in every human soul. This depth-psychological understanding of the grail myth has played an important role in the twentieth century, and its influence is more or less evident in most creative receptions of the grail material. The writings of C. G. Jung have had a lasting influence on the interpretations of Wagner's *Parsifal* in particular, especially in the case of Wieland Wagner's well known New Bayreuth production in 1951, which remained exemplary and influenced the style in which the work was produced for at least two decades. Even today every producer of *Parsifal* needs to take Wieland Wagner's production into consideration in some way or another. There is also a movie of Wagner's *Parsifal*, produced by Hans Jürgen Syberberg in 1982. One of the most interesting and exciting opera films ever made, this film consolidated the dominance of Wagner's influence on the German reception of the Arthurian legend (see Ulrich Müller 1991).

Given Wagner's dominance, it is not too surprising that there were so few German modifications of the Parzival/Parsifal material until well into the 1970s. Of course, there had been — after San Marte and Simrock — additional modern translations of Wolfram's poem, and there was also a growing number of adaptations of the Parzival/grail-story for young readers, for example by Gerhart Hauptmann (*Parsival. Mit Bildern von Ferdinand Staeger* [Berlin: Ullstein, 1914]), but most of these juvenile books were of modest quality. It was only after a relatively long break in the Parzival/grail reception, on the heels of the so-called "Middle Ages Boom" of the late sixties and seventies, that new approaches were attempted. Dieter Kühn, already well-known for several books — among them one about the late medieval singer Oswald von Wolkenstein — published *Der Parzival des Wolfram von Eschenbach* in 1986 (Frankfurt: Insel), which combines a very personal monograph and a modern translation, and which has become of great importance for the contemporary German reception of the Parzival story.

It was the ever-increasing number of English and American versions in the 1970s, the Arthurian films (especially John Boorman's *Excalibur* [1981]), Tankred Dorst's epic play *Merlin oder Das Wüste Land* (1981), as well as Christoph Hein's play *Die Ritter der Tafelrunde* (a key work in the so-called *Wende*, the political turning point in East Germany in 1989–1990) which awakened the knights of the Round Table from their long sleep in the German-speaking countries and also presented new views on Parzival. There were also two film versions of the story: the French movie *Perceval le Gallois* by director Eric Rohmer

(1979), and the German TV-play *Parzival* by Richard Blank (1980); both of them follow their medieval sources closely, Rohmer nearly word by word, Blank by combining the old legend with modern problems (see the edition of Harty 1991). The drama *Merlin* by Tankred Dorst (the leading West German dramatist), assisted by Ursula Ehler, became one of the central theatrical works of the eighties: it uses the whole Arthurian legend, according to Wolfram von Eschenbach and Malory, to depict a world of hope and war, of love and hatred, combining myth, history, and our present time. Although an unabridged version of the play would run about twelve hours or more, it has been produced in different versions with great success. A few sequels have followed: in 1984, Dorst and Ehler planned a television movie about Parzival (working title *Der Wilde*), which was printed in 1986 (and again in 1990) and which has yet to be made into a film. Besides this they published two more Parzival books, *Der nackte Mann* (Frankfurt: Suhrkamp, 1986) and *Parzival. Ein Szenarium* (Frankfurt: Suhrkamp, 1990), and they have also worked on Robert Wilson's sensational production *Parzival: Auf der anderen Seite des Sees*, which premiered on September 12, 1987 at the Hamburg Thalia-Theater. In this production — which follows the conception of Dorst's *Merlin* — the story of Parzival and his unsuccessful (!) search for the grail is portrayed for the most part visually rather than with words. Another work using Dorst as a model is the strongly pacifistic jazz version of the grail story, the jazz oratorio *The Holy Grail of Joy and Jazz*, composed by George Gruntz. It was performed in Austria in 1985 and was, like *Merlin*, also shown on Austrian television.

The year 1989 brought a veritable Parzival/grail "boom" to the German-speaking world. Besides Christoph Hein, the following authors should be mentioned here: the Austrian Peter Handke, *Das Spiel vom Fragen oder Die Reise zum sonoren Land* (Frankfurt: Suhrkamp, 1989; premiere January 16, 1990 at the Vienna Burgtheater); the above-mentioned Tankred Dorst/Ursula Ehler, *Parzival. Ein Szenarium* (announced for 1989, but first published in Frankfurt by Suhrkamp in 1990); and a novel by the Swiss Adolf Muschg called *Der Rote Ritter. Eine Geschichte von Parzivâl* (Frankurt: Suhrkamp, 1993). Parzival and the grail have also become more visible outside of German-speaking countries in the recent past. In the French and lately also in the English-speaking areas there has been a growing interest in the Perceval-grail material that mostly follows the French and English Arthurian traditions. One need only remember works such as the above mentioned *Perceval* film by Eric Rohmer (1979), and the *Graal Théâtre* by Jacques Roubaud/Florence Delay (1977–1981) in France.

In English there are the Parzival romances by Michael Moorcock (*The War Hound and the World's Pain* [New York: Timescape Books, 1981]), by Richard Monaco (*Parsival or a Knight's Tale* [New York: Macmillan, 1977], *The Grail War* [New York: Pocket Books, 1979], *The Final Quest* [New York: Putnam, 1980], and *Blood and Dreams* [New York: Berkley, 1985] — crude retellings with explicit references to Wolfram!), and by Peter Vansittart (*Parsifal. A Novel* [London: P. Owen, 1990]). One also thinks of the suggested, but not explicitly formulated Parzival structure in Bernard Malamud's *The Natural* (New York: Harcourt & Brace 1952), and in 1989 there was a highly successful American adventure movie about a modern American Perceval and his grail-quest: Steven Spielberg's *Indiana Jones and the Last Crusade*.

The stories of Arthur and Parzival have even been used to discuss recent issues in Eastern Europe such as *glasnost* and *perestroika*. The dramatist Christoph Hein, one of the leading East German writers, wrote a drama entitled *Die Ritter der Tafelrunde* (*The Knights of the Round Table*), for which he used the German Parzival tradition, i.e. Wolfram's romance and, probably, Dorst/Ehler's *Merlin*. Hein's drama had its opening night in March 1989 at the "Staatschauspiel" of Dresden/GDR. The play depicts a senile group of knights, sitting at a damaged "Round Table" (at Camelot, of course, not in Berlin, Moscow, or Warsaw), lamenting their failures, the ruin of their politics, and the discontented young people. Among them is Parzival, a modest nonconformist, who is the publisher of a critical journal at Arthur's court. The audience quickly realizes the modern political meanings behind the medieval conversations (e.g., "Round Table"= "Politbüro"). The director of the Dresden theater has been said to have experienced some difficulties because of the performance of this drama, and the publication of the text was delayed. Seen from today's perspective, subsequent to the astonishing events in the two Germanys and in Eastern Europe since the fall of 1989, Hein's drama seems to have been a prophetic piece of literature with respect to political developments, although it is also clear that Hein's play is not merely related to specific political problems, but — in a more general way — to collapsing social orders and the archetypal conflict between the generations. A common aspect of the dramas by Dorst/Ehler, Handke, and Hein, and of the novel by Muschg is that it is no longer the grail itself (which is said to have only little value or even not to exist at all) which is of supreme importance, but rather the quest. Here can be found the beginning of a new German Parzival tradition, adjacent to Wagner and contending with Wagner's dominance.

Works Cited

Editions and Translations of Wolfram's Works

Titurel and The Songs. Ed. Trans. Marion E. Gibbs and Sidney M. Johnson. New York: Garland, 1984.

Willehalm. Trans. Marion E. Gibbs and Sidney M. Johnson. Harmondsworth: Penguin, 1984.

Wolfram von Eschenbach. Ed. Albert Leitzmann. Altdeutsche Textbibliothek Vol.15: *Willehalm Buch I bis V* and Vol.16: *Willehalm Buch VI bis IX; Titurel; Lieder.* 5th revised edition by Albert Dienert. Tübingen: Niemeyer, 1963.

Wolfram von Eschenbach. Parzival. A Romance of the Middle Ages. Ed. Helen M. Mustard and Charles E. Passage. New York: Vintage Books, 1961.

Wolfram von Eschenbach. Parzival. Ed. Karl Lachmann. 6th ed. Berlin/Leipzig: de Gruyter, 1926. Reprinted 1965.

Wolfram von Eschenbach. Parzival. Trans. A. T. Hatto. Harmondsworth: Penguin, 1980.

Other Cited Editions and Translations

Altdeutsche Genesis. Ed. V. Dollmayr. Halle/S.: Niemeyer, 1932.

Aliscans, Kritischer Text. Ed. Erich Wienbeck, Wilhelm Hartnacke, and Paul Rasch. Tübingen: Niemeyer, 1903.

Andreas Capellanus. *The Art of Courtly Love.* Translated, with an Introduction and Notes, by John Jay Parry. New York: Norton, 1969.

Boccaccio, Giovanni. *Genealogy of the Gentile Gods.* Quoted from: *Medieval Literary Criticism. Translations and Interpretations.* Ed. O. B. Hardison, Jr., Alex Preminger, Kevin Kerrane, and Leon Golden. New York: Ungar, 1985. 192–212.

Chrétien de Troyes. *Arthurian Romances*. Trans. William Kibler. (*Erec and Enide* translated by Carleton W. Carroll.) New York: Penguin, 1991.

Chrétien de Troyes. *Le conte du graal (Perceval)*. Ed. Felix Lecoy. Paris: Champion, 1981.

Chrétien de Troyes. *Erec et Enide*. Ed. Trans. Jean-Marie Fritz. Paris: Le Livre de Poche, 1992.

Chrétien de Troyes. *Der Percevalroman (Li Contes del Graal)*. Ed. Alfons Hilka. Halle: Niemeyer, 1932.

Chrétien de Troyes. *The Story of the Grail (Li Contes del Graal) or Perceval*. Ed. Rupert T. Pickens. Trans. William W. Kibler. New York and London: Garland, 1990.

The Continuations of the Old French Perceval of Chrétien de Troyes, Volume I. Ed. William Roach. Philadelphia: U of Pennsylvania P, 1949.

Cyprian of Carthage. *De lapsis and De ecclesiae catholicae unitate*. Ed. Trans. Maurice Bénevot. Oxford: Clarendon, 1971. (Also Migne, ed. *Patrologia Latina* 4,477–536.)

Dante Alighieri. *La Vita Nuova (Poems of Youth)*. Translated with an Introduction by Barbara Reynolds. London: Penguin, 1969.

Enchiridion Symbolorum. Ed. Heinrich Denzinger and Clemens Bannwart 27th ed. by J. B. Umberg. Freiburg i. Br.: Herder, 1928.

Fasisculus Morum. A Fourteenth-Century Preacher's Handbook. Ed. Trans. Siegfried Wenzel. University Park: Pennsylvania State UP, 1989.

Geoffrey of Monmouth. *The History of the Kings of Britain*. Trans. Lewis Thorpe. London: Penguin Classics, 1966.

Gottfried von Straßburg. *Tristan*. Ed. Karl Marold. Berlin: de Gruyter, 1977.

Gottfried von Straßburg. *Tristan*. Trans. A. T. Hatto. Harmondsworth: Penguin, 1960/1984.

Hartmann von Aue. *Der arme Heinrich*. Ed. H. Paul. 15th ed. by G. Bonath. Tübingen: Niemeyer, 1984.

Hartmann von Aue. *Gregorius*. Ed. H. Paul. 13th ed. by B. Wachinger. Tübingen: Niemeyer, 1984.

Hartmann von Aue. *Iwein*. Ed. G. F. Benecke and Karl Lachmann. 7th revised edition by Ludwig Wolff. Berlin: de Gruyter, 1968.

Hermann von Sachsenheim. *Die Mörin*. Ed. Horst Dieter Schlosser. Wiesbaden: Brockhaus, 1974.

Historia Welforum. Ed. Erich König. 2nd ed. Sigmaringen: Thorbecke, 1978.

Malory, Sir Thomas. *The Works of Sir Thomas Malory*. Ed. Eugène Vinaver. 3 vols. Oxford: Clarendon, 1947. Rep. with corrections 1948.

Marie de France. *Lais*. Paris: Flammarion, 1994.

Mechthild von Magdeburg. *Flowing Light of the Divinity*. Trans. Christiane Mesch Galvani. Edited with an Introduction by Susan Clark. New York and London: Garland, 1991.

Otto von Freising and Rahewin. *Gesta Frederici*. Ed. Franz-Josef Schmale. Darmstadt: Wissenschaftliche Buchgesellschaft, 1965.

Patrologiae curses completus . . . Series Latina. Ed. Jacques Paul Migne. Paris, 1844–64.

Peredur. Ed. Trans. James J. Wilhelm. *The Romances of Arthur II*. New York: Garland, 1986. 29–61.

Perlesvaus. English. The High Book of the Grail. Trans. Nigel Bryant. Ipswich: Rowman and Littlefield, 1978.

La Queste del Saint Graal. Ed. Albert Pauphilet. Paris: Champion, 1980.

Robert de Boron. *Le roman de l'estoire du graal*. Ed. William A. Nitze. Paris: Champion, 1927.

Wirnt von Gravenberg. *Wigalois*. Ed. J. M. N. Kapteyn. Bonn: Klopp, 1926.

Studies

Adorno, Theodor W. (1981). *In search of Wagner*. Trans. Rodney Livingstone. London: NLB. (Original German edition: *Versuch über Wagner*. Berlin: 1952)

Agena, Kathleen (1983). "The Return of Enchantment." *The New York Times*, Magazine Desk, 27 Nov. 1983, Sec. 6, p.66, col.1.

Allen, Peter L. (1992). *The Art of Love. Amatory Fiction from Ovid to the 'Romance of the Rose.'* Philadelphia: U of Pennsylvania P.

Arnold, Benjamin (1985). *German Knighthood 1050–1300*. Oxford: Oxford UP.

Bakhtin, Michael (1981). *The Dialogic Imagination. Four Essays by M. M. Bakhtin*. Ed. Michael Holmquist. Trans. Caryl Emerson and Michael Holmquist. Austin: U of Texas P.

Baldwin, John W. (1994). *The Language of Sex. Five Voices from Northern France around 1200*. Chicago: U of Chicago P.

Barber, Richard (1961). *King Arthur: Hero and Legend*. New York: St. Martins.

Barber, Richard (1973). *King Arthur in Legend and History*. Boydell: Ipswich.

Barber, Richard and Juliet Barker (1989). *Tournaments: Jousts, Chivalry and Pageantry in the Middle Ages*. Woodbridge: Boydell.

Bayer, Hans (1976). "Soziale Struktur-Sprache-Ethos: Zur Soziologie der sozialethischen Begriffswelt des deutschen Mittelalters." *Wirkendes Wort* 5: 334–55.

Benton, John F. (1968). "Clio and Venus: An Historical View of Medieval Love." *The Meaning of Courtly Love*. Ed. F. X. Newman. Albany: State U of New York P. 19–42.

Bertau, Karl (1983). *Wolfram von Eschenbach. Neun Versuche über Subjektivität und Ursprünglichkeit in der Geschichte*. Munich: Beck.

Bindschedler, Maria B. (1984). "Der Ritter Gawan als Arzt oder Medizin und Höflichkeit." *Schweizer Monatshefte für Politik, Wirtschaft, Kultur* 64: 729–743.

Blair, Claude (1979). *European Armour circa 1066 to circa 1700*. 3rd ed. London: Batsford.

Blamires, David (1965). *Characterization and Individuality in Wolfram's 'Parzival.'* Cambridge, Cambridge UP.

Bloom, Harold (1994). *The Western Canon. The Books and School of the Ages*. New York: Riverhead Books.

Boeheim, Wendelin (1890). *Handbuch der Waffenkunde*. Leipzig: Seemann.

Boigs, Lotte (1992). "Versuch einer entstehungsgeschichtlichen Einordnung der sogenannten Selbstverteidigung." *Zeitschrift für Deutsche Philologie* 111: 1–23.

Boor, Helmut de (1953). *Die höfische Literatur: Vorbereitung, Blüte, Ausklang 1170–1250*. Volume 2 of Helmut de Boor and Richard Newald, *Geschichte der deutschen Literatur: Von den Anfängen bis zur Gegenwart*. Munich: Beck.

Borst, Arno (1959). "Das Rittertum im Hochmittelalter. Idee und Wirklichkeit." *Saeculum* 10: 213–31.

Bossy, John (ed.) (1989). *Disputes and Settlements. Law and Human Relations in the West*. Cambridge: Cambridge UP.

Bradbury, Jim (1992). *The Medieval Siege*. Woodbridge: Boydell.

Brewer, D. S. (1996). *Medieval Comic Tales*. Ed. Derek Brewer. 2nd ed. Cambridge: Brewer.

Brooks, Peter (1992). *Reading for the Plot: Design and Intention in Narrative*. Cambridge (MA): Harvard UP.

Brunner, Horst (1983). "Artus der wise höfsche man. Zur immanenten Historizität der Ritterwelt im *Parzival* Wolframs von Eschenbach." *Germanistik in Erlangen. Hundert Jahre nach der Gründung des Deutschen Seminars*. Ed. Dietmar Peschel. Universitätsbund Erlangen-Nürnberg. 61–73.

Brunner, Otto (1970). *Land und Herrschaft. Grundfragen der territorialen Verfassungsgeschichte Österreichs im Mittelalter.* 6th ed. Darmstadt: Wissenschaftliche Buchgesellschaft.

Bumke, Joachim (1977). *Studien zum Ritterbegriff im 12. und 13. Jahrhundert.* 2nd ed. Heidelberg: Winter.

Bumke, Joachim (1986). *Höfische Kultur. Literatur und Gesellschaft im hohen Mittelalter.* Munich: Deutscher Taschenbuch Verlag.

Bumke, Joachim (1991). *Wolfram von Eschenbach.* 6th ed. Stuttgart: Metzler.

Bumke, Joachim (1994). "Geschlechterbeziehungen in den Gawanbüchern von Wolframs *Parzival.*" *Amsterdamer Beiträge zur älteren Germanistik* 38–39: 105–21.

Burdach, Konrad (1938). *Der Gral. Forschungen über seinen Ursprung und seinen Zusammenhang mit der Longinuslegende.* Stuttgart: Kohlhammer, 1938. Rpt. Darmstadt, 1974.

Busby, Keith (1980). *Gauvain in Old French Literature.* Amsterdam: Rodopi.

Busby, Keith (1993). *Chrétien de Troyes: Perceval: Le Conte du Graal.* London: Grant and Cutler.

Camargo, Martin (1996). "Where's the Brief?: The *Ars Dictaminis* and the Reading/Writing Between the Lines." *Disputatio* 1: 1–17.

Camille, Michael (1985). "Seeing and Reading: Some Visual Implications of Medieval Literacy and Illiteracy." *Art History* 8: 26–49.

Camille, Michael (1989). "Visual Signs of the Sacred Paper: Books in the *Bible moralisée.*" *Word & Image* 5, 1: 111–130.

Campbell, Joseph (1959). *The Masks of God: Primitive Mythology.* New York: Viking.

Casey, John (1990). *Pagan Virtue: An Essay in Ethics.* Oxford: Clarendon.

Christoph, Siegfried R. (1981). *Wolfram von Eschenbach's Couples.* Amsterdam: Rodopi.

Christoph, Siegfried R. (1981). "Wolfram's Sigune and the Question of Guilt." *Germanic Review* 56: 62–69.

Cirlot, J. E. (1991). *A Dictionary of Symbols.* 2nd ed. Trans. Jack Sage. New York: Dorset Press.

Clanchy, M. T. (1979). *From Memory to Written Record: England, 1066–1307.* London: Edward Arnold.

Clark, S. H. (1990). *Paul Ricoeur.* London and New York: Routledge.

Classen, Albrecht (1994). "Andreas Capellanus aus kommunikationstheoretischer Sicht. Eine postmoderne Auslegung von *De amore.*" *Mittellateinisches Jahrbuch* 29/1: 45–60.

Classen, Albrecht (1996). "Spiritual and Existential Meanings of the Word: Strategies and Functions of Reading in the Middle Ages. With Special Emphasis on Hartmann von Aue's *Gregorius*." *Seminar* 32, 3: 221–239.

Coleman, Janet (1981). *Medieval Readers and Writers 1350–1400*. New York: Columbia UP.

Contamine, Philippe (1984). *War in the Middle Ages*. Trans. Michael Jones. Oxford: Blackwell.

Cormeau, Christoph and Wilhelm Störmer (1985). *Hartmann von Aue: Epoche, Werk, Wirkung*. Munich: Beck.

Couratin, A. H. (1969). "Liturgy." *Historical Theology*. Ed. J. Daniélou, A. H. Couratin, and John Kent. Harmondsworth: Penguin. 131–240.

Curtius, Ernst Robert (1990). *European Literature and the Latin Middle Ages*. Trans. Willard R. Trask. Afterword by Peter Godman. Princeton: Princeton UP.

Czerwinski, Peter (1975). *Die Schlacht- und Turnierdarstellungen in den deutschen höfischen Romanen des 12. und 13. Jahrhunderts*. Dissertation, Freie Universität Berlin.

Dahlgrün, Corinna (1991). *Hoc fac ut vives (Lk 10, 28) — vor allen dingen minne got*. Frankfurt/M.: Lang.

Dallapiazza, Michael (1985). "Häßlichkeit und Individualität. Ansätze zur Überwindung der Idealität des Schönen in Wolframs von Eschenbach *Parzival*." *Deutsche Vierteljahrsschrift für Literaturwissenschaft und Geistesgeschichte* 59, 3: 400–421.

Darrah, John (1981). *The Real Camelot: Paganism and the Arthurian Romances*. London: Thames.

Deinert, Wilhelm (1960). *Ritter und Kosmos im 'Parzival.' Eine Untersuchung der Sternkunde Wolframs von Eschenbach*. Munich: Beck.

Deutsche Literaturgeschichte. Von den Anfängen bis zur Gegenwart (1979). Ed. Wolfgang Beutin et. al. Stuttgart: Metzler.

DeVries, Kelly (1992). *Medieval Military Technology*. Peterborough, Ont.: Broadview Press.

Dick, Ernst (1978). "*Katabasis* and the Grail Epic: Wolfram von Eschenbach's *Parzival*." *Res Publica Litterarum. Studies in the Classical Tradition* 1: 57–87.

Dimler, G. Richard (1970). "Parzival's Guilt: A Theological Interpretation." *Monatshefte* 62: 123–34.

Dinzelbacher, Peter (1996). "Hauptlinien einer Religionsgeschichte Deutschlands im Hochmittelalter." *Saeculum* 47: 67–88.

Draesner, Ulrike (1993). *Wege durch erzählte Welten. Intertextuelle Verweise als Mittel der Bedeutungskonstitution in Wolframs 'Parzival'.* Frankfurt a.M.: Lang.

Duby, Georges (1988). *La société chevaleresque: Hommes et structures du Moyen Age I.* Paris: Flammarion.

Duckworth, David (1980). *The Influence of Biblical Terminology and Thought on Wolfram's 'Parzival.'* Göppingen: Kümmerle.

Duckworth, David (1987/88). "Herzeloyde and Antikonie, Some Aspects Compared." *German Life and Letters* 41: 332–341.

Ebenbauer, Alfred (1984). "*Es gibt ain mörynne vil dick suss mynne*: Belakanes Landsleute in der deutschen Literatur des Mittelalters." *ZfdA* 113: 16–42.

Ehrismann, Gustav (1928). "Er heizet lapsit exillis, Parz. 469,7." *ZfdA* 65: 62–63.

Elias, Norbert (1976). *Über den Prozeß der Zivilisation. Soziogenetische und psychogenetische Untersuchungen.* 2 vols. Frankfurt a.M.: Suhrkamp.

Ernst, Ulrich (1985). "Kyot und Flegetanis in Wolfram's *Parzival*. Fiktionaler Fundbericht und jüdisch-arabischer Kulturhintergrund." *Wirkendes Wort* 35: 176–195.

Fleckenstein, Josef (1977). "Das Rittertum der Stauferzeit." *Die Zeit der Staufer. Geschichte- Kunst- Kultur.* Ed. Reiner Hausherr. Katalog der Ausstellung. 4 vols. Stuttgart: Württembergisches Landesmuseum. Vol 3. 103–9.

Fleckenstein, Josef (ed.) (1985). *Das ritterliche Turnier im Mittelalter. Veröffentlichungen des Max-Planck-Instituts für Geschichte 80.* Göttingen: Vandenhoeck & Ruprecht.

Fletcher, Robert Huntington (1965). *Arthurian Material in Chronicles.* New York: Haskell.

Frappier, Jean (1957). *Chrétien de Troyes.* Paris: Hatier-Boivin, 1957.

Gamber, Ortwin (1977). "Die Bewaffnung der Stauferzeit." *Die Zeit der Staufer. Geschichte- Kunst- Kultur.* Ed. Reiner Hausherr. Katalog der Ausstellung. 4 vols. Stuttgart: Württembergisches Landesmuseum. Vol. 3. 113–18.

Gaunt, Simon (1989). *Troubadours and Irony.* Cambridge: Cambridge UP.

Gellrich, Jesse M. (1985). *The Idea of the Book in the Middle Ages. Language Theory, Mythology, and Fiction.* Ithaca and London: Cornell UP.

Gernhuber, Joachim (1952). *Die Landfriedensbewegung in Deutschland bis zum Mainzer Reichslandfrieden von 1235.* Bonn: Bouvier.

Gervinus, G. G. (1853). *Geschichte der Deutschen Literatur.* Vol.1. 4th ed. Leipzig: Enzelmann.

Gibbs, Marion E. (1972). *'Wiplîchez Wîbes Reht': A Study of the Women Characters in the Works of Wolfram von Eschenbach*. Pittsburgh: Duquesne UP.

Gibbs, Marion E. (1976). *Narrative Art in Wolfram's 'Willehalm.'* Göppingen: Kümmerle.

Gibbs, Marion E. (1980). "Ampflise im *Parzival* und im *Titurel*." *Wolfram-Studien* 6: 48–53.

Goedeke, Karl (1884). *Grundrisz zur Geschichte der deutschen Dichtung aus den Quellen*. Vol.1. 2nd ed. Dresden: Ehlermann.

Goetinck, Glenys (1975). *Peredur. A Study of Welsh Tradition in the Grail Legends*. Cardiff: U of Wales P.

Green, D. H. (1970). "Der Auszug Gahmurets." *Wolfram-Studien I*. Berlin: Schmidt. 62–86.

Green, D. H. (1978). "Homicide and Parzival." *Approaches to Wolfram von Eschenbach*. By D. H. Green and L. Peter Johnson. Berne: Lang. 11–82.

Green, D. H. (1979). *Irony in the Medieval Romance*. Cambridge: Cambridge UP.

Green, D. H. (1982). *The Art of Recognition in Wolfram's 'Parzival.'* Cambridge: Cambridge UP.

Green, D. H. (1994). *Medieval Listening and Reading: The Primary Reception of German literature 800–1300*. Cambridge: Cambridge UP.

Green, Miranda (1995). *Celtic Goddesses: Warriors, Virgins and Mothers*. London: British Museum Press.

Grimm, Reinhold R. (1972). "Die Paradisesehe. Eine erotische Utopie des Mittelalters." *Getemperet und gemischet (Festschrift für Wolfgang Mohr)*. Ed. F. Hundschnurcher and Ulrich Müller. Göppingen: Kümmerle. 1–25.

Groos, Arthur (1975). "Time Reference and the Liturgical Calendar in Wolfram von Eschenbach's *Parzival*." *Deutsche Vierteljahrsschrift* 49: 43–65.

Groos, Arthur (1993). "Dialogic Transpositions: The Grail Hero Wins a Wife." *Chrétien de Troyes and the German Middle Ages*. Ed. Martin H. Jones and Roy Wisbey. Woodbridge/ Rochester: 1993. 257–276.

Groos, Arthur (1995). *Romancing the Grail: Genre, Science and Quest in Wolfram's 'Parzival.'* Ithaca and London: Cornell UP.

Gruenter, Rainer (1955). "Der *paradisus* der *Wiener Genesis*." *Euphorion* 49: 121–44.

Grünkorn, Gertrud (1994). *Die Fiktionalität des höfischen Romans um 1200*. Berlin: Schmidt.

Gürttler, Karin (1976). *'Künec Artus der guote.' Das Artusbild der höfischen Epik des 12. und 13. Jahrhunderts*. Bonn: Bouvier.

Gutman, R. W. (1968). *Richard Wagner. The Man, His Mind, and His Music.* New York/London: Harcourt, Brace & World.

Haage, Bernhard D. (1992). *Studien zur Heilkunde im 'Parzival' Wolframs von Eschenbach.* Göppingen: Kümmerle.

Haas, Alois M. (1964). *Parzivals 'tumpheit' bei Wolfram von Eschenbach.* Berlin: Schmidt.

Haferland, Harald (1988). *Höfische Interaktion: Interpretationen zur höfischen Epik und Didaktik um 1200.* München: Fink.

Halford, Mary-Bess (1980). *Illustration and Text in Lutwin's 'Eva und Adam.' Codex Vindob. 2980.* Göppingen: Kümmerle.

Hart, Thomas Elwood (1989). "Crestien, the Quadrivium, Kyot, and Katabasis: New Evidence of Mathematical Design Techniques in Wolfram's *Parzival*." *'in hôhem prise.' A Festschrift in Honor of Ernst S. Dick, presented on the Occasion of his Sixtieth Birthday: April 7, 1989.* Ed. Winder McConnell. Göppingen: Kümmerle. 83–127.

Harty, Kevin J. (ed.) (1991). *Cinema Arthuriana. Essays on Arthurian Film.* New York/London: Garland.

Haskins, Charles Homer (1957). *The Renaissance of the Twelfth Century.* Cleveland and New York: Meridian Books.

Hasty, Will (1994). "*Daz priset in, und sleht er mich*: Knighthood and *gewalt* in the Arthurian Works of Hartmann von Aue and Wolfram von Eschenbach." *Monatshefte* 86: 7–21.

Hasty, Will (1995). *Adventures in Interpretation: The Works of Hartmann von Aue and their Critical Reception.* Columbia, South Carolina: Camden House.

Hatto, A. T. (1940). "Archery and Chivalry: A Noble Prejudice." *Modern Language Review* 35: 40–54.

Hatto, A. T. (1945). "Parzival 183,9 ... *und arger schützen harte vil.*" *Modern Language Review* 40: 48–49.

Hatto, A. T. (ed.) (1965). *Eros. An Enquiry into the theme of Lovers' Meetings and Partings at Dawn in Poetry.* The Hague: Mouton.

Hatto, A. T. (1980). "An Introduction to a Second Reading." *Wolfram von Eschenbach. 'Parzival.'* Trans. A. T. Hatto. Penguin: Harmondsworth, 1980. 412–438.

Haug, Walter (1992). *Literaturtheorie im deutschen Mittelalter von den Anfängen bis zum Ende des 13. Jahrhunderts.* 2nd ed. Darmstadt: Wissenschaftliche Buchgesellschaft.

Haug, Walter (1995). *Brechungen auf dem Weg zur Individualität: kleine Schriften zur Literatur des Mittelalters.* Tübingen: Niemeyer.

Hausherr, Reiner (1972). "Sensus litteralis und sensus spiritualis in der Bible moralisée." *Frühmittelalterliche Studien* 6: 356–380.

Heninger, S. K., Jr. (1974). *Touches of Sweet Harmony. Pythagorean Cosmology and Renaissance Poetics*. San Marino, CA: The Huntington Library.

Horgan, A. D. (1974). "The Grail in Wolfram's *Parzival*." *Medieval Studies* 36: 354–381.

Huby, Michel (1989). "Nochmals zu Parzivals Entwicklung." *Studien zu Wolfram von Eschenbach. Festschrift für Werner Schröder*. Ed. Kurt Gärtner. Niemeyer: Tübingen. 257–269.

Illich, Ivan (1993). *In the Vineyard of the Text. A Commentary to Hugh's 'Didascalicon.'* Chicago and London: U of Chicago P.

Irvine, Martin (1994). *The Making of Textual Culture: 'Grammatica' and Literary Theory, 350–1100*. Cambridge: Cambridge UP.

Jackson, William H. (1994). *Chivalry in Twelfth-Century Germany: The Works of Hartmann von Aue*. Cambridge: Brewer.

Jackson, William H. (1994). "Lance and Shield in the buhurt." *German Narrative Literature of the Twelfth and Thirteenth Centuries. Studies Presented to Roy Wisbey*. Ed. Volker Honemann et al. Tübingen: Niemeyer. 39–54.

Jackson, William H. (1995). "Zank und Zwist bei Waffenspielen." *'bickelwort' und 'wildiu maere.' Festschrift für Eberhard Nellmann*. Ed. Dorothee Lindemann et al. Göppingen: Kümmerle. 408–423.

Jaeger, C. Stephen (1985). *The Origins of Courtliness. Civilizing Trends and the Formation of Courtly Ideals 939–1210*. Philadelphia: U of Pennsylvania P.

Johnson, L. Peter (1968). "Lähelin and the Grail horses." *MLR* 63 (1968): 612–617.

Johnson, L. Peter (1972). "Dramatische Ironie in Wolframs *Parzival*." *Probleme mittelhochdeutscher Erzählformen*. Berlin: Schmidt. 133–152.

Johnson, L. Peter (1978). "Sine klâwen. An Interpretation." *Approaches to Wolfram von Eschenbach*. By D. H. Green and L. Peter Johnson. Berne: Lang. 295–334.

Johnson, Sidney M. (1958). "Gawan's Surprise in Wolfram's *Parzival*." *Germanic Review* 33: 285–292.

Johnson, Sidney M. (1970). "Parzival and Gawan: Their Conflicts of Duties." *Wolfram-Studien* 1: 98–116.

Jones, Martin H. (1972). "Parzival's Fighting and his Election to the Grail." *Wolfram-Studien* 3: 52–71.

Jones, Martin H. (1988). "The Depiction of Battle in Wolfram von Eschenbach's *Willehalm*." *The Ideals and Practice of Medieval Knighthood II. Papers from the third Strawberry Hill Conference 1986.* Ed. Christopher Harper-Bill and Ruth Harvey. Woodbrige: Boydell. 46–69.

Jones, Martin H. (1989). "*die tjostiure uz vünf scharn* (Willehalm 362,3)." *Studien zu Wolfram von Eschenbach: Festschrift für Werner Schröder.* Ed. Joachim Heinzle et al. Tübingen: Niemeyer. 429–441.

Jung, Carl Gustav (1972). *The Spirit in Man, Art, and Literature.* Trans. R. F. C. Hull. Princeton: Princeton UP.

Jung, Carl Gustav (1977). *Mysterium Coniunctionis. An Inquiry into the Separation and Synthesis of Psychic Opposites in Alchemy.* 2nd ed. Trans. R. F. C. Hull. Princeton: Princeton UP.

Jung, Carl Gustav (1980). *The Archetypes of the Collective Unconscious.* 2nd ed. Trans. R. F. C. Hull. Princeton: Princeton UP.

Jung, Carl Gustav (1980). *Psychology and Alchemy.* 2nd ed. Trans. R. F. C. Hull. Princeton: Princeton UP.

Jung, Carl Gustav (1984). *Psychology and Western Religion.* Trans. R. F. C. Hull. Princeton: Princeton UP.

Jung, Carl Gustav (1989). *Aspects of the Masculine.* Trans. R. F. C. Hull. Introduction and Headnotes by John Beebe. Princeton: Princeton UP. 9–23. (Includes "The Battle for Deliverance from the Mother.")

Jung, Emma, and Marie-Louise von Franz (1986). *The Grail Legend.* 2nd ed. Trans. Andrea Dykes. Boston: Sigo Press.

Kahane, Henry and Renée (1959). "Wolfram's Gral und Wolframs Kyot." *ZfdA* 89: 202–213.

Kaiser, Gert (1991). Introduction. *An den Grenzen höfischer Kultur: Anfechtungen der Lebensordnung in der deutschen Erzähldichtung des hohen Mittelalters.* Ed. Gert Kaiser. München: Fink. 7–8.

Kant, Karl (1878). *Scherz und Humor in Wolframs von Eschenbach Dichtungen.* Heilbronn: Henninger.

Karg, Ina (1993). *'sîn süeze sûrez ungemach': Erzählen von der Minne in Wolframs 'Parzival.'* Göppingen: Kümmerle.

Karnein, Alfred (1985). *De Amore in volkssprachlicher Literatur. Untersuchungen zur Andreas-Capellanus-Rezeption im Mittelalter und Renaissance.* Heidelberg: Winter.

Katz, Jacob (1986). *The Darker Side of Genius: Richard Wagner's Anti-Semitism.* Hanover and London: UP of New England. (Original German edition: *Richard Wagner. Vorbote des Antisemitismus.* Königstein, 1985.)

Kermode, Frank (1979). *The Genesis of Secrecy: On the Interpretation of Narrative.* Cambridge (MA) and London: Harvard UP.

Knapp, F. P. (1996). "Von Gottes und der Menschen Wirklichkeit. Wolframs fromme Welterzählung *Parzival*." *Deutsche Vierteljahrsschrift* 70: 351–368.

Knefelkamp, Ulrich (1986). *Die Suche nach dem Reich des Priester Johannes, dargestellt anhand von Reiseberichten und anderen ethnographischen Quellen des 12. bis 17. Jahrhunderts.* Gelsenkirchen: Andreas Müller.

Kolb, Herbert (1986). "Guido militiae Templi magister." *Archiv* 223: 337–344.

Kratz, Henry (1973). *Wolfram von Eschenbach's 'Parzival': An Attempt at a Total Evaluation.* Bern: Francke.

Kühnel, Jürgen (1991). "Wagners *Parsifal* — ein antisemitisches Werk?" Programmheft *Parsifal* der Wiener Staatsoper. 49–55.

Kunitzsch, Paul (1984). "Der Orient in Wolframs *Parzival*." ZDA 113: 79–111.

Lacey, Norris J. (ed.) (1996). *The New Arthurian Encyclopedia* New York: Garland.

Le Goff, Jacques (1965). *Das Hochmittelalter.* Trans. Sigrid Metken. Frankfurt a.M.: Fischer.

Le Goff, Jacques (1988). *The Medieval Imagination.* Trans. Arthur Goldhammer. Chicago and London: U of Chicago P.

Leixner, Otto von (1910). *Geschichte der deutschen Literatur.* Leipzig: Spanner.

Lewis, Gertrude Jaron (1975). "Die unheilige Herzeloyde. Ein ikonoklastischer Versuch." *Journal of English and Germanic Philology* 74: 465–485.

Lofmark, Carl J. (1972). "Wolfram's source references in *Parzival*." MLR 67: 820–844.

Lofmark, Carl J. (1977). "Zur Interpretation der Kyotstellen im *Parzival*." *Wolfram-Studien* 4: 33–70.

Loomis, Roger Sherman (1926). *Celtic Myth and Arthurian Romance.* New York, Columbia UP. Reprinted London, 1995.

Loomis, Roger Sherman (1949). *Arthurian Tradition and Chrétien de Troyes.* New York: Columbia UP.

Loomis, Roger Sherman (1991). *The Grail. From Celtic Myth to Christian Symbol.* Princeton: Princeton UP. Originally published in 1963.

Maksymiuk, Stephan (1996). *The Court Magician in Medieval German Romance.* Frankfurt a. M.: Peter Lang.

de Mandach, André (1995). *Auf den Spuren des Heiligen Gral.* Göppingen: Kümmerle.

Marchand, James (1977). "Wolfram's Bawdy." *Monatshefte* 69: 131–149.

Marx, Jean (1952). *La légende Arthurienne et le Graal*. Paris: Presses Universitaires de France.

McFarland, Timothy (1993). "Clinschor. Wolfram's Adaptation of the *Conte du Graal*: The Schastel Marveile Episode." *Chrétien de Troyes and the German Middle Ages. Papers from an International Symposium*. Ed. Martin H. Jones and Roy Wisbey. Cambridge: Brewer/London: Institute of Germanic Studies, University of London. 277–294.

Mielke, Andreas (1992). *Nigra sum et formosa. Afrikanerinnen in der deutschen Literatur des Mittelalters. Texte und Kontexte zum Bild des Afrikaners in der literarischen Imagologie*. Stuttgart: Helfant.

Miklautsch, Lydia (1991). *Studien zur Mutterrolle in den mittelhochdeutschen Großepen des zwölften und dreizehnten Jahrhunderts*. Erlangen: Palm & Enke.

Mohr, Wolfgang (1957). "Obie und Meljanz. Zum 7. Buch von Wolframs *Parzival*." *Gestaltprobleme der Dichtung. Günther Müller zu seinem 65. Geburtstag am 15. Dezember 1955*. Bonn: Bouvier. 1957. 9–20 (Reprinted in Rupp ed., 1966).

Mohr, Wolfgang (1958). "Parzival und Gawan." *Euphorion* 52: 1–22 (Reprinted in Rupp, ed. 1966).

Mohr, Wolfgang (1965). "Landgraf Kingrimursel. Zum VIII. Buch von Wolframs *Parzival*." *Philologia Deutsch. Festschrift zum 70. Geburtstag von Walter Henzen*. Ed. Werner Kohlschmidt and Paul Zinsli. Bern: Francke. 21–38.

Mohr, Wolfgang (1965). "Zu den epischen Hintergründen in Wolframs *Parzival*." *Mediaeval German Studies presented to Frederick Norman*. London: Institute of Germanic Studies. 174–87.

Mohr, Wolfgang (1970). "Parzivals ritterliche Schuld." *Der arthurische Roman*. Ed. Kurt Wais. Darmstadt: Wissenschaftliche Buchgesellschaft. 332–54. (First published in *Wirkendes Wort* 2, 1951–52: 148–60).

Müller, Jan-Dirk (1980). "Funktionswandel ritterlicher Epik am Ausgang des Mittelalters." *Gesellschaftliche Sinnangebote Mittelalterlicher Literatur*. Ed. Gert Kaiser. München: Fink. 1–11.

Müller, Ulrich (1980). "Parzival und Parsifal. Vom Roman Wolframs von Eschenbach und vom Musikdrama Richard Wagners." *Sprache-Text-Geschichte*. Ed. Peter K. Stein. Göppingen: Kümmerle. 479–502.

Müller, Ulrich (1991). "Blank, Syberberg, and the German Arthurian Tradition" Trans. Julie Giffin. *Cinema Arthuriana. Essays on Arthurian Film*. Ed. Kevin J. Harty. New York/London: Garland. 157–168.

Murdoch, Brian (1972). *The Fall of Man in the Early Middle High German Biblical Epic*. Göppingen: Kümmerle.

Murdoch, Brian (1974). *The Recapitulated Fall. A Comparative Study in Medieval Literature.* Amsterdam: Rodopi.

Murdoch, Brian (1975). "Das deutsche Adambuch und die Adamlegenden des Mittelalters." Ed. W. Harms and L. P. Johnson. *Deutsche Literatur des späten Mittelalters.* Berlin: Schmidt. 209–24.

Murdoch, Brian (1978). "Hartmann's *Gregorius* and the Quest of Life." *New German Studies* 6: 79–100.

Murdoch, Brian (1991). "The Origins of Penance: Reflections of Adamic Apocrypha and of the *Vita Adae* in Western Europe." *Annals of the Archive of Ferran Valls I Taberner's Library* 9/10: 205–228.

Nellmann, Eberhard (1966). "Produktive Mißverständnisse. Wolfram als Übersetzer Chrétiens." *Wolfram-Studien* 14: 134–148.

Nellmann, Eberhard (1994). "Stellenkommentar." *Wolfram von Eschenbach. Parzival.* Ed. Karl Lachmann. Revised and with commentary by Eberhard Nellmann. Trans. Dieter Kühn. 2 vols. Frankfurt am Main: Deutscher Klassiker Verlag. Vol.2. 443–837.

Neumann, Erich (1974). *The Great Mother. An Analysis of the Archetype.* Trans. Ralph Manheim. Princeton: Princeton UP.

Nicolle, David C. (1988). *Arms and Armour of the Crusading Era 1050–1350.* 2 vols. New York: Kraus.

Nitze, William A. (1949). "Perceval and the Holy Grail." *Univ. of Calif. Publ. In Mod. Phil.* 28: 281–332.

Noltze, Holger (1995). *Gahmurets Orientfahrt: Kommentar zum ersten Buch von Wolframs 'Parzival' (4,27–58,26).* Würzburg: Königshausen & Neumann.

Nykrog, Per (1996). *Chrétien de Troyes: Romancier discutable.* Geneva: Librairie Droz.

Ortmann, Christa (1973). "Ritterschaft. Zur Bedeutung der Gahmuret-Geschichte im *Parzival* Wolframs von Eschenbach." *Deutsche Vierteljahrsschrift für Literaturwissenschaft und Geistesgeschichte* 47: 664–710.

Patterson, Linda (1975). *Troubadours and Eloquence.* Oxford: Clarendon.

Paul, Hermann (1975). *Mittelhochdeutsche Grammatik.* 21st ed. Revised by Hugo Moser and Ingeborg Schröbler. Tübingen: Niemeyer.

Poag, James (1974). *"Diu verholnen mære umben gral* (Parz. 452, 30)." *Wolfram Studien* 2: 72–83.

Poag, James (1977). "Gawan's Surprise." *Wolfram-Studien* 4: 71–76.

Pütz, Hans Henning (1971). *Die Darstellung der Schlacht in mittelhochdeutschen Erzähldichtungen von 1150 bis um 1250.* Hamburg: Buske, 1971.

Rahn, Otto (1974). *Kreuzzug gegen den Gral: Die Tragödie des Katharismus.* Stuttgart: Gunther.

Ranke, Friedrich (1946). "Zur Symbolik des Grals." *Trivium* 4: 20–30.

Ranke, Friedrich (1952). *Gott, Welt und Humanität in der deutschen Dichtung des Mittelalters.* Ed. Maria Bindschedler. Basel: Schwabe.

Richey, Margaret F. (1923). *Gahmuret Anschevin: A Contribution to the Study of Wolfram von Eschenbach.* Oxford: Blackwell.

Ricoeur, Paul (1984). *Time and Narrative.* Vol 1. Trans. Kathleen McLaughlin and David Pellauer. Chicago and London: U of Chicago P.

Ruh, Kurt (1980). *Höfische Epik des deutschen Mittelalters. II. 'Reinhart Fuchs,' 'Lanzelet,' Wolfram von Eschenbach, Gottfried von Straßburg.* Berlin: Schmidt.

Rupp, Heinz (ed.) (1966). *Wolfram von Eschenbach.* Darmstadt: Wissenschaftliche Buchgesellschaft.

Rupp, Heinz (1983). "Die Bedeutung der Gawan-Bücher im *Parzival* Wolframs von Eschenbach." *London German Studies II.* Ed. J. P. Stern. London: Institute of German Studies London. 1–17.

Sacker, Hugh (1963). *An Introduction to Wolfram's 'Parzival.'* Cambridge: Cambridge UP.

Salmon, Paul (1963). "Der zehnte Engelchor in deutschen Dichtungen und Predigten des Mittelalters." *Euphorion* 57: 321–30.

Salzer, Anselm (1926). *Illustrierte Geschichte der Deutschen Literatur.* Vol.1. Regensburg: Habbel.

Schäfer-Maulbetsch, Rose-Beate (1972). *Studien zur Entwicklung des mittelhochdeutschen Epos. Die Kampfschilderung in 'Kaiserchronik,' 'Rolandslied', 'Alexanderlied,' 'Eneide,' 'Liet von Troye,' und 'Willehalm.'* 2 vols. Göppingen: Kümmerle.

Schirok, Bernd (1982). *Parzivalrezeption im Mittelalter.* Darmstadt: Wissenschaftliche Buchgesellschaft.

Schirok, Bernd (1985). *Wolfram von Eschenbach, 'Parzival.' Die Bilder der illustrierten Handschriften.* Göppingen: Kümmerle.

Schmid, Elisabeth (1993). "Wolfram von Eschenbach: *Parzival.*" *Interpretationen: Mittelhochdeutsche Romane und Heldenepen.* Ed. Horst Brunner. Stuttgart: Reclam. 173–195.

Schmolke-Hasselmann, Beate (1980). *Der arthurische Versroman von Chrestien bis Froissart. Zur Geschichte einer Gattung.* Tübingen: Niemeyer.

Schnell, Rüdiger (1974). "Vogeljagd und Liebe im 8. Buch von Wolframs *Parzival. Beiträge zur Geschichte der deutschen Sprache und Literatur (Tübingen)* 96: 246–269.

Scholz, Manfred G. (1980). *Hören und Lesen. Studien zur primären Rezeption der Literatur im 12. und 13. Jahrhundert.* Wiesbaden: Steiner.

Schröder, Walter Johannes (1952). *Der Ritter zwischen Welt und Gott.* Weimar: Böhlau.

Schröder, Walter Johannes (1963). *Die Soltane-Erzählung in Wolframs 'Parzival.' Studien zur Darstellung und Bedeutung der Lebensstufen Parzivals.* Heidelberg: Winter.

Schultz, Alwin (1889). *Das höfische Leben zur Zeit der Minnesinger.* 2nd ed. 2 vols. Leipzig: Hirzel.

Schweikle, Günther (1970). *Dichter über Dichter in Mittelhochdeutscher Literatur.* Tübingen: Niemeyer.

Schwietering, Julius (1969). "Parzivals Schuld." *Philologische Schriften.* Ed. Friedrich Ohly and Max Wehrli. Munich: Fink. 362–84. (Originally published in *Zeitschrift für deutsches Altertum* 81 [1944]: 44–68.)

Siberry, Elizabeth (1985). *Criticism of Crusading 1095–1274.* Oxford: Clarendon.

Simson, Otto Georg von (1966). "Über das Religiöse in Wolframs *Parzival.*" In: Heinz Rupp (ed.). 207–31.

Singer, Samuel (1898). "Zu Wolframs *Parzival.*" *Abhandlungen zur germanischen Philologie. Festgabe für Richard Heinzel.* Halle/S.: Niemeyer. 353–436.

Smail, R. C. (1956). *Crusading Warfare (1097–1193).* Cambridge: Cambridge UP.

Smalley, Beryl (1957). *The Study of the Bible in the Middle Ages.* Oxford: Oxford UP.

Spahr, Blake Lee (1991). "Gahmuret's Erection: Rising to Adventure." *Monatshefte* 83: 403–413.

Stauffer, Marianne (1959). *Der Wald. Zur Darstellung und Deutung der Natur im Mittelalter.* Berne: Francke.

Stein, Alexandra (1993). *'wort unde werc': Studien zum narrativen Diskurs im 'Parzival' Wolframs von Eschenbach.* Frankfurt: Lang.

Steiner, Gertraud. *Das Abenteuer der Regression: Eine Untersuchung zur phantasmagorischen Wiederkehr der verlorenen Zeit im 'Erec' Hartmanns von Aue.* Göppingen: Kümmerle, 1983.

Stevens, Adrian (1993). "Heteroglossia and Clerical Narrative." *Chrétien de Troyes and the German Middle Ages.* Ed. Martin H. Jones and Roy Wisbey. Woodbridge/Rochester: Brewer; Institute of German Studies. 241–255.

Stevens, Adrian (1994). "Memory, Reading and the Renewal of Love: On the Poetics of Invention in Gottfried's *Tristan*." *German Narrative Literature of the Twelfth and Thirteenth Centuries: Studies presented to Roy Wisbey on his Sixty-fifth Birthday*. Ed. Volker Honemann et al. Tübingen: Niemeyer, 1994. 319–336.

Sturges, Robert S. (1991). *Medieval Interpretation. Models of Reading in Literary Narrative, 1100–1500*. Carbondale and Edwardsville: Southern Illinois UP.

Sussman, Linda (1995). *The Speech of the Grail. A Journey toward Speaking that Heals and Transforms*. Hudson, NY: Lindisfarne Press.

Swinburne, Hilda (1955). "Parzival's Crisis." *Modern Language Review* 50: 181–6.

Swisher, Michael. "*Zorn* in Wolfram's *Parzival*." *Neuphilologische Mitteilungen* 93 (1992): 393–410.

Tax, Petrus (1965). "*Felix culpa* und *lapsit exillis*: Wolframs *Parzival* und die Liturgie." *MLN* 80: 454–69.

Tax, Petrus (1973). "Gahmuret zwischen Äneas und Parzival: Zur Struktur der Vorgeschichte von Wolframs *Parzival*." *ZDP* 92: 24–37.

Tax, Petrus (1973). "Wolfram von Eschenbach's *Parzival* in the Light of Biblical Typology." *Seminar* 9: 1–14.

Tennant, F. R. (1903) *The Sources of the Doctrines of the Fall and of Original Sin*. Cambridge: CUP.

Thomas, Neil (1989). *The Medieval German Arthuriad. Some Contemporary Revaluations of the Canon*. Berne: Lang.

Timpson, George F. (1959/60). "The Heraldic Element in Wolfram's *Parzival*." *German Life and Letters* N.S. 13: 88–93.

Tobin, Frank (1975). "Fallen Man and Hartmann's *Gregorius*." *Germanic Review* 50: 85–98.

Vale, Malcolm (1981). *War and Chivalry: Warfare and Aristocratic Culture in England, France and Burgundy at the End of the Middle Ages*. London: Duckworth.

Verbruggen, J. F. (1976). *The Art of Warfare in Western Europe during the Middle Ages*. Trans. S. Willard and S.C.M. Southern. Amsterdam: North-Holland; New York: American Elseview.

Vinaver, Eugène (1984). *The Rise of Romance*. Cambridge and New Jersey 1984: Barnes & Noble.

Vorderstemann, Jürgen (1974). *Die Fremdwörter im 'Willehalm' Wolframs von Eschenbach*. Göppingen: Kümmerle.

Wack, Mary F. (1984). "Wolfram's dawn song *Sîne klâwen*." *Traditio* 40: 235–249.

Wand, Christine (1989). *Wolfram von Eschenbach und Hartmann von Aue.* Herne: Verlag für Wissenschaft und Kunst.

Wapnewski, Peter (1955). *Wolframs 'Parzival.' Studien zur Religiosität und Form.* Heidelberg: Winter.

Wapnewski, Peter (1992). "The Operas as Literary Works." Trans. Peter Palmer. *Wagner Handbook.* Ed. Ulrich Müller and Peter Wapnewski. (Translation edited by John Deathridge.) Cambridge, MA: Harvard UP. (Originally published as *Richard-Wagner-Handbuch* [Stuttgart, 1986].)

Wehrli, Max (1966). "Wolfram's Humor." In Heinz Rupp, ed., 104–124.

Wehrli, Max (1975). "diu menscheit hât wilden art." *Verbum et signum: Beiträge zur mediävistischen Bedeutungsforschung.* Ed. Hans Fromm. 2 vols. Munich: Fink. Vol.2. 189–201.

Weigand, Hermann J. (1969). "Narrative Time in the Grail Poems of Chrétien de Troyes and Wolfram von Eschenbach." *Wolfram's 'Parzival': Five Essays with an Introduction.* By HW. Ed. Ursula Hoffmann. Ithaca and London: Cornell UP. 18–74. (Originally published in *PMLA* 53 [1938]: 917–50.)

Weiner, Marc A. (1995). *Richard Wagner and the Anti-Semitic Imagination.* Lincoln and London: U of Nebraska P.

Wells, Christopher J. (1985). *German. A Linguistic History to 1945.* Oxford: Clarendon.

Wells, David A. (1994). "Fatherly Advice. The Precepts of Gregorius, Marke, and Gurnemanz and the School Tradition of the *Disticha Catonis*." *Frühmittelalterliche Studien* 28: 296–332.

Wenzel, Horst (1980). "Zur Repräsentation von Herrschaft in mittelalterlichen Texten." *Adelsherrschaft und Literatur.* Ed. Horst Wenzel. Frankfurt: Lang.

Wessels, P. B. (1966). "Wolfram zwichen Dogma und Legende." In: Heinz Rupp, ed., 232–60.

Westernhagen, Curt von (1966). *Richard Wagners Dresdener Bibliothek 1842–1849.* Wiesbaden: Brockhaus.

Weston, Jessie L. (1920). *From Ritual to Romance.* Cambridge: CUP, 1920.

Wiedmer, Peter (1977). *Sündenfall und Erlösung bei Heinrich von Hesler.* Berne: Francke.

Wiles, Maurice (1977). *The Christian Fathers.* 2nd ed. London: SCM Press.

Willoughby, Harold R. (1929) *Pagan Regeneration. A Study of Mystery Initiations in the Graeco-Roman World.* Chicago: U of Chicago P.

Willson, Bernard (1962). "Das Fragemotiv in Wolframs *Parzival*." *Germanisch-Romanische Monatsschrift* 12: 139–50.

Wynn, Marianne (1962). "Parzival and Gawan — Hero and Counterpart." *Beiträge zur Geschichte der deutschen Sprache und Literatur (Tübingen)* 84: 142–172. (Reprinted in Wynn, *Wolfram's 'Parzival'*).

Wynn, Marianne (1976/77). "Orgeluse, Persönlichkeitsgestaltung auf chrestienschem Modell." *German Life and Letters* 30: 127–137.

Wynn, Marianne (1983). "Medieval Literature in Reception: Richard Wagner and Wolfram's *Parzival*." *London German Studies* 2: 94–114.

Wynn, Marianne (1984). *Wolfram's 'Parzival': On the Genesis of Its Poetry.* Frankfurt: Lang.

Wynn, Marianne (1994). "Wolfram von Eschenbach." *German Writers and Works of the High Middle Ages: 1170–1280.* Ed. James Hardin and Will Hasty. *Dictionary of Literary Biography.* Vol. 138. Detroit, Washington, DC, and London: Gale Research. 185–206.

Yeandle, David N. (1981). "Herzeloyde: Problems of Characterization in Book III of Wolfram's *Parzival.*" *Euphorion* 75: 1–28.

Yeandle, David N. (1985). *Commentary on the Soltane and Jeschute Episodes in Book III of Wolfram von Eschenbach's 'Parzival.'* Heidelberg: Winter.

Zelinsky, Hartmut (1976). *Richard Wagner — ein deutsches Thema. Eine Dokumentation zur Wirkungsgeschichte Richard Wagners 1876–1976.* Frankfurt: Zweitausendeins.

Zeydel, Edwin H. (1953). "Wolfram's *Parzival*, 'Kyot' und die Katharer." *Neophilologus* 37: 23–35.

Zimmermann, Gisela (1972). "Untersuchungen zur Orgeluseepisode in Wolfram von Eschenbachs *Parzival.*" *Euphorion* 66: 128–150.

Zimmermann, Gisela (1974). *Kommentar zum VII. Buch von Wolfram von Eschenbachs 'Parzival.'* Göppingen: Kümmerle.

Notes on Contributors

Albrecht Classen is Professor of German Studies at the University of Arizona. He has published many books and articles on medieval and early modern German literature and is editor of *Tristania*.

Francis G. Gentry is Professor of German and Co-Director of the Max Kade German-American Research Institute at the Pennsylvania State University. He has written and edited numerous books on medieval German literature.

Marion E. Gibbs is Reader in German at Royal Holloway, University of London. She has published books on Wolfram's *Parzival* and *Willehalm*, and is co-author of a Companion to Medieval German Literature (New York, 1997) and co-translator of Wolfram's *Willehalm* and *Titurel and the Songs* (with Sidney M. Johnson).

Will Hasty is Associate Professor in German at the University of Florida. He has written numerous books and articles on medieval German literature.

W. H. Jackson is Senior Lecturer in German at the University of St. Andrews. Among his many publications on medieval German literature is *Chivalry in Twelfth-Century Germany: The Works of Hartmann von Aue* (Cambridge 1994).

Sidney M. Johnson is Professor Emeritus of Germanic Studies at Indiana University. He has published numerous articles on medieval German literature, and is co-author of a Companion to Medieval German Literature (New York, 1997) and co-translator of Wolfram's *Willehalm* and *Titurel and the Songs* (with Marion E. Gibbs).

Martin Jones is Senior Lecturer in German at King's College London. He has published numerous articles and edited three volumes dealing with medieval German literature.

Winder McConnell is Professor of German and Director of Medieval Studies at the University of California, Davis. He has published numerous books and articles on German heroic epic and romance, and translated both *Kudrun* and *Nibelungenklage* for Camden House.

Ulrich Müller is Professor of German Studies at the University of Salzburg. He has published extensively on medieval German literature and on Richard Wagner.

Brian Murdoch is Professor of German at the University of Stirling. He has written books on the Adam legends in German and Celtic and on the Germanic Hero.

Adrian Stevens is Senior Lecturer in German at University College London. He has published numerous articles and co-edited several volumes on medieval German literature.

Neil Thomas is Lecturer in German at the University of Durham. He has published a book and numerous articles on medieval German literature and the medieval Arthurian tradition.

Index

Abel 122
Abenberg x
absolution 152–153, 194
Adam 112, 143–152, 154, 156–157, 218
Addanz 226
Adorno, Theodor W. 251, 254, 261
Aeneas 47, 57, 214
Agena, Kathleen 241, 261
Alain of Lille 155, 191
Albigensians 85
alchemy/alchemical symbolism xix, 203, 205, 214, 216–221, 255
Alexander-saga 92–93
Allen, Peter L. 189, 261
Altdeutsche Genesis 145, 151, 259
Ampflise (The Queen of France) 6, 8, 19, 27–28, 168, 200
Anchises 214
Andreas Capellanus 189–191, 201, 259
Anegenge 146
Anfortas 9, 16, 26, 33–34, 55–56, 59, 72, 84, 88–92, 105, 107, 112–113, 137, 150, 156, 180, 183, 198, 208–210, 214–216, 226, 235, 237, 239, 250, 252, 254
anger (*zorn*) xi, 15, 17, 22, 44, 60, 63, 155, 175, 229, 230–231, 238
anima 256
Anjou 37, 79, 112, 114, 228
Antanor 28
anthropology 193
Antikonie 22–25, 47–50, 73
apo koinou 128
Arabic xvi, 79, 85, 87–88, 91, 110–112, 193, 247
archers (*schützen*) 162, 172–174, 179
archetypal images 232
Arnive 40, 52, 58, 65, 69, 219
Arnold, Benjamin 162, 261
Arnold of Villanova 213–214
Arthur, King xiii, 6, 10, 41, 58, 65, 68–74, 89, 106, 112–113, 120, 129–131, 171, 179, 189, 200, 208, 223–224, 229, 231, 233, 240, 246, 258
Arthurian court/chivalry xiii, xviii–xix, 6, 8, 10, 26, 28–29, 39–42, 46, 47, 50, 52, 54, 57, 59, 61, 63–68, 73, 89–90, 106, 131–132, 169, 175, 179–180, 200, 203–204, 207–208, 214–215, 221, 223–231, 233, 239
Arthurian romance/narratives/works ix, xiii–xiv, xix, 3, 30, 38, 40, 78, 84, 99–101, 104, 113, 118, 125, 130–131, 159, 169, 176, 178, 203, 223–225, 227, 232, 234, 240–241
ascetic/asceticism xvi, 33, 226, 233, 236–238, 240, 250
Astor 175
astronomy ix, 193
Augustine, Saint 136, 144, 147–148, 151, 155
Avalon 225, 233
aventiure/aventure xiii, 22, 79, 90, 100, 136, 177, 209, 232
Avitus 155

Baghdad 205
Bakhtin, Mikhail 125, 128, 130, 261
Baldwin, John W. 189, 261
Balin 235
banner (*vanen/baniere*) 170
baptism 21, 27, 89, 137–138, 143,

145–146, 150, 153, 157, 183, 195, 199, 233
Barber, Richard 166–168, 179, 226, 241, 261
barbican (*barbigân*) 174
Barbigoel 50
Barker, Juliet 166–168, 179, 261
Baruc, the xii, 200, 232
Bataille d'Aliscans xii, 136, 259
Bayer, Hans 225, 262
Bayreuth Festspielhaus 246
Beacurs 70
Bearosche 23, 42–43, 45–46, 49, 54, 71, 73–74, 76, 169–177, 183
Belacane 5–8, 11, 19–22, 26–27, 56, 112–113, 121–122, 138, 168, 198–200, 205–206, 232
bellum iustum 136
Bene 53, 55, 60, 65, 68–69, 215
Benton, John F. 189, 262
Bernard Silvestris 191
Bertau, Karl ix, 9, 127, 206, 220, 226, 233, 262
Bindschedler, Maria B. 58, 262
black magic 195
Blair, Claude 162–163, 262
Blamires, David 13, 19, 40, 157, 262
Blank, Richard (German TV-play *Parzival*) 257
Blanschefleur (Chrétien's *Perceval*) 31–32
Blood and Dreams (Richard Monaco) 258
Blood in the snow 22–23, 33, 41
Bloom, Harold ix, xiv, 203, 262
Boccaccio, Giovanni 194, 259
Bodel, Jean 99
Boeheim, Wendelin 162, 262
Boigs, Lotte 227, 262
Boor, Helmut de xvii–xviii, 262
Boorman, John (*Excalibur*) 256
Bors 226, 237
Borst, Arno 183, 262
Bossy, John 160, 262

Boulez, Pierre 254
Bow metaphor 138
Bradbury, Jim 161, 171, 173, 262
Brandelidelin 68–70
Brewer, D. S. 126, 262
Brickus 112
Brobarz 166, 209
Brooks, Peter 102–103, 262
Brun von Schönebeck 179
Brunhilde 249
Brunner, Horst 71, 73, 227, 262
Brunner, Otto 161, 263
Buddhism 250
buhurt 164–66
Bumke, Joachim ix, xi, 8, 26, 40, 45, 54, 56, 62, 104, 110, 162–166, 168–169, 176–177, 182, 193, 224, 235, 263
Burdach, Konrad 84, 263
Busby, Keith 40, 120, 263

Cain 122–123
Camargo, Martin 199, 263
Camelot 10, 246, 258
Camilla (the Story of Aeneas) 57
Camille, Michael 192, 263
Campbell, Joseph 203, 234, 263
Carduel 106
caritas 150, 156
Casey, John 238, 263
Castis 148
Catharism 152, 220
Cato (*Distichs*) 149
Celan, Paul 125
Celtic sources 86, 99, 193
Chanson de Geste xii, 74, 133
Chanson de Roland 245
Charles Martel xii
Chaucer 137, 139
chivalric ethics 179–184
chivalry/knighthood x–xi, xv, xvii–xix, 5, 10, 20, 22, 24, 27, 32–33, 41, 43, 53–54, 59, 63, 74–75, 91, 117–123, 148, 160, 162, 164–165, 171–172, 179–184, 199, 205, 207, 223, 226,

INDEX 283

228, 230, 235, 237–239, 240
Chrétien de Troyes ix, xii–xv, 3, 9,
  25, 38–39, 78–87, 99–106,
  108–110, 113, 115–120, 122,
  133, 138, 159, 166, 223, 227,
  234–235, 240
Chrétien de Troyes, works by:
  Erec and Enide xv, 38–39, 86,
    99–106, 119, 260
  Lancelot xii, 260
  Li Contes del Graal (Perceval)
    xii, 3, 28–29, 31–32, 38–39,
    55, 78–86, 88, 91, 103–
    110, 112–113, 115–122,
    131–132, 159, 162, 164–
    166, 169–170, 172–174,
    176, 178, 181, 193, 213,
    219, 232–233, 235, 240,
    246–247, 250, 260
  Yvain xv, 39, 84, 86, 99, 260
Christ 83–84, 89, 91, 144–145,
  149, 153–154, 157, 192, 217,
  252
Christian moral consciousness 238
Christoph, Siegfried R. 13, 16, 21,
  263
chronicle 80, 112, 114–116, 161,
  195, 213
Chronicle of Heliandus 213
Cidegast 26, 51, 56, 62–64, 69–
  70, 72
Cirlot, J. E. 210–212, 218, 263
Cistercian order 226, 240
Clamide 28, 30, 171–173, 178–
  179
Clanchy, M. T. 118, 191, 263
Clark, S. H. 103, 263
Classen, Albrecht 124, 190–191,
  263, 279
clerical culture/learning/books x,
  xiv–xv, xviii–xix, 100–101,
  118–120, 159, 190–191, 193
Clias the Greek 52
Clinschor 51–55, 58, 209, 215,
  217–219, 221, 250
Coleman, Janet 192, 264

collective unconscious 209
Condwiramurs 5–6, 8, 15, 21–22,
  26, 28, 30–34, 56, 89–90,
  123, 173, 179, 208–210, 229
confession 90, 152–153, 156
conjunture/conjointure 101–104,
  112, 123
Contamine, Philippe 161–162,
  174, 264
Continuations of Chrétien de
  Troyes's *Perceval* 81–82, 86,
  138, 260
contrition 142, 152, 156–157, 230
Cormeau, Christoph (and Wilhelm
  Störmer) 146, 264
Couratin, A. H. 157, 264
crisis of chivalry 10
"crooked" German 127
Crusades, the xii– xiv, 85, 87, 139,
  174
Cundrie (Gawan's sister) 52, 70,
  72
Cundrie (la surziere) 8–9, 16, 34,
  41–42, 52, 59, 87–88, 90, 92,
  151, 156, 193, 208, 210, 214–
  215, 219, 221, 229–231
Cunneware 28–29, 179
Curtius, Ernst Robert 192, 201,
  264
Cyprian of Carthage 147, 151,
  154, 157–158, 260
Czerwinski, Peter 167, 170–171,
  264

Dahlgrün, Corinna 148, 264
Dallapiazza, Michael 193, 264
Dante Alighieri ix, 202, 245, 260
Danto, Arthur 117
Darrah, John 235, 264
death in chivalry (see also
  homicide) 4, 6–8, 10, 16–17,
  20–21, 23, 26, 33, 37, 41, 56,
  112, 121–122, 136, 165, 170,
  175, 178, 180–181, 199, 201,
  205–206, 226, 228, 232–237,
  239

Debussy, Claude 254
Decian persecutions 147
defensionis audacia 152
Deinert, Wilhelm 221, 264
Delay, Florence 257
demotic registers 125
Der saelden hort 146
development 9, 19–20, 22, 93, 203–204, 207–209, 229–231, 229–231, 239, 254
DeVries, Kelly 162, 264
dialectic (liberal arts) 119
Dick, Ernst 205–206, 210, 215, 264
Dido 47
Dimler, G. Richard 156, 264
Dinzelbacher, Peter 197, 264
Dollnstein (the women shopkeepers of) 48, 235
Dolorous Stroke 235
Dorst, Tankred 256–258
Draesner, Ulrike 41, 47, 169, 265
Duby, Georges 112, 265
Duckworth, David 25, 147, 152, 154, 156–158, 265

Ebenbauer, Alfred 5, 265
Ehcunaht 51
Ehler, Ursula 257–258
Ehrismann, Gustav 92, 265
Eleanor of Aquitaine xii
Eliade, Mircea 205
Elias, Norbert 183, 225, 265
Elsa, duchess of Brabant (Richard Wagner's *Lohengrin*) 249
Enchiridion Symbolorum 143, 260
Enite (Hartmann von Aue's *Erec*) 30
Enygeus (Sister of Joseph of Arimathea) 83
epilogue (of *Parzival*) 113
epitaph (Gahmuret) 8, 199–200
epitaph (Wolfram) x
Erlösung, the 146
Ernst, Ulrich 85, 265
Eve 144–146, 149–152, 154

Excalibur (John Boorman) 256
Ezzos Gesang 146

fabula/fable 102–103, 114
Fasisculus Morum 155, 260
Faust 220, 255
Feirefiz xii, 5, 9, 15, 17, 21, 27, 33, 89, 95, 112–113, 121–123, 137–139, 150, 157, 167, 178, 180, 182, 199–200, 206, 219, 221, 231
feuds/feuding xiv, 160–161, 166, 171, 175, 225
fiction/fictionality 99–104, 107–110, 112–114, 116–117, 194, 196
The Final Quest (Richard Monaco) 258
First Knight (film) 240
Fisher King 80–81, 84, 87, 109, 150
Fleckenstein, Josef 166, 177, 265
Flegetanis 111, 195
Fletcher, Robert Huntington 224, 265
Florant von Itolac (the Turkoite) 61–62, 67, 70, 72, 74, 182, 219, 221
flühtesal 17–18, 206
Fouqué, Baron Friedrich de la Motte 254–255
Franz, Marie-Louise von (and Emma Jung) 209–210, 212–213, 216–218, 226, 255, 269
Frappier, Jean 86, 265
Frederick I, Emperor x, 175
Frederick II, Emperor x, 247, 253
Frederick II of Prussia 247
French xii–xiii, xv, 7, 25, 29, 32, 39–40, 78–80, 82, 87–88, 101–102, 104, 110–114, 116, 118, 128, 133, 136, 159, 162–163, 165, 167, 174, 193, 198–200, 225, 245–247, 253–254, 256–257
Frimutel 114, 210

INDEX

Gahmuret 3–12, 16–21, 27–28, 37–38, 107–108, 112–113, 117–118, 121–122, 148, 164–171, 178, 198–200, 205–206, 226–229, 232–235, 239
Galahad 226, 237, 240
Galoes 4, 226, 228
Gamber, Ortwin 162, 265
Gandin 4, 199, 226, 228, 232, 239
Gaunt, Simon 127, 265
Gauvain 39–40, 81–82, 87
Gawan xvii–xix, 3, 11, 22–26, 28, 33, 37–55, 57–76, 89–90, 110, 131, 169–175, 178, 182–183, 205, 209, 214–219, 221, 226, 229, 250
Gellrich, Jesse M. 192, 265
genealogy/genealogical 38, 112–113, 116, 205
Gentry, Francis G. 279
Geoffrey of Monmouth xiii, 113–114, 120, 223–224, 260
geography ix, 193, 204
Gereint 86
germaine cousine (Chrétien's *Perceval*) 80
Gernhuber, Joachim 160, 265
Gervinus, G. G. xv–xvi, xviii, 265
Gibbs, Marion E. 9, 136, 259, 266, 279
Gilgamesh 214
Ginover 57–58, 200
glasnost 258
God as a book 191–192
Goedeke, Karl xv, 266
Goethe, Johann Wolfgang von 124–125, 220
Goetinck, Glenys 86, 266
Good Friday xiv, 78, 83, 88, 132, 152–154
Gornemant (Chrétien's *Perceval*) 30
Görres, Joseph 247, 249
Gottfried von Straßburg xiv–xv, 12, 31, 120, 124–128, 139, 196, 203, 249, 253, 260
graal (Chrétien's grail) 82
Graal Théâtre (Jacques Roubaud and Florence Delay) 257
Graharz 204
grail xiii–xiv, xvi, xviii–xx, 3, 15–16, 20, 40, 43, 46, 50, 56, 74, 76–95, 108–111, 115, 122–123, 138, 150, 180, 192, 195–198, 201, 208, 210–211, 213–214, 216, 230–231, 234–235, 240, 251–252, 255, 258
grail as a book 196–198
The Grail War (Richard Monaco) 258
grammar (liberal arts) xiv, 119
Gramoflanz 43, 51–52, 56, 61–65, 67–73, 182–183, 200–202, 210, 221
Great Mother (*magna mater*) 208, 234
Green, D. H. 3, 48, 51–52, 65, 70, 72, 107, 109, 115, 127, 130, 132, 136, 178, 180, 182, 191, 266
Green, Miranda 233–234, 236, 266
Gregory the Great 151
Grey Knight (Kahenis) xiv, 132, 152–153, 230
Grimm, Reinhold R. 148, 266
Groos, Arthur xviii–xix, 32, 130, 132, 153, 155, 174, 180–181, 190, 193, 200, 266
Gruenter, Rainer 149, 266
Grünkorn, Gertrud 99, 110, 266
Gruntz, George (*The Holy Grail of Joy and Jazz*) 257
Guenevere 225
Guillaume Durandus (Bishop of Mende) 192
Guillaume of Toulouse, Count xii
Guiot de Provins 84
Gundacker von Judenburg 146
Gurnemanz 10, 30, 149–150, 152,

164, 178, 180–182, 196, 208–209, 229, 250
Gürttler, Karin 227, 266
Gurzgri 226
Gutman, R. W. 251, 267
Gyburg (Wolfram's *Willehalm*) 21, 136–138

Haage, Bernhard D. 154, 267
Haas, Alois M. 20, 147, 267
Haferland, Harald 225, 267
Halford, Mary-Bess 149, 267
Handke, Peter (*Das Spiel vom Fragen oder Die Reise zum sonoren Land*) 257–258
Hardiz, King of Gascony 5
Hart, Thomas Elwood 213, 220, 267
Hartmann von Aue ix, xiii–xv, 12, 39, 99, 105, 118–119, 124–125, 127, 146, 155, 169, 223–224, 227, 240
  Der arme Heinrich xiv, 118, 146, 155, 260
  Erec xiii, xv, xviii, 41, 99, 105, 118–119, 169
  Gregorius 146, 148–149, 155, 260
  Iwein xiii–xv, xviii, 30, 39, 41, 99, 118–119, 169, 177, 234, 238, 260
Harty, Kevin J. 257, 267
Hawkins, Charles Homer 191, 267
Hasty, Will xv, 180–181, 267, 279
Hatto, A. T. 120, 129, 133, 139, 144, 172, 227, 235, 249, 259, 267
hauberk (*halsberc, harnasch*) 163
Haug, Walter 99, 101, 107, 116, 121, 267
Hauptmann, Gerhart 256
Hausherr, Reiner 192, 268
healing/curing/*nêren* 58, 153–154, 156, 210
Hebron/Bron (Legend of Joseph of Arimathea) 83

Hein, Christoph (*Die Ritter der Tafelrunde*) 256–258
Heinrich VI x
Heinrich von dem Türlin 213
Heinrich von Morungen 133
Heinrich von Neustadt 146
Heinrich von Veldeke xiv, 3
Helinand de Froidmont (Chronicle of Helinandus) 80, 213
Heliopolis, altar of the sun 82
Heninger, S. K., Jr. 212–213, 268
Henry II of England 224
Henry the Lion x
Heracles 214
heraldry 160, 164
Hermann of Thuringia ix, xi, 136, 176
Hermann von Sachsenheim (*Die Mörin*) 178, 260
heroic epic/literature 128, 176, 183
Herzeloyde 3–12, 14–22, 25–27, 29, 33, 56, 105, 108, 112–113, 122, 137, 148–149, 152, 166, 168, 199, 206–209, 226, 232–236, 239, 250
Herzog Ernst 204
Hesler, Heinrich 146
Hildebert of Lavardin 191
Historia Welforum 161, 260
Hohenstaufen dynasty 245
The Holy Grail of Joy and Jazz (George Gruntz) 257
Homer xvi, 245
homicide (see also death in chivalry) 132, 136, 181
Honorius 148
Horace 101
Horgan, A. D. 90–91, 268
horse cover (*decke/kovertiure*) 163
Huby, Michel 229, 231, 268
Hugh of St. Victor 192
humanity/humaneness xii, 11, 46, 54, 64, 75–76, 139, 192
humor xviii, 48, 116, 118, 120, 126–127, 130, 137–139, 164,

168, 176, 182
hyperbaton 128

Illich, Ivan 192, 268
illiteracy 118, 124, 128–129, 190, 193, 195
Indiana Jones and the Last Crusade (film) 214, 258
individuation 204, 209, 222
Ingliart (Gawan's horse) 46
Innocent III (Pope) 143
integration of masculine and feminine 208, 221
inventio 119
irony xviii, 27, 106, 118, 126–127, 130, 132–133, 139, 150, 168, 182, 190, 193
Irot (father of Gramoflanz) 62
Irvine, Martin 109, 268
Isenhart 6–7, 21, 23, 121–122, 205–206
Isidore of Seville 109, 151
Ither of Gaheviez (The Red Knight) 4, 10, 46, 122–123, 132, 164, 173, 181–182, 226, 229, 239
Itonje 52, 61–63, 65, 67–72, 200, 221

Jackson, William H. 162, 164, 166, 168, 227, 268, 279
Jaeger, C. Stephen 159, 268
James, Henry 76
javelin (*gabilôt*) 121, 172
Jerome 212
Jeschute 10, 26, 28–29, 89, 125–127
Joflanze 52, 54, 63–68, 70, 72–73, 75, 200
Johannes von Frankenstein 146
John the Baptist 89, 153
Johnson, L. Peter 130, 132, 135, 268
Johnson, Sidney M. 65, 150, 154, 259, 268, 279
Jones, Martin H. 26, 162, 170, 180, 227–228, 238, 268–269, 280
Joseph of Arimathea 83, 91, 232, 252–253
Josephus 87
jousting xix, 5–7, 27, 41, 50, 52, 67, 108, 121, 165, 167, 171, 175, 177, 179, 182, 186, 217, 227
Jung, Carl Gustav 203–206, 214, 216–218, 220, 255–256, 269
Jung, Emma (and Marie-Louise von Franz) 209–210, 212–213, 216–218, 226, 255, 269

Kahane, Henry 85, 269
Kahane, Renée 85, 269
Kahenis (Grey Knight) xiv, 132, 152–153, 230
Kaiser, Gert 226, 269
Kalogreant (Hartmann von Aue's *Iwein*) 30
Kant, Karl 127, 269
Kanvoleiz 40, 108, 166–170, 172, 177, 187
Kardefablet 172
Kardeiz 6
Karg, Ina 10, 269
Karnahkarnanz 207
Karnein, Alfred 189, 269
katabasis 214
Katz, Jacob 251, 269
Kaylet 4, 121
Keie 41, 61, 66–67, 74
Kennedy, John F. 224
Kermode, Frank 117, 269
Keu (Chrétien's *Perceval*) 28
Kingrimursel 42, 48–51, 63
Kingrun 30, 32
Klingsor 250
Klopstock, Friedrich Gottlieb 125
Knapp, F. P. 231, 270
Knefelkamp, Ulrich 139, 270
knighthood/chivalry x–xi, xv, xvii–xix, 5, 10, 20, 22, 24, 27, 32–33, 41, 43, 53–54, 59, 63, 74–

75, 91, 117–123, 148, 160, 162, 164–165, 171–172, 179–184, 199, 205, 207, 223, 226, 228, 230, 235, 237–239, 240
knightly equipment 160–162, 164, 177
Knights Templar xiv, 79–80, 87–89, 178
Köhler, Erich 131
Kolb, Herbert 85, 270
Konrad of Hirsau 109
Koralus (Hartmann von Aue's *Erec*) 30
Kratz, Henry 19, 26, 130, 157, 270
Kriemhilde 56, 249
Kudrun 204
Kühn, Dieter 256
Kühnel, Jürgen 251, 270
Kundry (Richard Wagner's *Parsifal*) 250
Kunitzsch, Paul 232, 270
Kurtz, Hermann 249
Kyot (postulated source) xii, xv–xviii, 9, 78–79, 84–86, 91, 106–107, 110–116, 119, 130, 194–196

Lacey, Norris J. 234, 270
Lachmann, Karl xi, 82, 247, 259
Lähelin 132
Lambekin 167
lance, bleeding 80, 84, 86–87, 210, 212
Lancelet (*Perlesvaus*) 87
Lancelot 225, 240, 246
Lanval 225, 233–234
lapidary science 193, 198
lapsit exillis 78, 80, 82, 92, 150, 213, 216
Lascoyt 226
Last Supper 83, 138, 252
Latin x, xiv, xviii, 79–80, 83, 86, 92, 100, 111–112, 114–116, 118–120, 129, 143, 146, 148, 151, 155, 158, 189, 193, 195, 216
Laudine (Hartmann von Aue's *Iwein*) 39, 234
lay culture/literacy xiii, 139, 152, 184, 193–196, 200–201, 224–225
Lazaliez 112
Le Goff, Jacques xiv, 270
Leixner, Otto von xvi, xviii, 270
Lessing 139
Lewis, Gertrude Jaron 17–18, 233–234, 270
Li gweiz prelljus 62, 64
Liaze 26, 30–32
Liddamus 49–50, 60, 75
lion (in *Schastel Marveile*) 218
Lischoys Gwelljus 57, 59–61, 70, 72, 74, 182, 215, 221
Lit Marveile 53–54, 215, 217
litotes 130
liturgy/liturgical 79, 132, 145, 153–154, 157, 198
Loathly Damsel 87
locus amoenus 204
Lofmark, Carl J. 85, 106, 130, 270
Logroys 43, 51, 56–57, 64, 66
Lohengrin 246–247
Loherangrin 6, 22, 180, 246, 249
Longinus 84, 91, 212, 235
Loomis, Roger Sherman 86–87, 235, 270
Lot, King of Norway 40, 62–63, 66, 70, 73
Louis VII of France xii
Lucas, George 203
Lucifer 144, 154, 238
Luther, Martin 129
Lutz, Bernd xviii
Lyppaut 43–45, 49, 175

mabinogion 86–87
Mabonagrin 234
magna mater (Great Mother) 208, 234–235
Mahabharata 245
mail chausses (*hosen*) 163

INDEX 289

mail coif/hood (*hersenier/hèrsenier*) 163
Maksymiuk, Stephan 217, 270
Malamud, Bernard (*The Natural*) 258
Malcreatiure 59, 219
Malory, Sir Thomas 233–235, 240, 257, 260
de Mandach, André 85, 270
Manesse Codex xi, 159–160, 185–188
Marchand, James 125, 271
Marie de Champagne xii
Marie de France 225, 233, 260
Marx, Jean 86, 271
Mary, The Virgin 19, 150, 233
matière de Bretagne 86, 99, 100,
Maximilian II of Bavaria x
Mazadan 112, 114, 195
McConnell, Winder 53, 131, 280
McFarland, Timothy 52–53, 271
Mechthild von Magdeburg 192, 261
mêlée 167, 187
Meljacanz 43, 182
Meljanz 23, 43, 45–47, 49, 73–74, 171, 175
Mentelin, Johann ix, 247
merchants (*koufman*) 44, 59, 172–173
Mercury 218
Merlin 219
Merlin oder Das Wüste Land 256–257
Middle High German literary language 124
Mielke, Andreas 198, 271
Miklautsch, Lydia 9, 271
minne/minnedienst (love service) xii–xiii, 7, 25–26, 45, 50, 60–61, 117, 133, 135, 137, 223, 229, 232, 236
Mohr, Wolfgang 40, 46, 57, 176, 181, 271
Monaco, Richard (*Parsival or a Knight's Tale, The Final Quest,*

and *Blood and Dreams*) 258
mons salvationis 151
Moorcock, Michael (*The War Hound and the World's Pain*) 258
moors 168, 205, 253
Mordred 233
Morgan le Fay 233–234
Moses 91, 147, 197
Müller, Jan-Dirk 225, 271
Müller, Ulrich xvi, 250, 256, 271, 280
Munsalvaesche/grail castle/grail kingdom xiii, xviii–xix, 6, 8, 10, 16–17, 20, 22, 26, 39, 55–56, 74, 77–79, 81–82, 87, 89–90, 108, 113–114, 149–152, 155–156, 166, 178, 180, 194–198, 204, 206, 208–210, 212, 214–216, 219, 221, 226, 229–230, 232, 234, 237, 239, 250
Murdoch, Brian 144, 146, 149, 153–155, 239, 271–272, 280
Muschg, Adolf 257–258
Muslims xii, xiv
Mustard, M. 205, 259
Myller, Christoph Heinrich 245, 247
myth/mythic/mythological elements 87, 204, 225–227, 233–236, 241, 245–246, 253, 256–257

Der nackte Mann (Tankred Dorst and Ursula Ehler) 257
Nantes 106
The Natural (Bernard Malamud) 258
Nellmann, Eberhard 48, 54, 66, 84, 163, 167, 178, 272
neologism 125
Neumann, Erich 208, 235, 272
neutral angels 78, 92
Nibelungenlied 12, 56, 136, 204, 245, 249
Nicolle, David C. 162, 272

Nietzsche, Friedrich 254
Nitze, William A. 86, 272
Noltze, Holger 3, 163, 272
Nördlingen x
numerology 205, 210, 213
Nykrog, Per 113, 120, 272

Obie 22–25, 43–45, 47, 59
Obilot 22–24, 44–45, 47, 74
obscurity xvi, 104, 127–128
occult sciences 193
Odysseus 214
Old High German 154
Orgeluse 22–27, 33, 51–67, 69–76, 90, 170, 174, 182–183, 219, 221
Orilus 7, 28–29, 164, 177, 179
Orpheus 214
Ortmann, Christa 181, 272
Oswald von Wolkenstein 256
Otfried von Weissenburg 149
otherworlds/otherworldly landscapes xix, 203–209, 214–216, 225, 232–234, 239
Otto IV (Otto of Brunswick) ix–x
Otto von Freising (*Gesta Frederici*) 175, 261
Outremer 10
Ovid xii
Owein 86

Paneth, Ludwig 211
Paris 189
Parsifal. A Novel (Peter Vansittart) 258
Parsival or a Knight's Tale (Michael Moorcock) 258
Parzival xiv, xviii–xix, 3–12, 14–23, 25–26, 28–46, 50–51, 54–56, 58–59, 61, 67–70, 72, 74–78, 83–84, 89–90, 92–94, 105–106, 108, 112–115, 122–123, 125–128, 130–132, 137–138, 144, 146–157, 164–166, 169, 171–174, 177–183, 194, 196–198, 201, 203–210, 214–219, 221, 226–231, 233–240, 246–247, 249–250, 253–258
Parzival (German TV-play by Richard Blank) 257
Parzival: Auf der anderen Seite des Sees (Robert Wilson) 257
Parzival. Ein Szenarium (Tankred Dorst and Ursula Ehler) 257
Passage, Charles E. 205, 259
Patelamunt 5, 169–172, 205
patelierre 172
Patterson, Linda 129, 272
Paul, Hermann 124, 230, 272
pax dei xiv
peace movements xiv, 160, 225
peacock feathers (symbolism) 210, 216
Pellam 235
Pelrapeire 6, 33, 127, 169–173, 176, 209
penance 16, 144–146, 149, 151–153, 155–156, 237
Perceval xiii, 28, 30–32, 39, 80, 84, 108, 120–122, 132, 165, 170, 174, 178, 226, 233, 237, 246
Perceval le Gallois (Eric Rohmer) 256
Peredur 86, 261
perestroika 258
Perlesvaus 86, 261
Philip of Alsace, Count of Flanders xii, 86, 103, 104, 113, 116
Philip of Swabia ix–x, 176
philosophical stone 216
Phineas (Numbers 25:1–15) 91
phoenix 78, 155
Pilate 83
pillar, the magic 55, 218–219
plate armor (*plate*) 163
plate armor for knees (*poleyns/schinnelier/schillier*) 163
Plippalinot 52–54, 60, 215–216
plot 103, 115
Poag, James 65, 72, 138, 272

INDEX

poinder (jousting) 165
politburo 258
Poydiconjunz 173, 175–176
Prester John 113, 139
prologue (of *Parzival*) 11, 13, 119, 201
Prose Tristan 225
Prothizilas 205
psychoanalysis 233
Pütz, Hans Henning 170, 272
Pythagoras 212–213, 220–221

quarter (*sicherheit*) 178, 237
Queste del Saint Graal 226, 233, 237, 240, 261
question, the healing xvi, 8, 16, 33–34, 55, 72, 80, 84, 87, 89, 150, 155–156, 182, 196, 198, 214, 229, 250, 254

rabbîn (jousting) 165
Rahewin (*Gesta Frederici*) 175, 261
Rahn, Otto 85, 272
Ramayana 245
Ranke, Friedrich 92–93, 146, 273
realism/historical transparency 30, 77, 130–132, 135, 164, 169, 224, 227
Red Knight, the (Chrétien) 121–122
redemption 144–145, 147
redoubts (*zingel*) 174
regeneration 232–236
Reichslandfrieden 225
reine de la Terre Gaste 233
Reinmar (Minnesänger) 133
Repanse de Schoye 15, 27, 82, 87, 94–95, 113, 137, 150, 183, 211, 219
rhetoric (liberal arts) xiv, 44, 58, 100–102, 114, 119–120, 200
Richey, Margaret F. 9, 273
Ricoeur, Paul 102–103, 273
Die Ritter der Tafelrunde (Christoph Hein) 256, 258

Robert de Boron 82–84, 86, 232, 261
Rohmer, Eric (*Perceval le Gallois*) 256–257
Rosarium philosophorum 213
Rosche Sabins 51
Der rote Ritter: Eine Geschichte von Parzival (Adolf Muschg) 257
Roubaud, Jacques (*Graal Théâtre*) 257
Round Table xiii, 37, 41, 63, 68, 73, 75, 210, 246, 258
Round Table tournaments 179
Ruh, Kurt 40, 54, 190, 193, 273
Rupp, Heinz 40, 273

Sacker, Hugh 40, 130, 146, 152, 157, 273
sacraments 143
St. Gall manuscript of *Parzival* xi
Salmon, Paul 144, 273
Salzer, Anselm xvii, 273
San Marte (Alfred Schulz) 247, 249, 251, 256
Sangive 52, 70, 72, 221
Sant near Nuremberg x
Schaeffer, Albrecht 255
Schäfer-Maulbetsch, Rose-Beate 170, 273
Schanpfanzun 42–43, 45, 47, 50–51, 60, 73, 75, 110
Schastel Marveile 3, 51–55, 58, 61–67, 73–76, 204, 206, 208–209, 211–212, 215–216, 218–219, 221
Schentaflurs 226
Schiller, Friedrich 124
Schionatulander xii, 6–7, 15–16, 23, 33, 57, 122, 135, 201, 226
Schirok, Bernd 178–179, 273
Schmid, Elisabeth 121–122, 144, 273
Schmolke-Hasselmann, Beate 273
Schnell, Rüdiger 47, 50, 273
Schoette 4, 27
Scholz, Manfred G. 191–193, 273

Schopenhauer, Arthur 250
Schröder, Walter Johannes 19, 152, 157, 206–207, 274
Schultz, Alwin 162–163, 165, 173, 274
Schulz, Alfred (San Marte) 247, 249, 251, 256
Schweikle, Günther 124, 274
Schwietering, Julius 144, 274
Secundille 27, 219
Segramors 41, 61
Selbstaussagen xv, xviii
"self-defense" x, 13, 117, 190, 227
sergeants (*sarjande*) 172–173
Seth 144, 150
Shakespeare 134, 139
Siberry, Elizabeth 139, 274
siege engines 173, 179, 188
sieges 161, 173, 188
Siegfried 245
Sigune xii, 6–7, 14–16, 19–20, 22–23, 25–27, 33–34, 56–57, 77, 89, 112, 121, 135, 137, 151–152, 201, 208, 236, 247
Simon de Montfort 85
Simrock, Karl 247, 249, 256
Simson, Otto Georg von 152, 274
sin 92, 122, 143–149, 151–152, 154–156, 158, 229, 231, 239
Singer, Samuel 144, 274
slingmen (*slingaere*) 172
Smail, R. C. 174, 274
Smalley, Beryl 131, 274
Solomon 221
Soltane 3, 10, 206–208, 234–235
sorcery 219
Spahr, Blake Lee 9, 11, 274
Das Spiel vom Fragen oder Die Reise zum sonoren Land (Peter Handke) 257
spiritual commentators in grail quests 237
squires (*knappen*) 42–44, 166, 168, 177, 182, 200, 210, 212
Star Wars 203
Stauffer, Marianne 206, 274

Stein, Alexandra 3, 274
Steiner, Gertraud 226, 274
Steiner, Rudolf 255
Stevens, Adrian 32, 118–119, 124, 130, 159, 176, 274–275, 280
stone/stones 22, 53, 78–82, 87–88, 90–94, 155, 197–198, 213–214, 216, 218–219, 234, 251, 253
Störmer, Wilhelm (and Christoph Cormeau) 146, 264
Sturges, Robert S. 201, 275
style 120, 124–139
stylization 164, 168–169, 176
Suite du Merlin 235
sujet/discourse 102, 115
Summa Theologiae 146
superbia/pride/*Hochfahrt* 90, 92, 155, 182, 237–238, 241
Sussman, Linda 217, 219, 275
Swinburne, Hilda 156, 275
Swisher, Michael 229, 231, 275
Syberberg, Hans Jürgen 256
syntax 125
synthesis of opposites 221

Tannhäuser 246, 248–250
Taurian's spear 29
Tax, Petrus 3, 145, 153–154, 156, 275
templeise xiv, 79, 89, 178
ten (symbolism of number) 212
Tenabroc 106, 211
Tennant, F. R. 143, 275
Terdelaschoye 112
Terre de Salvaesche 78
Terre Marveile 43, 51–52, 64, 215
Terrible Mother 208
tetrads (in *Parzival*) 208, 211–212
Thomas, Dylan 11
Thomas, Neil 120, 275, 280
Thomas of Britain 196
Thomas of Celano 191
Thucydides 134
Tilo von Kulm 146
time references in *Parzival* 132

Timpson, George F. 164, 275
Titurel 14, 78, 112, 114, 197, 201
Tobin, Frank 144, 275
Toledo xvi, 79, 111, 195
tournaments 166, 169, 177
treuga dei xiv
Trevrizent xviii, 4–5, 10, 14–15, 19, 21–22, 29, 34, 40, 51, 78, 80, 83, 88, 90, 92, 115, 122, 127, 132, 148, 152, 154–156, 166, 180–182, 194, 197, 208, 213–214, 216, 219, 231–232, 236–238
Tristan 31, 246
triuwe 12–17, 24–25, 34, 153
trobar clus 130
troubadours 130
truth of fiction/poetry 109–110, 194
tumpheit 20, 29–30, 122, 147
Turcopoles 174
Twelfth Century Renaissance xix

Ulrich von Lichtenstein 179
Ulrich von Zatzikhoven (*Lanzelet*) 163
unconscious mind 226
unverzaget mannes muot 228, 239
Urban II, Pope xiv
Urjans 57–58, 60, 64
Utependragun 108, 112, 120, 167

Vale, Malcolm 177, 275
ventail (*fintâle*) 163
Verbruggen, J. F. 162, 275
Vergulaht 47–51, 73–75
Vespasian 83
veve fame de la gaste forest 233
Vienna Genesis 145
Vinaver, Eugène 99, 275
vineyards of Erfurt 176
violence xvi, 43, 58, 64, 74, 120, 122, 135, 165
Virgil ix, 214, 245
visionary works of art 204
Vorderstemann, Jürgen 163, 275

Vulgate Cycle 225–226

Wace xiii, 120, 224
Wack, Mary F. 135, 275
Wagner, Richard xvi, xix, 245–256, 258; anti-Semitism 251; assessment of Wolfram 252–254; Dresden library 248, 253
Wagner, Richard, works by:
  Die Feen 246
  Der fliegende Holländer 246
  Lohengrin 247–251
  Die Meistersinger von Nürnberg 246
  Parsifal 246, 248–254, 256
  Rienzi 246
  Der Ring des Nibelungen 246, 249, 251
  Tristan und Isolde 246, 249–252
Wagner, Wieland 256
walap (jousting) 165
Walther von der Vogelweide 133
Wand, Christine 146, 276
Wapnewski, Peter 147, 152, 229, 276
The War Hound and the World's Pain (Michael Moorcock) 258
warfare 160–162, 169, 227
Wartburg castle xi
wasteland 209, 214, 235
Wehrli, Max 193, 276
Weigand, Hermann J. 6, 131–132, 153, 276
Weiner, Marc A. 251, 276
Wells, Christopher J. 124, 276
Wells, David A. 149, 276
Wenzel, Horst 225, 276
Wertheim, Count of xi, xvi, 176
Wesendonck, Mathilde 250–251, 253
Wessels, P. B. 152, 276
Westernhagen, Curt von 248, 276
Weston, Jessie L. 150, 235, 276
White, T. H. 240
Wiedmer, Peter 146, 276

Der Wilde (Tankred Dorst and Ursula Ehler) 257
wilder funt 119–120
Wiles, Maurice 143, 276
Wilhelm, James J. (Translation of *Peredur*) 86, 261
Willehalm 21
William of Tudela 85
William of Tyre 161
Willoughby, Harold R. 234, 276
Willson, Bernard 150, 276
Wirnt von Gravenberg (*Wigalois*) 124–125, 261
Wolfram von Eschenbach ix–xxii, 3, 6–7, 9–19, 21–34, 37–41, 46, 49, 54–55, 60–61, 74–93, 99–100, 104–139, 143, 146–147, 151–153, 159–170, 172–174, 176, 178–183, 185, 190–198, 200–206, 208, 210–211, 213–214, 216, 218–221, 223, 226–230, 232, 235–236, 238–241, 246–257; biography ix–x; illumination of xi; lyrics xii, 133–134
Wolfram von Eschenbach, works by:
  Parzival ix–xii, xiv–xix, 1, 3, 6–7, 9, 12, 19–21, 28, 38–39, 47, 53, 56, 74–76, 81, 83, 86, 88–92, 96, 99–100, 104–112, 114–123, 127, 129–130, 135–138, 146–148, 150, 157, 159–160, 162–166, 168–170, 172, 174–181, 183, 186, 19 0–191, 196–197, 200–201, 203–206, 208, 213, 218–221, 223, 226–227, 230–232, 235–241, 247–250, 252–257
  Parzival, books of:
    Book I 3, 10–12, 20–21, 37–38, 169, 198, 205, 226
    Book II x, 3, 10–11, 37–38, 40, 52, 107, 117, 190, 199, 226–227
    Book III xii, 13–14, 17–18, 37, 39, 106, 125, 149, 226, 233
    Book IV xi–xii, 37, 169
    Book V xiii, 15, 30, 37, 77, 150, 216
    Book VI xi, xiii, 37, 39–41, 44, 52, 59, 61, 73, 75, 191, 228
    Book VII xi, xiii, 37, 39–40, 42, 59, 131, 169, 183
    Book VIII xiii, 37, 40, 42–43, 47, 50–51, 105, 110, 131
    Book IX xiii–xiv, xviii, 14, 24, 30, 38–39, 51, 78, 105, 111, 115, 131–132, 144, 151–152, 156–157, 194, 206, 214, 216, 230–231
    Book X xiii, 37, 40, 43, 50–51, 55, 131
    Book XI xiii, 37, 40, 43, 51–52, 55, 131
    Book XII xiii, 37, 40, 43, 51, 55, 131, 200, 210
    Book XIII xiii, 37, 39–40, 43, 51, 55, 131
    Book XIV 15, 28, 33, 37, 39–40, 43, 51, 55, 183, 231
    Book XV 37, 106, 122, 156, 230
    Book XVI 37, 78, 137, 231
  Selbstaussagen xv, xviii
  Titurel xii, 6, 16, 28, 135, 201
  Willehalm ix, xii, 21, 84, 88, 136, 138, 169–170, 190
Wolfram von Eschenbach Museum x
Wolframs-Eschenbach (Obereschenbach) x, 48
Wynn, Marianne xii, 7–10, 26, 40, 55, 57, 131, 135, 190, 193, 232, 250, 277

Yeandle, David N. 17–18, 20, 233, 277

Zazamanc 170–171, 205
Zelinsky, Hartmut 251, 277
Zeydel, Edwin H. 85, 277
Zimmermann, Gisela 56, 163, 171, 174, 176, 183, 277

Wolfram von Eschenbach's *Parzival* expands and transforms the Arthurian tradition into a grand depiction of the medieval cosmos around 1200. Standing between clerical and chivalric cultures and articulating the interests and values of both, Wolfram produced the most popular vernacular work in medieval Germany and one of the most vibrant of the High Middle Ages. The brilliance, boldness, and astonishing originality of *Parzival,* along with the allure of its elusive author and his enigmatic grail, have continued to fascinate modern audiences since the nineteenth century. And in the late twentieth century, as the study of literature becomes increasingly interdisciplinary, Wolfram's masterpiece continues to hold forth a seemingly inexhaustible supply of cultural knowledge and insights. The original essays in this volume, written by more than a dozen Wolfram experts working in Europe and the United States, provide a definitive treatment in English of significant aspects of Wolfram's incomparable rendering of the quest for the grail (Wolfram's modes of narrative presentation, his relationship to his sources, his portrayal of the grail), and of some of the broader social and cultural issues it raises (the theology of the Fall, the status of chivalric self-assertion, the characterization of women, the modern reception of *Parzival*). These and other essays, ranging from new readings of significant episodes (the story of Herzeloyde and Gahmuret, the Gawan-books) to analyses of material culture (tournaments and battles), point in new directions for the future study of Wolfram's poem, and demonstrate that *Parzival* deservedly occupies a central position in our understanding of the High Middle Ages.

WILL HASTY is Professor of German at the University of Florida. He is the editor of *German Literature of the High Middle Ages* (2006; Camden House History of German Literature, volume 3); *A Companion to Gottfried von Strassburg's "Tristan"* (2002), and author of *Adventures in Interpretation: The Works of Hartmann von Aue and Their Critical Reception* (1996), all published by Camden House.

The essays are well written and insightful, and the authors bring a sense of their own delight in a way that will be contagious among a broad readership.
COLLOQUIA GERMANICA

A very usable introduction to various aspects of Wolfram's *Parzifal*.
JOURNAL OF ENGLISH AND GERMANIC PHILOLOGY

www.ingramcontent.com/pod-product-compliance
Lightning Source LLC
Chambersburg PA
CBHW031706230426
43668CB00006B/128